THE END
OF LIBERALISM

*The Second Republic
of the United States*

SECOND EDITION

Also by Theodore J. Lowi

At the Pleasure of the Mayor
The Pursuit of Justice, with Robert F. Kennedy
Private Life and Public Order, editor
The Politics of Disorder
Poliscide, with Benjamin Ginsberg
American Government: Incomplete Conquest
Legislative Politics U.S.A., editor with Randall B. Ripley
Public Policies in America

THE END
OF LIBERALISM

*The Second Republic
of the United States*

THEODORE J. LOWI

SECOND EDITION

W · W · NORTON & COMPANY
NEW YORK   LONDON

Published simultaneously in Canada by Stoddart,
a subsidiary of General Publishing Co. Ltd,
Don Mills, Ontario.

W. W. Norton & Company, Inc., 500 Fifth Avenue, New York, N.Y. 10110
W. W. Norton & Company Ltd., 37 Great Russell Street, London WC1B 3NU

Library of Congress Cataloging in Publication Data
Lowi, Theodore J
    The end of liberalism, second edition
    Includes bibliographical references.
    1. Liberalism—United States.   I. Title.
HM276.L57   1979   320.5'1'0973   78–27093
ISBN 0-393-09000-0 pbk.
      7 8 9 0

TO
Alvin Lowi, Jr.

CONTENTS

PREFACE TO THE SECOND EDITION

I wrote this book in the 1960s with the conviction that the ideologies and policies at that time were threatening to produce a deep and permanent change in the American constitution. The Democrats, guided by a new public philosophy—interest-group liberalism—had sought to build a modern state upon good intentions and the support of organized privilege. Such a structure, they felt, could give the state the legitimacy of a broadly representative popular base, and at the same time could provide that state with sufficient independence to insure that it could intervene justly into private affairs.

Fundamental changes in policies and institutions could readily be observed and have been widely accepted as inevitable or good or both. This book was part of a small minority which treated these changes as part of a national crisis of public authority. The First Edition was subtitled accordingly. The view of the Second Edition is that we had our crisis and did not survive it. These changes turned out to be a series of adjustments our political system was making to a still more fundamental change of government and of the basis of rule. Through these adjustments we had actually remade ourselves, politically speaking, to such an extent that I have called the results the Second Republic. And, although this Second Republic is operating under an unwritten constitution, the cumulative changes and adjustments of the past two decades can be pieced together into a sketch of a constitution:

PREAMBLE. There ought to be a national presence in every aspect of the lives of American citizens. National power is no longer a necessary evil; it is a positive virtue.

Article I. It is the primary purpose of this national government to provide domestic tranquility by reducing risk. This risk may be physical or it may be fiscal. In order to fulfill this sacred obligation, the national government shall be deemed to have sufficient power to eliminate threats from the environment through regulation, and to eliminate threats from economic uncertainty through insurance.

Article II. The separation of powers to the contrary notwithstanding, the center of this national government is the presidency. Said office is authorized to use any powers, real or imagined, to set our nation to rights by making any rules or regulations the president deems appropriate; the president may sub-delegate this authority to any other official or agency. The right to make all such rules and regulations is based upon the assumption in this constitution that the office of the presidency embodies the will of the real majority of the American nation.

Article III. Congress exists, but only as a consensual body. Congress posses-ses all legislative authority but should limit itself to the delegation of broad grants of unstructured authority to the president. Congress must take care never to draft a careful and precise statute because this would interfere with the judgment of the president and his professional and full-time adminis-trators.

Article IV. There exists a separate administrative branch composed of per-sons whose right to govern is based upon two principles: (1) the delegations of power flowing from Congress; and (2) the authority inherent in professional training and promotion through an administrative hierarchy. Congress and the courts may provide for administrative procedures and have the power to review agencies for their observance of these procedures; but in no instance should Congress or the courts attempt to displace the judgment of the ad-ministrators with their own.

Article V. The judicial branch is responsible for two functions: (1) to pre-serve the procedural rights of citizens before all federal courts, state and local courts, and administrative agencies; and (2) to apply the Fourteenth Amendment of the 1787 Constitution as a natural-law defense of all sub-stantive and procedural rights. The appellate courts shall exercise vigorous judicial review of all state and local government and court decisions, but in no instance shall the courts review the constitutionality of Congress's grants of authority to the president or to the federal administrative agencies.

Article VI. The public interest shall be defined by the satisfaction of the voters in their constituencies. The test of the public interest is reelection.

Article VII. Article VI to the contrary notwithstanding, actual policy-making will not come from voter preferences or congressional enactments but from a process of tripartite bargaining between the specialized administrators, relevant members of Congress, and the representatives of self-selected or-ganized interests.

The only redeeming feature of the Second Republic constitution is that it does not correspond fully to reality. This was of course also true of the Con-

stitution of 1787, but there the comparison ends. The constitution of our
Second Republic is a poor constitution, made worse by a lack of recognition *the 2nd*
of its existence. In the late 1970s there was more grumbling than ever against / *Rep*
the heavy-handed and irrational interferences of big government. And President Jimmy Carter was elected in 1976 on a campaign against big government, its ever-expanding bureaucracy, its special favors to special interests,
and especially the swollen and conspiratorial White House. Yet, despite all
that, and despite the contribution of these very facts to the failure of two of his
four precedessors, President Carter was hardly in office when he began to
cope with the ungovernable Second Republic as though he were deliberately
imitating them. He sought legislation providing the president with still more
discretion and responsibility; he sought to reorganize the bureaucracy so that
more responsibility than ever culminated in the presidency; he assumed responsibility for the entire fight against inflation without even bothering with
legislation; and he began building a public relations and advertising staff in
the White House. President Carter has been operating as though he were
thirty-ninth president of the republic of 1787 when actually he is the fifth
president of the Second Republic. Apparently he has not learned any better
than his four precedessors that the historic continuity of American national
politics has been broken.

The Second Edition of this book is dedicated to the proposition that the
most fundamental political problem of our time *is* our politics. Our solution
ultimately lies not in piecemeal reform or in more vigorous participation. It
will be found only by withdrawal from action long enough to analyze and to
understand the reasons for our discontents.

A year of leave at the Center for Advanced Study in the Behavioral Sciences
in 1977–78 provided time for the completion of the research for and writing of
the Second Edition. For their sponsorship I am deeply indebted to the Center
and to the Ford Foundation and the National Endowment for the
Humanities. But I am especially indebted to the Center, because it provided
me not only with the time and space, but with the most conducive intellectual environment imaginable. To the Center fellows as a collectivity I want to
express my thanks and my hope that I made a proportionate contribution to
their year. Among them were of course several individuals who were particularly helpful to me. These were Joseph Sax of the University of Michigan Law
School; Richard Epstein of the University of Chicago Law School; James
Rule of the Department of Sociology at the State University of New York at
Stony Brook; and Yaron Ezrahi (Department of Political Science, University
of Jerusalem), Kent Jennings (Department of Political Science, University of

Michigan), Anthony King (Department of Government, University of Essex, England), and Robert Keohane and Paul Sniderman (Department of Political Science, Stanford University).

During the ten years the First Edition was in print I encountered innumerable students, colleagues, and friends whose influences on the Second Edition are incalculable. A sketch of these encounters would provide an interesting map of part of the terrain of political science in the United States and Europe. From this community a few names stand out; but I list them in full awareness of the inadequacy of the listing, not only because of the names it neglects entirely but also because of its failure to convey fully my debt to those who are identified. Some gave me advice and guidance on specific chapters or issues: Richard Bensel and Michael Levy (Department of Political Science, Texas A & M University), Roger Marz (Department of Political Science, Oakland University, Michigan), Stephan Leibfried (University of Bremen, Germany), Sotirios Barber (Department of Political Science, University of South Florida), Paul Peterson and David Greenstone (Department of Political Science, University of Chicago), and M. M. Glosser (superintendent of schools of "Iron City"). They and others provided me in a more general way with new ideas or fresh insights into old ones: David Kettler (Department of Political Science, University of Trent, Canada), Benjamin Ginsberg, Sidney Tarrow, and Douglas Ashford (Department of Government, Cornell University), Francesco Kjellberg (Institute of Politics, University of Oslo, Norway), Samuel Beer (Department of Government, Harvard University), Norton Long (Department of Political Science, University of Missouri at St. Louis), Alan Stone (Department of Political Science, University of Houston), David Vogel (School of Business, University of California, Berkeley), Lewis Lipsitz and Duncan MacRae (Department of Political Science, University of North Carolina). I would also like to thank the Fondation Nationale des Sciences Politiques of Paris for the opportunity they provided during their observance of the American Bicentennial to try out some of my ideas on the Second Republic. And, although he is very probably unaware of this book and of my work in general, I want to express a very belated thanks to Friedrich A. Hayek. His work had much more of an influence on me than I realized during the writing of the First Edition. I neither began nor ended as a Hayekist but instead found myself confirming, by process of elimination and discovery, many of his fears about the modern liberal state. Finally, it is probable that my largest debt of gratitude is to my students who heard me lecture on these subjects. They were always first to hear and often last to be convinced.

Ithaca, New York
November 1978   THEODORE J. LOWI

PREFACE TO THE
FIRST EDITION

The End of Liberalism is a deliberately ambiguous title intended to convey at
least two purposes. First, it is an inquiry into the actual character of contemporary liberalism, its tenets, its origins, and the state and policies it is responsible for. That is to say, it is an analysis of the end or ends of the liberal state in
the 1960s. I have for this purpose tried to write a textbook, in which the reader
will find enough data and exposition through which to make analyses and
draw conclusions for himself.

Second, the book is a polemic. It is a textbook with a point of view, a strong
point of view. As a polemic, its principal target is the modern liberal state itself, its outmoded ideology, and its self-defeating policies. But the polemic is
addressed, too, to academic political science and its fellow disciplines of history, sociology, and economics. The tie between the modern liberal state and
political science parallels the older tie between the capitalist system and
laissez-faire economics. Like classical economics, contemporary political
theory is good theory elevated into bad ideology through repetition of its hypotheses as though they were inviolable principles. And, like criticisms of laissez-faire economics, criticisms of political science theory often make difficult
reading. But there is a need to break the thirty-year moratorium on consideration of first premises that has characterized modern political science. Controversy must be opened on questions of theory and ideology, not merely on
questions of methodology and practice.

Almost exactly thirty years ago the contemporary liberal state was founded
on the basis of two overwhelming national elections and a series of Supreme
Court decisions that seemed to validate new constitutional principles. But in
United States history there have always been two dimensions to the problem
of what constitutes acceptable constitutional government. The first has concerned the actual scope of governmental power; the second, the forms by
which governmental power, whatever its scope, could be exercised. The
Roosevelt revolution conclusively settled only the first, by establishing the

principle for all time in the United States that in a democracy there can be no effective limit to the scope of governmental power. The idea of government limited to a specific set of activities had been a characteristically American invention which, characteristically, was discarded once it became too confining. The second issue—essentially the issue of due process of law—was not settled in the 1930s. Instead, the new theory and jurisprudence of the liberal state defined it away. This was done by borrowing from political science the pluralist notion that the pulling and hauling among competing interests is sufficient due process. Pluralism became the model and the jurisprudence of the good society. In the liberal state all formalisms were effectively set aside, as though formalism were the enemy of democracy.

The result—which only at first exposure appears paradoxical—was not the strong, positive government of which the pluralists spoke but impotent government, no less impotent because it was getting bigger. Government that is unlimited in scope but formless in action is government that cannot plan. Government that is formless in action and amoral in intention (i.e., *ad hoc*) is government that can neither plan nor achieve justice.

Two images of contemporary liberal government will probably emerge from the ensuing pages. In some instances it will appear as a gigantic prehistoric beast, all power and no efficacy. In other instances it will appear as another case of Casey at the Bat, power with purpose but without definition, finesse, discrimination, ending in disappointment. Together the two images capture the essence of contemporary liberal government.

It should thus be clear that the issues with which the book deals are remote from the mere question of more government or less government. We already have more, and twentieth-century democracies will tolerate nothing less. It is my hope that such a question will be completely discarded, along with a great number of the other intellectual burdens of the past several decades. Instead, the issues will be the still older and almost forgotten ones of what kind of government, what ends of government, what forms of government, what consequences of government—for our time and for the future, as the United States faces the revolution of human relations. Since these are the questions to which contemporary liberalism has refused to address itself—and in so refusing has failed to found a potent or a just regime—perhaps the way out of the crisis might be discovered by returning to such questions. Therefore they are the primary sources of my polemic, the primary subjects of my textbook, and the primary goals of the alternative ideology—juridical democracy—proposed at the end of the volume.

A polemic poses special problems for the members of the intellectual community who helped shape it. I am therefore especially grateful for the good-natured assistance of my colleagues, and must with greater than usual emphasis absolve them all of any responsibility for my errors. However, they are responsible for many improvements in the draft. My only regret is in not having followed their advice more carefully and more frequently. Wallace S. Sayre of Columbia University and Winston Fisk of Claremont Men's College read the entire manuscript and provided a view of the whole without which many important revisions would not have taken place. Many colleagues read parts of the book and were most generous in giving me the benefit of their skills. It is impossible to overestimate the value of the community of scholars of the University of Chicago, but it is possible to single out a few of those who made the environment so productive for me: David Easton, Richard Flathman, David Greenstone, Morris Janowitz, Grant McConnell, Paul Peterson, and, from the Law School, Kenneth C. Davis. There were many excellent students at Chicago and also at Cornell, among whom the most influential were Isaac Balbus, Elliott Feldman, Warren Olson, Lawrence Pierce, L. John Roos, and Peter Sharfman, by virtue of their research or their disagreement, or both. I am also indebted to a great many professional associates in other universities. Among them I must single out a few: Alan Altshuler, Massachusetts Institute of Technology; Daniel Bell, Columbia; Jean Blondel, Essex, England; James Davis, Wisconsin; L. A. Froman, Jr., University of California, Irvine; E. Pendleton Herring, Social Science Research Council; Henry Kariel, Hawaii; Anthony King, Essex, England; Walter LaFeber, Cornell; George LaNoue, Teachers College; Paul Oren, Centre Universitaire International; Annick Percheron, Fondation National des Sciences Politiques; Austin Ranney, Wisconsin; Randall Ripley, Ohio State; James Rosenau, Rutgers; Charles Roig, Grenoble; Edward V. Schneier, City College of the City University of New York; Harry Scoble, University of California, Los Angeles; Nicholas Wahl, Princeton; William Wallace, Manchester, England.

I would also like to take this opportunity to thank the editors of the following reviews and presses for having given me the opportunity to publish articles that became trial runs for the book: *American Political Science Review*, *The Reporter*, *Challenge*, The Free Press, and the University of Chicago Press.

Without institutional assistance all possible individual assistance might have been wasted. A Social Science Research Council Fellowship in 1963–64 and a Guggenheim Foundation Fellowship in 1967–68 made it possible for me to undertake the long-range analyses of public policies of which the present volume is the second installment. The first, *Private Life and Public Order* (Norton, 1967), is a companion book of readings and bibliography. The third, in progress, entitled *Arenas of Power*, is a somewhat less normative study of the processes of policy formulation and implementation in the

United States and France. The University of Chicago, Social Science Division, and the Centre Universitaire International of the University of Paris are two other institutions whose assistance has been invaluable.

Among all my many debts, however, my strongest is to my brother, Alvin Lowi, Jr. In a real sense, this book is merely an episode in an argument that began over a decade ago. I dedicate it to him in full knowledge that it will only cause a temporary quiet between rounds.

THEODORE J. LOWI

Paris
August 1968

Part I

THE ORIGIN AND DECLINE OF LIBERAL IDEOLOGY IN THE UNITED STATES

"[T]he ideas of economists and political philosophers, both when they are right and when they are wrong, are more powerful than is commonly understood. . . . Practical men, who believe themselves to be quite exempt from any intellectual influences, are usually the slaves of some defunct economist. Madmen in authority, who hear voices in the air, are distilling their frenzy from some academic scribbler of a few years back."

Lord Keynes

1

THE OLD PUBLIC
PHILOSOPHY
Capitalist Ideology
and the Automatic Society

The United States is a child of the Industrial Revolution. Its godfather is capitalism and its guardian Providence, otherwise known as the "invisible hand."

Capitalism is an ideology because it is a source of principles and a means of justifying behavior; that is, it is something Americans believe in. It is a liberal ideology because it has always participated in positive attitudes toward progress, individualism, rationality, and nationalism. It is capitalism because its foundation is a capitalistic economic theory and because its standards of legitimacy are capitalistic. It was the public philosophy during the nineteenth century because it dominated all other sources of belief in the formulation of public policy. It is the old public philosophy because it no longer dominates other sources of belief.

In a very important sense, of course, capitalism is not an ideology at all. It is a bundle of economic and technological processes. In this sense capitalism is not something one believes in but rather something one does. One simply amasses wealth and tries to make it produce in the most rational manner by ruthlessly submitting it to the principles of human organization, machines, and double-entry bookkeeping.[1] Objectively it can be done by private or by public means; capitalistic practices are adopted whenever and wherever rational economic order is sought. But when these objective capitalistic practices are successfully employed privately for many years, as in the United States, institutions develop around them, classes of wealth emerge, power centers or-

---

1. See Max Weber, *General Economic History* (New York: Collier Books, 1961), pp. 207 ff. Reprinted in my *Private Life and Public Order* (New York: Norton, 1968). See also Herbert Muller: "Few have heard of Fra Luca Pacioli, the inventor of double-entry bookkeeping; but he has probably had much more influence on human life than has Dante or Michael Angelo." *The Uses of the Past* (New York: Oxford University Press, 1952), p. 257.

ganize. Then words are spoken on behalf of these patterns. When repeated often and spread widely these justifying words become the ideology of the thing. When these words end up coloring the Constitution, influencing policies of government, and shaping the very criteria of worth as well as wealth, they constitute a public philosophy.

Capitalism as public philosophy had an immensely strong theoretical core. Karl Marx as economist is an amateur and an imitator in comparison to Adam Smith. Smith's kind of economics appealed to the nineteenth-century American builders for a number of obvious reasons. The most important reason, it seems in retrospect, must have been the reliance of his theory on an automatic, self-regulating society. The second most important reason was, obviously, that it was purely commercial at a time when "being in trade" was still something despicable. In sum, left entirely to their own devices, commercial interests could provide the greatest possible wealth for a nation:

[When the entrepreneur] intends only his own gain . . . he is . . . led by an invisible hand to promote an end which was no part of his intention. . . . By pursuing his own interest he frequently promotes that of the society more effectually than when he really intends to promote it. . . . The statesman, who should attempt to direct private people in what manner they ought to employ their capitals, would not only load himself with a most unnecessary attention, but would assume an authority which could . . . nowhere be so dangerous as in the hands of a man who had folly and presumption enough to fancy himself fit to exercise it.[2]

There were other reasons for its appeal. Laissez-faire, as the theory became identified during its elevation to ideological status, made a happy fit with the native American fear of political power. Smith gave systematic reasons for opposition to government, but his reasons merely supplemented and confirmed reasons already widely embraced before and during our Revolution. And why not such confirmation? American grievances were as much against mercantilism as against colonialism. Smith was known and debated during the formative years of the Republic perhaps better in the new country than among the educated classes in England at that time. Hamilton in his *Report on Manufactures* (1791) must have had good reasons to spend the bulk of his first section attempting to refute Smith as regards the application of laissez-faire principles to the new country.[3] Hamilton won his battles but lost his war. If the principles of nineteenth-century economics had not existed the Americans would most certainly have invented them. The Americans accepted the view that there was a natural economic harmony which could only be harmed if touched. The dismal laws of Smith's colleagues Malthus and Ricardo made little difference, for any effort to repeal them could only do still greater injury.

This was the underlying dynamic. Strongly and logically related to it at the

2. Adam Smith, *The Wealth of Nations*, Book IV, reprinted in Lowi, *Private Life*, p. 12.
3. Reprinted in part in Lowi, pp. 111 ff.

level of behavior were the sanctity of property and the binding morality of contract. These notions were justified by the classical economics and were, at one and the same time, additional bulwarks against tyranny. Already imbedded in common law, property and contract were flexible enough to survive the changes in actual property and actual contract as corporations split the property atom into millions of anonymous parts and anonymous corporate giants entered into sacred contracts with tiny suppliers and individual laborers.

Insofar as it also shaped objective constitutional practices and governmental life, capitalist ideology can also be said to have constituted the public philosophy during the same period. Beliefs about popular rule, decentralization of power, and the evils of government were strong; but the case for capitalism as the stronger doctrine can be fairly convincingly documented. Happily for both, the tenets of popular rule and of capitalism generally reinforced each other; but in instances of conflict, American government and public policy were decidedly unresponsive to popular rule ideology. The issue could be *Dred Scott* v. *Sanford*, in which slaves were incorporated into the system by confirmation that they are property under the Fifth Amendment. Or the issue could be popularly enacted state regulatory laws, invalidated as unreasonable restraints on contract; many were invalidated as interference with even the process by which contracts are made. Or the issue could be that of the corporation itself, which was given two advantages in nineteenth-century jurisprudence; taken together they strain heavily upon one's sense of logic. On the one hand corporations were merely property, for which the owners, the shareholders, received for themselves total protection and full claim to all profits. On the other hand corporations were defined as persons separate from their owners, so that the death of a corporation affected no owner beyond his shares—because stockholders are not responsible for the debts of the corporation—and yet this "person" was held to enjoy almost all the rights of citizenship under the Bill of Rights and the Fourteenth Amendment.

Following the Civil War, conflicts between capitalism and popular rule increased. But whatever the issue during all of the nineteenth century and part of the twentieth, capitalism won out in a straight fight. In his famous dissent in *Lochner* v. *New York*, Justice Holmes proclaimed, "The Fourteenth Amendment does not enact Mr. Herbert Spencer's Social Statics. . . . [A] constitution is not intended to embody a particular economic theory." This doctrine makes Justice Holmes one of the better prophets and one of the worst historians of his day. Spencer was extreme, but his vision of laissez-faire fairly represented an ideology of capitalism that shackled popular-rule ideology, ordaining in effect that popular rule was all right so long as popular institutions chose to do nothing. As soon as state assemblies and Congress became captured by majorities favorable to regular and frequent state intervention, the inconsistencies between the demands of capitalistic ideology and the demands of popular-rule ideology became clear. By the end of the nineteenth century the two were no longer reinforcing at all, and the entire constitutional epoch of 1890–1937 can, and will in Chapter 3, be characterized as a dialogue between the two.

In the course of that dialogue, capitalism declined as ideology and died as public philosophy. It came to be called conservatism, but that is an incredibly obtuse misnomer that in no way contributes to an understanding of the decline. Capitalism never became conservative. It went into a decline because it became irrelevant and erroneous. The intellectual and theoretical core of the ideology became weakened by generations of belief in itself. Smith and the nineteenth-century liberal economists who followed him were not wrong; in fact, they still hold up for the phenomena with which their theories deal. Capitalist ideology became irrelevant and error-ridden because capitalist ideologues became disloyal to the intellectual spirit of liberal economics. Rather than risk incorporating the new facts of twentieth-century economics and society they closed their minds.

Capitalism as Economic Theory and Sociological Monstrosity

How did nineteenth-century capitalism view society? It necessarily had social views, for no mere economic theory was broad enough to provide ideological support for the new social classes, the new sources of power. What were its weaknesses? Weaknesses it must have had if it lost its place as public philosophy.

The competitive, or "supply-and-demand," or market model of capitalist economics has been criticized from a number of points of view. No criticism has ever satisfactorily cracked the logic of the theory or its applicability to the cases that lie within its assumptions. Successful criticism takes the form of arguing toward a larger frame of reference. Theories of imperfect competition, macroeconomics, national income, "systems," and notions of that sort suggest the different dimensions from which twentieth-century criticisms are hurled back at nineteenth-century truths.[4]

There is, however, still another dimension of the problem which is of greatest relevance to the connection between nineteenth-century liberal eco-

4. The relevant literature is too vast to sample here. A clever review of Keynes and his American disciples can be found in a review article of John Kenneth Galbraith, reprinted as "Came the Revolution" in Lowi, *Private Life*, pp. 142 ff. For a well-balanced assessment of many other features, written with particular regard for social scientists other than professional economists, see R. A. Dahl and C. E. Lindblom, *Politics, Economics, and Welfare* (New York: Harper & Brothers, 1953), especially Chapters 6 and 7, including their most helpful bibliography.

nomics and the rise and fall of capitalist public philosophy. This dimension is the more strictly social views of capitalism. Based upon the same dynamic of competition, the notion spread from Smith that the market produced extremely important social as well as narrowly economic benefits. The "equilibrium" of which such economists spoke came to mean not merely stability of prices near actual costs but also to mean social stability—that is, harmony, felicity, public order.[5] Smith was optimistic. Perhaps the gloomy political economists who followed him also believed that it would be difficult to improve upon a society governed largely by the principle that selfish interests produce the public interest. But it is equally clear that their economics did not commit them or us to the sociology developed in their name in succeeding generations. Herein lies the key to understanding the success and eventual decline of laissez-faire ideology. Four great political economists captured the basic developmental truths about their century. But the clear implications of their laws of development lead in directions irrelevant to or inconsistent with the model of the automatic society erected by the laissez-faire ideologues. Review of these laws of development reveals that the society they anticipate is not automatically provided for by market competition. Review shows a contrary feature that the market mechanism in the economy assumes a society whose institutions have adjusted themselves to the market mechanism. Modern society must become capable of controlling, suppressing, and absorbing market forces or the market becomes menace rather than good provider.

THE LAWS OF DEVELOPMENT

The division of labor • Adam Smith began his great classic, *The Wealth of Nations* (1776), not with a disquisition about market competition but with an inquiry into the division of labor. To Smith the division of labor was the cause of "improvement in the productive powers of labour." It would spread if men were free to apply rationality to their self-interest, and there would be an immense increase in productivity, far beyond anything public policy might try to ordain.

Smith expected the division of labor to spread toward every aspect of industry because it was the only rational way of organizing. But how far would the division of labor actually spread and how extremely would it be applied? In Figure 1.1 the tendency is expressed as an S-curve, which suggests that the rate of application of the principle of the division of labor is very high but then slackens up after a certain point. That makes the phenomenon appear to be naturally harmonious with other needs, suggesting, for example, that the principle would not be applied to such a runaway extreme that workers com-

5. The most brilliant as well as most orthodox contemporary version of laissez-faire theory is Ludwig von Mises, *Human Action* (New Haven: Yale University Press, 1949). Note the title. To Mises, market economics is a science of society. See passages reprinted in Lowi, pp. 70 ff.

pletely lost touch with their product. But in truth there is no naturally harmonious tendency to be found here. The division of labor curve has been given an S-shape because it is a ratio, and the tendency of all such ratios may be an S. Operationally, the division of labor is a ratio of the actual number of diffrent tasks in a given work force to the total personnel in the work force. The *rate* by which a given task is broken into two or three separate tasks will probably decline as the ratio approaches 100 percent. But that is only for a given size of work force at a given level of technology. Smith himself, for example, observed that the full potential of specialization can begin to be realized only as a work force or market reaches large size and is growing. Moreover, new machines and processes open new possibilities for specializing labor in a given work force. This means that even if the division of labor tendency is an S-curve, the rate of specialization may not slow up until society is submerged in specialties. Economic rationality and market pressure may dictate this, but those same factors do not specify when society—mankind—is suffering under the weight. Specialization may, therefore, reach an automatic equilibrium, but not necessarily at a level that other social needs will tolerate.

The law of population • Thomas Malthus in his *Essay on the Principle of Population* (1798) produced one of the most influential and clearly the most dismal of the laws of industrial society: As the supply of food goes up at an arithmetic rate, the population goes up at a geometric rate. Consequently, poverty, pestilence, and war are inevitable unless society learns "moral restraint." Population growth is expressed as an S-curve in Figure 1.1 although it is not a ratio subject to statistical tendency. It is drawn as an S-curve because that has been the actual history of population growth in the West.[6] However, again we have a tendency that does not relate in any naturally harmonious way with society at large.[7] In the first place, reduction of the population growth rate by poverty and pestilence, and at least a few of the wars, must represent a malfunctioning rather than a proper functioning of the economic system. Secondly, the market economy depends upon the very pressure of the Malthusian law for the proper operation of a labor market. That is where Ricardo comes in.

The iron law of wages • David Ricardo's formulation, in *Principles of Political Economy and Taxation* (1817), is an extension of Smith and Malthus. In Ricardo's hands the two tendencies, division of labor and population growth, support each other not in the harmonious way seen by Smith but in a vicious relationship due to insufficiently expanding productivity. The amount of product available for distribution is never enough; moments of prosperity are either short-lived or create new population pressure which, through competi-

6. For an interesting discussion of the population S-curve and its significance for society, see David Riesman et al., *The Lonely Crowd* (Garden City: Doubleday, 1953), pp. 21 ff.

7. Von Mises, *Human Action*, argues forcefully that an unfettered market is the best natural birth control, but it is only a hypothesis logically derived from restating the market model in more general terms. See reprinted portion in Lowi, *Private Life*.

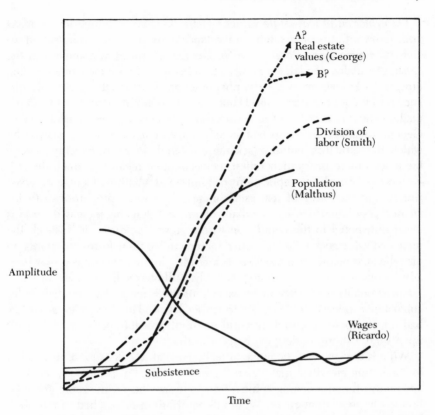

A?
Real estate
values (George)

B?

Division of
labor (Smith)

Population
(Malthus)

Wages
(Ricardo)

Amplitude

Subsistence

Time

FIGURE 1.1 The Nineteenth-Century Laws of Political Economy: A Diagrammatic
Survey

tion for work, reduce the price of labor. This was a close relationship, not
dependent upon lengthy birth cycles, because new supplies of labor came into
cities from the countryside, and they came with only slight incentive once the
feudal relation to land ended. A fluid and expansive labor supply has been a
major factor in the development of commerce and industry.

To Ricardo the tendency toward declining wages was limited only by the
absolute necessities of survival.[8] The curve takes its S-shape (upside down)
from the assumption that the rate of population growth will directly affect
pressure on wages. The bottom horizontal is drawn to suggest fluctuation
around subsistence, with the tendency always toward subsistence—*if other
things are left equal and no deliberate effort is made to interfere.* Here is another
equilibrium, or leveling off, that may be natural but is certainly not necessarily reached at a level supportive of equilibrium in all other realms of social
life.

8. In Figure 1.1, subsistence level is drawn on a slight upward slant to suggest historical
changes in the level considered to be bare subsistence.

The explosion of real estate values • Henry George, although less appreciated, ranks with the others in the importance of his insights into industrial society. In *Progress and Poverty* (1879), George attempted to grapple with the
apparent paradox of a large class of unattached poor in a society of increasing
prosperity. Pauperism as a mass phenomenon was something virtually un-
known to the preindustrial world, but it was recognized by many of George's
predecessors. The factor of rent was also appreciated by economists before
George; Ricardo's criticisms had already helped convert it into a weapon by
which the capitalists could attack the old landholders. But Henry George
brought to these issues their fullest socioeconomic meaning, much the way
Ricardo had fused the implications of Smith and Malthus. George observed
simply that the value of real estate increases in some proportion with increased population density or urbanization, and that this increased value is
never distributed to the population whose growth produced it. Instead, the
increased value goes as an "unearned increment" to those fortunate enough to
own the land before urbanization. As a result, "in the new city you may have
a luxurious mansion, but among its public buildings will be an almshouse."
Unquestionably there were many exceptions to his thesis. Real estate bubbles
could burst; prices could tumble to earlier levels. However, George's book
had hit a responsive chord in world opinion, probably because he had hit
upon such a strong underlying basis of truth.

What is the shape of the curve of real estate values? Because of its relation
to population growth it may be an S-curve; but due to speculation, anxiety,
and many other nondemographic factors, rent may bear some geometric relation to the population curve. Would its equilibrium be reached, if rent were
left to its natural course, in time to avoid revolution? When we add to rent the
costs of other factors of production, the phenomenon about which George
concerned himself is seen to be fundamental, fully worthy of consideration in
the context of revolution. We do not have to believe with George that rent is
original sin. We need only take his thesis as cause for inquiry into possibly
self-destructive aspects of capitalism.[9] Capitalism produces industrialization
and urbanization. These two phenomena are the sources of stresses and
strains that will not necessarily be solved by more capitalism, industrialization, and urbanization. Yet to have less of them would require interference with the natural tendency of a market-governed economy to expand.

AUTOMATIC ECONOMY VERSUS AUTOMATIC SOCIETY

These four basic tendencies do not represent runaway factors. Industrial
societies have had, despite their many problems, impressive histories. But the

9. Only the social consequences are explored here. For a fascinating speculation into certain
self-destructive economic features, see Joseph Schumpeter on capitalism in his classic *Capitalism, Socialism and Democracy* (New York: Harper & Brothers, 1942).

problems are as often as not attributable to the very same forces that produce
the impressive histories. As has already been suggested, these tendencies,
expressed in the four curves, have an aggravating effect on each other. Once
industrialization began there seemed to be no stopping Western societies from
the fullest pursuit of all its implications: Advances in the division of labor
demanded more population; increased productivity made greater population
possible as well as necessary, but populations were badly affected as productivity brought on concentration. Increasing concentration of population put
great pressure on for still more output, but productivity rates declined as the
price of real estate and other factors of production went up. Inventions only
postponed the moment when more masses of labor were needed, because new
levels in the division of labor required more workers, and more population
pressure was needed to keep the price of labor down and consumption up.
The price of labor was of special importance because it was far easier to manipulate than the price of real estate and capital.

This is only a partial statement of the system but it suggests how the parts of
the system related to each other. It takes something of an optimist to believe
that such relationships, if left alone, produce nothing but felicity.

In the modern city we can observe without difficulty how these forces must
have worked themselves out. The growth curves in Figure 1.2 suggest that
once a society enters upon industrialization—or, in the terms of W. W. Rostow, begins its "takeoff"—its central cities become creatures of these forces.
The population of Old London had reached 225,000, according to the best estimates, by 1600. Two centuries later, on the eve of the Industrial Revolution, London had grown only to about 900,000.[10] By 1800, in fact, a rather
small proportion of the population of England or the United States lived in
cities. From that point the story is one of incredible urban-industrial growth,
despite slow progress in public health and the amenities in cities. For example, between 1800 and 1890 the proportion of the U.S. population living
in cities of 8,000 or larger increased 87 times, while the general population
increased 12 times. But the story is more vividly told in Figure 1.2. Separated
by a time lag of about twenty years, New York and London show enormous
rates of growth. Following by about the same time lag are three other large industrial cities.

Even more striking than the consistently high rates of growth is the fact that
all five cities grew at almost *identical* rates once their takeoff had begun. Every
industrializing city seems to be under the same intensity of pressure to realize
the fullest potential of its resources and culture. The extreme and parallel

10. Figures for London (1800–41) are taken from Adna F. Weber, *The Growth of Cities in the
Nineteenth Century* (Ithaca: Cornell University Press, 1899; republished 1963), p. 46. His figures
include territory in the county that is not included in the official definition of Registration London. The differences are negligible. They are noted here only to avoid confusion over the slight
lack of correspondence with figures on London taken from other sources, cited below.

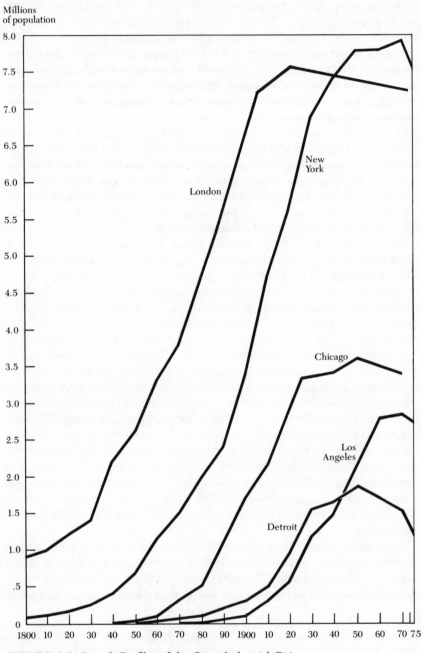

Millions of population

FIGURE 1.2 Growth Profiles of the Great Industrial Cities

rates of growth seem to confirm the universality of aggravating relations among the developmental tendencies of industrialization. This is further confirmed by the very structure of those large cities that were built after the advent of capitalism. The structure of each reveals that it was built fundamentally as a producing and marketing unit. Only Washington, which was designed to be a capital city, shows any influence of noncapitalistic values in the building of the great American cities. It was designed and built with defense of the White House and Capitol buildings in mind. Its back is the Potomac, and one side is the "Eastern Branch" (Anacostia River), with the Capitol on a hill above the fork. The street layout is a nearly perfect grid cut across by major arterials that converge on each other to form sixteen intersections (now called circles) at strategic points in every direction around the White House and Capitol. This was an ideal defense against the movement of cavalry and heavy artillery. However, no other major modern city bears the stamp of such noncapitalist preoccupations. New York has its Battery, but New York's development was overwhelmingly toward encouraging movement, not defending against it. Still more have inland cities been, even according to their boosters, gateways to this and that. The same tracings can be made in England and France although they may be somewhat confused by the fossil remains of precapitalist values in old cities. Paris is the exception proving the rule: Paris is a royal city, an anticapitalist city. Not only are most cities in other countries now built for access, they, like the American cities, were created as economic capitals, not government or esthetic capitals. They were built for functional specialization. They were and are still built for efficiency. One particularly antisocial form of this is the practice of building for a life expectancy of around forty years. Once the structures are "amortized" they can be destroyed or abandoned to other uses, the most important of which is the very profitable entity called the slum. Manchester, England, might as well be in New Jersey. How many times have capitalist economies renewed and recreated the slums that Engels saw? Contemporary France, even with its stronger statist tradition, displays most of the same values today. If not in Paris, this is true even of the Paris suburbs, where so much of the industry and industrial proletariat were relocated. French cities rebuilt after World War II damage suggest that capitalist values are still preeminent.[11]

The trend lines in Figure 1.2 suggest that the cities have, except for Los Angeles, reached their upper levels of expansion. But this does not mean equilibrium, and certainly not natural, felicitous, and self-maintaining equilibrium. In the first place, expansion continues toward a scale and complexity

11. Max Weber's essay *The City*, edited by Don Martindale (New York: Free Press, 1958), and Lewis Mumford's *The City in History* are useful corroborative studies. However, the most fascinating, due to the richness of the data, is Adna F. Weber, *The Growth of Cities*, especially Chapter 3.

impossible to imagine. It does not show up in the population curves simply because the population living beyond the city's legal boundaries erected political barriers to further city expansion. Each metropolitan region continues in its pace. Soon most of the land east of the Mississippi and west of the Divide will be megalopolis. Half the population of France will someday live in the region of Paris.[12] In the second place, the processes of specialization and amortization, as well as progress and poverty, continue as the pace of invention makes these changes possible without local population increases. The end is not in sight, though the forms may change.

What of the capitalist vision of the automatic society? The structure and life of industrial cities, as well as the logic of the tendencies of industrial development, suggest that the market system is *simply one and only one adjustment industrial society made to the demands of industrialization.* Market systems were vital to industrialization, they remain indispensable, and they clearly do generate benefits beyond the mere provision of rational information and control among entrepreneurs. But the market system falls far short of including within its sphere all of the fallout of industrialization. It, moreover, makes its own distinct contribution to those pressures: In history, competition tended to reduce prices toward the irreducible costs of production. Such reduction put irresistible pressures upon the entrepreneur to reduce his costs wherever he could. That meant reduction of production costs. Population pressure gave the entrepreneur no control over the price of land, but it gave him a great opportunity in his relation to labor; hence, increased pressure for more population and cheaper labor costs. Pressure, too, for more invention; free competition probably did produce many of the technological advances of the epoch. But invention is a postponement, not a repeal, of the workings of industrial forces.

If the United States and other industrializing societies maintained some semblance of public order during their developmental ordeals, it could not have been due entirely to some self-correcting characteristic of the very factors in the process of development. The capitalistic assumption that capitalistic processes produce their own social solutions is sheer mythology—that is, it bears no necessary relation to the truth. Since there is some truth to it—since the economic forces of capitalism produced some social benefit—the influence of capitalist ideology was strengthened and spread, ultimately to become accepted by an entire governing class. But in the extension of this image of an automatic society lay the seeds of its decline. As capitalist society galloped into the twentieth century its intellectual weaknesses strained belief. At some undetermined point capitalism ceased to constitute the public philosophy, although it remains a strong ideological force.

12. See below, Chapter 7.

AUTOMATIC SOCIETY VERSUS THE VISIBLE HAND

The intellectual core of capitalist public philosophy became corrupted by complacent insistence upon its own universal applicability. It reinforced itself largely in a manner resembling primitive magic—when it did not seem to be working the answer lay in some devilish outside interference with the long run, just as the medicine man might explain drought as the wages of insufficiently passionate rain dancing. The fact of the matter is that capitalist theory assumed society would somehow adjust to take up the social slack created by the market. Society did in fact adjust, but it did not do so in patterns remotely explicable in terms of self-regulating commercial mechanisms. Quite the contrary; modern industrialized society can be explained as an effort to make the "invisible hand" as visible as possible. The tendencies represented by the curves in Figure 1.1. are laws of development in societies that operate according to capitalist principles. But the capitalistic principles alone will only guarantee that production will be maximal and that prices will tend toward their lowest levels; that says nothing about the society except that its average members will probably enjoy improved comforts and choices. The question of whether and at what point the curves become S-curves is representative of the social problems left unsolved. As long as the laws of development cannot be repealed, the aggravating and unpredictable interrelations among them suggest that they must be taken not as problems somehow automatically solved but rather as "functional prerequisites" that must somehow be regularly fulfilled in industrial societies if such societies hope to maintain themselves at all. That is to say, the industrializing societies had to develop institutions that would, as a regular matter, adjust themselves and their members to the requirements of capitalism.

If the adjustment was successful, it was due to the successful application of a trait essential to market economies—rationality. But rationality was used *on* markets as well as *in* them. Rationality came to be set above all other values. Smith unassailably attributed the market and the division of labor to man's "faculties of reason." But it is hard to imagine rational man happy to submit under all conditions to so nonrational and mechanistic an expression of rationality as a self-regulating market. Humans did not, of course, submit; and their universal application of rationality created a history which stands in strong contrast to the claim to universality of capitalist theory, ideology, and public philosophy.

Rationality was product as well as prerequisite of industrialization, but it was at no point limited to markets. Rationality can be seen in virtually all the larger forms of social activity. While we cannot actually see a thing called rationality, we can see its most important application. This is *differentiation*, which is simply rationality in the organization of conduct.

Differentiation can be defined as the articulation of parts, or, with Herbert

Spencer, the "unlikeness of parts." It can be thought of as the principle of the division of labor applied to any and all aspects of life. However differentiation is defined, two critical things can be said of it. First, it is immediately and intimately bound up in the process of development in the West. And second, it is, or quickly becomes, a phenomenon whose workings and consequences are far removed from anything resembling a market mechanism.

There are at least four forms of differentiation: (1) multiplication of individual roles; (2) multiplication and specialization of the units of production and distribution; (3) multiplication and specialization of the units of social control; and (4) spatial differentiation. A brief treatment of each will reveal the significance of differentiation as the prime response to the curves of development and the primary means by which the curves are leveled out into S's.

1. The division of labor, despite its undoubted importance, is but a part of the process of multiplication of individual roles in industrial society. For, in addition to the separation of people by tasks, there is also subdivision of individuals according to their various realms of life. The week is divided into employment, family life, church, association; and in each realm a person varies in role, status, and identity. Early in industrial development work is separated from the home. People become involved in workplace associations that are separate from neighborhood associations, and there is little continuity among these and the roles of father, husband, deacon, and son. The "urbane person" is one who is admired for the ease with which he or she lives with and passes easily among a large number of separate roles. Sociology in an advanced society can with justification define a human being as a bundle of roles. Sir Henry Maine's evaluation of society as passing "from status to contract" captures with incredible efficiency a society whose roles are so conscious and so well defined as to provide a basis for specific, contractual fulfillment.[13]

2. The multiplication and specialization of the units of production is as important an economic phenomenon as the division of labor into specialized tasks for individuals within the units. There is probably a period of years in every industrializing country when the total number of producing units declines, because the evolution of industry usually passes through and destroys such preindustrial systems of production as the household or family system, the guild or handicraft system, and the domestic or cottage system.[14] But once

---

13. Developments in the medical profession show clearly that even a narrowly economic multiplication of roles is not merely a phenomenon of centralized and bureaucratized big industry. Most professional specialization in medicine has occurred in the last hundred years, during which time it passed from a simple profession to one in which, by 1942, there were twenty-three basic medical specialties available for the prospective resident. Here is a dramatic case of differentiation in the free professions. See Victor A. Thompson, *Modern Organization* (New York: Knopf, 1961), pp. 49 ff.

14. See, for example, Adna F. Weber, *The Growth of Cities*, p. 185. Weber's statistics show, for example, that in Germany between 1882 and 1895 (the period of Germany's greatest industrialization) the number of persons working on their own account dropped by 5.3 percent while

production becomes more centralized in factories, the actual number of separate units within factories increases, these units specialize, and the likelihood of any one unit producing a whole item for a market goes down accordingly. Countless firms grow deliberately larger in order to be able to differentiate sufficiently to provide for their own specialized services. But an equally important type of unit specialization is the growth of autonomous special service firms. One of the vital functions of central business districts has become provision of the most highly specialized economic services. The best known examples are communications, information, advertising, legal, and stenotyping services, professional employment agencies, and consulting firms. Still another form of specialization of units is in the legal and capital structure of the firm itself. A most important example during the past fifty years is the separation of ownership and control. As stock became a basic means of accumulating capital, ownership spread to many, while operating control of policy and management was necessarily retained by a few. Ultimately control and management become split too, so that many top managers of large firms are no more than highly paid professional employees. Even the fullest exercise of every stock option would give few managers the dominant voice in policy-making on the board of directors.

3. Of equal importance in the rational adjustment to the incessant forces of industrialization is the specialization of the units of social control. This applies to virtually every institution in society that is not included under "units of production" above. The decline of the family as a producing unit was accompanied by the loss to the family of other functions as well. The family no longer functions as an agency of self-defense, or as a holder of property in perpetuity. It does little even to educate children beyond the age of five. As a unit, the family narrows down to the dual functions of procreation and child-rearing, and even these receive narrower and narrower definition with expansion of hospitals and day-care centers, kindergartens and nursery schools, the folkways of babysitting at one end of life and institutions for the aged at the other end. Gaetano Mosca and others note the parallel development of separation of public and private roles and institutions, and an extreme narrowing down of the functions performed by any one of them. Mosca's distinction between the "feudal state" and the modern state rests largely upon this type of differentiation.[15] In the feudal state "all the executive functions of society—the economic, the judicial, the administrative, the military—are exercised simultaneously by the same individuals, while at the same time the state is made up of small social aggregates, each of which possesses all the organs that are required for self-sufficiency."[16] In the modern bureaucratic state, the mil-

---

the number working in establishments rose as follows: Establishments of 5 or fewer, + 23 percent; of 6 to 50, + 76.3 percent; of more than 50, + 88.7 percent (p. 188).

15. See Gaetano Mosca, *The Ruling Class* (New York: McGraw-Hill, 1939), Chapter 3. This is a classic essay in the politics of development.

16. Ibid., p. 81.

itary becomes a totally public instrument, but all administrative and judicial powers are withdrawn from it. Administrative and judicial functions become separated. Offices become separated from holders of office; "*L'état c'est moi*" becomes an impossibility even in modern absolutisms. Specialization of political functions among administrative, elitist, and elective elements makes the modern system of representative government "the most complex and delicate type of political organization that has so far been seen in world history."[17] Meanwhile, many nongovernmental institutions have displaced or supplemented family *and* government. Obvious examples are philanthropic and social-service organizations, unions and trade associations, political parties, fraternities, and social registers. Specialization leaves the church as simply one more example.

4. Finally, there is spatial differentiation, which contributes its own advantages and disadvantages. A famous analysis shows how Chicago developed its concentric circles of land uses emanating from the central business district through warehouse and skid rows to lower-, middle-, and then upper-income housing districts.[18] If Chicago's concentric circle pattern is not universal, it is at least an interesting case of a universal—the specialization of land uses in one form or another. This, like the other forms of specialization, is a rational ordering of things. Jane Jacobs has argued that along with such rational use of space we run the risk of grave social problems, but that only points immediately toward the general problem created by all differentiation.[19] This is that *the rational organization of conduct produces new social problems, and these in turn require a rational approach to social control.*

Thus differentiation in all its forms was productive of responses appropriate to industrialization. But at what cost? There seem to be at least three regular and intimate consequences of differentiation. They need little explication beyond what is evident in the mere listing: (1) multiplication of dependencies (interdependence); (2) multiplication of statuses; and (3) multiplication of interests.

1. A person who is able to produce a surplus due to the increased productivity of his or her own specialization also becomes unable to live without the many who provide his or her other needs. Observers from Smith to Émile Durkheim have celebrated this interdependence as the basis of a new kind of social solidarity. But, as we shall see, other conclusions are equally supportable. The only unassailable generalization seems to be the truism that men lose their independence and their autonomy. When President Dwight Ei-

17. Ibid., p. 389.

18. E. W. Burgess, in Robert E. Park et al., *The City* (Chicago: University of Chicago Press, 1925).

19. For a fascinating account of some of the serious problems of spatial differentiation in cities see Jane Jacobs, *The Death and Life of Great American Cities* (New York: Random House, 1963). Ponder with Jacobs the consequences of the simple fact that large parts of the city go empty and unattended for several hours each day.

senhower left public life, he faced two ordinary but irritating problems—learning how to drive again and learning how to tie his shoelaces. It is difficult to imagine a modern American housewife plucking her own chicken. Workers no longer have the family plot to return to and would not know how to use it if it still existed.

2. One form of differentiation earlier noted was the multiplication of roles. Each role defines a particular set of functions and an obligation to carry out the functions. But inevitably, statuses also come to be involved; persons are identified by their roles, and some roles are considered more important than others. The more roles there are, the more occasions for invidious distinctions among roles, among types of roles, and among the people who are identified with each role. There are still some social values, such as wealth, social standing, popularity, around which major pecking orders are established. But there has nevertheless been a great increase of special status orders, so much so that a given individual may enjoy many different status positions during one waking day.[20]

3. Finally, it seems almost unnecessary to say that as people become separated by their specialties and by the roles and statuses that develop around the specialties (without mentioning the many nonoccupational roles and statuses), their view of the outside world and of their own relation to it is bound to be shaped accordingly. The more complex is the society, the more numerous and complex will be the distribution of interests. There are enormous varieties of relations to the market. There are proportionate numbers of economic and noneconomic groupings.

By this route we are led to a confrontation with the two central sources of disequilibrium in industrial societies. They cannot be eliminated, but rather must somehow be controlled. These are alienation and conflict. They seem to be as much a part of capitalistic practice as is the market. Moreover, they seem to increase along with the expansion of the market system, a factor which bears heavily against the argument that markets solve their own social problems.

Some may define alienation as the narrow issue of work and its meaning; but the problem is obviously broader than that. Specialization reduces a person's chances of developing a whole personality; it can twist and depersonalize him or her. People thus become alienated from themselves; they become anomic. They also become alienated from other people—from their own families, from friends, from the community. Work becomes a mere matter of compulsion. People no longer own their own tools. Their labor, therefore *they*, become a commodity. Work can become separated from life, and life can become so divided and subdivided that one loses the human meaning of living. To any Marxist, the Smithian and the Ricardian curves (in Figure 1.1)

20. For the effect of this on general social class stratification, see Sir Ernest Barker's observations in Chapter 2.

are the curves of alienation. But such interpretations are not the exclusive invention of Marxist ideologues. Thoreau, for example, objected "to the division of labor since it divided the worker, not merely the work, reduced him from a man to an operative, and enriched the few at the expense of the many." Tocqueville, as we shall see, was equally concerned.[21]

Increased potential for conflict is hardly more than another way of looking at alienation. Specialization, extreme mobility, large markets, enormous ranges of choice (far greater for the commoner today than to the king of antiquity), discontinuities between each generation, renewal every forty years, vastly increased scale—these are a few of the things one usually has in mind when one tries to capture the difference between modern and premodern communities. No longer do people grow up together, know exactly what to expect of one another, move in easy interactions by unconscious cues. Yet they must somehow interact, indeed more frequently and over a wider range of infinitely more complex expectations. Many conflicts settle themselves if they are at all subject to an economic calculus. But the others, the majority certainly, are either settled by informal, individual endeavor, or, increasingly, are dealt with administratively. It is clear that neither of these methods of settlement depends upon automatic forces.

Karl Mannheim best captured the meaning of alienation and conflict with his formulation, "displacement of self-regulating small groups."[22] To Mannheim, society literally entered into a process of disintegration when it expanded from "a parochial world of small groups . . . into a Great Society [sic] in a comparatively short time."[23] Mannheim was strongly confirmed by on-the-scene observers, as suggested already by Marx, Maine, and de Tocqueville. Jefferson was another, a man far less optimistic than his French, British, or American contemporaries that some sort of commercial calculus would be sufficient in the dreaded urban society. To Mannheim—and others—self-regulation could not work beyond families, local markets, traditions. The very requirements of the expanded markets of commercial societies prevent them from being fully sufficient as social forces.

We need not go all the way with Marx and Mannheim—and many like-minded theorists during the years between them—in order to accept their hypotheses. We do not have to use the term *alienation* to see that differentiation, interdependence, multiplied statuses and interests, etcetera, etcetera, might tend to weaken the automatic or self-regulating social mechanisms. Yet those same factors—all of the forces discussed in this chapter—increase the

21. Quoted in C. Wright Mills, *White Collar* (New York: Oxford University Press, 1951), p. 225. See an analysis of de Tocqueville, in Chapter 2, below.

22. Karl Mannheim, *Freedom, Power and Democratic Planning* (New York: Oxford University Press, 1950), p. 11.

23. Ibid., p. 4. Many a modern antisocialist agrees wholly with Mannheim's diagnosis. See, for example, a fascinating field study by Baker Brownell, *The Human Community* (New York: Harper & Brothers, 1950).

number of situations in which people with different goals must deal with each other. Thus we run into the final dilemma: *There is an inverse relation between the need and the availability of informal and automatic social controls. Those societies most in need of automatic social controls have fewer of them to bank on.*

The fact of the matter seems to be that the immense complexities of development and control in the industrial society are too powerful for thoughtless institutions. Leaders, seeking to reap the incredible benefits of technology, apply rationality to production and exchange. But it seems impossible to imagine that the effort to reap such benefits would stop there. The various forms of differentiation suggest that rationality quickly comes to be applied to virtually every personality, institution, group, and function in the social process.[24]

To suppose that rationalization stops merely with tasks, units of work, and markets is to suppose that modern society, after one revolutionary round of organizing, is just as mindlessly automatic as ever. In such a case our distance from the medieval would merely be a step from the organic to the mechanistic. Far newer arrangements must be accounted for. The modern method of social control involves the application of rationality to all social relations. In production we call it technology. In exchange it is called commerce or markets. In social structure we have here called it differentiation. *Rationality applied to social control is administration.* Administration may indeed be the *sine qua non* of modernity.

Administration is a necessary part of capitalism and capitalist society. But it never was incorporated into capitalist ideology. In fact, the idea of conscious and systematic application of legitimate controls on conduct, by public or private institutions, is rejected altogether by orthodox capitalist theory. Here was a gap between myth and reality that would inevitably weaken the myth. At a minimum it meant that public leadership would have to have a new public philosophy. Capitalist ideology could not last as the public philosophy because it could not accept capitalism in any other except the most orthodox commercial world. Orthodox capitalist theory recognized only one legitimate type of modern social control—competition. Yet capitalism is third only to the Church and warfare in its contribution to the rational approach to control, administration. Obviously an orthodox capitalist position that society must cease to change after an entrepreneurial revolution is no less absurd than an orthodox Marxist position that society must cease to change after a proletarian society is established.

24. It is applied even to our concept of time, according to Lewis Mumford, to whom "the clock, not the steam-engine, is the key-machine of the modern industrial age." The clock fathered the notion of orderly nature and regularity of behavior. See Mumford's *Technics and Civilization* (New York: Harcourt, Brace, 1934).

2

PLURALISM AND THE TRANSFORMATION OF CAPITALIST IDEOLOGY

Administration presents two basic dilemmas to capitalist theory. First, the predominance of administration proves that conscious control rather than mechanistic, automatic, self-control is the predominant fact about modern conduct. Second, it proves that even the remaining self-regulating mechanisms, still a substantial factor, have shifted in very large part from market competition to group competition—from self-regulation through economics to self-regulation through politics. These two factors became a sort of one-two punch. The first led finally to an acceptance of *statism*; that is, the overwhelming proportion of leaders embraced positive government. With its rise began a long dialogue with laissez-faire over the value of public control that led to the reclassification of laissez-faire as a conservative doctrine. The second led to *pluralism*, the intellectual core of the new liberalism which would eventually replace capitalism as the public philosophy by a process of absorption. The new public philosophy, interest-group liberalism, is the amalgam of capitalism, statism, and pluralism. The amalgam is evaluated in Chapter 3 and beyond. Here it is necessary to see how the parts could possibly fit together.

The Administrative Component and the Inevitability of Government

Administration is a process of self-conscious, formal adaptation of means to ends. Administered social relations are all those self-conscious and formal efforts to achieve a social end, whether expressed as a general condition like predictable conduct, legality, productivity, public order, or as a more concrete organizational goal. Many traditional social patterns continue to fulfill vital control functions in society. Economic and political competition are also vital controls. But the modern overlay upon all this is not so automatic. It is administration.

Many influential observers maintain that technology is the key to what is modern in the revolutionary Western civilization.[1] But this seems to beg the question, which is how and with what result men come to live peacefully and productively with each other in the presence of this technical complexity and scale and yet in the absence of complete familiarity. Karl Polanyi provided an appropriate riposte:

Social not technical invention was the intellectual mainspring of the Industrial Revolution. . . . The triumphs of natural science had been theoretical in the true sense, and could not compare in practical importance with those of the social sciences of the day. . . . The discovery of economics was an astounding revelation which hastened greatly the transformation of society . . . while the decisive machines had been the inventions of uneducated artisans some of whom could hardly read or write. It was both just and appropriate that not the natural but the social sciences should rank as the intellectual parents of the mechanical revolution which subjected the powers of nature to man.[2]

This is not to deny technology. It is only to ask for the social inventions through which a technical invention became revolutionary instead of a museum curiosity. Administration takes a machine and makes it a "man-machine" system. The increased pace of technological change in our epoch seems only to make the need for administration more intense—or else the technological change would be wasted.

In a sense, the administrative component is a fifth form of differentiation to go along with the four earlier identified. This fifth form is a differentiation of social units that perform "system maintaining" functions. Moreover, there are several dimensions. Units within groups are separated out to administer to the internal needs of the group. In the literature of administrative science these are usually referred to as staff, auxiliary, or overhead functions. Then there is a large category of groups and institutions whose entire function is to administer services to nonmembers and groups, services once performed automatically—or not at all. Thirdly, while most groups and institutions are not founded especially to do these good works, they tend just the same to spend a great deal of their time and resources administering against some possible social disequilibrium. Some may call these "latent functions."

ADMINISTRATION BY GOVERNMENTS

By far the most important mechanism of administered social relations is modern government. The rise of large government with a large administrative

1. See Michael Harrington, *The Accidental Century* (New York: Macmillan, 1965), and John Kenneth Galbraith, *The New Industrial State* (Boston: Houghton Mifflin, 1967), for expressions of this view.
2. Karl Polanyi, *The Great Transformation* (Boston: Beacon Press, 1957), p. 119.

core came relatively late in the United States but its coming is undoubted. Per capita dollar outlays by federal, state, and local governments are impressive when 1878 and 1908 are compared to 1938 and 1978. Also of great significance is the rise in administrative personnel in government. But of far greater significance is the nature of the outlays of dollars and the activities of the administrative personnel. Neither budgets nor bureaucrats will measure personnel. Neither budgets nor bureaucrats will measure the importance of such agencies as the Federal Reserve Board, the Interstate Commerce Commission (ICC) and its sister public service commissions in all the states, the rest of the "alphabetocracy" begun in the 1930s, and the research, service, and fiscal components added largely since then. Their administrative role in the fate of persons and properties is important beyond measure.

Any comparison of federal, state, and local government pre- and post-New Deal, as made frequently in Chapters 3–10, will indicate that the overwhelming proportion of government responsibility is administrative operation of facilities and services that a century ago were left primarily to family, neighborhood, local church, guild, and individual initiative.[3] Public schools have expanded downward to kindergarten and then to nursery school, toward further and further incorporation of family functions. They have expanded upward to take over more and more of the preparation for life that once was done in the labor market by the "School of Hard Knocks." And they have expanded outward, toward subjects and types of training never thought of as the province of school or anything else very public—sex hygiene, family finance, psychological and occupational guidance, and so on. (One of the basic undergraduate courses at Michigan State University for many years was Effective Living.) Along with this, the expansion of public welfare administration, with the federal Social Security programs, suggests the extent to which many other problems outside the realm of rudimentary socialization have ceased to be a normal part of the everyday life of traditional social units. The "problem of the aged" is a simple and poignant expression of the almost total disappearance of the extended family. We are faced here with two quite different methods of performing one of society's natural and inevitable duties. Obviously the contemporary form is administrative.

PRIVATE ADMINISTRATION

The governmental response to industrialization was very late in the United States, but when it did come it was swift, massive, and administrative. How-

3. Even as late as 1900 public education was slipshod and far from universal. There were no standards or administrative controls regarding teacher recruitment, and every school and local district was an operation in and of itself. Only around 71 percent of the children between 5 and 17 years of age were enrolled (compared to 84 percent in public schools alone in 1964), and an overwhelming proportion of these were attending part-time, one-room schools. These and many other significant figures are reported in Thomas R. Dye, *Politics, Economics, and the Public* (Chicago: Rand-McNally, 1966), Chapter 4.

ever, since the rise of modern administrative government was so late, it would be too easy to come to the erroneous conclusion that for most of our modern history public order was being maintained by the self-regulating mechanisms. On the contrary, it would be closer to the truth to propose that at no time in the past century or more was there a period when society in the United States was anywhere nearly self-regulating. Allowing for a time lag during the early consolidation of capital, the administrative component has developed in hand with the technological, the commercial, and the pluralistic components. The development was simply taking place in the private sector.

The rise of administration in the private sphere began early and has been dramatic. One measure of its importance can be seen in the employment picture given in Figures 2.1–2.3. In less that half a century, administrative em-

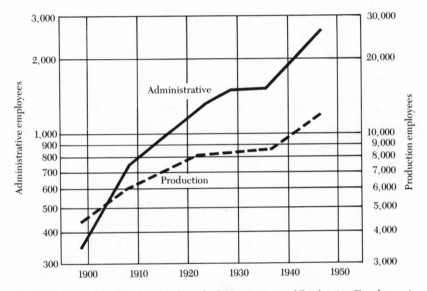

FIGURE 2.1 Increase in the Number of Administrative and Production Employees in Industry, the United States, 1899–1947 (in thousands)

ployees in the United States increased from below 6 percent to nearly 25 percent of all production employees.[4] The rise of this aspect of the administrative component has been even more extreme in Sweden and Great Britain. The rate of change has been a good deal less extreme in Germany (from 5 to about 12 percent) and in France (a rate which was static at the relatively high level of over 12 percent). However, these two latter cases are significant because France and Germany have had the largest and most authoritarian public sectors among the five. Perhaps the quantum of administrative need, public and private, was close to the same in all five.

4. The source for the following statistics and the graphs is Rinehart Bendix, *Work and Authority in Industry* (New York: Harper Torchbooks, 1963), pp. 216 ff.

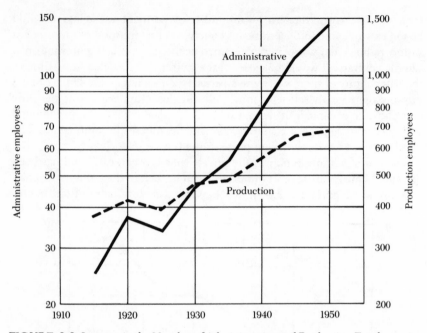

FIGURE 2.2 Increase in the Number of Administrative and Production Employees in Industry, Sweden, 1915–50 (in thousands)

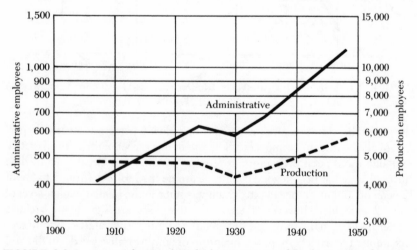

FIGURE 2.3 Increase in the Number of Administrative and Production Employees in Industry, Great Britain, 1907–48 (in thousands)

A look inside the larger corporations in the United States helps specify the elements of the private administrative component. Pricing and production decisions have long been removed from the market by an immense planning, programming, and research apparatus. Undoubtedly many an American giant had the equivalent of a Five-Year Plan earlier than did the Soviet government. Daniel Bell reports that as of 1956 white-collar workers outnumbered blue-collar workers. While not all white-collar workers are administrative, they do reflect the extent to which production works by shuffling papers, handling routines, and supervising or facilitating the conduct of others.[5]

As much as the administrative employee and internal bureaucratic apparatus help to measure the administrative component in production, so does the *trade association* indicate the degree to which the commercial dimension of the system—that is, the market economy itself—has come also to be an administrative process. The trade association is basically an administrative structure whose most important mission is regularizing relations among participants in the same industry, trade, or sector. Where the market seeks competition, the trade association seeks to administer. Trade associations have been widely defined erroneously as pressure groups first and foremost. While they are ubiquitous in Washington and the state capitols, their basic function is administering to their members.[6] For example, Raymond Bauer and associates were struck by the amount of time and energy trade associations spend informing and consulting their own members relative to the time spent in political bargaining and coalition-building, even when they are involved in a highly political issue.[7]

The population of trade associations began to mushroom in the late nineteenth century. From a few guilds and rate bureaus, formalized economic cooperation expanded to at least 12,000 national, state, and local trade associations in 1940, when an official census was taken.[8] Taking a complete contemporary census would be extremely complicated; but it is difficult to imagine any product, process, or service in the United States whose operatives are not represented and served by at least one of these agencies of private administration. Single firms of more than modest size usually find it desirable to

5. Daniel Bell, "Notes on the Post-Industrial Society," *The Public Interest* (Winter 1967), p. 28. In this fascinating essay Bell also suggests that the postindustrial society will be typified by even the administration of knowledge and innovation: "In one sense, chemistry is the first of the 'modern' industries because its inventions—the chemically-created synthetics—were based on theoretical knowledge of the properties of macromolecules, which were 'manipulated' to achieve the planned production of new materials" (p. 29).

6. See Melvin Anshen and Francis D. Wormuth, *Private Enterprise and Public Policy* (New York: Macmillan, 1954), p. 319. Their entire Chapter 11 is an excellent discussion of the various devices of "business self-government" administered by trade associations.

7. Raymond Bauer et al., *American Business and Public Policy* (New York: Atherton, 1963), especially pp. 315 ff.

8. Trade Association Survey, TNEC Monograph No. 18 (Washington, D.C.; U.S. Government Printing Office, 1941).

belong to several associations. Imagine the total number of associations if General Electric claims among its active affiliations a Porcelain Enamel Institute.[9]

Trade associations cannot be cast off as evils of overbureaucratized, overcentralized, and oligopolistic business that would disappear if some semblance of competition could be reintroduced. The fact is, the administrative functions of trade associations become even more necessary in decentralized markets. The number of firms is greater, the fear of competition is stronger; and the need for research and marketing services, trained personnel, and so on turns smaller firms to outside forms of administration where bigger firms can provide much of this internally. Three of the most famous trade associations—the National Association of Real Estate Boards, the National Association of Retail Druggists, and the American Medical Association—administer to highly decentralized markets.

The rise of private administration is not manifested only in economic phenomena. In the first place, many of the functions of all trade associations are noneconomic. Moreover, many thousands of groups that are not trade associations perform administrative services vital to the stability of the society. For example, regular social service becomes attached as a "latent function" to most groups. Robert Merton observes best how the old-time urban machine was rooted not merely in control of office but more solidly still in its displacement of impersonal controls with informal and personalized, yet systematic, controls.[10] Then there is the proliferation of groups—"do-gooder" groups—manifestly dedicated to ministering to one problem or another of socialization or social control. Between church school and public school and all related activities, almost nothing is left to the family, clan, neighborhood, or guild—or to chance. Even sandlot baseball has given way to Little Leagues, symptomatic of an incredible array of parental groups and neighborhood businesses organized to see that the child's every waking moment is organized, unprivate, wholesome, and, primarily, oriented toward an ideal of adjustment to the adult life of rationality that comes all too soon.

All of the larger voluntary associations, as well as most of the smaller ones have given up their sponteneity for a solid administrative core. The study of groups limited to capitols and city halls tends to exaggerate the political over the socioadministrative. Life in the cities would be hard to imagine without the congeries of service and charitable agencies that, systematically, help keep our streets clean of human flotsam and jetsam. Of growing importance are the

9. For good treatments see Robert A. Brady, *Business as a System of Power* (New York: Columbia University Press, 1943), pp. 189 ff.; and David B. Truman, *The Governmental Process* (New York: Knopf, 1951), pp. 55–62. Note particularly the second level of administration, the "peak association," an organization whose members are mainly other organizations.

10. Robert Merton, *Social Theory and Social Structure* (New York: Free Press, 1957), Chapter 1.

family-service agencies, agencies for the elderly, for adoption, and for maternal and child care, all of which in turn draw financial support from still other (for instance, Community Chest, United Fund) agencies that are still more tightly administrative. To repeat, all such groups naturally possess potential political power, but only occasionally are they politicized. The rest of the time they administer.

Another all-too-little appreciated example of private administration is the nonprofit sector of our economy and its phenomenal expansion in the past generation. In other countries many of these units are governmental, but that only emphasizes the administrative importance of their function in the United States. This sector includes mutual insurance companies, savings and loan associations, professional societies, foundations, cooperatives, health insurance programs, research organizations, private universities, and so on. Each deals administratively with some vital element of social relations. Each receives special privileges in tax law and in other ways precisely because as a category they are all considered to be dedicated more to community than to competitive goals. Together they employed 3.3 million people, or 4.9 percent of the labor force, in 1960. The growth of these organizations between 1950 and 1960 accounted for nearly one out of every two net new jobs, one in three of *all* new jobs.[11] These jobs are administrative, as are the organizations.

Perhaps the most unappreciated service in that sector, although by no means all of it is classified as nonprofit, is insurance. Most studies have catalogued the impressive rise of insurance as a mere part of the general phenomenon "concentration of economic power."[12] Or they give it no treatment at all.[13] But the insurance companies are far more socially significant in that we rely upon them to administer our conflicts, with each other or with nature, rather than leave these to spontaneous confrontation or traditional litigation. Companies set up to run death benefits and pensions have helped further to replace the family. Fire, automobile, theft, weather, travel, title, and other insurance is provided by companies that administer our liabilities.[14] The liability lawyer may not be so highly regarded as he goes after the big settlement and makes our premiums rise; but he is, for all that, no less important a functionary in the modern social apparatus. Ponder just for a moment the social implications of "liability insurance." Keeping these social accounts

11. Eli Ginzberg et al., *The Pluralistic Economy* (New York: McGraw-Hill, 1965), pp. 22, 61, 139. No equivalent study has been done since 1965, but there is little indication of change in these patterns.

12. This approach was inspired by the TNEC research of the late 1930s. For example, David Lynch, *The Concentration of Economic Power* (New York: Columbia University Press, 1946), pp. 122–23.

13. For example, W. W. Rostow, *The Stages of Economic Growth* (London: Cambridge University Press, 1960); and John Kenneth Galbraith, *American Capitalism* (Boston: Houghton Mifflin, 1952).

14. See Edgar S. and Jean C. Cahn, "What Price Justice: The Civilian Perspective Revisited," *Notre Dame Lawyer* (1966), pp. 936–38.

requires an incredibly large and intricate apparatus. The insurance industry is precisely that.

Finally, there is that category called interest groups, in the most orthodox pluralistic sense. Interest groups do compete and coalesce, as political scientists say. Yet they also possess an important administrative dimension. They would have no staying power at all if they did not have an efficient bureaucracy. This is particularly true of the large groups most frequently noted for their national political importance. Unions, like trade associations, administer and reduce competition within their own ranks. Job classification alone, despite such occasional absurdities as the electrician's helper who is forbidden to move a rug or a broom, is vital to industrial peace; and it is no less an administrative process because unions rather than government civil service commissions participate in the classification. Even when trade unions square off against employer groups the relationship is, at least since the 1930s, one in which the labor market is replaced by an administrative process. General demand affects collective bargaining, and together these two competitive mechanisms comprise part of the relationships. However, general demand and collective bargaining are most often marginal; in "labor-management relations," collective bargaining has become a brief, albeit critical, moment in a long process of administering the terms of the labor-management contract. In the strictly political realm fewer intergroup relations may be so strongly institutionalized; but the many notable examples suggest that the pattern is significant and increasing. From the National Association of Manufacturers (NAM) and the U.S. Chamber of Commerce and all the state chambers, to the Farm Bureau Federation, to the Federation of Jewish Philanthropies and the Council of Churches, to the AFL-CIO, we have layer upon layer of "peak associations," which exist to institutionalize relations among constituent groups. Each peak association and every major interest group started out as a coalition that eventually perpetuated itself by the development of a central administrative core. [15]

Stress on the administrative component is not an attempt to deny the existence of the self-regulating mechanisms of markets and pluralism. It is rather to stress what is still more modern about social control, including those very mechanisms. Groups, federations, insurance companies, corporations, and government agencies share at least one common trait; they impose an administrative process on as much of their internal structures and on as much of their environments as they possibly can. Whether one looks first at the Little League, the bureaucratization of philanthropy, or community psychiatry; or

15. See Truman, *The Governmental Process*, Chapters 2–4. See also Robert Michels, *Political Parties* (New York: Collier Books; first published 1915). His general theory of parties and pressure groups is based largely on this sort of development among European unions and democratic socialist parties. See also Wallace Sayre and Herbert Kaufman, *Governing New York City* (New York: Russell Sage Foundation, 1960), pp. 497 ff., for the composition of typical large groups in cities.

whether one comes first to appreciate the cheap insurance which is the real secret of farm bureaus and many other societies; or whether one starts with awareness of the indenturing of the middle classes in career and salary plans and retirement plans; or whether one looks at the staff of a powerful pressure group or the headquarters of a national trade association—one way or the other the true image of modern society emerges. In hardly more than two peaceful generations the great American prototype has passed from Andrew Carnegie to Dale Carnegie.

Pluralism, Its Influence, Its Fallacies

Central to capitalist theory is the belief that power and control are properties of the state and, therefore, should be feared and resisted. This proposition, while hard to deny, is patently one-sided; in fact it covers only one of at least three sides. It says nothing about who controls the state; and it says nothing about institutions other than the state that possess the same properties of power and control.

The Marxist critique of capitalism is overwhelming on the question of control of the state, especially when applied to the very period of industrial growth when fear of the state was so pervasive in the United States. Up to a point capitalist values were so directly expressed in the activities of federal and state governments that it would have been impossible to say where the one ended and the other began. The very idea of capitalist public philosophy can be accurately termed a euphemism for capitalist political power during most of the nineteenth century. It was not a question of influence *on* the policy-maker; capitalism was so pervasive because it operated as an influence *in* the policy-maker.

Important as the Marxist analysis has been, American history suggests that it, like capitalist theory, presents one-sided truths. The side left untouched by capitalism and falsely treated by Marxism is that of the nature and significance of the institutions other than the state in an industrial civilization. Here the pluralist model is overwhelmingly superior, at least for American society.

Pluralist theory begins with recognition that there are many sources of power and control other than the state. In our differentiated society, there will be many basic interests represented by organizations able and willing to use power. This is why the pluralist can accept government expansion with equanimity. But the significance of the pluralistic organization of the society goes beyond that. Since there are so many well-organized interests, there is, in pluralist theory, no possibility that a unitary society, stratified in two or three simple, homogenized classes, could persist. The result, however, is not the Marxist revolution where the big class devours the small, but an evolution in which the unitary society becomes a pluralistic one—that is, where the addition and multiplication of classes tends to wipe out the very notion of class stratification.[16] Stratification in two simple classes, bourgeoisie and proletariat, seems to have been a passing phase of early industrialization. Perhaps that is the reason why it figured so large in the sociology of Marx.

PLURALISM AS THEORY: UBIQUITY OF CONTROL, AUTONOMY OF POLITICS

Alexis de Tocqueville, over a decade before Marx, identified many of the fundamental features of the industrial society. He expressed strikingly similar concern about the sort of society which was emerging. In his essay "How an Aristocracy May Be Created by Manufactures," Tocqueville went to the core of the matter. He began by recognizing the importance of the division of labor and proceeded immediately to a consideration of what it does to human beings and social classes:

While the workman concentrates his faculties more and more upon the study of a single detail, the master surveys an extensive whole, and the mind of the latter is enlarged in proportion as that of the former is narrowed. . . . [I]n proportion as the mass of the nation turns to democracy, that particular class which is engaged in manufactures becomes more aristocratic. Men grow more alike in the one, more different in the other; and inequality increases in the less numerous class in the same ratio in which it decreases in the community.[17]

However, unlike Marx, Tocqueville provided more than a theory of alienation within simple social classes. He also paid attention to the composition of this industrial aristocracy. Tocqueville saw this new aristocracy as quite peculiar in comparison to its predecessors. While there are and will be extremes of wealth and poverty, the members of the new aristocracy do not constitute a unitary social class, for there develop no feelings of class, no consciousness of shared status:

To tell the truth, though there are rich men, the class of rich men does not exist; for these rich individuals have no feelings or purposes, no traditions or hopes, in common; there are individuals, therefore, but no definite class. . . . [T]he rich [are] not compactly united among themselves.[18]

This was the very basis of James Madison's argument half a century before—and nothing had happened between Madison and Tocqueville to alter

16. For a well-balanced discussion of the weakening of social class stratification in the United States and other industrializing societies, see Sir Ernest Barker, *Reflections on Government* (New York: Oxford University Press, 1942), pp. 108 ff.

17. Alexis de Tocqueville, *Democracy in America*. Reprinted in Lowi, *Private Life and Public Order* (New York: Norton, 1968), p. 15.

18. Ibid., p. 15.

the fact—that industrialization produces social diversity along with extremes of wealth and poverty: "A landed interest, a manufacturing interest, a mercantile interest, a moneyed interest, with many lesser interests."[19] Developments in the generations since *Federalist 10* would only require that we lengthen Madison's list. Pluralists do not have to deny the Marxian proposition that there is a conflict between those who own and those who work for those who own. They need only answer by adding to Marx's the other equally intense conflicts. Exporters cannot love importers, except perhaps on the Fourth of July—and, in fact, many people may still have misgivings about the patriotism of importers. Renters cannot love owners. Borrowers cannot love lenders, nor creditors debtors, and this is particularly interesting in our day, when the biggest debtors are not the poor but the rich. Retailers cannot love wholesalers. The black middle class loves neither the black lower class nor the white sellers of middle-class housing.

In this context the existence of the administrative component merely confirms the reality of the pluralist model of society. Groups amount to far more than a façade for a class. Administration gives each basic interest an institutional core, renders each interest less capable of being absorbed or neutralized, gives each interest the capacity to articulate goals, integrate members, provide for leadership and succession, in short, to perpetuate itself. The organization of interests is the first step, but after rudimentary organization comes staff, procedures, membership service, internal propaganda, addition of more permanent personnel, salaried help, files—corporate existence, staying power.

As alluded to above, the pluralist model cuts equally against capitalist theory. It renders absurd the capitalist notion that government is the only source of power and control. It rightly rejects any and all notions of a natural distinction between the functions of government and the functions of nongovernmental institutions. Power and control are widely distributed. They are in fact ubiquitous.

Sayre and Kaufman introduce a useful game for pursuing the problem of government and nongovernment.[20] Try to identify a governmental activity for which there is not an important counterpart in some private institution. The judiciary? Mediation and arbitration play a widespread and increasing role. Police? Pinkertons are famous in our history; today every large company and school has its own security force, and private eyes continue to be hired for peephole duty; many highly innovating industries have their own secret service working in the world of industrial espionage. Welfare? Any listing of private, highly bureaucratized and authoritative welfare systems would be as long as it is unnecessary. Armies? It is difficult to overestimate the significance of private armies in the past, or such present private armies as those possessed by the Mafia and other syndicates, not to mention the neighborhood gangs

19. Ibid., p. 19.
20. Sayre and Kaufman, *Governing New York City*, pp. 57–58.

and Minutemen. Society highly prizes the function they perform in administering the acceptable vices and keeping the violence associated with these vices subterranean. Obviously the game need not be carried into every realm.

Some activities may be found universally among modern governments; but they will not be found *only* in governments. Moreover, the complete pattern of functions associated with any given government is the result of time, chance, culture, and politics. Government is only one institution of social control, as it was and always will be. Government is distinguishable from other institutions, as we shall soon see. But the distinction is not the one upon which the American Constitution and the nineteenth-century liberals erected their defenses.

This in turn reflects critically still further upon the Marxist model. Central to the pluralist model of power is the anti-Marxist hypothesis that with the flowering of the system of autonomous groups the monopoly hold of capitalism, or of any other class, passes. Control of the state does not pass from the capitalists to another class but rather is dispersed. This breaks the deterministic link between economics and politics: *In the pluralist system, modern developments have brought about a discontinuity between that which is socioeconomic and that which is political.* Politics in the pluralist model ceases to be an epiphenomenon of socioeconomic life. Politics becomes autonomous as the number of autonomous and competing social units multiplies.

In these simple propositions, reaching back to James Madison, lies the pluralist critique of capitalism and of Marxism. To summarize: (1) Groups, of which corporations are merely one type, possess power directly over a segment of society and also a share of control of the state. (2) Groups, rather than entrepreneurs and firms, are the dominant reality in modern life. (3) As long as even a small proportion of all interests remains strong and active, no unitary political class, or "power elite," will emerge. That is, in the pluralist system it is highly improbable that a consensus across a whole class can last long enough to institutionalize itself.[21]

PLURALISM AS IDEOLOGY: ITS STRENGTH

A good social theory is always but a step away from ideology. The better it is as theory, the more likely it is to become ideology. The bigger the scope of the theory the greater the likelihood of becoming the public philosophy. Pluralism became a potent American ideology. It did not become the public phi-

---

21. The best treatments of the theory, even though limited to cities, will be found in Robert A. Dahl, *Who Governs?* (New Haven: Yale University Press, 1961), and Nelson W. Polsby, *Community Power and Political Theory* (New Haven: Yale University Press, 1963). For a review of the issues and bibliography at the national level, see my "American Business, Public Policy, Case Studies and Political Theory," *World Politics* (July 1964).

losophy, but it is the principal intellectual member in a neocapitalistic public philosophy, interest-group liberalism.

Short and few are the steps in the reasoning procedure by which pluralist theory becomes pluralist ideology: (1) Since groups are the rule in markets and elsewhere, imperfect competition is the rule of social relations. (2) The method of imperfect competition is not really competition at all but a variant of it called bargaining—where the number of participants is small, where the relationship is face-to-face, and/or where the bargainers have "market power," which means that they have some control over the terms of their agreements and can administer rather than merely respond to their environment. (3) Without class solidarity, bargaining becomes the single alternative to violence and coercion in industrial society. (4) By definition, if the system is stable and peaceful it proves the self-regulative character of pluralism. It is, therefore, the way the system works and the way it ought to work.

A closer look will show how potent these principles are in a country so traditionally concerned about power. Most obviously they show pluralism to be very much in line with the realities of modern life. Groups and imperfect competition are impossible to deny. Second, the reasoning suggests that pluralism can be strongly positive toward government without relinquishing the traditional fear of government. Since the days of Madison the pluralist view has been that there is nothing to fear from government so long as many factions compete for its favor. Modern pluralism turned the Madisonian position from negative to positive; that is, government is good because many factions do compete for its favor. A third and obvious feature of pluralist reasoning is that with pluralism society remains automatic. Pluralism is just as mechanistic as orthodox Smithian economics, and since the mechanism is political it reinforces acceptance of government. Pluralists believe that pluralist competition tends toward an equilibrium, and therefore that its involvement with government can mean only good. Use of government is simply one of many ways groups achieve equilibrium. Pluralist equilibrium is really the public interest.

Pluralism's embrace of positive government first put it at an ideological pole opposite capitalism. This is the foundation of the liberal-conservative dialogue that bridged the gap between the old public philosophy and the new. On the basis of these opposing positions, debate over great issues took place in the United States, even without socialism, for many years following 1890. But this situation was only temporary. The two apparent antitheses ultimately disappeared. The rhetoric continued, so that even today one may occasionally feel that the two poles represent substantial differences. But in reality they have come to represent a distinction without a difference. Capitalism and pluralism were not actually synthesized, however; in a sense, they absorbed each other.

PLURALISM AS IDEOLOGY: ITS FALLACIES

Here lies also the source of the weakness and eventual failure of interest-group liberalism, which has led us into a crisis of public authority in the United States in the 1960s more serious than any other in the twentieth century. Pluralism had helped bring American public values into the twentieth century by making the state an acceptable source of power in a capitalist society. Pluralism had also made a major contribution by helping to break down the Marxian notion of solidary classes and class-dominated government. But the zeal of pluralism for the group and its belief in a natural harmony of group competition tended to break down the very ethic of government by reducing the essential conception of government to nothing more than another set of mere interest groups.

The strength of pluralism rested in very great part upon the proposition, identified earlier, that a pluralist society frees politics by creating a discontinuity between the political world and the socioeconomic world. However, there is a related proposition that present pluralist theories either reject or miss altogether: *In a pluralist society there is also a discontinuity between politics and government.* The very same factors of competition and multiple power resources that frees politics from society also frees government from both society and politics. This is precisely why pluralism appealed to such constitutionalists as Madison. Group competition could neutralize many of the most potent power centers sufficiently to keep all of them within the formal structure of government. This was the Madisonian method of regulating groups and protecting the governmental authorities from control by any "majority," which could mean a class elite, a capitalist group, or a mass social movement. In contemporary pluralism this aspect of the pluralist argument has gone by the boards. Groups become virtuous; they must be accommodated, not regulated. Formalism in government becomes mere formality. Far from Madison, they could say, as the disappointed office seeker is supposed to have said to President Grover Cleveland, "What's a Constitution among friends?"

It should thus be evident that pluralist theory today militates against the idea of separate government. Separate government violates the basic principle of the automatic political society. This was reinforced by the scientific pluralist's scientific dread of such poetic terms as *public interest, the state,* and *sovereignty* that admittedly cannot be precisely defined and are closely associated aesthetically with the notion of separate government. But by such means pluralism gained a little and lost a lot. Only three of its losses are pursued here: (1) Pluralist theory achieved almost no additional scientific precision by insisting that government was nothing but an extension of the political process. (2) It could maintain this fiction, and the fiction of the automatic political society, only by elimination of *legitimacy*. (3) It could maintain those fictions only by elimination of *administration*.

1. In 1908, Arthur F. Bentley fathered the scier
as an interest that could be thought of "as an inte
preference for the immaculateness of the formu/
ever since felt the tug of limitation more than t'
the way concessions have been made, so t'
inclusive set of relationships that we call the sta.
tion did not seem to operate quite like a pressure g.
concept of a "potential interest group" whose interest is
game."[24] These formulations did not introduce precision. They
stituted an invitation to disregard those aspects of the political system ni.
ceptible to group interpretation and the hypothesis of natural equilibrium.
Even to the most sophisticated, government became "the political process."
We shall see the results in Chapter 3.

2. Competition and its variant, bargaining, are types of conflict distinguishable by the existence of rules. Rules convert conflict into competition.
But rules and their applications imply the existence of a framework of controls
and institutions separate from the competition itself. Whether we call this a
public or not, *there is a political context that is not itself competition* within
which political competition takes place.

A good way to approach the problem of the distinction is to return momentarily to the game of counterparts. It must have occurred to many already that
something was missing. Once while participating in the exercise a student
found the missing dimension by identifying prisons and imprisonment as a
public activity without private counterpart. Leaving aside a quibble over the
question of whether the Mafia has a prison system, it is easy to spot the essential point implied to the student in his choice of governmental activity. The
practice of imprisonment suggests simply that the intrinsic governmental feature is *legitimate use of coercion*.

Legitimacy is not easy to operationalize, but its problems are actually easier
to solve than those the pluralist solution offers, because our interest is not in
measuring the behavioral attribute in question but only in using the fact of its
existence as a criterion. It justifies our treating the state as a real thing apart
and not merely a group or a poetic figment. Thus, while governments can
rarely if ever perform any function that a nongovernmental institution cannot
also perform, governmentalization of a function—that is, passing a public
policy—is sought because the legitimacy of its sanctions makes its social controls more surely effective. This is what activates and motivates politics in the
pluralist system, but it is far from being part and parcel of pluralism.

3. Finally, rules and their enforcement do not merely exist. They must be
applied with regularity and some degree of consistency if pluralist competition

22. Quoted in Truman, *The Governmental Process*, p. 51.
23. Ibid., p. 52.
24. Ibid., pp. 51–52.

ist at all. This is administration. Administration is necessary to con-
and to change the system within which pluralism is to operate, yet
alism presupposes the existence of that favorable structure, just as laissez-
ire presupposed a social system favorable to itself. To pluralists, social
change in a pluralist system works in small increments. "Incrementalism" is
what moves the successful polity, and by definition that is how the successful
polity ought to be moved. This means that social oscillation in the pluralist
ideal is and ought to occur at a very narrow range around some point of equilibrium. But note how susceptible all of this is to the criticisms earlier heaped
upon capitalist theory. First, it takes a certain predefined equilibrium as good
and presupposes it in order to work the theory. Second, recall the problem of
market perfection: Even if you get your economic equilibrium it may not be
at anywhere near full employment. The political variant of this would be
equilibrium at something far less than an acceptable level of participation, or
satisfaction, or even public interest. Let us take a simple dimension to illustrate both points: expansion of membership in the system. This usually comes
from critical, as distinct from incremental, changes, and is usually imposed
administratively. One need only ponder the case of the blacks, who were first
kept out of the pluralist system for ages, and who are being only now introduced into it not only by fiat but by a fiat with force, accompanied by intricate and authoritative processes of administration. [25]

One of the most influential pluralist scholars, Robert A. Dahl, has made
the following proposition about the political system: "When two individuals
conflict with one another . . . they confront three great alternatives: deadlock,
coercion, or peaceful adjustment."[26] Deadlock is "no deal"; there is no
change of demands or behavior on either side. Coercion to Dahl means forc-
ible change of behavior by physical imposition. This he feels is an extremely
exceptional alternative, rarely involved even in governmental acts, all the
more rarely involved in the affairs of popular governments. Everything else,
including all other methods of government, comes under the rubric "peaceful
adjustment," by which he means consultation, negotiation, and the search
for mutually beneficial solutions.[27] Obviously this cannot possibly exhaust
the alternatives. It relies on an extremely narrow definition of coercion, giving
one to believe that coercion is not involved if physical force is absent. And it
depends on an incredibly broad and idealized notion of what is peaceful about
peaceful adjustment. A slight readjustment of Dahl's categories will reveal
what is missing. It will also reveal the ideological element just underneath the
skin of pluralist theory. What Dahl is really dealing with here are the logical

25. This will be further developed in Chapter 3, below; and Chapter 7 is a case of the unanticipated consequences of pluralistic influences on administration in racially significant areas of
policy.
26. Robert A. Dahl, *Modern Political Analysis* (Englewood Cliffs: Prentice-Hall, 1963), p. 73.
27. Ibid., p. 71.

relations between two continua—the extent to which coercion is involved and the extent to which adjustment is involved in any response to conflicting interests. This slight formalizing of his scheme yields the following results:

TABLE 2.1

THE PROPERTIES OF POLITICAL RELATIONSHIPS

| | | LIKELIHOOD OF PEACEFUL ADJUSTMENT | |
		LOW	HIGH
LIKELIHOOD OF COERCION	Remote	Deadlock	Negotiation
	Immediate	"Coercion"	?

What goes in the fourth cell of the four-cell table of properties of political relationships? It is a vast category. It must include virtually all of the public and private governmental processes in which people have internalized the sanctions that might be applied. The element of coercion may seem absent when in actuality the participants are conducting themselves in a certain way largely because they do not feel they have any choice.[28] Since it is well enough accepted to go unnoticed, this coercion can be called legitimate. Since it is regular and systematic, it can be called administration because an administrative component must be there if the conduct in question involves a large number of people making these peaceful adjustments. This immense fourth "great alternative" is missing from Dahl's scheme because it is beyond the confines of the theory of the perfect, self-regulating pluralist society. That fourth cell is actually the stable regime of legitimacy and effective administration without which neither the reality nor the theory of pluralism has any meaning.

THE PRINCIPLE OF SEPARATE GOVERNMENT AND THE CONSEQUENCES OF ITS REJECTION

Many social theorists earlier in the century stressed the distinction between nongovernment and government. Weber's definition of government is founded on the distinction.[29] Mosca based his classification of modern and traditional systems upon the distinction.[30] Robert McIver and many others

28. Grant McConnell, in a brilliant analysis of the myth of democracy in trade unions, aptly refers to the group phenomenon as "private government." *Private Power and American Democracy* (New York: Knopf, 1966), Chapter 5. This phenomenon is neither all peaceful adjustment nor all coercion. It seems to belong in the fourth cell, and it applies to many relations among groups and between groups and government, as well as to relations within the big groups.

29. A. M. Henderson and Talcott Parsons, *Max Weber: The Theory of Social and Economic Organization* (New York: Oxford University Press, 1947), p. 156.

30. See Gaetano Mosca, *The Ruling Class* (New York: McGraw-Hill, 1939), especially the part quoted above, Chapter 1.

based their liberal response to syndicalism upon the same distinction, passionately affirmed:

The extreme insistence of the guild socialists on functional representation becomes an attack on the state itself. . . . A nation is not simply composed of crafts and professions. These might logically elect an economic "parliament," but if it possessed also political sovereignty it would be a denial of the whole process which has differentiated economic and political centres of power. The state is retained in name but disappears in fact. . . . Political representation is real only because it is not based on any function but citizenship.[31]

E. Pendleton Herring, although one of the key figures in developing pluralist political science, was still able to warn in the 1930s that while the "government of the democratic state reflects inescapably the underlying interest groups of society . . . the very fact that the state exists evinces a basic community of purpose."[32]

These authors were defending the notion of a distinguishable government from the doctrines of fascists, syndicalists, corporativists, and guild socialists because it was these doctrines and experiments that sought to destroy the distinction. Not very much later American liberalism began to develop in the same direction, but these features of it tended to escape attention precisely because American pluralists had no explicit and systematic view of the state. They simply assumed it away. Such negative intellectual acts seldom come in for careful criticism.

Concern for government was an American culture trait. Yet, ironically, once the barriers to its expansion were broken, government ceased almost altogether to be a serious issue. Destruction of the principle of separate government, the coerciveness of government, the legitimacy of government, the administrative importance of government, was necessary if capitalist ideology was to be transformed rather than replaced. The fusion of capitalism and pluralism was a success; destruction of the principle of separate government was its secret.

As this aspect of pluralism becomes dominant in the new public philosphy its more repulsive features can more easily be seen. The new liberal public philosophy was corrupted by the weakness of its primary intellectual component, pluralism. The corrupting element was the myth of the automatic society granted us by an all-encompassing, ideally self-correcting, providentially automatic political process. This can hardly be more serviceable than the nineteenth-century liberal (now conservative) myth of the automatic society granted us by the total social equilibrium of freely contracting individuals in

31. Robert M. McIver, *The Modern State* (New York: Oxford University Press, 1964; first published 1926), pp. 465–66.
32. E. Pendleton Herring, *Public Administration and the Public Interest* (New York: McGraw-Hill, 1936), p. 397.

the market place. The pluralist myth helped bring about the new public philosophy, but the weaknesses of the myth made certain the degeneration of the public philosophy. What has it degenerated into? What kind of liberalism can be formulated to take its place?

3

THE NEW PUBLIC
PHILOSOPHY
Interest-Group Liberalism

Why Nineteenth-Century Liberalism Declined

The decline of capitalist ideology as the American public philosophy took the form of a dialogue between a private and a public view of society. This dialogue, between a new liberalism and an old liberalism (redefined as conservatism) comprises the constitutional epoch immediately preceding our own, ending in 1937. During this period there was no prevailing public philosophy but rather two bodies of competing ideology. Liberal and conservative regimes derived their specific uses of government and policy from their general positions, and differences between the two national parties were for the most part clear within these terms. The perennial issue underlying the dialogue was the question of the nature of government itself and whether expansion or contraction of government best produced public good. Expansion of government was demanded by the new liberalism as the means of combating the injustices of a brutal world that would not change as long as we passively submitted ourselves to it. The mark of the new liberalism was its assumption that the instruments of government provided the means for conscious inducement of social change and that outside the capacity for change no experimentation with new institutional forms would be possible. Opposition to such means, but not necessarily to the proposed forms themselves, became the mark of contemporary conservatism.

Across all disagreements there was unanimity on the underlying criteria. These basic criteria were attitude toward government and attitude toward social change. There was also agreement, which persists today, that these two attitudes are consistent and reinforcing, both as guides for leaders in their choices among policies and as criteria for followers in their choices among leaders. For example,

Conservatism is committed to a discriminating defense of the social order against change and reform (liberalism). . . . By the Right, I mean generally those parties and movements that are skeptical of popular governments, oppose the bright plans of the reformers and dogooders, and draw particular support from men with a sizable stake in the established order. By the Left, I mean generally those parties and movements that demand wider popular participation in government, push actively for reform, and draw particular support from the disinherited, dislocated and disgruntled. As a general rule, to which there are historic exceptions, the Right is conservative or reactionary, the Left is liberal or radical.[1]

These two criteria arose out of a particular constitutional period, were appropriate to that period, and provided a mutually reinforcing basis for doctrine during that period. After 1937, the Constitution did not die from the Roosevelt revolution, as many had predicted, but the basis for the liberal-conservative dialogue did die. Liberalism-conservatism as the source of public philosophy no longer made any sense. Once the principle of positive government in an indeterminable but expanding political sphere was established, criteria arising out of the very issue of expansion became irrelevant.

LIBERALISM-CONSERVATISM: THE EMPTY DEBATE

The old dialogue passed into the graveyard of consensus. Yet it persisted. Old habits die hard. Its persistence despite its irrelevance means that the liberal-conservative debate has become almost purely ritualistic. And its persistence even in ritualistic form has produced a number of evil effects among which the most important is the blinding of the nation to the emergence of a new and ersatz public philosophy. The coexistence of a purely ritualistic public dialogue and an ersatz and unrecognized new public philosophy has produced most of the political pathologies of the 1960s and 1970s. The decline of a meaningful dialogue between a liberalism and a conservatism has meant the decline of a meaningful adversary political proceedings in favor of administrative, technical, and logrolling politics. In a nutshell, politics became a question of equity rather than a question of morality. Adjustment comes first, rules of law come last, if at all. The tendency of individuals to accept governmental decisions simply because these decisions are good has probably at no time in American history, save during the Civil War, been less widely distributed and less intensely felt. Cynicism and distrust in everyday political processes have never been more widespread. The emerging public

1. Clinton Rossiter, *Conservatism in America* (New York: Knopf, 1955), pp. 12, 15. The term *conservative* came to be attached to nineteenth-century liberals because they favored the government and social order that had become the established fact of the nineteenth-century United States. There is other conservatism in America—racial, aristocratic, ethnic, perhaps even monarchic and feudalistic. But the major part of it is nineteenth-century liberalism grown cold with success. This already suggests the narrow span of the ideological gamut in the United States.

philosophy, interest-group liberalism, has sought to solve the problems of public authority in a large modern state by defining them away. This has simply added the element of demoralization to that of illegitimacy. Interest-group liberalism seeks to justify power by avoiding law and by parceling out to private parties the power to make public policy. A most maladaptive political formula, it was almost inevitably going to produce a crisis of public authority even though its short-run effects seem to be those of consensus and stabilization.

A brief look at a few hard cases will expose the emptiness of the old liberal-conservative dialogue and the kinds of pathology it was likely to produce. Table 3.1 shows at a glance how irrelevant the old criteria are to present policies.[2] In the table there are a number of public policies and private policies (or widely established private practices) that have been arranged according to the two fundamental dimensions of liberalism-conservatism. Above the line is the public sphere containing public policy; below the line are the policies and established group practices associated with the private sphere. This vertical dimension is a simple dichotomy; therefore, the "liberal" dimension is supposedly above the line and the "conservative" dimension is below the line. The horizontal axis is a continuum whereupon each policy or practice is placed along the line from left to right roughly according to its probable impact upon the society. To the left is the liberal direction, where policies are placed if they are likely to produce a direct social change. To the right is the conservative direction because the policies and practices placed there are thought to militate against change and to support the status quo.[3]

If the two dimensions—attitude toward government and attitude toward change—were consistent, and if together they described and justified all public policy, then liberal policies would be concentrated in the upper left corner and conservative policies in the lower right. In reality these policies range all across the continuum, below and above the line. Little reflection is necessary to perceive the fact that policy-makers are being guided by criteria very different from those underlying Table 3.1. Obviously the liberal-conservative dialogue made no sense after the principle of positive government was established.[4]

2. The method of analysis is drawn from R. A. Dahl and C. E. Lindblom, *Politics, Economics, and Welfare* (New York: Harper & Brothers, 1953), Chapter 1, although the two of them may not necessarily agree with the particular uses here.

3. Placement along the continuum is gross and informal. However, it is very doubtful that any placement of these policies could reduce the spread from left to right. Moreover, differences of opinion as to the effect of a policy upon society would lead to the very kind of policy analysis political scientists need to get involved in.

4. Some readers will argue that there is still another dimension of difference, attitudes toward equality and welfare. Adding a third dimension to a diagram of this sort would overly complicate matters, but some response to this kind of objection can be made textually: (1) The equality dimension is already implicitly present in the sense that the policies to the left of the continuum

TABLE 3.1
Selected Public and Private Policies Arranged According to Probable Effect on Society

GRADUATED INCOME TAX (POTENTIAL)						HIGH AND RIGID FARM PRICE SUPPORTS
Social Security programs based on graduated income tax	Luxury taxes	Growth fiscal policies	Countercyclical fiscal policies	Social Security programs based on insurance principles (U.S.)	Existing farm programs	High tariffs
Civil rights package	Real antitrust	Graduated income tax (United States)	Sales taxes	Direct regulation (e.g., FCC, ICC, CAB, etc.)	Restraint of competition (NRA, fair trade, antiprice discrimination)	Import quotas
Low tariffs	"Yardstick" regulation (TVA)		Aids to small business	Antitrust by consent decree	Tax on colored margarine	Utilities
						Group representation on boards
						Strict gold standard with no bank money
Competition in agriculture	*Competitive business*	*Oligopoly with research competition*	*Oligopoly without competition (steel, cigarettes)*	*Trade associations*		*Monopoly*
New interest groups	*Corporate philanthropy*		*Brand names*	*Pools*		*Old interest groups (NAM, AFL-CIO, TWU, etc.)*
	Merit hiring and promotion		*Ethnic appeals of political campaigns*	*Basing points*		
				Price leadership		
				Fair trade policies		
				Union unemployment and automation policies		

Above the line: Public policies ("liberal")
Below the line: Private policies or practices ("conservative")

Toward the left side: Policies likely to produce change ("liberal")
Toward the right side: Policies likely to maintain existing practices ("conservative")

LIBERALISM-CONSERVATISM: THE PUBLIC POLICIES

Although the distance above or below the line on Table 3.1 is not meant to convey additional information about the degree of public involvement, it is worthwhile to consider that dimension. This can be done by cross-tabulating each of the public policies according to the actual degree of government involvement against the probable degree of social change likely to be produced by that policy (Table 3.2). This particular look at government should be most unsettling to those who have assumed that political power is all one needs in order to achieve important humanitarian goals. Note especially how many government policies seem to congregate in cells labeled with a minus sign (hypothesized as likely to "militate against change"). Note also that government's relation to social change does not appear to increase as government involvement increases from one to two to three pluses. On the contrary, there almost seems to be an inverse relationship, suggesting that *government is most effective and most frequently employed when something in society has been deemed worthy of preservation.* This is why the notion of "maintaining public order" is more suitable than humanitarianism or egalitarianism as the initial hypotheses for an inquiry into the nature of contemporary government.

Analysis of the real or potential impact of public policies shows how incomplete is the fit between the old liberal-conservative public philosophies and the policies they were supposed to support and justify. The analysis reveals that those who espouse social change in the abstract, especially government-engineered social change, are seldom favoring policies that would clearly effect any social change. Conversely, the analysis shows that those who harangue on principle against government and against social change are frequently in real life supporting policies that would give us strong doses of both. If the guiding criteria do not really guide the leadership, they can certainly offer no plausible justification to the intelligent follower. A few examples will show why.

The income tax • All taxes discriminate. The political question arises over the kind of discrimination to choose. The graduated or progressive income tax is capable of effecting drastic changes in the relationships between social classes and between individuals and their property. According to the two dimensions governing Table 3.1, a steeply progressive income tax is "liberal" both because it is governmental and because it effects social change. Our own

---

tend to produce "change toward equality." However, (2) "equality" is a tendency produced by some private policies as well as public policies. Furthermore, (3) many public policies *reduce* the forces of equality (as well as change). Those in the upper right quadrant of the chart serve as examples. Welfare is no better a basis for distinguishing positions. (1) No definition of welfare could put it strictly within the province of the public or of the private sphere. And (2), no definition of "effect on welfare" would eliminate the enormous spread of public policies from left to right along the continuum.

TABLE 3.2

SELECTED PUBLIC POLICIES, TABULATED BY DEGREE OF SOCIAL CHANGE AND DEGREE OF GOVERNMENT INVOLVEMENT

Impact of Policy:
Likelihood of Significant Social Change

DEGREE OF GOVERNMENT INVOLVEMENT	CHANGE VERY LIKELY +++	CHANGE PROBABLE ++	+	−	MILITATES AGAINST CHANGE −	−−−
+++ Sustained and active intervention	Title VI of 1964 Civil Rights Act Civil Rights Act, 1965 Fully Progressive Income Tax (Hypothetical)	Walsh-Healy Civil Rights Act, 1964 Reciprocal Trade	TVA 1964 Tax cuts	Countercyclical fiscal policy Manpower Training Tax Revision 1961–62 Tax Cuts	FTC Area Redevelopment Nationalized industry	Defense construction Public Housing Farm Parity Old tariff ICC Utilities
++ Substantial involvement	1962 Trade Act	Aid to Education	COMSAT Appalachia	Patents Urban redevelopment	FCC CAB Social Security French & Italian public corporations War on Poverty	Farm extension NRA codes Robinson-Patman of FTC Monopolies
+ Low but measurable involvement	Head Start Free trade (Hypothetical)	Education grants-in-aid Title I Housing Research Subsidy			SEC	

income tax structure can be called only mildly progressive because of the varieties of exemptions written into the law. It is generally understood that the effective ceiling on taxes is not 91 percent or 75 percent but a good deal less than 50 percent, with many large corporations not paying any taxes at all. And taking all our taxes together, from the local property taxes to the federal luxury and inheritance taxes, it seems fairly clear that they are a bastion against rather than a weapon for fluidity among economic classes in the society. This is not an argument in favor of one tax structure or the other but rather an attempt to assess the general tendency as an illustration of the virtual irrelevance of old liberal-conservative principles. With virtually every new administration, there is vigorous talk of tax reform, but the interests in maintaining the present structure seem always to be too strong to be overcome.[5]

The Social Security system • This is a bundle of policies, and an accurate account would require classification of each program. On balance, however, Social Security programs in the United States are "liberal" only because they are governmental. Otherwise they are quite conservative in their impact on the social structure and upon the behavior of individual clients. If the general welfare is promoted by our Social Security system it is only because a basically conservative policy *can* promote welfare. Nevertheless these programs are conservative in at least two senses of the term. First, welfare policies are fiscal policies and as techniques of fiscal policy they are countercyclical; that is to say, they are automatic stabilizers that work systematically to maintain demand, and therefore existing economic relationships, throughout the business cycle. Second, Social Security programs are techniques of social as well as economic control. Government's role is essentially paternalistic. For those basic Social Security programs that depend upon employee contributions, the government is saying in essence, "This much of your income we will not trust you to spend but will hold it for you until you really need it." The discretionary and noncontributory social welfare programs are also paternalistic to the extent that they are making judgments about the relative need of each applicant and whether the family situation deserves governmental assistance.[6]

Farm policy • Farm programs provide an equally good case of the irrelevance of actual policies to the old criteria. High price supports with crop controls—the central feature of farm policy for a generation—are supported by so-called liberals despite the fact that the basic purpose of these programs has been to restore or maintain a pre-1914 agriculture in the face of extremely strong contrary economic developments. So-called conservatives have made it

---

5. For an effort to assess dispassionately the economic significance of tax exemptions and the political difficulties of reforming the tax structure, see Stanley S. Surrey, *Pathways to Tax Reform* (Cambridge, Mass.: Harvard University Press, 1973). For a lively account of some of the same problems, see Philip M. Stern, *The Rape of the Taxpayer* (New York: Random House, 1973).

6. Many more details will be found in Chapter 8. For an independent but related critique, see Francis Piven and Richard Cloward, *Regulating the Poor* (New York: Pantheon, 1971).

a point to oppose these programs despite the fact that the quick elimination of price supports would probably revolutionize the agriculture industry.[7]

The private sector • It is equally bizarre to rate as "conservative" support on principle of practices in the private sector. Competitive business enterprise is a highly dynamic force that usually makes change normal, innovation necessary, and influence by ordinary individuals over economic decisions possible. For these reasons many forms of competitive enterprise should warrant the support of real liberals. However, except for occasional martyrs, such as Thurman Arnold, who have sought vainly to use government to decentralize industry, the net impact of attitudes toward business from conservatives as well as liberals has been to put restraints on the most dynamic aspects of the private sphere. One could say that the only difference between old-school liberals and old-school conservatives is that the former would destroy the market through public means and the latter through private means.

As shown on Table 3.1, organized competition in the private sphere is highly dynamic and is one of the most important sources of change in society. But it is of equal importance to stress that holding companies, pools, market sharing, nonprice competition, and trade associations are strongly opposed to change; indeed they are usually organized for the purpose of resisting change. On the other hand, they are in no way functionally distinguishable from such government policies as basing-point laws, fair-trade laws, fair-competition laws, industrial-safety codes, and monopoly-rate regulation (see especially Chapter 5). Note also that interest groups have been placed on Table 3.1. Although they are not policies, strictly speaking, interest groups, especially trade associations and unions, are formed and supported as a matter of policy by entrepreneurs and corporations. Putting old groups on the right and new groups on the left suggests a very important political tendency, which is that new groups, regardless of their program, tend to have a very innovative effect on society while all established interest groups tend to be conservative.[8]

The old public philosophy, drawn from the liberal-conservative dialogue, became outmoded in our time because elites simply no longer disagree whether government should be involved. Therefore, they neither seek out the old criteria for guidance through their disagreements, nor do they really have need of the criteria to justify the mere governmental character of their policy proposals. But this does not mean that public leaders are free of ideology. Leaders need ideology because they need guidance, and more importantly in a democratic society, they need rationalization. If they are no longer governed by their old public philosophy, it is highly probable that another one is emerging to take its place but may not be clearly enough formulated to be fully appreciated by themselves or by the public at large.

7. See Chapter 4.
8. This particular tendency is pursued elaborately in a book of mine, *The Politics of Disorder* (New York: Basic Books, 1971); see especially Chapters 1 and 2.

Interest-Group Liberalism

The frenzy of governmental activity in the 1960s and 1970s proved that once the constitutional barriers were down the American national government was capable of prompt response to organized political demands. However, that is only the beginning of the story, because the almost total democratization of the Constitution and the contemporary expansion of the public sector has been accompanied by expansion, not contraction, of a sense of distrust toward public objects. Here is a spectacular paradox. It is as though each new program or program expansion had been an admission of prior governmental inadequacy or failure without itself being able to make any significant contribution to order or to well-being. It is as though prosperity had gone up at an arithmetic rate while expectations, and therefore frustrations, had been going up at a geometric rate—in a modern expression of Malthusian Law. Public authority was left to grapple with this alienating gap between expectation and reality.

Why did the expansion of government that helped produce and sustain prosperity also help produce a crisis of public authority? The explanation pursued throughout this volume is that the old justifications for expansion had too little to say beyond the need for the expansion itself. An appropriate public philosophy would have addressed itself to the purposes to which the expanded governmental authority should be dedicated. It would also have addressed itself to the forms and procedures by which that power could be utilized. These questions are so alien to public discourse in the United States that merely to raise them is to be considered reactionary, apolitical, or totally naïve.

Out of the emerging crisis of public authority developed an ersatz political formula that bears no more relation to those questions than the preceding political formula. The guidance the new formula offers to policy formulation is a set of sentiments that elevated a particular view of the political process above everything else. The ends of government and the justification of one policy or procedure over another are not to be discussed. The *process* of formulation is justified in itself. As observed earlier it takes the pluralist notion that government is an epiphenomenon of politics and makes out of that a new ethics of government.

There are several possible names for the new public philosophy. A strong candidate would be *corporatism*, but its history as a concept gives it several unwanted connotations, such as conservative Catholicism or Italian fascism. Another candidate is *syndicalism*, but among many objections is the connotation of anarchy too far removed from American experience. From time to time other possible labels will be experimented with, but, since the new American public philosophy is something of an amalgam of all of the candidates, some new terminology seems to be called for.

The most clinically accurate term to capture the American variant of all of these tendencies is _interest-group liberalism_. It is liberalism because it is optimistic about government, expects to use government in a positive and expansive role, is motivated by the highest sentiments, and possesses a strong faith that what is good for government is good for the society. It is interest-group liberalism because it sees as both necessary and good a policy agenda that is accessible to all organized interests and makes no independent judgment of their claims. It is interest-group liberalism because it defines the public interest as a result of the amalgamation of various claims. A brief sketch of the working model of interest-group liberalism turns out to be a vulgarized version of the pluralist model of modern political science: (1) Organized interests are homogeneous and easy to define. Any duly elected representative of any interest is taken as an accurate representative of each and every member.[9] (2) Organized interests emerge in every sector of our lives and adequately represent most of those sectors, so that one organized group can be found effectively answering and checking some other organized group as it seeks to prosecute its claims against society.[10] And (3) the role of government is one of insuring access to the most effectively organized, and of ratifying the agreements and adjustments worked out among the competing leaders.

This last assumption is supposed to be a statement of how a democracy works and how it ought to work. Taken together, these assumptions amount to little more than the appropriation of the Adam Smith "hidden hand" model for politics, where the group is the entrepreneur and the equilibrium is not lowest price but the public interest.[11]

These assumptions are the basis of the new public philosophy. The policy behavior of old liberals and old conservatives, of Republicans and Democrats, so inconsistent with the old dialogue, is fully consistent with the critieria drawn from interest-group liberalism: _The most important difference between liberals and conservatives, Republicans and Democrats, is to be found in the interest groups they identify with. Congressmen are guided in their votes, presidents in their programs, and administrators in their discretion by whatever organized interests they have taken for themselves as the most legitimate; and that is the measure of the legitimacy of demands and the only necessary guidelines for the framing of the laws._

It is one thing to recognize that these assumptions resemble the working

9. For an excellent inquiry into this assumption and into the realities of the internal life of organized interests, see Grant McConnell, _Private Power and American Democracy_ (New York: Knopf, 1966); S. M. Lipset et al., _Union Democracy_ (New York: Anchor, 1962); and Raymond Bauer et al., _American Business and Public Policy_ (New York: Atherton, 1963).

10. It is assumed that countervailing power usually crops up somehow, but when it does not, government ought help create it. See John Kenneth Galbraith, _American Capitalism_ (Boston: Houghton Mifflin, 1952). Among a number of excellent critiques of the so-called pluralist model, see especially William E. Connolly, ed., _The Bias of Pluralism_ (New York: Atherton 1969).

11. See also Chapters 2 and 11.

methodology of modern political science. But it is quite another to explain how this model was elevated from a hypothesis about political behavior to an ideology about how our democratic polity ought to work.

THE APPEALS OF INTEREST-GROUP LIBERALISM

The important inventors of modern techniques of government were less than inventive about the justifications for particular policies at particular times. For example, Keynes was neither a dedicated social reformer nor a political thinker with an articulated vision of the new social order.[12] Keynes helped discover the modern economic system and how to help maintain it, but his ideas and techniques could be used to support a whole variety of approaches and points of view:

Collective bargaining, trade unionism, minimum-wage laws, hours legislation, social security, a progressive tax system, slum clearance and housing, urban redevelopment and planning, education reform, all these he accepted but they were not among his preoccupations. In no sense could he be called the father of the welfare state.[13]

These innovators may have been silent on the deeper justification for expanding government because of the difficulty of drawing justification from the doctrines of popular government and majority rule. Justification of positive government programs on the basis of popular rule required, above all, a belief in and support of the supremacy of Congress. The abdication of Congress in the 1930s and thereafter could never have been justified in the name of popular government; and, all due respect to members of Congress, they made no effort to claim such justification. Abdication to the Executive Branch on economic matters and activism in the infringement of civil liberties produced further reluctance to fall back upon Congress and majority rule as the font of public policy justification. Many who wished nevertheless to have majority rule on their side sought support in the plebiscitary character of the presidency. However, presidential liberals have had to blind themselves to many complications in the true basis of presidential authority, and their faith in the presidency as a representative majority rule came almost completely unstuck during the late 1960s and thereafter.[14]

This is precisely what made interest-group liberalism so attractive. It had the approval of political scientists because it could deal with so many of the realities of power. It was further appealing because large interest groups and large memberships could be taken virtually as popular rule in modern dress.

12. Alvin H. Hansen, *The American Economy* (New York: McGraw-Hill, 1957), p. 152.
13. Ibid., pp. 158–59. Keynes himself said, "the Class War will find me on the side of the educated bourgeoisie" (Ibid., p. 158).
14. For a critique of the majoritarian basis of presidential authority see Willmoore Kendall, "The Two Majorities," *Midwest Journal of Political Science* 4 (1960): 317–45. The abdication by Congress to the Executive Branch will come up again and again throughout this volume.

And it fit the needs of corporate leaders, union leaders, and government officials desperately searching for support as they were losing communal attachments to their constituencies. Herbert Hoover had spoken out eloquently against crass individualism and in favor of voluntary collectivism. His belief in this kind of collectivism is what led him to choose, among all his offers, to be Secretary of Commerce in 1921.[15] And the experts on government who were to become the intellectual core of the New Deal and later Democratic administrations were already supporting such views even before the election of Franklin D. Roosevelt. For example,

[The national associations] represent a healthy democratic development. They rose in answer to certain needs. . . . They are part of our representative system. . . . These groups must be welcomed for what they are, and certain precautionary regulations worked out. The groups must be understood and their proper place in government allotted, if not by actual legislation, then by general public realization of their significance.[16]

After World War II, the academic and popular justifications for interest-group liberalism were still stronger. A prominent American government textbook of the period argued that the "basic concept for understanding the dynamics of government is the multi-group nature of modern society or the modern state."[17] By the time we left the 1960s, with the Democrats back in power, the justifications for interest-group liberalism were more eloquent and authoritative than ever. Take two examples from among the most important intellectuals of the Democratic Party, writing around the time of the return of the Democrats to power in 1960. To John Kenneth Galbraith, "Private economic power is held in check by countervailing power of those who are subjected to it. The first begets the second."[18] Concentrated economic power stimulates power in opposition to it, resulting in a natural tendency toward equilibrium. This is not merely theoretical for Galbraith, although he could not possibly have missed its similarity to Adam Smith; Galbraith was writing a program of positive government action. He admitted that effective countervailing power was limited in the real world and proposed that where it was absent or too weak to do the job, government policy should seek out and support it and, where necessary, create the organizations capable of countervailing. It should be government policy to validate the pluralist theory.

Arthur Schlesinger summarized his views for us in a campaign tract written in 1960. To Schlesinger, the essential difference between the Democratic and

15. For an account of Herbert Hoover's political views and his close relationship to the New Deal, see Grant McConnell, *Private Power*, pp. 62 ff.; and Peri Arnold, "Herbert Hoover and the Continuity of American Public Policy," *Public Policy* (Autumn 1972).

16. E. Pendleton Herring, *Group Representation before Congress* (Baltimore: Johns Hopkins Press, 1929), p. 268. See his reflections of 1936 in Chapter 2 of that book.

17. Wilfred Binkley and Malcolm Moos, *A Grammar of American Politics* (New York: Knopf, 1950), p. 7. Malcolm Moos became an important idea man in the Eisenhower Administration.

18. Galbraith, *American Capitalism*, p. 118.

Republican Parties is that the Democratic Party is the truly multi-interest party:

What is the essence of multi-interest administration? It is surely that the leading interests in society are all represented in the interior processes of policy formation—which can be done only if members or advocates of these interests are included in key positions of government. [19]

Schlesinger repeated the same theme in a more sober and reflective book written after John Kennedy's assassination. Following his account of the 1962 confrontation of President Kennedy with the steel industry and the later decision to cut taxes and cast off in favor of expansionary rather than stabilizing fiscal policy, Schlesinger concludes,

The ideological debates of the past began to give way to a new agreement on the practicalities of managing a modern economy. There thus developed in the Kennedy years a national accord on economic policy—a new consensus which gave hope of harnessing government, business, and labor in rational partnership for a steadily expanding American economy. [20]

A significant point in the entire argument is that the Republicans would disagree with Schlesinger on the *facts* but not on the *basis* of his distinction. The typical Republican rejoinder would be simply that Democratic administrations are not more multi-interest than Republican. In my opinion this would be almost the whole truth.

The appeal of interest-group liberalism is not simply that it is more realistic than earlier ideologies. There are several strongly positive reasons for its appeal. The first is that it helped flank the constitutional problems of federalism that confronted the expanding national state before the Constitution was completely democratized. A program like the Extension Service of the Department of Agriculture got around the restrictions of the Interstate Commerce clause by providing for self-administration by a combination of land-grant colleges, local farmer and commerce associations, and organized commodity groups (see Chapter 4). These appeared to be so decentralized and permissive as to be hardly federal at all. With such programs we begin to see the ethical and conceptual mingling of the notion of organized private groups with the notions of local government and self-government. Ultimately, direct interest-group participation in government became synonymous with self-government; but at first it was probably a strategy to get around the inclination of the Supreme Court to block federal interventions in the economy.

A second positive appeal of interest-group liberalism, strongly related to the first, is that it helped solve a problem for the democratic politician in the

19. Arthur Schlesinger, Jr., *Kennedy or Nixon—Does It Make Any Difference?* (New York: Macmillan, 1960), p. 43.

20. Arthur Schlesinger, *A Thousand Days*, as featured in the *Chicago Sun-Times*, January 23, 1966, section 2, p. 3.

modern state where the stakes are so high. This is the problem of enhanced conflict and how to avoid it. The contribution of politicians to society is their skill in resolving conflict. However, direct confrontations are sought only by so-called ideologues and outsiders. Typical American politicians displace and defer and delegate conflict where possible; they face conflict squarely only when they must. Interest-group liberalism offered a justification for keeping major combatants apart and for delegating their conflict as far down the line as possible. It provided a theoretical basis for giving to each according to his claim, the price for which is a reduction of concern for what others are claiming. In other words, *it transformed access and logrolling from necessary evil to greater good.*

A third and increasingly important positive appeal of interest-group liberalism is that it helps create the sense that power need not be power at all, control need not be control, and government need not be coercive. If sovereignty is parceled out among groups, then who is out anything? As a major *Fortune* editor enthusiastically put it, government power, group power, and individual power may go up simultaneously. If the groups to be controlled control the controls, then "to administer does not always mean to rule."[21] The inequality of power and the awesome coerciveness of government are always gnawing problems in a democratic culture. Rousseau's General Will stopped at the boundary of a Swiss canton. The myth of the group and the group will is becoming the answer to Rousseau and the big democracy. Note, for example, the contrast between the traditional and the modern definition of the group: Madison in *Federalist 10* defined the group ("faction") as "a number of citizens, whether amounting to a majority or minority of the whole who are united and actuated by some common impulse of passion, or of interest, *adverse to the right of other citizens, or to the permanent and aggregate interests of the community*" (emphasis added). Modern political science usage took that definition and cut the quotation just before the emphasized part.[22] In such a manner pluralist theory became the handmaiden of interest-group liberalism, and interest-group liberalism became the handmaiden of modern American positive national statehood, and the First Republic became the Second Republic. (This is the first of many references to the passage of the United States into a new republic. The detailed analysis of this transformation is in Chapter 10.)

Evidence of the fundamental influence of interest-group liberalism can be found in the policies and practices of every Congress and every administration since 1961. The very purpose of this book is to identify, document, and assess the consequences of the preferences that are drawn from the new public philosophy. President Kennedy is an especially good starting point because his

21. Max Ways, " 'Creative Federalism' and the Great Society," *Fortune*, January 1966, p. 122.

22. David Truman, *The Governmental Process* (New York: Knopf, 1951), p. 4.

positions were clear and because justification was especially important to him. His actions were all the more significant because he followed the lines of interest-group liberalism during a period of governmental strength, when there was no need to borrow support from interest groups. But whatever he did in the name of participation, cooperation, or multi-interest administration, and whatever President Johnson did in the name of "maximum feasible participation" and "creative federalism," so did President Eisenhower and Presidents Nixon and Ford do in the name of "partnership." This posture was very much above partisanship, and that is precisely what makes it the basis of what we can now call the Second Republic. *Fortune* could rave its approval of the theory of "creative federalism," despite its coinage by Lyndon Johnson, as "a relation, cooperative and competitive, between a limited central power and other powers that are essentially independent of it . . . a new way of organizing Federal programs . . . [in which simultaneously] the power of states and local governments will increase; the power of private organizations, including businesses, will increase; the power of individuals will increase."[23] Similarly, one of the most articulate officials during the Kennedy-Johnson years could speak glowingly of the Republican notion of partnership: "To speak of 'federal aid' simply confuses the issue. It is more appropriate to speak of federal support to special purposes . . . [as] an investment made by a partner who has clearly in mind the investments of other partners—local, state, and private."[24]

In sum, leaders in modern, consensual democracies are ambivalent about government. Government is obviously the most efficacious way of achieving good purposes, but alas, it is efficacious because it is coercive. To live with that ambivalence, modern policy-makers have fallen prey to the belief that public policy involves merely the identification of the problems toward which government ought to be aimed. It pretends that through "pluralism," "countervailing power," "creative federalism," "partnership," and "participatory democracy" the unsentimental business of coercion need not be involved and that unsentimental decisions about how to employ coercion need not really be made at all. Stated in the extreme, the policies of interest-group liberalism are end-oriented but ultimately self-defeating. Few standards of implementation, if any, accompany delegations of power. The requirement of standards has been replaced by the requirement of participation. The requirement of law has been replaced by the requirement of contingency. As a result, the ends of interest-group liberalism are nothing more than sentiments and therefore not really ends at all.

23. Ibid., p. 122. See also *Wall Street Journal,* March 16, 1966, for another positive treatment of creative federalism.

24. Francis Keppel, while assistant secretary for education, quoted in *Congressional Quarterly, Weekly Report,* April 22, 1966, p. 833.

THE FLAWED FOUNDATION OF INTEREST-
GROUP LIBERALISM: PLURALISM

Everyone operates according to some theory or frame of reference, or paradigm—some generalized map that directs logic and conclusions, given certain facts. The influence of a paradigm over decisions is incalculably large. It helps define what is important among the multitudes of events. It literally programs the decision-maker toward certain kinds of conclusions. People are unpredictable if they do not share some elements of a common theory. Pragmatism is merely an appeal to let theory remain implicit, but there is all too much truth in Lord Keynes's epigram, which was for this reason chosen as the opening quotation to Part I. Interest-group liberals have the pluralist paradigm in common and its influence on the policies of the modern state has been very large and very consistent. Practices of government are likely to change only if there is a serious reexamination of the theoretical components of the public philosophy and if that reexamination reveals basic flaws in the theory. Because they guide so much of the analysis of succeeding chapters, contentions about the fundamental flaws in the theory underlying interest-group liberals ought to be made explicit here at the outset. Among the many charges to be made against pluralism, the following three probably best anticipate the analysis to come.

1. The pluralist component has badly served liberalism by propagating the faith that a system built primarily upon groups and bargaining is self-corrective. Some parts of this faith are false, some have never been tested one way or the other, and others can be confirmed only under very special conditions. For example, there is the faulty assumption that groups have other groups to confront in some kind of competition. Another very weak assumption is that people have more than one salient group, that their multiple or overlapping memberships will insure competition, and at the same time will keep competition from becoming too intense. This concept of overlapping membership is also supposed to prove the voluntary character of groups, since it reassures us that even though one group may be highly undemocratic, people can vote with their feet by moving over to some other group to represent their interests. Another assumption that has become an important liberal myth is that when competition between or among groups takes place the results yield a public interest or some other ideal result. As has already been observed, this assumption was borrowed from laissez-faire economists and has even less probability of being borne out in the political system. One of the major Keynesian criticisms of market theory is that even if pure competition among factors of supply and demand did yield an equilibrium, the equilibrium could be at something far less than the ideal of full employment at reasonable prices. Pure pluralist competition, similarly, might produce political equilibrium,

but the experience of recent years shows that it occurs at something far below an acceptable level of legitimacy, or access, or equality, or innovation, or any other valued political commodity.

2. Pluralist theory is also comparable to laissez-faire economics in the extent to which it is unable to come to terms with the problem of imperfect competition. When a program is set up in a specialized agency, the number of organized interest groups surrounding it tends to be reduced, reduced precisely to those groups and factions to whom the specialization is most salient. That almost immediately transforms the situation from one of potential competition to one of potential oligopoly. As in the economic marketplace, political groups surrounding an agency ultimately learn that direct confrontation leads to net loss for all the competitors. Rather than countervailing power there is more likely to be accommodating power. Most observers and practitioners continue to hold on to the notion of group competition despite their own recognition that it is far from a natural state. Galbraith was early to recognize this but is by no means alone in his position that "the support of countervailing power has become in modern times perhaps the major peace-time function of the Federal government."[25] Group competition in Congress and around agencies is not much of a theory if it requires constant central government support.

3. The pluralist paradigm depends upon an idealized conception of the group. Laissez-faire economics may have idealized the enterprise and the entrepreneur but never more than the degree to which the pluralist sentimentalizes the group, the group member, and the interests. We have already noted the contrast between the traditional American or Madisonian definition of the group as adverse to the aggregate interests of the community with the modern view that groups are basically good things unless they break the law or the rules of the game. To the Madisonian, groups were a necessary evil much in need of regulation. To the modern pluralist, groups are good, requiring only accommodation. Madison went beyond his definition of the group to a position that "the regulation of these various interfering interests forms the principal task of modern legislation." This is a far cry from the sentimentality behind such notions as "supportive countervailing power," "group representation in the interior processes of . . . ," and "maximum feasible participation."

THE COSTS OF INTEREST-GROUP LIBERALISM

The problems of pluralist theory are of more than academic interest. They are directly and indirectly responsible for some of the most costly attributes of modern government: (1) the atrophy of institutions of popular control; (2) the

25. *American Capitalism*, p. 136.

maintenance of old and the creation of new structures of privilege; and (3) conservatism in several senses of the word. These three hypotheses do not exhaust the possibilities but are best suited to introduce the analysis of policies and programs in the next six chapters.

1. In *The Public Philosophy*, Walter Lippmann was rightfully concerned over the "derangement of power" whereby modern democracies tend first toward unchecked elective leadership and then toward drainage of public authority from elective leaders down into the constituencies. However, Lippmann erred if he thought of constituents as only voting constituencies. Drainage has tended toward "support-group constituencies," and with special consequences. Parceling out policy-making power to the most interested parties tends strongly to destroy political responsibility. A program split off with a special imperium to govern itself is not merely an administrative unit. It is a structure of power with impressive capacities to resist central political control.

When conflict of interest is made a principle of government rather than a criminal act, programs based upon such a principle cut out all of that part of the mass of people who are not specifically organized around values salient to the goals of that program. The people are shut out at the most creative phase of policy-making—where the problem is first defined. The public is shut out also at the phase of accountability because in theory there is enough accountability to the immediate surrounding interests. In fact, presidents and congressional committees are most likely to investigate an agency when a complaint is brought to them by one of the most interested organizations. As a further consequence, the accountability we do get is functional rather than substantive; and this involves questions of equity, balance, and equilibrium, to the exclusion of questions of the overall social policy and whether or not the program should be maintained at all. It also means accountability to experts first and amateurs last; and an expert is a person trained and skilled in the mysteries and technologies of that particular program.[26]

Finally, in addition to the natural tendencies, there tends also to be a self-conscious conspiracy to shut out the public. One meaningful illustration, precisely because it is such an absurd extreme, is found in the French system of interest representation in the Fourth Republic. As the Communist-controlled union, the Confédération Générale du Travail (CGT), intensified its participation in postwar French government, it was able to influence representatives of interests other than employees. In a desperate effort to insure that the interests represented on the various boards were separated and competitive, the government issued a decree that "each member of the board must be *independent of the interests he is not representing*."[27]

26. These propositions are best illustrated by the ten or more separate, self-governing systems in agriculture, in Chapter 4.
27. Mario Einaudi et al., *Nationalization in France and Italy* (Ithaca: Cornell University Press, 1955), pp. 100–101. (Emphasis added.)

2. Programs following the principles of interest-group liberalism tend to create and maintain privilege; and it is a type of privilege particularly hard to bear or combat because it is touched with a symbolism of the state. Interest-group liberalism is not merely pluralism but is *sponsored* pluralism. Pluralists ease our consciences about the privileges of organized groups by characterizing them as representative and by responding to their "iron law of oligarchy" by arguing that oligarchy is simply a negative name for organization. Our consciences were already supposed to be partly reassured by the notion of "overlapping memberships." But however true it may be that overlapping memberships exist and that oligarchy is simply a way of leading people efficiently toward their interests, the value of these characteristics changes entirely when they are taken from the context of politics and put into the context of pluralistic government. The American Farm Bureau Federation is no "voluntary association" if it is a legitimate functionary within the extension system. Such tightly knit corporate groups as the National Association of Home Builders (NAHB), the National Association of Real Estate Boards (NAREB), the National Association for the Advancement of Colored People (NAACP), or the National Association of Manufacturers (NAM) or American Federation of Labor-Congress of Industrial Organizations (AFL-CIO) are no ordinary lobbies after they become part of the "interior processes" of policy formation. Even in the War on Poverty, one can only appreciate the effort to organize the poor by going back and pondering the story and characters in *The Three Penny Opera*. The "Peachum factor" in public affairs may be best personified in Sargent Shriver and his strenuous efforts to get the poor housed in some kind of group before their representation was to begin (see especially Chapter 8).

The more clear and legitimized the representation of a group or its leaders in policy formation, the less voluntary its membership in that group and the more necessary is loyalty to its leadership for people who share the interests in question. And, the more widespread the policies of recognizing and sponsoring organized interest, the more hierarchy is introduced into our society. It is a well-recognized and widely appreciated function of formal groups in modern society to provide much of the necessary everyday social control. However, when the very thought processes behind public policy are geared toward these groups they are bound to take on the involuntary character of *public* control.

3. The conservative tendencies of interest-group liberalism can already be seen in the two foregoing objections: weakening of popular control and support of privilege. A third dimension of conservatism, stressed here separately, is the simple conservatism of resistance to change. David Truman, who has certainly not been a strong critic of self-government by interest groups, has, all the same, provided about the best statement of the general tendency of established agency-group relationships to be "highly resistant to disturbance":

New and expanded functions are easily accommodated, provided they develop and operate through existing channels of influence and do not tend to alter the relative importance of those influences. Disturbing changes are those that modify either the content or the relative strength of the component forces operating through an administrative agency. In the face of such changes, or the threat of them, the "old line" agency is highly inflexible.[28]

If this already is a tendency in a pluralistic system, then agency-group relationships must be all the more inflexible to the extent that the relationship is official and legitimate.

Innumerable illustrations will crop up throughout the book. They will be found in new areas of so-called social policy, such as the practice early in the War on Poverty to co-opt neighborhood leaders, thereby creating more privilege than alleviating poverty (see Chapter 8). Even clearer illustrations will be found in the economic realm, so many, indeed, that the practice is synthesized in Chapter 10 as "a state of permanent receivership." Old and established groups doing good works naturally look fearfully upon the emergence of competing, perhaps hostile, new groups. That is an acceptable and healthy part of the political game—until the competition between them is a question of "who shall be the government?" At that point conservatism becomes a matter of survival for each group, and a direct threat to the public interest. Ultimately this threat will be recognized.

The New Representation: A Second Republic?

If ambivalence toward government power is a trait common to all democracies, American leaders possess it to an uncommon degree. Their lives are dedicated to achieving it, and their spirits are tied up with justifying it. They were late to insist upon the expansion of national government, and when the expansion finally did begin to take place, it only intensified the ambivalence. *With each significant expansion of government during the past century, there has been a crisis of public authority. And each crisis of public authority has been accompanied by demands for expansion of representation.*

The clearest case in point is probably the first, the commitment by the federal government, beginning with the Interstate Commerce Act of 1887, to intervene regularly in the economic life of the country. The political results of the expansion were more immediate and effective than the economic consequences of the statutes themselves. The call went out for congressional reform of its rules, for direct election of senators, for reform in nominating processes, for reform in the ballot, for decentralization of House leadership, and so on.

28. *The Governmental Process*, pp. 467–68.

The results were dramatic, including "Reed's Rules" in the House, direct election of senators, the direct primary movement, the Australian ballot, and the "Speaker Revolt." This is also the period during which some of the most important national interest groups were organized.

Expansion of government during the Wilson period was altogether intertwined with demands by progressives for reform and revision in the mechanisms of representation: female suffrage (Nineteenth Amendment), the short ballot, initiative, referendum and recall, great extensions of direct primaries, the commission form of city government, and the first and early demands for formal interest representation—leading to such things as the formal sponsorship of the formation of Chambers of Commerce by the Commerce Department, government sponsorship of the formation of the Farm Bureau movement, the establishment of the separate clientele-oriented Departments of Labor and Commerce, and the first experiments with "self-regulation" during the World War I industrial mobilization.

The Roosevelt revolution brought on more of the same but made its own special contribution as well. Perhaps the most fundamental change in representation to accompany expanded government was the development and articulation of the theory and practice of the administrative process (see Chapter 5). Obviously the more traditional demands for reform in actual practices of representation continued. Reapportionment became extremely important; demands for reform produced the Administrative Procedure Act and the congressional reforms embodied in the 1946 LaFollette-Monroney Act. But probably of more lasting importance during and since that time has been the emergence of interest-group liberalism as the answer to the problems of government power. The new jurisprudence of administrative law is a key factor, to me the most important single factor. The new halo words alone indicate the extent to which new ideas of representation now dominate: *interest representation, cooperation, partnership, self-regulation, delegation of power, local option, creative federalism, community action, maximum feasible participation,* Nixon's *new federalism,* and even that odd contribution from the 1960s New Left—*participatory democracy.*

In whatever form and by whatever label, the purpose of representation and of reform in representation is the same: to deal with the problem of power—to bring the democratic spirit into some kind of psychological balance with the harsh reality of government coerciveness. The problem is that the new representation embodied in the broad notion of interest-group liberalism is a pathological adjustment to the problem. Interest-group liberal solutions to the problem of power provide the system with stability by spreading a *sense* of representation at the expense of genuine flexibility, at the expense of democratic forms, and ultimately at the expense of legitimacy. Prior solutions offered by progressives and other reformers built greater instabilities into the system by attempting to reduce the lag between social change and government policy.

But that was supposed to be the purpose of representation. Flexibility and legitimacy could only have been reduced by building representation upon the oligopolistic character of interest groups, reducing the number of competitors, favoring the best organized competitors, specializing politics around agencies, ultimately limiting participation to channels provided by preexisting groups.

Among all these, the weakest element of interest-group liberalism, and the element around which all the rest is most likely to crumble, is the antagonism of interest-group liberal solution to formalism. The least obvious, yet perhaps the most important, aspect of this is the antagonism of interest-group liberalism to law (see Chapters 5 and 11). Traditional expansions of representation were predicated upon an assumption that expanded participation would produce changes in government policies expressed in laws that would very quickly make a difference to the problems around which the representation process had been activated. Since the "new representation" extends the principle of representation into administration, it must either oppose the making of law in legislatures or favor vague laws and broad delegations that make it possible for administrative agencies to engage in representation. This tends to derange almost all established relationships and expectations in a republic. By rendering formalism impotent, it impairs legitimacy by converting government from a moralistic to a mechanistic institution. It impairs the potential of positive law to correct itself by allowing the law to become anything that eventually bargains itself out as acceptable to the bargainers. It impairs the very process of administration itself by delegating to administration alien material—policies that are not laws and authorizations that must be made into policies. Interest-group liberalism seeks pluralistic government, in which there is no formal specification of means or of ends. In a pluralistic government there is, therefore, no substance. Neither is there procedure. There is only process.

Part II

WHY LIBERAL GOVERNMENTS CANNOT PLAN

"You must first enable the government to control the governed; and in the next place oblige it to control itself."

James Madison

4

THE ORIGIN AND FIRST
CONSEQUENCES OF
PLURALISTIC GOVERNMENT
Agriculture, Commerce, Labor

Liberal governments cannot plan. Planning requires the authoritative use of authority. Planning requires law, choice, priorities, moralities. Liberalism replaces planning with bargaining. Yet at bottom, power is unacceptable without planning.

Application of pluralist principles in the construction of liberal government has made it possible for government to expand its efforts but not to assemble them. We can invent ingenious devices like the Executive Budget, the Executive Office of the President, Legislative Clearance, Program Budgeting, and Computerized Routines, but we do not use them to overcome the separatist tendencies and self-defeating proclivities of the independent functions. Liberal government seems to be flexible only on the first round of a response to political need. It allows for a certain expansion of functions to take place and then militates against any redistribution of those functions as needs change. New needs therefore result in expansions, never in planning. James Madison could have been writing for our times when he observed that government control and government self-control go together. The lack of rationale in our modern government has tended to vitiate its potential for good by sapping the strength and impairing the legitimacy of its authority.

Nowhere are the consequences of pluralist principles better seen than in those agencies in which the principles were first applied. Agriculture policy set the pattern of organizing the government along pluralist lines. Its influence spread far and wide, most notably to the Departments of Commerce and Labor, when these were created. Together the three provide the limiting extremes by which other programs and agencies can be analyzed. With these three departments one can begin to appreciate the extent to which the alienation of public authority has taken place, why it has taken place, and how this is reducing the capacity of modern government to govern responsibly, flexibly, and determinatively. The pattern will be established through observations on the practices of the Democratic 1960s, with side-glances at a few antecedents. It will then be tested for continuity against the Republican 1970s.

Agriculture: The New Feudalism

Agriculture is that field of American government where the distinction between public and private has come closest to being completely eliminated. This has been accomplished not by public expropriation of private domain— as would be true of the nationalization that Americans fear—but by private expropriation of public authority. That is the feudal pattern: fusion of all statuses and functions and governing through rigid but personalized fealties. In modern European dress, that was the corporativistic way; it is also the pluralist way, the way of contemporary liberalism in the United States. However, the best definition is one which puts the reader in the very presence of the thing.

THE PRESENT ESTATE OF AGRICULTURE

On December 18, 1963, President Lyndon Johnson summoned a conference of the leaders of major agriculture interests and interest groups. These representatives were asked to formulate a program by which they and their supporters could be served and regulated. The president's call for an agriculture congress was followed on January 31 with a Farm Message. In the message the president proposed the establishment of a bipartisan commission to investigate the concentration of power in the food industry and "how this greatly increased concentration of power is affecting farmers, handlers and consumers." Such investigations are always popular in farm states in helping spread the blame for high prices despite large subsidies. As one Administration spokesman explained, "We're not making a whipping boy out of anybody, but we're receiving repeated charges that certain retailers are setting market prices and it is clear that some chains do have large concentrations of market power." In the same message the president also called for new legislation to strengthen farmer cooperatives, to encourage their expansion through merger and acquisition, and to provide them with further exemptions from the antitrust laws.

The summoning of an agriculture congress was a call to agriculture to decide for itself what it wants from government. The president's attack in his Farm Message on concentration of market power, coupled with his proposals for expanded and stronger farm cooperatives, was obviously not an attack so much on concentration itself as on the intervention of nonagricultural power into strictly agricultural affairs.

That agricultural affairs should be handled strictly within the agricultural community is a basic political principle established before the turn of the century and maintained since then without serious reexamination. As a result, agriculture has become neither public nor private enterprise. It has been a system of self-government in which each leading farm interest controls a segment of agriculture through a delegation of national sovereignty. Agriculture has emerged as a largely self-governing federal estate within the federal structure of the United States.

President Johnson recognized these facts within three weeks of his accession when he summoned the conference of agricultural leaders. The resulting concession to agriculture's self-government was the wheat-cotton bill of 1964. Because cotton supports were too high, the cotton interests wrote a bill providing for a subsidy to mills of six to eight cents a pound in order to keep them competitive with foreign cotton and domestic rayon without touching the price supports. On the other hand, wheat supports were too low because wheat farmers in the 1963 referendum had overwhelmingly rejected President John Kennedy's plan to provide some federal regulation along with supports. The wheat section of the new act called for a program whereby wheat farmers would voluntarily comply with acreage reduction for subsidies of up to seventy cents a bushel but without the federal supply regulations. The press called this a major legislative victory for Mr. Johnson. But the victory really belonged to organized cotton and wheat and testified to the total acceptance by the president, press, and public of the principle that private agriculture interests alone govern agriculture. It is a sturdy principle; its inheritance by President Johnson was through a line unbroken by personality or party in the White House. For example, in one of President Kennedy's earliest major program messages to Congress, on March 16, 1961, he proposed:

The Soil Conservation and Domestic Allotment Act . . . should be amended to provide for the establishment of national farmer advisory committees for every commodity or group of related commodities for which a new supply adjustment program is planned [as proposed in the same message]. Members of the committees would be elected by the producers of the commodities involved or their appropriate representatives. In consultation with the Secretary of Agriculture, they could be charged with the responsibility for considering and recommending individual commodity programs. . . .

In order to insure effective farmer participation in the administration of farm programs on the local level, the Secretary of Agriculture is directed to revitalize the county and local farmer committee system and to recommend such amendments as may be necessary to safeguard such farmer participation.

ORIGINS IN ECONOMICS AND TACTICS

The reasons for agricultural self-government are deep-rooted, and the lessons to be drawn from it are vital. For a century agriculture has been out of joint with American economic development. Occasional fat years have only created unreal expectations, making the more typical lean years less bearable. As industries concentrated, discovered the economies of scale and how to control their markets, agriculture remained decentralized and subject to the market. As industries showed increasing capacity to absorb technology and to use it to increase profit, agriculture took on technology only with net debt. Profit from increased productivity was either neutralized with lower prices or absorbed by the processing, distributing, and transporting industries interposed between agriculture and its markets. After the Civil War America's largest and most basic industry was never for long out of trouble. At the beginning of World War I, for example, net farm income was $3.6 billion. By 1919, it was $9.3 billion; but two years later it was back down to $3.7 billion. It rose slowly to $6.1 billion in 1920–30 and had fallen off to $1.9 billion by 1932. At a higher level, these fluctuations have beset agriculture since World War II as well. The only things stable about agriculture have been (1) its declining relative importance in the census and in the economy, (2) the reverence it enjoys in the American mythology, and (3) the political power it possesses despite (1) and largely because of (2).

Organized agriculture was early to discover the value of political power as a counterweight to industrial wealth. The land-grant and homesteading acts were followed by governmental services in research, quarantine, and education. But continuing distress despite governmental support led to bolder demands. First the movement was for a redistribution of wealth and power toward agriculture. As a debtor class, farmers saw inflation as the solution; William Jennings Bryan was one of many spokesmen for cheaper money and easier credit. Farmers also sought government regulation of those economic forces they had identified as the causes of their problems. The monopolies, the railroads, the grain merchants and other processors, the banks, and the brokers were to be deprived of market power by dissolution or by severe restraints upon the use of that power. Finally farmers sought solutions by emulating the business system. Almost simultaneously they hit upon the cooperative to restrain domestic trade, and international dumping over high tariff walls to restrain international trade.

All these mechanisms failed the farmers. The blunderbuss—inflation of the whole economy—failed both for want of enough legislation and because more and more of the national debt was held by the industrial rich. Regulation of industry failed for want of will and power to administer it; a governing elite opposed to inflating the business system could not be expected to dismantle it. International dumping never was given the test; Coolidge and Hoover vetoed the Smoot-Hawley tariff bills that would "make the tariff work for agriculture." The cooperative movement did not fail; it simply did not succeed on a large enough scale.

By a process of elimination, organized agriculture turned then to another way: *the regulation of itself.* In the Democratic Party of 1930 and the Democratic Party philosophy, to be called the New Deal, agriculture found an eager handmaiden. And in the modest government assistance programs of the pre-New-Deal period the appropriate instrumentalities and precedents were found. After the 1932 election all that remained was to ratify in legislation the agreements already reached. The system created then has remained with only a few marginal additions and alterations. Bitter political conflicts within the agriculture community have been fought out over the margins, but on the system itself there is almost total consensus among the knowledgeable minority and total apathy and ignorance among the nonagricultural majority.

The principle of self-regulation might have taken several forms, the most likely one being a national system of farm representation within a farmer's type of National Recovery Administration (NRA). Instead, a more elaborate and complicated system of "cooperation" or local self-government developed largely for constitutional reasons. There was already experience with local districts in the Extension Service that had become a proven way for the federal government to get around the special constitutional problem of regulating agriculture. Agriculture was the most "local" of the manufactures the government was attempting to reach. The appearance if not the reality of decentralizing federal programs through local, farmer-elected committees helped to avoid straining the Interstate Commerce Clause and to escape the political charge of regimentation.

Eventually, many separate programs were created within the government-agriculture complex. Each constituted a system in and of itself. The programs were independently administered and often had conflicting results. But underneath all the complexity of parity, forestry, conservation, electrification, education, extension, and credit there was a simple principle: It amounted to the loan of governmental sovereignty to the leadership of a private sector to accomplish what other sectors could accomplish privately. Agriculture was so decentralized and dispersed that private, voluntary agreements to manipulate markets were obviously too difficult to reach and impossible to sustain. Therefore it was not going to be possible to emulate business. So, in a travesty of the Declaration of Independence, to secure these rights governments were instituted among farmers. Administrative agencies were created to facilitate agreements, and, once reached, public authority was expected to be employed where necessary to sustain them.

THE SYSTEM: BUILDING ON LOCAL COMMITTEES[1]

The prototype, the Federal Extension Service, is "cooperative" in the sense that it shares the expense of farm improvement with the states, the land-grant

1. The following studies were invaluable in locating the several separate agriculture systems, although none of the authors necessarily shares my treatment of the cases or the conclusions I have drawn: Grant McConnell, *The Decline of Agrarian Democracy* (Berkeley: University of Cali-

colleges, the county governments, and the local associations of farmers. The county agent is actually employed by the local associations, which are required by law. In the formative years, the aid of local chambers of commerce was enlisted; the local association was the farm bureau of the chamber. In order to coordinate local activities and to make more effective claims for additional outside assistance, these farm bureaus were organized into state farm bureau federations. The American Farm Bureau Federation, formed at the Agriculture College of Cornell University in 1919, was the offshoot. A filial relationship between farm bureau, land-grant college, and the Extension Service continues to this day. This transformation of an administrative arrangement into a political system has been repeated in almost all agriculture programs since that time. The Extension Service exercises few sanctions over the states and colleges, which in turn leave the localities alone. All are quick to scream "Federal encroachment!" at the mere suggestion that the Department of Agriculture should increase supervision or investigation, or that it should attempt to coordinate extension programs with other federal activities.

As other agriculture programs came along, most were similarly organized. Any inconsistency of purpose or impact among programs has been treated as nonexistent or beyond the jurisdiction of any one agency. The Soil Conservation Service operates through its soil conservation districts, of which there were 2,936 in 1963 and 2,950 in 1976, involving over 90 percent of the nation's farms. These districts are actually considered units of local government, and each is in fact controlled by its own farmer-elected committee, which is not to be confused with other farmer associations or committees. Agreements between the farmer and the service for acre-by-acre soil surveys, for assistance in instituting soil-conserving practices, and for improving productivity are actually made between the farmer and the district committee. Enforcement of the agreements is handled also by the district committee.

Additional aid to the farmer channels through the cooperatives, which are in turn controlled by farmer-elected boards. Four out of five farmers belong to at least one co-op. The Farmer Cooperative Service touches the farmer only through the boards of directors of the cooperatives as the boards see fit.

When the stakes get larger, the pattern of local self-government remains the same. Price support, the parity program, is run by the thousands of farmer-elected county committees of farmers, which function alongside but quite independently of the other local committees. Acreage allotments to bring

fornia Press, 1953); M. R. Benedict, *Farm Policies of the United States, 1790–1950* (New York: Twentieth Century Fund, 1953); Charles Hardin, *The Politics of Agriculture* (Glencoe: The Free Press, 1952). However, the most important source was the U.S. Code. The secret of agriculture success, as well as the significance of interest-group liberalism, lies in the extent to which pluralism is written into the statutes. No specific citations are made in the chapter because each system was pieced together from elements of all of the above sources.

supply down and prices up are apportioned among the states by the Agricultural Stabilization and Conservation Service. (The ASCS is the lineal descendant, thrice removed, of the Agricultural Adjustment Act [AAA].) State committees of farmers apportion the allotment among the counties. The farmer-elected county Stabilization and Conservation Committees receive the county allotment. The county committees made the original acreage allotments among individual farmers back in the 1930s, and they now make new allotments, bring about any adjustments and review complaints regarding allotments, determine whether quotas have been complied with, inspect and approve storage facilities, and act as the court of original jurisdiction on violations of price-support rules and on eligibility for parity payments. The committees are also vitally important in campaigning for the two-thirds-vote acceptance of high price-support referenda. Congress determines the general level of support, and the secretary of Agriculture proclaims the national acreage quotas for adjusting supply to guaranteed price. But the locally elected committees stand between the farmer and the Congress, the secretary, the ASCS, and the Commodity Credit Corporation.

In agriculture credit, local self-government is found in even greater complexity. The Farmers Home Administration (FHA, but not to be confused with Federal Housing Administration) and the Farm Credit Administration are, in essence, banks; and as banks they are unique. Credit extended by the FHA is almost entirely controlled by local FHA farmer committees. There is one per county, and again these are not to be confused with the other committees. The much larger Farm Credit Administration, an independent agency since 1953, was within the Department of Agriculture from 1938 until 1953 and was autonomous before that. But its departmental status is irrelevant, because it also operates through local farmer control. There is not one but three bodies politic within the FCA.

1. Membership in the mortgage loan body politic requires the purchase of stock in a local land-bank association. Broad participation is so strongly desired that it has been made mandatory. The farmer borrower must purchase an amount of voting stock equal to 5 percent of his loan in one of the 750 land-bank associations.

2. In the short-term loan body politic, 487 separate production credit associations own virtually all the stock, and the farmer-owners or their representatives pass upon all requests for loans within their respective districts. It is a point of pride in the FCA that ownership and control of these banks has passed from government to local, private hands.

3. The third body politic within the FCA is the cooperative system, controlled by elected farmer-directors and operated by credit available from the FCA's Central Bank for Cooperatives and its twelve district Banks for Cooperatives.

THE TEN SYSTEMS AND POLITICS

Taking all the agriculture programs, there are as many as ten separate, autonomous, self-governing systems—each with its own local constituencies, private support groups, and participation routines that give it consensus and legitimacy, and help maintain its separation from the others and from the department and the White House. In fiscal 1962, $5.6 billion of the total $6.7 billion Department of Agriculture budget were accounted for by these self-governing systems. An additional $5.8 billion in loans were handled by these systems. In fiscal 1976, because of a cyclical drop in price-support payments, $6 billion of a $15 billion budget went through these same systems, essentially unchanged thirteen years after the first visit. Loans administered through these systems (mainly through the Commodity Credit Corporation, the Farmers Home Administration, and the Farm Credit Administration) amounted to $25 billion in fiscal 1976. A better sense of the continuing importance of these self-governing systems can be conveyed by subtracting from the total expenditure budget the $7.5 billion food-stamp program because this is basically part of the welfare system ancillary to Aid to Families of Dependent Children (AFDC) and other welfare programs (see Chapter 8). This means that 80 percent of agriculture policy was still lodged in these systems. They are the state of agriculture.

Due to the special intimacy between federal agriculture programs and private agriculture, each administrative organization becomes a potent political instrumentality. Each of the self-governing local units becomes one important point in a definable political system which both administers a program and maintains the autonomy of that program in face of all other political forces emanating from other agriculture systems, from antagonistic farm and nonfarm interests, from Congress, from the secretary, and from the president.

The politics of each of these self-governing programs is comprised of a triangular trading pattern, with each point complementing and supporting the other two. The three points are: the central agency, a congressional committee or subcommittee, and the local or district farmer committees. The latter are also usually the grass-roots element of a national interest group.

The classic case is Extension. The Extension Service at the center of this system is supported in Congress by the long-tenure Farm Bureau members of the agriculture committees, particularly in the Senate. The grass-roots segment is composed of the Farm Bureau Federation and the local extension committees around which the Farm Bureau was originally organized and to which the Bureau continues to contribute assistance. Further interest-group support comes from two intimately related organizations, the Association of Land-Grant Colleges and Universities and its tributary, the National Association of County Agricultural Agents.

Another such triangle unites the Soil Conservation Service with Congress primarily through the Subcommittee on Agriculture of the House Committee on Appropriations, through which SCS managed to double its appropriations between 1940 and the early postwar years while severely limiting the related activities of the FHA and the old AAA and its successors. The third point is the local soil-conservation districts, which speak individually to the local congressman and nationally to Congress and the president through the very energetic National Association of Soil Conservation Districts. The SCS draws further support from the Soil Conservation Society of America (mainly professionals) and the Izaak Walton League of America (formerly Friends of the Land, mainly urban well-wishers).

Similar but much more complex forms characterize the price-support system. The Agriculture Stabilization and Conservation Service ties into Congress through the eight (formerly ten) commodity subcommittees of the House Agriculture Committee and the dozens of separately organized interest groups representing each of the single commodities. (Examples: National Cotton Council, American Wool Growers Association, American Cranberry Growers Association.) These in turn draw from the local price-support committees.

As in geometry and engineering, so in politics the triangle seems to be the most stable type of structure. There is an immense capacity in each agriculture system, once created, to maintain itself and to resist any type of representation except its own. These self-governing agriculture systems have such institutional legitimacy that they have become practically insulated from the three central sources of democratic political responsiblity: (1) Within the Executive Branch they are autonomous. Secretaries of agriculture have tried and failed to consolidate or even to coordinate related programs. (2) Within Congress, they are sufficiently powerful within their own domain to be able to exercise an effective veto or to create stalemate. (3) Agriculture activities and agencies are almost totally removed from the view of the general public. Upon becoming the exclusive province of those who are most directly interested in them, programs are first split off from general elective political responsibility. (Rarely has there been more than one urban member on the House Committee on Agriculture, sometimes not even one.) After specialization there is total submersion.

THE CORPORATE STATE

Important cases illustrate the consequences. In fact, in even a casual reading of the history of agriculture policy such cases are impossible to avoid.

Case 1 • In 1947, Secretary of Agriculture Clinton P. Anderson proposed a consolidation of all soil-conservation, price-support, and FHA programs into one committee system with a direct line from the committees to the secretary. Bills were prepared providing for consolidation within the price-support committees. Contrary bills were produced providing for consolidation under soil-conservation districts. Stalemate, 1947. In 1948, a leading farm senator proposed consolidation of the whole effort under the local associations of the Extension Service. Immediately a House farm leader introduced a bill diametrically opposed. The result, continuing stalemate.

Case 2 • In Waco, Texas, on October 14, 1952, presidential candidate Dwight Eisenhower said, "I would like to see in every county all federal farm agencies under the same roof." Pursuant to this promise, Secretary of Agriculture Ezra Taft Benson issued a series of orders during early 1953 attempting to bring about consolidation of local units as well as unification at the top, mainly by appointing some professional agriculture employees to membership in local committees. Finally, amid cries of "sneak attack" and "agricat," Benson proclaimed that "any work on the further consolidation of county and state offices . . . shall be suspended."

Case 3 • From the very beginning, Secretary Benson sought to abandon rigid price supports and bring actual supports closer to market prices. In 1954, as he was beginning to succeed, Congress enacted a commodity set-aside by which $2.5 billion of surplus commodities already held by the government were declared to be a "frozen reserve" for national defense. Since the secretary's power to cut price supports depends heavily upon the amount of government-owned surplus carried over from previous years, the commodity set-aside was a way of freezing parity as well as reserves. Benson eventually succeeded in reducing supports on the few commodities over which he had authority. But thanks to the set-aside, Congress, between fiscal 1952 and 1957, helped increase the value of commodities held by the government from $1.1 billion to $5.3 billion. What appeared, therefore, to be a real Republican policy shift amounted to no more than giving back with one hand what had been taken away by the other.

Case 4 • President Eisenhower's first budget sought to abolish farm home-building-and-improvement loans by eliminating the budgetary request and by further requesting that the 1949 authorization law be allowed to expire. Congress overrode his request in 1953 and each succeeding year, and the president answered Congress with a year-by-year refusal to implement the farm housing program. In 1956, when the president asked again explicitly for elimination of the program, he was rebuffed. The Subcommittee on Housing of the House Banking and Currency Committee added to the president's omnibus housing bill a renewal of the farm housing program, plus an authorization for $500 million in loans over a five-year period, and the bill passed with a congressional mandate to use the funds. They were used thereafter at a rate of about $75 million a year.

Case 5 • On March 16, 1961, President Kennedy introduced a "radically different" farm program in a special message to Congress. For the first time in the history of price supports, the bill called for surplus control through quotas placed on bushels, tons, or other units, rather than on acreage. An acreage allotment allows the farmer to produce as much as he can on the reduced acreage in cultivation. For example, in the first ten years or so of acreage control, acreage under cultivation dropped by about 4 percent, while actual production rose by 15 percent. The Kennedy proposal called for national committees of farmers to be elected to work out the actual program. This more stringent type of control was eliminated from the omnibus bill in the Agriculture Committees of both chambers and there were no attempts to restore them during floor debate. Last-minute efforts by Secretary Orville L. Freeman to up the ante, offering to raise wheat supports from $1.79 to $2.00, were useless. Persistence by the Administration led eventually to rejection by wheat farmers in 1963 of all high price supports and acreage controls.

The politics of this rejected referendum is of general significance. Despite all the blandishments and inducements of the Administration, the farmer had had his way. The local price-support committees had usually campaigned in these referenda for the Department of Agriculture, but this time they did not. And thousands of small farmers, eligible to vote for the first time, joined with the local leadership to help defeat the referendum. It is not so odd that wheat farmers would reject a proposal that aimed to regulate them more strictly than before. What is odd is that only wheat farmers were allowed to decide the matter. It seems that in agriculture, as in many other fields, the regulators are powerless without the consent of the regulated.

Economic Policy for Industrial Society: The Empty Houses

The Departments of Commerce and Labor, along with Agriculture, are very special units of government. From the very beginning, these departments were founded upon their dependence, not their independence. Widely known as clientele departments, they are organized around an identifiable sector of the economy and are legally obliged to develop and maintain an orientation toward the interests that comprise this sector. While there are other governmental agencies of the same type, these are the only three of Cabinet status and scope. All other departments of Cabinet rank are organized around some governmental process or function rather than around a set of persons legally identified as desirable.

As clientele agencies the Departments of Commerce and Labor are not meant to be governing agencies except in some marginal way. They are and were meant to be agencies of representation. They were, in other words, set up not to govern but to be governed. In a manner not unlike the early German and Italian Councils of Corporations, these departments provide functional representation, to be contrasted to the geographical representation provided for in Congress under the Constitution. With Agriculture, these departments are three Economic Parliaments; they constitute a true Fourth Estate in our governing order. Since Agriculture possesses many powers along with its representation function, largely because it represents the class in retreat, Commerce and Labor are left as the pure cases of functional representation.

The Departments of Commerce and Labor were founded simultaneously in 1903 as a single Department of Commerce and Labor "to foster, promote, and develop the foreign and domestic commerce, the mining, manufacturing, shipping, and fishing industries, and the transportation facilities of the United States." But this arrangement was not at all satisfactory to the newly organizing AFL, which rightly saw itself as the poor relative in the family. Labor had been seeking representation in a Cabinet department for many years. They had taken only minor satisfaction in the Bureau of Labor, established in the Department of Interior in 1884; and no improvement was seen in making that bureau an independent but non-Cabinet agency in 1888.

Labor was not to get its full representation until 1913, when the separate Department of Labor was created to "foster, promote, and develop the welfare of the wage earners of the United States, to improve their working conditions, and to advance their opportunities for profitable employment."

Merged or separate, however, the entire history of Commerce and Labor attests to their special character and function in the governmental scheme. From the beginning they were both feedback agencies. Both were charged with any and all research and statistical work necessary to make certain that the problems and needs of their clients were known at every turn. The original Bureau of Labor, a research agency, was the core of the new department, and long after Cabinet elevation, references were frequently made to the Department of Labor Statistics. Commerce always housed our census, geographical surveys, weights and measures, domestic and international business surveys, and other research activities essential to commercial enterprise.

While the pattern of development has not been exactly the same in the two departments, neither has departed from its original responsibility for being an official collectivity of unofficial economic interests.

As the national government grew in size and power, these two departments grew also, but consistently in a way reflecting their special legal and political character: They grew through expansion of services and promotional activities. Neither department took on more than one or two of the functions involved in the new relationships between government and the economy. The revolution of the modern state bypassed them almost completely.[2]

2. See, for example, Chapter 5, below.

COMMERCE: GOVERNMENT ITALIAN STYLE

Functional representation in the Department of Commerce quickly expanded after 1903 in response to business needs. To its research activities was very early added the mission of encouraging business representation in government through one of the most significant of business institutions, the trade association. Trade associations, which were just beginning to form in significant numbers after 1903, are essentially legalized restraints of trade. Each serves its members and helps regularize relations among competitors by sharing information, eliminating cutthroat competition, standardizing products, pooling advertising, and so on.

The Department of Commerce fostered the trade associations where they already existed and helped organize them where they did not yet exist. Thus the department took the initiative in founding the U.S. Chamber of Commerce. Without official endorsement in 1912, the fusion of local chambers into one national business association would more than likely never have taken place. Most of the negotiating sessions among local leaders, the National Association of Manufacturers, and others were arranged by, and took place in, the office of the secretary of Commerce and Labor. The final organization charter was written there.

The practice of official recognition and representation of trade associations in the inner processes of policy formulation was established, very much in a manner to anticipate NRA, during the war years of the Wilson Administration. This was fostered and given doctrinal support in the 1920s, primarily by Secretary of Commerce Herbert Hoover. In 1924, Secretary Hoover observed, "Legislative action is always clumsy—it is incapable of adjustment to shifting needs. . . . Three years of study and intimate contact with associations of economic groups convince me that there lies within them a great moving impulse toward betterment."[3] Even then the vision was one of codes of business practice formulated by trade-association processes and promulgated by the Department of Commerce. This Hoover saw as "the strong beginning of a new force in the business world."[4]

These relationships were further formalized early in the New Deal when Roosevelt's first secretary of Commerce organized the Business Advisory Council to guide the department on "matters affecting the relations of the Department and business." This group, under the Kennedy name of Business Council, remained central to the *modus operandi* in the department. During the 1950s a new agency, the Business and Defense Services Administration

---

3. Quoted in Grant McConnell, *Private Power and American Democracy* (New York: Knopf, 1966); see also Peri Arnold, "Herbert Hoover and the Continuity of American Public Policy," *Public Policy* (Autumn 1972), p. 525.

4. McConnell, p. 66.

(BDSA), was set up around a vast network of specialized business advisory committees to determine cold-war industrial policies.

LABOR: LITTLE SIR ECHO

Although growth in the Department of Labor produced a different pattern, it fulfilled the same purpose of bringing private interests into the interior processes of government. Here it did not take the form of fostering a trade association movement because, ironically, labor was more laissez-faire than business. Labor unions lacked status, but they had their Magna Carta in the Clayton Act and were, following Samuel Gompers, officially opposed to government intervention in the affairs of collective bargaining.

As a consequence, the department remained quite small, and the primary addition to statistics in its functional representation was the evolution of the office of the secretary itself. During the first twenty years, that Cabinet post was filled with people taken directly from the leadership ranks of organized labor. The appointments of Frances Perkins, Louis Schwellenbach, and Maurice Tobin during the New Deal-Fair Deal period did not really constitute a change from this tradition since labor representation continued to be lodged in the office of the secretary. And the contemporary role of the secretary in intervening in disputes, settling strikes, and helping with guidelines is a natural result of the department's evolution.

COMMERCE, LABOR, AND THE MAINSTREAM

The histories of these two departments present a stunning contrast to the history of American government. The twentieth-century political revolution has erected an enormous apparatus for public control of economic life, and the end is apparently not in sight. Yet, the Departments of Commerce and Labor have been bypassed almost altogether. As clientele agencies they are simply not to be entrusted by anyone with significant direct powers over persons and property. The existence of functional representation meant that the growth of new functions of government would almost have to take place outside the Cabinet and, therefore, in a piecemeal and uncoordinated fashion.

The original Department of Commerce and Labor included a Bureau of Corporations, armed with power to make the Sherman Antitrust Act more effective. Within a decade this had become the core of an independent Federal Trade Commission, and its removal took from Commerce the only significant regulatory and planning powers it was ever to have. One by one, and with increasing frequency, new powers and agencies of public power over business were created outside the department and outside the Cabinet. Regulation of railroads in the Interstate Commerce Commission (ICC) predated Commerce by sixteen years. However, positive planning for a national railway system, a function not necessarily consistent with rate regulation, also passed to ICC when the rails were returned to private ownership after 1920. For forty-six years this anomalous situation continued, until the new Transportation Department was created—outside Commerce, independent of and equal to Commerce, larger than Commerce, too late to influence the shape of transportation.

Radio communication, from the beginning a part of commerce near the very center of public domain, was also from the beginning made the responsibility of a new agency—outside and independent of Commerce. Commerce got a small piece of civil aeronautics control under the 1934 act, but by 1938 even this had been lost to the semiautonomous Civil Aeronautics Administration and then to the fully autonomous Federal Aviation Agency. The entire realm of securities, credit, banking, and currency are outside Commerce. The power industry, including civilian atomic development, got its own, non-Cabinet agencies.

True, Commerce did get the Maritime Administration in 1950, but this is a semiautonomous subsidizing agency with an altogether independent tradition and constituency. The Bureau of Public Roads was Commerce's only significant traditional exercise of commerce power, and it is clear that the secretary's authority over the bureau was almost nonexistent. For example, the April 8, 1967, release of $1.1 billion in highway construction funds was authorized by the president and the budget director without any reference whatsoever to the secretary of Commerce.

Governmental responses to the civil-rights revolution also bypassed Commerce, despite the deep involvement of civil-rights laws in business decisions. The only part of the historic 1964 Civil Rights Act going to Commerce was the Community Relations Service, which is essentially a center for communications, conciliation, and conference holding. The only part of the New Frontier-Great Society in which Commerce participated was the Area Redevelopment Administration, an important but relatively declining feature of the new social legislation which, by 1965, as the Economic Development Administration, had become essentially a public-works program. The Appalachia Program was developed in Commerce but immediately became the property of the Appalachian states. In sum, almost every significant commerce power of the federal government has been lodged somewhere other than in Commerce.

The Department of Labor is a pint-sized version of the same story. On the eve of the Roosevelt revolution, Labor was a microscopic Cabinet department whose only significant governing activity was the Immigration and Naturalization Service. (This unusual responsibility for controlling the noncitizen competitors for jobs comprised 80 percent of the department's budget.) During the 1930s, government expanded its relation to the laboring man in many ways, but little of this involved the laboring man's department. On the contrary, the department declined relative to virtually every other sector of public activity.

Over the protest of Frances Perkins, almost all New Deal labor programs escaped her department. The 1934 railway labor legislation came early in her incumbency and set the tone for what was to follow. A board was set up with thirty-six representatives, outside Labor, to deal with railway labor disputes in a gray area somewhere between private arbitration and public adjudication. The National Labor Relations Board became an independent commission. All but one of the Social Security programs, the least important one, were organized outside the Department of Labor. The National Bituminous Coal Commission, with its many labor responsibilities, escaped both Labor and Commerce.

The only major governmental responsibilities entrusted to Labor by Roosevelt were the regulatory programs under the Walsh-Healy and Fair Labor Standards Acts, now administered by the one Wages and Hours and Public Contracts Division. But while Labor was gaining those tasks, it was losing still more. Of its four original core jurisdictions—labor statistics, immigration, conciliation, and children—Labor lost as follows: Immigration went to the Department of Justice in 1940; the Children's Bureau went to the Federal Security Agency (now the Department of Health, Education and Welfare) in 1946; the Federal Mediation and Conciliation Service was converted by the Taft-Hartley Act into an independent agency. Labor even lost the Bureau of Employment Security in 1939, regaining it in 1950 only after a long struggle.

In general, Labor participated almost as little as Commerce in the social revolution of the 1960s. This includes almost all the most significant features of the New Frontier-Great Society programs. The Office of Economic Opportunity (OEO), VISTA, and the antidiscrimination provisions of the civil-rights and antipoverty legislation are in the labor field but not in the Labor Department. About half of the manpower training program of 1962 comprises all of Labor's share of the government explosion of the 1960s.

Pluralistic Power and Pluralistic Government

In 1967 President Johnson made a serious but vain proposal to merge once again the Departments of Commerce and Labor, just over half a century after their original union was dissolved. Some types of merger can be significant. Merger of the National Guard with the Reserve would be significant. Merger of Nassau County with New York City would be significant. The very insignificance of the proposed Commerce-Labor merger raises all sorts of fundamental questions about the politics and administration of economic policy in the national government of the United States.

Nothing possible could have been changed by making a duplex out of the House of Labor and the House of Commerce. Nothing would have been subtracted except one voice from Cabinet meetings. Nothing would have been added except frustrated expectations. No additional order, coordination, purpose, or policy could have come out of the merger *because the really important controls over economic life would not have been involved.*

This only barely suggests the state of things. The insignificance of the Commerce and Labor Departments is a monument to the overwhelming innocence of the liberal spirit in America, which has justified the tangle of government controls as necessary for maximum flexibility, maximum expertise, and maximum insurance for keeping control out of politics. The real economic powers of government are nonpolitical if Humpty-Dumpty is your lexicographer. They seem flexible only because they are numerous. They seem rational only because they are specialized. Control over the American economic system is split up among the Treasury, the Office of Management and Budget, the Council of Economic Advisers through the president, the Joint Committee on Internal Revenue Taxation, the Federal Reserve Board, the Social Security System, the ten or more agriculture systems, the many specialized regulatory agencies, the Office of the Secretary of Defense—and others. All of them exist separately and independently. There is hardly a scintilla of central control, because no such control could ever be entrusted to any one of them. No governing institution possesses central control, because in the liberal state a virtue is made of its absence.

Commerce and Labor are on the periphery still further because they were captured by too narrow a range of interests. As a consequence their very existence works a positive harm. They have done little more than help prevent expansion of the Cabinet toward an attempt at central control. And the two departments not only helped prevent development of an integrated and rational economic policy establishment; the harm goes further. The processes of functional representation in Labor and Commerce have helped to blind national leadership to the need for integration by creating and reporting business consensus and labor solidarity when the only consensus was that among the very special interests established therein. Merger of Commerce and Labor would have created false hopes and expectations. A bold approach to economic policy can be begun only with their abolition.

There will also be little rationality to national economic policy until somehow agriculture is integrated, and this is an even more difficult problem, because the Department of Agriculture administers real government programs and therefore cannot simply be abolished. Political responsibility and the prospect of planning were destroyed when agriculture policy-making was parceled out to the most interested parties. No progress toward correcting that situation can be made until it is fully realized that over $10 billion of government-agriculture intimacy per year is too much agriculture policy to be entrusted to agriculturalists.

Reversing the situation in agriculture is made still more difficult by the fact that the autonomy of agriculture is grounded in the still more legitimated local committees. To attack them is to chip away at idols. This legitimacy reinforces the very considerable political power of agriculture interests, the source of which is often misunderstood. The problem of rural versus urban political power was never really one of simply poor legislative apportionment. Rural interests hold sway because of the specialization of their concerns and the homogeneity of interests within each agriculture system. Rural congressmen and state assemblymen, for example, are recruited by and owe their elections to the same forces that operate the quasi-public committees, and each level of activity reinforces the other. Mere legislative reapportionment is not likely to change this as long as there is no direct confrontation between agriculture interests and nonagriculture interests.

This confrontation could not take place as long as interest-group liberal values prevailed. The cases of Agriculture, Commerce, and Labor suggest that weakened national efficacy and impaired political responsibility—the incapacity to plan—are not recent developments. However, special responsibility rests with the Eisenhower, Kennedy, and Johnson Administrations. Pluralistic solutions may have been thrust upon the New Deal due to the seriously weakened state of public confidence and public finance. The weakened state of the presidency and the Democratic Party under Truman made fresh departures in domestic affairs close to impossible.[5] But after 1952 there was peace, confidence, and efficacy. In Europe and the United States in the 1930s pluralist solutions were turned to out of weakness. The state was forced to share its sovereignty in return for support. *In the 1960s pluralist solutions were not forced upon national leaders but were voluntarily pursued as the highest expression of their ideology.* This must change before the pattern will change.

Republican Succession: No Change, More of the Same Thing

Yet, during the late 1960s the character of the clientele departments was further confirmed. Their extreme resistance to change seems to have succeeded beyond merely the avoidance of change. Despite the rumors that agriculture power had been waning or that union and corporate power were being fragmented by stagflation, the pattern of the 1970s seems to have been no change *and* more of the same thing. In the country at large, even in the rhetoric of

5. Despite this weakness, the Fair Deal may have been less pluralistic than the programs of Eisenhower, Kennedy, and Johnson.

the Nixon Administration, there was a vast preoccupation with poverty, hunger, and a variety of specific ills for which a Department of Agriculture, a Department of Labor, a Department of Commerce, and other related clientele departments might have been a focus for appropriate action. It probably comes as a surprise to few that no such actions came from or through those departments.

THE STATE OF AGRICULTURE

Take the Department of Agriculture to begin with. The 1969 bill of the Nixon Administration, although touted as an Omnibus Farm Bill, extended the basic features of the legislation of previous Democratic administrations. As enacted in 1970, the Nixon Administration program actually added a few reinforcing twists of its own. The only sign that the class and racial turmoils of the 1960s had been recognized at all in the Agriculture Department or related congressional committees or in the White House was the ceiling of $55,000 on the price-support payments the government could make to any one farmer. (Title I. This was lowered to $20,000 in 1973.) Although this ceiling may have established a principle of fundamental reform for the future, and although the principle was to come up for debate again and again in succeeding years, the realities of 1970–73 produced so many loopholes that the principle was virtually overturned. And these loopholes are consistent with the established interest-group liberal pattern in the field of agricultural policy. For example, the law permits farmers to sell or lease part of their acreage allotment (the number of acres on which any farmer can raise a surplus crop) and to receive income from that sale or lease without counting that income against the government price-support payments. This means that a large farmer, who has acreage allotments on which he can receive no further price-support payments can sell or lease the allotments for further income while the purchaser or lessee of those allotments can either grow the crop or himself receive price-support payments—up to the ceiling. Meanwhile, the original farmer, having shed the unneeded allotment, can grow certain alternate (non-surplus) crops and again not have to count the income received from those crops against the total price permissible for support payments.

The rest of the Republican formula for agriculture was wholly consistent with approaches of the 1960s. Title II continued federal milk marketing orders. Title III extended the National Wool Act for three more years, retaining the high "incentive price" for wool growers. Title IV continued the price-support structure for wheat and in fact liberalized the supports by suspending acreage quotas through 1973. The Eisenhower soil-bank approach to acreage reduction was extended under a new name, set-asides. And the elaborate committee system described earlier was left completely untouched.

Another indication of the continuation of established patterns of policy and government in agriculture was the posture of the 1970 act toward government sponsorship of private interests. The act went further than merely continuing the Cotton Board established during the Johnson Administration (affectionately called Cotton Inc.); it actually authorized the Commodity Credit Corporation (CCC) to pay Cotton Inc. up to $10 million per year to enable it to "enter into agreements with [a contracting organization] for the conduct of domestic and foreign markets, of market development, research or sales promotion programs, and programs to aid in the development of new and additional markets" (section 610). The only proviso in this section of the act was that none of these funds could be used to try to influence future agriculture legislation. Cotton Inc. brought on a clamor of demands for equivalent promotional programs for other commodities. One was for funds to pay for advertising and promotion for milk; another was for funds for the promotion of apples and papayas. Two demands succeeded extremely well: Late in 1970 Congress passed the Potato Research Promotion Act creating a National Potato Promotion Board to engage in potato research, development, advertising, and promotion. It was to be financed by an assessment of up to 1 percent per hundredweight of potatoes produced commercially in the United States. The act also added tomatoes to the list of commodities for which the Agriculture Department could run paid advertisements. (Others on the list, going as far back as 1937, were peanuts and cotton.)

In 1974, Congress established the Egg Board to accomplish these same purposes for the egg producers. The official legislative history on this act explicitly recognized that government sponsorship was necessary because

the egg producing industry has been unable to organize itself independently for [these] purposes. A basic impediment has been the wide variation in the size of the nation's egg producers. . . . The bill is specifically designed for the participation of only commercial egg producers with laying flocks of more than 3,000. Even though small producers will not participate, . . . benefits from the program will accrue to all egg producers.[6]

In the grand tradition, membership on these new boards was to be composed of representatives of producers designated by the secretary of Agriculture from nominations made by producers in a manner prescribed by the secretary.

The 1973 Agricultural and Consumer Protection Act continued most of the existing 1970 and pre-1970 provisions, despite the context of extremely high domestic and world demand for agricultural products. The government took no significant steps to bring agriculture prices down; in fact, agriculture price increases were not brought within the wage-and-price-control system established after 1970 for virtually all nonagricultural commodities during that period. The important innovation in the 1973 legislation was the adding of target prices against which to compare actual prices paid to the farmer. The

6. U.S. Code, Congressional and Administration News (1974), pp. 5418-19.

difference between the two would be made up for by direct government support payments for farmers participating in the set-aside program. This is reminiscent of the very generous Brannan Plan of the late 1940s, and the Republicans were lucky enough to be saved from its full budgetary implications by the high world demand for U.S. produce. And although in greatest part this high demand was natural, part of it was artificially induced by still another, purely interest-group liberal victory, the famous 1972 trade agreement providing for the sale of over $1 billion of American grain to the Russians through low-interest credit plus a heavily subsidized per bushel price. This story is related in detail in Chapter 6 as part of the analysis of the Republican approach to foreign policy.

One other significant piece of legislation during the Republican period was the creation of the Commodity Futures Trading Commission, which consolidated government control over speculation in agricultural products and their prices. This effort to enhance and clarify regulatory power was in no way a sign of political defeat for agriculture but rather was a reaction to the explosive growth of commodity trading and a blow against the many exploiters of instability in agriculture prices working in the major exchanges in the large cities. What is really significant politically about this act is the fact that the new Commodity Futures Trading Commission, which was established to take over all authority of the Commodity Exchange Commission, was withdrawn from the Department of Agriculture and made into an independent regulatory commission.[7]

INTEREST-GROUP LIBERALISM IN LABOR AND COMMERCE

The Republican administration was not at all reluctant to intervene in matters affecting the nation's commercial life. Although President Nixon had not wanted wage and price control, he utilized this authority with vigor not very long after it was handed to him by Congress through the Economic Stabilization Act of 1970 (see Chapters 5 and 10). Characteristically, this most important single government intervention of the decade—possibly any decade before or since the 1930s—was formulated and implemented outside the Departments of Labor and Commerce. Nixon's Ash Commission (the President's Advisory Council on Executive Organization) recognized the lack of utility of these departments by proposing their abolition through reorganizing their constituent agencies into a new superdepartment. Although the Watergate crisis killed any chance of serious departmental reorganization, the

7. For a recent statement of farm politics in Congress and related agencies, see Roger Davidson, "Representation and Congressional Committees," *Annals of the American Academy* 411 (January 1974). For a good review of the world and domestic economic and political context of Republican agriculture legislation, see "Leading Farmer's Market," *The Economist*, February 24, 1973.

Nixon and Ford Administrations continued to view the Departments of Labor and Commerce as nothing more than the channels for interest accommodation they had always been. Revenue sharing not only bypassed the departments but weakened them still further by reducing the needs of local governments to seek their specific assistance.

The Commerce Department had the most barren record of all departments in the 1970s. By Executive Orders in 1969 and 1971, President Nixon established the Office of Minority Business Enterprise (OMBE). Its job is to coordinate federal efforts to strengthen minority business. But the agency has no direct authority over other agencies in the federal government or over the activities of local agencies receiving federal assistance. Thus the only White House moves of any importance in matters affecting commerce or the Commerce Department were the Rail Passenger Service Act in 1970 and the Consumer Product Safety Act of 1972. The former created Amtrak (the National Railroad Passenger Corporation). The latter created the Consumer Product Safety Commission. Both were made almost completely independent of the Commerce Department. The Consumer Product Safety Commission is a classic independent regulatory commission. Amtrak is an independent enterprise attempting to bail out and operate the nation's passenger rail service. It is independent of the Department of Commerce and the Department of Transportation. Its board of directors is composed of nine public members appointed by the president without need of Senate approval and three members actually selected by the various railroad companies which own Amtrak stock.[8]

The Labor Department got a bit more attention during the 1970s, not because it received any authority to implement wage-and-price controls—which it did not—but because of two particular programs—OSHA and CETA. OSHA (Occupational Safety and Health Administration) is a rare instance of a regulatory program housed in a regular departmental agency rather than set up as or within an independent commission. OSHA has also been one of the more maligned and caricatured government agencies (not without justification—for example, one OSHA regulation uses several pages to define a safe ladder; another regulation requires steel workers to wear life jackets even when building bridges over dry riverbeds in the Southwest). However, what is most significant about OSHA—and what may explain why it was housed as a regular agency within the Department of Labor—is its au-

8. The railroad companies continue to own the tracks and to maintain the trains, for a fee paid to them by Amtrak. Legislation allowed the railroads either to receive Amtrak's stock for their fees or to treat their payment as a cost and take a tax write-off. Most chose the latter option, but four, who were in such bad shape they could not get an advantage from a tax write-off, chose to take stock. These four troubled companies became Amtrak's only shareholders. (The four were the Burlington Northern, Penn Central, Milwaukee, and Grand Trunk Western.) They also became the companies authorized to elect the three railroad representatives to the Amtrak board. Several of the so-called public members of the Amtrak board are also railroad or affiliated executives. See *Fortune*, May 1974, pp. 272–90. More on Consumer Products Safety will be found in Chapter 5.

thority under the 1970 act to adopt "national consensus standards." The act states explicitly that a

national consensus standard [is] any occupational safety and health standard or modification which (1) has been adopted and promulgated by a nationally recognized standards-producing organization under procedures whereby it can be determined by the Secretary that persons affected have reached substantial agreement on its adoption; (2) and formulated after an opportunity for consideration of diverse views; (3) and designated as such a standard by the Secretary, after consultation with other appropriate Federal agencies.[9]

CETA (Comprehensive Employment and Training Act of 1973) is even more an indication of the continuity of values from Democrats to Republicans, because it was a legislative culmination of a four-year effort by the Nixon Administration. Although CETA probably did clarify the lines of administrative authority among manpower programs, the CETA legislation, long and detailed as it was, failed to set any guidelines or limits on the decisions of its newly created Office of Comprehensive Employment Development Programs (OCED). CETA defined OCED's authority in terms that were completely open-ended: "Comprehensive manpower services may include, *but shall not be limited to*." The act then went on to identify at least two dozen things the OCED might do, but in any case this was in the context of the opening clause that the OCED was not limited to just these things.[10] Therefore, for almost any purposes within the judgment of the agency, OCED could make grants to states or units of local government on the basis of applications made by those state and local units to OCED. OCED was to have no plan but was obliged (sections 104–5) to consider only those applications based upon (1) a "comprehensive manpower plan produced by the applying unit and (2) a local planning council consisting, to the extent practicable, of members who are representative of the client community and the community-based organization, the employment service, educational and training agencies and institutions, business, labor and, where appropriate, agriculture." Some critics, especially congressional Democrats, accused President Nixon of hiding a drastic reduction of manpower dollars behind a bid for rational administration. Possibly so; nevertheless, Nixon's method of cutting

9. *U.S. Code*, vol. 3 (1970), pp. 5,202–3. This means that many of the health and safety standards in this industry-wide safety program were to be those already developed and agreed upon by leading members of a trade association. To add insurance that standards would be acceptable to each industry, the law provided for a three-member Occupational Safety and Health Review Commission, an independent, quasi-judicial agency with power to review and set aside OSHA actions. The act also set up a National Institute for Occupational Safety and Health in the Department of Health, Education and Welfare to serve as a source of information on industry health standards. For further references to OSHA, see Chapter 5. For a reinforcing interpretation of OSHA see James E. Anderson, *Public Policy-Making* (New York: Praeger, 1975), pp. 116 and 129–30.

10. *U.S. Code*, vol. 42 (1973), section 101 and part A of Title III and Title IV. (Emphasis added.)

down the budget could hardly have been more consistent with Democratic ways and means of using government.

CETA may best be understood as part of Nixon's general plan as expressed in revenue sharing to push more federal activities down to local levels. As discussed elsewhere (in Chapter 7), General Revenue Sharing, provided for in the State and Local Fiscal Assistance Act of 1972, went a step further than the Democrats but in exactly their direction. This is true regardless of the inclination of Republicans to spend less or to consolidate, reduce, or terminate some programs. For example, despite, or through, a few programs like CETA, Nixon did cut back drastically on "categoric aid" (federal grants that are given to state and local governments on condition that the money be spent only in the prescribed subject-matter area, such as grants-in-aid or soil conservation, education, vocational rehabilitation, and so forth). But rather than cut further, Nixon diverted the remaining federal assistance and grants-in-aid to revenue sharing. This meant that Nixon was removing the remaining limits on the discretion of administrative agencies to make policy as they saw fit. Under categoric aid programs, there were already no explicit standards to delimit or guide administrative decision-making. Yet, there is a bit of limitation on discretion inherent in the subject-matter categories themselves. Under General Revenue Sharing, even these limitations were abolished. When a local government gets money under revenue sharing, it can choose almost without any constraint whether to spend that money to pay the interest on its local bonds or to spend that money to buy a General Sherman tank. Thus, here again Nixon's New Federalism turned out to be no change, more of the same thing. Republicans in the 1970s were simply more niggardly interest-group liberals.

It is quite misleading to try to explain the politics of the Departments of Agriculture, Commerce, Labor, and, for that matter, the other clientele departments such as Interior and Transportation, in terms of the power of the respective groups or sectors of the economy. First of all, power begs the question. Having seen results that look like success—access, favorable policies, appropriations, holding actions—observers then use *power* as the ancient scientist used phlogiston to explain combustion: "Something must have been present. Let's give it a name." In the second place, power implies an exercise of some kind of influence or force by the outside interest upon the agency or legislature. It is probably closer to the truth to deny altogether the role of influence *upon* the government and to look instead for the influence that is *within* the policy maker. What we see mostly in the policies and in the administrative practices of a whole succession of administrations and their agencies and support blocs in Congress is a congruence of values and ideologies. And this is by far the most insidious of types of influence, especially when the influence is so internalized and all-inclusive as to go unrecognized as ideology and be accepted as a natural phenomenon—indeed accepted not merely as

the truth (in the sense of a confirmed hypothesis) but actually as
that is inherent in the system itself. Political scientists and practiti
what they see the political process without recognizing that *process* b
fair and misleading connotations from its use in biology. Politics may   ....u-
ral, but particular forms are artificial. They can be made and remade.

Few who are familiar with the United States are surprised to learn that
agribusiness, with 5 percent of the population, determines whether the other
95 percent will eat and how much they will have to pay for the privilege. Few
will be surprised with the assertion that a tiny minority of workers—those
organized in a few of the larger unions—call the tune on labor and employment legislation. Most knowledgeable observers will also shrug off as truistic
any reports that all the procedural and most of the policy decisions toward
commerce and industry are precleared with the National Association of Manufacturers (NAM) and related business interests. What is likely to surprise and
disturb most observers is the mere contention that none of this is natural or inherent. Few have stopped even to ask whether *process* is fair terminology in
society, especially in government. Pluralistic politics, as observed in these
programs of the Departments of Agriculture, Labor, and Commerce, is not a
process at all, if this is meant to imply something natural and inevitable.
What we have seen is the result of actual government sponsorship of pluralism. It is not natural; it is simply repeated, through a succession of Democratic and Republican administrations. Pluralism as we can observe it in the
actual conduct of American government is nothing but an artifact, an expression of widely shared ideology. It is the furthest thing from a natural and inevitable expression of capitalism; it is not even a necessary expression of what
could be called pluralist democracy. It is simply one pathological expression
of pluralist democracy. The fact that Democratic patterns are picked up and
repeated by as partisan an anti-Democrat as Richard Nixon proves not that the
observed patterns are inherent but only that they have become institutionalized. And if they are artificial patterns rather than natural processes,
these patterns can be changed. If the supportive ideology of interest-group
liberalism can be changed, then the pattern it supports will also change. However, it must be admitted that changing the ideology and the patterns will be
more difficult after the 1970s than it appeared to be at the end of the 1960s.
Succession from partisan Democrats to partisan Republicans nails the pattern
down more firmly in the heads and habits, and eventually in the mores of
American leaders, American active publics, and the ordinary American citizen. Indeed, it is all so well established in our minds and in our legitimized
and government-sponsored power patterns that we are obliged to call it the
Second Republic. Consequently, only a radical, organized constitutional
revolt will succeed now where once a sustained intellectual attack might have
been sufficient.

5
LIBERAL JURISPRUDENCE
Policy without Law

Liberal jurisprudence is a contradiction in terms. Liberalism is hostile to law. No matter that it is motivated by the highest social sentiments; no matter that it favors the positive state only because the positive state is the presumptive instrument for achieving social good. The new public philosophy is hostile to law.

In a country with a strong rule-of-law tradition, those who are hostile to law are doomed to silence. Thus perhaps the most damning evidence of the liberal position on law is that there will be disagreement over the mere description of its jurisprudence as well as disagreement over its meaning and consequences.

Interest-group liberalism has little place for law because laws interfere with the political process. The political process is stymied by abrupt changes in the rules of the game. The political process is not perfectly self-correcting if it is not allowed to correct itself. Laws change the rules of the game. Laws make government an institution apart; a government of laws is not a simple expression of the political process. A good clear statute puts the government on one side as opposed to other sides, it redistributes advantages and disadvantages, it slants and redefines the terms of bargaining. It can even eliminate bargaining, as this term is currently defined. Laws set priorities. Laws deliberately set some goals and values above others.

In brief, law, in the liberal view, is too authoritative a use of authority. Authority has to be tentative and accessible to be acceptable. If authority is to be accommodated to the liberal myth that it is not power at all, it must emerge out of individual bargains.

The legal expression of the new liberal ideology can be summed up in a single, conventional legal term: *delegation of power*. Delegation of power refers technically to actions whereby a legislature confers upon an administrative agency certain tasks and powers the legislature would and could itself exercise if that were not impracticable. Delegations can be narrow or broad, but the practice under the liberal state has most generally and consistently been broad. As Kenneth Davis put it, Congress in effect says, "Here is the problem: deal with it."[1] Delegation of power provides the legal basis for rendering a statute tentative enough to keep the political process in good working order all the way down from Congress to the hearing examiner, the meat inspector, the community action superviser, and the individual clients with which they deal. Everyone can feel that he is part of one big policy-making family.

Delegation of power enjoys strong standing in the courts. The broadest applications of the doctrine have been accepted by the Supreme Court for over thirty years. The last major statute invalidated for involving too broad a delegation to either public agencies or private associations was the "sick chicken case" of 1935.[2] The 1935 decision has never been reversed, but the Supreme Court has not seen fit to apply it since that time. Policy without law is what a broad delegation of power is. Policy without law is clearly constitutional, according to present judicial practice.

The doctrine of delegation of power also meets with strong support among academic political scientists and historians. Too much law would obviously be intolerable to scientific pluralist theory. In a vitally important sense, *value-free political science is logically committed to the norm of delegation of power because delegation of power is a self-fulfilling mechanism of prediction in modern political science.* Clear statutes that reduce pluralistic bargaining also reduce drastically the possibility of scientific treatment of government as simply part of the bundle of bargaining processes and multiple power structures. A good law eliminates the political process at certain points. A law made at the center of government focuses politics there and reduces interest elsewhere. The center means Congress, the president, and the courts. To make law at a central point is to centralize the political process. If this is too authoritative for interest-group liberalism it is too formal for modern political science.

Hostility to law, expressed in the principle of broad and unguided delegation of power, is the weakest timber in the shaky structure of the new public philosophy. This, more than any other single feature of interest-group liberalism, has wrapped public policies in shrouds of illegitimacy and ineffectiveness. This, more than any other feature, has turned liberal vitality into governmental and social pathology.

It is of course impossible to imagine a modern state in which central authorities do not delegate functions, responsibilities, and powers to administrators. Thus the practice of delegation itself can hardly be criticized. The practice becomes pathological, and criticizable, at the point where it comes to be considered a good thing in itself, flowing to administrators without guides,

---

1. See below, Chapter 11.
2. A.L.A. *Schechter Poultry Corporation* v. *U.S.*, 295 U.S. 495. The Court held that the National Industrial Recovery Act, in giving the president the authority to promulgate codes of fair competition, had gone too far in delegating lawmaking power which was "unconfined and vagrant . . . not canalized within banks to keep it from overflowing." The ruling was confirmed in a major case in 1936 but not seriously applied thereafter.

checks, safeguards. Historically, delegation had a rather technical meaning that emerged as the price to be paid in order to reap the advantages of administration. Delegation today represents a bastardization of earlier realities, and it is the bastardization that is at issue.

Evolution of Public Controls in the United States: The Delegation of Powers and Its Fallacies

Delegation of power did not become a widespread practice or a constitutional problem until government began to take on regulatory functions. The first century was one of government dominated by Congress and virtually self-executing laws. Congressional government, as Woodrow Wilson could view it in the 1880s, was possible for two reasons: Either its activity was insignificant, or it sought only to husband private action. Between 1795 and 1887, the key federal policies were tariffs, internal improvements, land sales and land grants, development of a merchant fleet and coastal shipping, the post offices, patents and copyrights, and research on how the private sector was doing. Thus, after a short Hamiltonian period when the Economic Constitution was written—including assumption and funding of debts, the taxation system, currency and banking structure, establishing the power to subsidize—the federal government literally spent one century in the business of subsidization. It was due to this quite special and restricted use of government that Congress could both pass laws and see to their execution. There must have been considerable corruption in this method, but it did build a nation, and it did, after a century, make possible the following characterization by Lord Bryce, on the very eve of the revolution in public control and in congressional government:

It is a great merit of American government that it relies very little on officials [i.e., administrators] and arms them with little power of arbitrary interference. The reader who has followed the description of Federal authorities, state authorities, county and city or township authorities, may think there is a great deal of administration; but the reason why these descriptions are necessarily so minute is because the powers of each authority are so carefully and closely restricted. It is natural to fancy that a government of the people and by the people will be led to undertake many and various functions for the people, and in the confidence of its strength will constitute itself a general philanthropic agency for their social and economic benefit. There has doubtless been of late years a tendency in this direction. . . . But it has taken the direction of acting through the law rather than through the officials. That is to say, when it prescribes to the citizen a particular course of action it has relied upon the ordinary legal sanctions, instead of investing the administrative officers with inquisitorial duties or powers that might prove oppressive.[3]

3. James Bryce, *The American Commonwealth* (1888), from the chapter "The Strength of American Democracy."

DELEGATION DEFINED

The American system Bryce was describing was one whose regulations were few, whose resources were many, and whose central government was unobtrusive.[4] It was a system ideally suited for congressional government. When this system was revolutionized, beginning in 1887, it was one no longer susceptible to direct rule by legislature. Means had to be found to insure that even with the decline of the legislature there would be no equivalent decline in law. This would be no minor achievement, if it were at all possible. Involved was no less than reducing the hallowed role of the legislature and revising the even more hallowed separation of powers, while yet maintaining a sense that we were a government of laws and not of men.

The first move, so strongly feared, was made only in response to terrifying agrarian agitation and a Supreme Court decision which abolished all state efforts to deal with the problem.[5] This move, the Interstate Commerce Act of 1887, reflects all of the problems and all of the concerns that have plagued government regulation ever since. In this famous act, Congress (1) delegated its own power to regulate an aspect of interstate commerce (2) to an administrative agency (3) designed especially for the purpose. However, as will be emphasized strongly below, debate over the problem of delegation and how to delegate began before the passage of the act and continued until the question of delegation became a dead issue with interest-group liberalism.

Congressmen were intensely concerned with constitutional issues during this first step toward a new venture in federal government. They were obviously aware that the Interstate Commerce Commission was an innovation, even if they did not altogether appreciate its significance as a model for the future. Fifty years later James Landis best captured its significance in two passages of his classic essay:

In terms of political theory, the administrative process springs from the inadequacy of a simple tripartite form of government to deal with modern problems. . . . (p. 1)

[I]t is obvious that the resort to the administrative process is not, as some suppose, simply an extension of executive power. Confused observers have sought to liken this development to a pervasive use of executive power. But the administrative differs not only in regard to the scope of its powers [a special sector or industry defined by statute]; it differs most radically in regard to the responsibility it possesses for their exercise. In

4. The prescribing to which Bryce refers was almost all state and local practice. Therefore, the problem of delegation to an administrative process began earlier in the states. Unfortunately, coverage of these developments would overly complicate the presentation here. For a short treatment, yet one of the best, see Robert E. Cushman, *The Independent Regulatory Commissions* (New York: Oxford University Press, 1941), Chapter 2.

5. *Wabash, St. L. & P.R. v. Illinois*, 118 U.S. 551 (1886). The Supreme Court in this case made railroads an interstate problem, whether Congress liked it or not, by declaring that the states could not regulate interstate railroad traffic within their own borders even in the absence of congressional action. This was indeed the categorical imperative for the commitment of the federal government at long last to an interventionist role. See Cushman, p. 38.

the grant to it of that full ambit of authority necessary for it in order to plan, to promote, and to police, it presents an assemblage of rights normally exercisable by government as a whole. . . . (p. 16)[6]

Constitutional concerns of the sort implied in Landis's definition of the administrative process were addressed in the Interstate Commerce Act in two ways. First, there was a fairly clear specification of standards regarding jurisdiction of the commission and regarding the behavior of the railroad deemed unlawful. There was no rigid codification, but conduct central to railroad abuses was specified quite sufficiently. These included such practices as rate discriminations, rebating, pooling, long-versus-short-haul adjustments. The commission's power to enjoin railroad rates that were "undue or unreasonable" was guided, therefore, by standards in the act. Second, however, the act itself was the culmination of a long history of public efforts vis-à-vis rail service and rates, efforts in state law and in the common law. In effect, congressional language, even where vague, had been "freighted with meaning" by history.[7] As a consequence, it was possible for Judge Friendly in 1962 to view the original 1887 act as a paragon of delegation. The fact that the commission was hobbled for over a decade by a hostile Supreme Court may only attest to the need for administrative tribunals to overcome anachronistic courts in the industrial age. The act was good law, because standards concerned with goals, clientele, and methods of implementation were clear, and it bred good legal behavior in the commission by keeping pressure on for further and further exegesis of explicit rules and definitions by the commissioners.[8] As we will see shortly, the commission became "old" and was captured by its railroad clientele only after it was given new and entirely different responsibilities in 1920.

To summarize: In the Interstate Commerce Act, there was delegation of the "full ambit of authority"—executive, legislative, and judicial—in a single administrative body. It was given the power to be flexible, but it was relatively well shackled by clear standards of public policy, as stated in the statute and as understood in common law. From the beginning, the whole notion of vesting great authority in administrative tribunals was never separated from the expectation that standards of law would accompany the delegation. Much fun has been made of the myth the courts tried to create, that agencies were merely "filling in the details" of acts of Congress. But neither the myth nor the mirth can hide the fact that when a delegation was broad, positive rules of law attached themselves to it.

Many have argued that restriction on delegation was never intended. They reason that prior to the Panama and Schechter cases in 1935 the Supreme Court had not declared delegations of power unconstitutional, that after 1936

6. James M. Landis, *The Administrative Process* (New Haven: Yale University Press, 1938).
7. Quoted in Henry J. Friendly, *The Federal Administrative Agencies* (Cambridge, Mass.: Harvard University Press, 1962), p. 13.
8. See Friendly, p. 29 ff.

no further delegations were invalidated, and therefore is it not possible that "Schechter is only of historical significance."[9] However, the question is badly put. The question of proper standards can be posed, and was indeed posed, without necessarily involving constitutionality. Obeying its own rule of restraint on constitutional issues, the Court merely filled in the congressional and presidential void with specifications of its own—or so construed the statute as to render the agency powerless. Jaffe himself provides the best example. The Federal Trade Commission Act of 1914 so poorly defined the key term, "unfair method of competition," that the Supreme Court invalidated order after order issued by the FTC through most of the first twenty years of its life.[10] The question of accompanying delegations with proper standards of law did not become a dead issue—in the courts or in congressional debate—until the 1930s and 1940s.

DELEGATION TO THE ADMINISTRATIVE PROCESS:
A DEVELOPMENTAL ANALYSIS

Throughout the formative period of federal control of economic life, delegation was considered a problem. It had to be encountered because an administrative component had to be added to government, and delegation was the only way to accomplish it. Delegation was nonetheless the central problem, and it was faced with various partial solutions. However, a curious thing happened in the history of public control after 1887: As public control extended to wider and more novel realms, delegation became a virtue rather than a problem. *The question of standards disappeared as the need for them increased.* To pursue this proposition it is necessary first to pursue the actual developments in the practice of delegation itself.

The diagrammatic summary, Table 5.1, attempts to capture developments in the logic and practice of public control. From top to bottom the diagram is roughly but not exclusively chronological. There is an underlying logical progression among public controls, but Congress moved within this order in something slightly less than an orderly fashion, inventing techniques once in a while somewhat before their time. For example, the granting of overall market powers to the Interstate Commerce Commission (ICC) in the Transportation Act of 1920 anticipated a certain type of control by over a decade. However, it will be clear that the order is chronological in terms of the frequency and effectiveness in the use of each type of control.

At the federal level, modern public control—*administered* public control—began with the ICC and was followed up quickly by the Sherman Antitrust

9. The cases are *Panama Refining Company* v. *Ryan*, 293 U.S. 388 and *Schechter Poultry Corporation* v. *U.S.* The quote is Louis L. Jaffe, *Administrative Law* (Englewood Cliffs: Prentice-Hall, 1959), p. 49.

10. Jaffe, pp. 60–61; see also Cushman, *Independent*, p. 412, and especially *Federal Trade Commission* v. *Gratz*, 253 U.S. 421 (1920).

Act (1890). These early instances were not any less regulative than anything that came later. They added the stick of direct coercion to the carrot of subsidies. The peculiarity to be emphasized for purposes of later comparison is this: In both these early instances, the objects to be regulated were known entities easy to designate. In the case of ICC jurisdiction, the objects were quite clearly the railroads. Similar legislation in the states extended to grain elevators and public conveyances and services of various sorts, suggesting that the

TABLE 5.1

THE DEVELOPMENT OF PUBLIC CONTROLS
IN THE U.S.

An Analytic Summary

SCOPE OF CONTROL	OBJECTS OF CONTROL	DEVELOPMENTAL CHARACTERISTICS
A. The Railroads in Interstate Commerce (1887–)*	The railroads	concrete specific traditional rule-bound proscriptive
B. The Trusts (1890–)	Oil trust, sugar trust, liquor trust, cottonseed oil trust, etc.	concrete general† traditional rule-bound proscriptive
C. Goods (1906–)	Qualities of things. Substandard foods, impure drugs, immoral women, obscene literature, etc.	abstract specific traditional rule-bound proscriptive
D. Commerce (1914–)	Relationships. Competition, fair and unfair. Qualities of commerce.	abstract general traditional discretionary prescriptive
E. Factors (1933–)	Qualities of commodities behind commerce. Qualities of land, capital, labor and relations relevant to them.	abstract general novel discretionary proscriptive

* Dates given may often disregard some antecedent, but these are provided only to suggest when a particular phase seems to have begun in earnest.
† The major innovation of each phase is underlined.

SCOPE OF CONTROL	OBJECTS OF CONTROL	DEVELOPMENTAL CHARACTERISTICS
F. Exchange (1933–)	Qualities of relationships. Open-ended.	abstract universal novel discretionary prescriptive
G. Markets (1934–)	Structures of relationships. Open-ended.	abstract universal novel discretionary categoric
H. System (1946–)	The environment of conduct.	concrete universal traditional redistributive‡ categoric

‡ See my "Four Systems of Policy, Politics, and Choice," *Public Administration Review* (July/August 1972). This issue is beyond the scope of the present inquiry.

general category, insofar as we can say there is a category at all, is utilities. These are the so-called natural monopolies, which must be regulated because it was felt they could not and ought not be subject to normal competition.

In the second case, antitrust, another concrete category was involved, not really any more abstract and in need of definition than the first. *Trusts* referred to all large companies and company combinations, but the actual category in practice was comprised of a numerous but namable collection of companies and identifiable conducts. (Therefore, *The* Trusts.) The category was further specified by the fact that it fit into an established legal-governmental tradition, as did the concepts of rails and utilities. That is to say, two factors helped solve the problem of how to guide delegations with standards. The statute could easily identify scope and jurisdiction for the administrator because these were so close to real quantities. Second, the task of definition was eased still further by the fact that history had "freighted them with meaning."[11]

The third stage of development (C. in the table) constitutes a new twist relative to the first two, although at first glance nothing seems special. Here the

11. For an extended and balanced treatment, see Donald Dewey, *Monopoly in Economics and Law* (Chicago: Rand-McNally, 1959), Chapters 9–11. Dewey shows that the sanctions at common law were much too confused to have constituted a sufficient approach to enforcement without aid of positive, statutory law. But his review of concepts and cases shows that the contracts and practices that were considered part of the category, restraint of trade, were unmistakably clear.

objects of regulation were goods in commerce. The now time-honored techniques were regulatory taxation,[12] inspection, publicity, and outright prohibition and seizure of goods that were of low quality[13] or were considered to be immoral[14] or harmful to health.[15] The new twist was that for the first time scope and/or jurisdiction were to be defined not by mere designation of known companies and behaviors but by *abstract categorization*.

Rather than by actual designation the effort was to identify the objects of regulation through definition of a quality or characteristic that inheres in all of a defined or designated class of objects. Following that, flexible but effective guides could be set down for the administrator's decision on how to designate the actual objects below the cutoff point of *sub*standard, *im*moral, *un*healthy. Obviously the ability of Congress to guide and control the administrator is far more limited at this point, for definition by abstraction and categorization involves philosophic and philological as well as technological and empirical and just plain unpredictable dimensions. At what point of smell or bacteriological content is meat spoiled or are apples rotten? What kinds of actions define the point at which a woman's movement across state lines becomes immoral?

The difference between regulation of goods and that of railroads and trusts may seem slight as a matter of degree, but it is great in principle. The step may not have appeared so great at the time, as indeed it might not today, because control of certain goods was an old state and local practice, and had traditions which, again, "freighted with meaning" these early congressional efforts. Appreciation of the difference and its significance increases in light of later developments. The move from concreteness to abstractness in the definition of public policy was probably the most important single change in the entire history of public control in the United States. Certainly it is the most important step to those concerned for rule by law.

The very next phase in the development of government controls underscores the significance of the effort made in regulating goods, and also represents significant changes in its own right. The very definiteness of the Sherman Antitrust Act was beginning to cause strains on the Court and Congress. The language, tradition, and plain meaning of the act seemed clearly to forbid all conspiracies to restrain trade. Yet, the burgeoning of multimillion-dollar firms through patents, through growth, and through consolidation at

12. For example, we once dealt with liquor by prohibiting its manufacture and sale. We now control its use by setting upon it a tax so high that presumably people will be led to use it in moderation. Some regulatory taxes constitute an actual prohibition whenever the article has an elastic demand curve (for example, oleomargarine, goods made by child labor) rather than an inelastic one (liquor).

13. Examples range from rotten apples to sick chickens.

14. There are, fortunately, few examples of such goods, the most famous being immoral women, kidnapped children, sawed-off shotguns, narcotics, and liquor.

15. The best-known examples are drugs, cosmetics, and cigarettes.

that very time gave the Court and many others second thoughts.[16] As the Court retreated one step after another by drawing distinctions among reasonable and unreasonable restraints, the trust category became more and more muddied. In 1914 Congress made a stab at systematically defining what it had only had to point at in 1890. The Clayton Act and the Federal Trade Commission Act constitute valiant but vain efforts of Congress to define competition and to enumerate the actions that were to constitute restraints upon it.[17] The Clayton Act did manage to list three specific evils,[18] but all told these acts contributed a new and grievous characteristic to government control. Although regulation of goods (C.) was based upon abstractions, the standards governing implementation were quite specific. Congress had tried to be specific in Clayton, but ultimately failed. The language of Clayton and FTC was abstract *and* general. Taking these two attributes of law together, the result was inevitably an enormous grant of discretion to the new commission. This was new, this unguided discretion involved in the grant of power to enforce the law against "unfair methods of competition . . . and unfair or deceptive acts or practices." Note that the language creates an abstract category of behavior (commerce), decrees an abstract characteristic which is to adhere to all such behavior (competition), and provides an abstract standard to guide decisions (fairness). This may sound identical to the abstract category "goods" and the characteristics standard-substandard or healthy-unhealthy, but obviously there is a difference. In the regulation of goods, both the categories (beef, apples, morphine) and the qualities (this was even true of the notion of morality applied to transporting women, that is, prostitution) possessed both a plain meaning and some capacity for measurement. Laws governing competition could have very little of either (although some tradition still adhered at that time). Therefore, the need was for greater and greater definition in the act, and, clearly, definition was not being provided.

Almost identical actions were taken regarding the new grant of powers to the ICC by the Transportation Act of 1920. Briefly, the act added the power over minimum rates to the ICC's existing power over maximum rates.[19] Perhaps it is true that Congress did not appreciate what it was doing, but it is no less true that the change in ICC power at that time, when the railroads were passed back to private ownership, totally altered the commission. Power over maximum rates was specified fairly clearly by the lists in the 1887 act, by

16. Compare the radically purist position of the Court in 1897 in *U.S.* v. *Trans-Missouri Freight Association* 166 U.S. 290, one of the first test cases, with *Standard Oil Co.* v. *U.S.*, 221 U.S. 1, and *U.S.* v. *American Tobacco Co.*, 221 U.S. 106, in 1911.

17. Richard W. Taylor, "Government and Business," in Jack W. Peltason and James M. Burns, eds., *Functions and Policies of American Government* (Englewood Cliffs: Prentice-Hall, 1967), p. 230; and Cushman, *Independent*, pp. 186–87.

18. These were price discrimination, exclusionary agreements, and interlocking directorates or ownership of stock in competing firms.

19. For a detailed treatment, with which this section is fully in accord, see Friendly, *The Federal Administrative Agencies*, Chapter 4.

the 1906 Hepburn Amendment, and in common law. This was particularly true of the core of the ICC's jurisdiction—discrimination, exclusiveness, intimidation, and such matters as attended monopoly power. Power to raise minimum rates was granted with no such specification. The 1920 act was a grant to the agency to find out the meaning of the act itself, because the ICC was instructed only to act on what was "just and reasonable." In effect this meant case-by-case bargaining (called "on the merits"), the results putting the commission on every side of every issue. As we shall see, this totally altered the meaning of the ICC.

Much as the courts fought the FTC,[20] the 1914 and 1920 acts changed the entire practice and concept of regulation in ways from which there were to be no later departures. The next phase involved the move to include the factors of production that lay behind interstate commerce. While some of these factors might themselves have been in interstate commerce (currency), most were not so but rather were known to bear some intimate relation to the national—interstate—economy. Thus the big change here was not in the logical structure of the statute but in substantive expansion of the scope of federal authority. This turn of events got far more attention than either the FTC acts or the Transportation Act of 1920, but it involved no more important an innovation in government. It emphasizes once again an earlier observation, that there are two meanings to the term *limited government*, and that Americans were concerned about only one of them. So, the only question was whether the federal government had the power to reach such things as forest lands, child labor, working conditions, wages, and so on.[21] The issue of whether power existed required years to settle and involved some of the finest constitutional minds. Few except a Court of old men gave notice to the *other* dimension of limited government—how the power was to be exercised—and they were eagerly replaced.

Regulation of a few factors of production had been trifled with during the Wilson Administration. But conservation legislation and child-labor legislation were minor precursors of attempts to regulate factors of production during the Roosevelt Administration. The invalidation of child-labor legislation twice by the Supreme Court and the reaffirmation of that attitude during twelve Republican years in the White House slackened the pace of development. Therefore the most serious federal legislation in this area came almost simultaneously with the next step in the process of development—regulation of commercial exchange. This is a more advanced stage of development because it is a more abstract characterization of commerce. It is no further

20. For example, in the *Gratz* case (see note 10 above) the courts intervened to prevent the FTC from defining the scope and nature of its own powers and thus inhibited FTC development for twenty years.

21. Currency management involves no such problems because power to create a Federal Reserve is explicitly granted by the Constitution via *McCulloch* v. *Maryland*.

back along the flow of commerce, but that is a small part of the complexity of government's relation to economic life. Abstraction requires definition, and that is precisely what is absent from these more contemporary forms of regulation. Furthermore, this phase seems to carry to greater conclusiveness another feature that had been expressed only as a tendency before—the more positive or prescriptive character of the regulation. The regulation in question included the exercise of power over stock and grain exchanges, holding companies, agriculture land-use, and key aspects of marketing of both agricultural and processed commodities. All of this legislation emanated from virtually universal, not merely general, categories of jurisdiction, as well as, typically, the most abstract of indications, if any, of the characteristics of the objects to be included.[22] They moved away from the more restricted realm of activities already on the verge of hurting trade (1) into the sum total of all transactions and (2) toward certain qualities of all actions and transactions that may be deemed hurtful. The Robinson-Patman addition to the FTC constituted a significant expansion of FTC jurisdiction toward the hypothetical realm of all pricing, by defining the jurisdiction as price discrimination "between purchasers of like grade and quality," with differentials permitted for "due allowance for difference in cost of manufacture, sale, or delivery."[23] Under this legislation the FTC need only find "reasonable possibility of injury" from what it identifies as a price discrimination. This compounds and confounds abstraction by piling one hypothetical universe upon another. Similarly, regulation of securities extended to the complete universe of exchange, and certain qualities thereof, in that particular sector. Regulation of marketing, pricing, and acreage in the price-support field constitutes a less abstract definition of scope but one no less universal in intention. Its concept of the total structure of agriculture links up this phase of regulation with the last regulatory phases on the diagram. Price-support regulation also stands as the best example, although far from the earliest, of prescriptive control. Predicating quota and marketing controls upon a referendum does not alter the fact that the powers of the old Agricultural Adjustment Administration (AAA; see Chapter 4) include "thou shalts" as well as "thou shalt nots." There is also prescription of varying degrees and types in securities, holding-company, and fair-trade regulation.

Finally, the most advanced development in administrative process is the effort to reach the structure and/or composition of markets themselves. Licensing and franchising are old and established instruments of local regulation. However, while cities and states usually stipulate some conditions prior to

22. This I have tried to indicate on the diagram with the term *open-ended*. That is, a category of scope of jurisdiction is indicated but its limits are not defined. "Factors affecting competition," for example, is part of a long causal chain. Attempts are made to reduce universality with provisos, "due allowance for . . .," etc., but great abstractions are too powerful to be easily limited by small abstractions.

23. Section 2 of the Clayton Act as amended by the Robinson-Patman Act.

granting the license, the market concept involved at the federal level has been significantly different.[24] The essence of the difference is that federal regulation is based on an abstract concept of the whole market—that is, what practices ought to constitute it and which and how many participants ought to be involved. The practices and numbers are not specified, but the concept implies them; certification according to convenience and necessity implies them. The Transportation Act of 1920 was obviously searching for a concept of a whole transportation market,[25] but the real examples began with radio, then communications, where chaos over the airwaves dictated a whole-system concept with absolute control over entry, prescription of certain behavior in the public interest, and meticulous prescription of territory and range through control of frequencies and transmission strength. The whole-market approach was then applied to airways, maritime traffic, motor-carrier traffic (after 1935), domestic atomic energy, and satellite communication. This type of regulation went beyond the abstract, universal, nontraditional (novel), prescriptive character of the earlier phase by bringing entry and ownership—the very condition of livelihood—into the public domain. The term *categoric* seems appropriate, although it is not supposed to suggest that these agencies quit proscribing and prescribing conduct.[26]

There is still another step on the diagram, but this is actually a quantum step into another type of public control altogether. Approach to the whole economic system is not regulation or administrative process in any ordinary sense, in that it does not seek to specify conduct directly. Conduct is indeed influenced, but the influence is exerted through the environment of conduct rather than conduct itself. This final step is included on the diagram only to define the limits of the development of public control through regulation. No developmental characteristic is identified as novel simply because this phase constitutes a return (with a vengeance) to the Hamiltonian or constitutional period briefly identified earlier in this chapter. The federal government was expected all along to create and maintain the whole system or environment of conduct. The real difference here is that by the time we returned to such tasks two new developments had taken place: (1) The system had become so integrated that considerable manipulation (as distinct from mere maintenance) was now possible. And (2) economic science had developed new insights and

24. State occupational licensing comes closest to being an antecedent. Licensing of doctors, barbers, and the like is both a means of securing quality and of keeping control of the number who can participate. The local utility is another analogue, except that here the market is usually filled up by one entrant.

25. This act came closest to the concept described here in the granting of power to the ICC to forbid abandonment or construction of lines on the basis of "present or future public convenience and necessity," but the rail market was virtually stabilized by then anyway.

26. It is also not supposed to suggest a new extreme in coercion, but only a new method of delegation of broad administrative discretion. While the potential for heavy public control is there, in practice, as we have already seen in agriculture, the permissive statute has allowed for private expropriation of public domain, not the reverse.

manipulatory techniques. Social Security (Chapter 8) is an early and rudimentary case of a system concept, but it was formalized first in the Employment Act of 1946. The central techniques of this phase—fiscal and monetary policies—are dealt with in Chapters 10 and 11.

SUMMARY: THE RISE OF DELEGATION, THE DECLINE OF LAW

Empirically, the stages of development in the administrative process can be summarized as follows:

1. There is an expansion of the scope of federal control in the sense of the number and types of objects touched by directly coercive federal specification of conduct. This is what has been meant traditionally by the expansion of government.

2. There has also been an expansion of the scope of power in the more philosophical sense of expansion to the whole universe of objects or qualities of objects in a predefined category. This expansion proceeds as categories grow larger, eventually to include certain characteristics (such as trade) which any and all persons in the country might at one time or another possess. (On the diagram this is indicated by the move from "general" to "universal.")

3. Implied in (2) and necessary to it is the development from the concrete to the abstract. This development was observed at two levels. First, the jurisdictional categories became more and more abstract. Second, the standards by which actual qualities are designated moved rather quickly from the specific to the general.

4. The development also involved changes in sanctions. The movement seemed to be from the negative to the positive, the proscriptive to the prescriptive. The latter did not replace the former but only supplemented them.

Taking these few dimensions together, other realities emerge from slightly below the surface to show how much the relation between citizens and public control actually changed even though such labels as "regulation" and "administrative process" remained the same and implied a false sense of continuity throughout the entire century. As regulation moved from the denotation to the connotation of what is subject to public policy, discretion inevitably increased; and the process unavoidably centered on administration. This factor seems far more important in the rise of administrative power than the usual cry of how complex and technological a new field is. Thus the same citizen might receive the same injunction under phase E as under phase B, but the problems involved in his relation to the injunction would not be the same. The command under B is issued to him for an act he committed against a law dealing with that act. Under E, or even D, he receives the command not because of who he is or what he does but because abstractly he belongs to a type, or his behavior is of a type, that comes within public policy.

"Get off the grass" under A or B is an order a policeman issues to an elephant because an elephant hurts the grass. More and more, as we move down the diagram, the "get off the grass" order becomes derived from a definition of the "grassness" of the behavior. Establish grass as part of a category of public policy, then state grassness (without quite defining it) as a quality adhering or not adhering to acts, and you have the essence of modern regulation.

Obviously *modern law has become a series of instructions to administrators rather than a series of commands to citizens.* If at the same time (1) public control has become more positive, issuing imperatives along with setting limits, and if at the same time (2) application of laws and sanctions has become more discretionary, by virtue of having become more indirect as well as more abstract, why should we assume we are talking about the same governmental phenomena in 1968, and 1978 as in 1938, or 1918, 1908? The citizen has become an *administré,* and the question now is how to be certain he remains a citizen.

As has been said already, and as will be reiterated thematically, delegation has been elevated to the highest of virtues, and standards have been relegated to the wastebasket of history because that is the logic of interest-group liberalism. Bargaining—or, as Schlesinger might call it, participation in the "interior processes of policy-making"—must be preferred over authority at every level and phase of government. The idea that the universal application of bargaining solves the problem of power was just appealing enough to win out over alternative doctrines that appeared so conservative in light of the desperation of the 1930s. Victory can be measured by the almost universal application of the principle of broad delegation in regulatory policies and the meekness of the otherwise activist Supreme Court. The conversion of delegation from necessity to virtue also led to the spread of the practice to nonregulatory programs—in the name of partnership, creative federalism, and the like.

As late as 1938 James Landis could still express ambivalence. On the one hand he could exclaim that when government seeks to regulate business it

vests the necessary powers with the administrative authority it creates, not too greatly concerned with the extent to which such action does violence to the traditional tripartite theory of governmental organization. . . . The administrative process is, in essence, our generation's answer to the inadequacy of the judicial and the legislative processes.[27]

On the other hand he agonized over the need and the problem of accompanying delegation with standards. Although he insisted that a general principle applicable to standards for any delegation could not be enunciated, he went on to give a horrible example of a situation where no standards existed. The House version of the Public Utility Holding Company Act of 1935 would have granted the SEC power to exempt holding companies from the death

27. Landis, *The Administrative Process,* pp. 12, 46.

sentence if such exemption were found to be in the public interest. Such a delegation, turning over

the whole burning issue . . . to the Commission . . . was an impossible responsibility. It meant nothing less than that the Commission, rather than Congress, would become the focal point for all the pressures and counter-pressures that had kept the Congress and the press at a white heat for months. Instead of the controversy being concluded, it would have been protracted interminably.[28]

By 1968, perhaps even by 1958 or 1948, none of this reserve was left. There was only untarnished exuberance for a system built upon unregulated regulation. By 1978 these attitudes were fully congealed into the intellectual components of a Second Republic.[29]

Law versus Liberalism

A close review of developments in the administration of public controls turns present conventional wisdom on its head. It is widely assumed that the administrative process is an emergent phenomenon all of a single piece. It is also assumed that after more than three-quarters of a century of experience and after the development of still greater complexity of social organization, it is no longer possible to require that broad delegations of power be accompanied by clear legislative standards. It is further assumed that standards are not desirable anyway. But the truth seems to lie almost completely the other way around. In our day it is possible to enunciate effective standards precisely because businessmen, economists, and government officials have had more than three-quarters of a century's experience with the problems of modern industrial practice. Standards are both necessary and desirable today except for those who wish to see the power of the democratic state drained away. The drainage would not be, as Walter Lippmann feared, down into electoral constituencies. It would not be, as congressmen hope, back into Congress—for legislative oversight and review are forms of committee privilege, not lawmaking. And it would not be a drainage, as interest-group liberals expect, into a benign equilibrium. At its best the system is a hell of administrative boredom. At its worst, it is a tightly woven fabric of legitimized privilege.

Nonetheless, many express concern lest the revival of law destroy bargaining. Bargaining, they say, is one of the great virtues of democracy. It maintains flexibility, and this is supposedly the way to avoid turning citizen into *administré*. But this concern only reveals the extent to which an interest-group-liberal view disorders meanings and narrows vision. An attack on dele-

28. Ibid., pp. 55–56.
29. See especially Chapters 10 and 11.

gation is an attack not on bargaining but on one type of bargaining—logrolling. The attack is on a confusion of the two meanings of bargaining and the consequent misapplication of the whole idea. First, there can be bargaining over the decision on a particular case. This type of bargaining over the stakes is logrolling. It has to do with whether certain facts are to be defined as identical to some earlier set of facts. It has to do with whether the case will be prosecuted at all, and with how much vigor. It has to do with whether monetary sanctions apply; if so, how much; whether contrition plus compliance in the future are sufficient. Second, and worlds apart, there can be bargaining on the rule or rules applicable to the decision. This can take the form of simple insistence that the authority state some rule. It can be a quibble over the definition of a concept or a profound analysis of what Congress could possibly have intended. It could be a process of defining the agency's jurisdiction.

Once this distinction between two kinds of bargaining is stated it is impossible to imagine how they could possibly become fused or confused. The differences in their consequences ought to be clear. In any libertarian, unmobilized society, some logrolling is likely to occur on every decision at every stage in the governmental process. However, if by broad and undefined delegation you build your system in order to insure the logrolling type of bargain on the decision, you are very likely never to reach bargaining on the rule at all. If, on the other hand, you build the system by stricter delegation to insure bargaining on the rule, *you will inevitably get logrolling on the decision as well*.

These propositions are not true merely because the morality of the general rule is weaker than the stakes of the individual case. Bargaining on the rule is especially perishable because broad delegation simply puts at two great disadvantages any client who wishes to bargain for a general rule rather than merely to logroll his case. Here is what he faces: First, the broad delegation enables the agency to co-opt the client—that is, to make him a little less unhappy the louder he complains. On top of that, the broad delegation reverses the burden of initiative and creativity, the burden of proof that a rule is needed. If the client insists on making a federal case out of his minor scrape, he must be prepared to provide the counsel and the energy to start a rule-making process himself. This means that the individual must stop his private endeavors and for a while become a creative political actor. Most behavioral research agrees that this is an unlikely exchange of roles.

Case 1 is an only slightly fictionalized dialogue. It is the first of four cases of the consequences of policy without law.

Wages and Hours Regional: Mr. Employer, we find that you owe your ten employees a total of $10,000 in back wages, plus fines, for having them take telephone messages while having lunch on the premises.
Employer: I object. You interrogated my employees without my knowledge, and did not interrogate me at all. And, besides, where do you get off saying my boys were "on call" because they heard the phone ring? Talk to my lawyer.

Regional: How about $5,000 in back pay and no fines?

Employer: Good God, now I'm really disgusted. I want in writing your official interpretation governing such a case. And aren't there rules about notice and hearings?

Regional: How about $2,500 in back pay?

Employer: Well, hell, I . . .

Regional: How about an exchange of memoranda indicating future compliance?

Employer: Mmm . . . [aside: Lawyers' fees . . . trips to testify . . . obligations to that damned congressman of ours . . .]

Official memo from Regional, weeks later: You are hereby directed to cease . . .

Posted in employees' toilet: You are hereby directed to eat lunch off the premises.

This drama could have taken place in one long-distance call or in half a dozen letters strung out over many weeks. However, the demoralizing part is not what one might expect. It isn't bureaucracy. The parable depends little on red tape and the like. It was hardly even a question of being caught. The employer is not a sweatshop operator. Perhaps he even agrees with the purpose and spirit behind Regional's case, and he in any event demurred on the facts. Disgust, disappointment, and distrust would arise in such a case because the agency appears gutless. Its effort to avoid enunciating a rule may be rationalized as flexibility, but to most intelligent people directly involved in such a problem it can end in reduced respect—for the agency and for government. And meanwhile, no rule.

Case 2 is a real case on a much higher level. It involves the history of the Interstate Commerce Commission from 1920, when it received general power over minimum rates, first over the railroads and later over motor transport as well.[30] From that moment on, the ICC fell into a bargaining relation to rail and trucking companies that produced most of the deleterious effects now regularly identified by ICC critics. It was after 1920 that the ICC developed the only principle to which it has held consistently, and that is the principle of bargaining on each decision; each case involving reasonable rates had to be decided "on its own merits in light of the facts of record in the case." With principle operating in the context of a vague enabling statute, it was impossible for the ICC to avoid developing what later came to be called congenital schizophrenia.[31] The commission has been on all sides of its own rules and rationalizations. Often, for example, it has operated as though its governing rule were maximization of profits for the transportation system as a whole. However, it may be fortunate that this was never fully articulated, because the ICC has often (but not consistently, of course) denied rate reductions below what was necessary for a carrier to gain or maintain a fair share, despite the fact that a yet lower rate would still have been remunerative to the carrier without disrupting the market. *Fair share* itself sounds like a rule too, and the above instance sounds at first like the application of this rule to a group of truckers to keep the railroads happy. But it rarely works that way, simply

30. Reported in detail in Friendly, *The Federal Administrative Agencies*, Chapter 6.
31. Ibid., p. 129.

because much of the traffic deserting the railroads is due rather to commis-sion-imposed, carrier-approved, artificially high rail rates, which if lowered would have resulted in increases of shares all around.[32]

On the other hand, any assumed rule relating to fair profits or fair shares vi-olates another rule long assumed, at least in Congress, yet never clearly enun-ciated by anyone; it has been applied, but never consistently. This is the origi-nal notion that through power over maximum and minimum rates the ICC could plan an integrated transportation system. Obviously this goal would require occasional deliberate reductions of rates and fair shares in order to achieve a balance of factors. But a closer look at the ICC reveals the impossi-bility of applying such a principle, even if the commission espoused it. The ICC staff is not in any way equipped to assess the real value and functions of the carriers and carrier systems. It acquires little data completely indepen-dently. Often it appears as though a regional ICC official calls a carrier repre-sentative and asks, "By the way, what are you worth today?" Worse, the ICC has no data, is equipped to get no data, and seems to feel no need to acquire data, on transportation investments, costs, or expenses below the level of total companies. It would thus be impossible for the ICC to assess fair shares or fair profits to help work out a balanced transportation system in a given metropoli-tan region. It is obvious, as most specialized observers have concluded, that decisions are bargained out between the ICC and each individual contender, and then "the Commission selects whatever theory appears best to fit the case at hand."[33]

This sort of situation is not flexible, only loose. It is not stable, only static. The phenomena are the same, but the significance is far different. The ab-sence of bargaining at the level of rule and principle has destroyed the capac-ity of the government to grow in this particular area of control. Decision-oriented bargaining, that is, logrolling, deprived the commission's history of any experience by which Congress, or even the ICC commissioners them-selves, might have been pushed into the formulation of improved rules or stat-utory standards. To state the case as generally as possible, Congress is less likely to be able or willing to work by successive approximations toward decent statutory treatment of complex modern problems to the extent that problems of rule-formulation are successfully avoided in administrative bargaining.[34] Thus, after twenty years of presumed experience, Congress in the Transpor-tation Act of 1940 "created as many contradictions as were dissipated"; and, following still another eighteen years in which the commission made deci-sions "without reference to any . . . general objective," Congress in the

32. Ibid., p. 130, especially the case and study cited in note 12.
33. Quoted in ibid., p. 139. See also ibid., note 98, quoting results of still another scholarly review.
34. See below, this chapter and Chapter 11, especially the discussion of the work of Kenneth C. Davis.

Transportation Act of 1958 gave back to the commission with one hand the ambiguities it had tried to remove with the other.[35] *Decision-oriented bargaining is noncumulative experience.* Since 1920 in the transportation industry this has meant that Congress benefits not from fifty years' experience but from one year's experience fifty times.

Case 3 reveals the same tendency in other fields by comparing the histories of the Federal Trade Commission and the National Labor Relations Board. The immense grant of undefined discretion in the two organic acts of the FTC—the Federal Trade Commission Act of 1914 and the Clayton Act of 1914—dictated immediate involvement of the new commission with each client in decision-oriented bargaining. The FTC was given power to make lists of unfair practices, which it proceeded to do in regular consultation with industries in industrial conferences. Thus from the very beginning the FTC developed an intimacy with trade associations and their codes of fair competition that was to become the practice and precedent for NRA corporatism during the New Deal, as well as the apple of Herbert Hoover's eye.[36]

The weakness of FTC law and practice in the antitrust field led to the rise of the still more undefined and corporativistic consent-decree method in the Department of Justice Antitrust Division. The consent decree is the name given to individual bargains on monopoly and restraint-of-trade issues; it is made on promise that no prosecution on the same alleged infractions will take place at a later time.[37] In the FTC itself, discretion led to weakness, and weakness led to the adoption of, essentially, a policy of no policy.

As a consequence, Congress has had neither experience nor doctrine to guide it. Congress's first FTC action after 1914 came twenty-four years later, with the Robinson-Patman Act of 1938. But two things are most peculiar about it. First, it was merely an amendment to Section 2 of the Clayton Act and did not touch other aspects of the organic law at all. Second, the Robinson-Patman Law, both in letter and in spirit, tended to forbid competitive practices rather than restraints on trade.[38] It is fantastic that nothing in the twenty-four-year history of FTC cast any particularly inconsistent light upon

35. Friendly, p. 140. See especially Friendly's sources, in notes 86–101.

36. See Hoover's opinions quoted in Chapters 3 and 4, below, and at greater length in Grant McConnell, *The Decline of Agrarian Democracy* (Berkeley: University of California Press, 1953); and in McConnell, *Private Power and American Democracy* (New York: Knopf, 1966).

37. See Jaffe, *Administrative Law*, pp. 59 ff., and citations. Incentive to enter consent-decree bargaining is sweetened by court-backed protection against triple damage suits by injured parties. The "consent decree amounts to an innoculation against a number of legal difficulties." See William D. Rogers, "Is It Trust Busting or Window Dressing?" *Reporter*, November 1, 1956, p. 21.

38. See Robert Bork and Ward S. Bowman, "The Crisis in Antitrust," reprinted in Randall B. Ripley, ed., *Public Policies and Their Politics* (New York: Norton, 1965), pp. 90 ff. Even the more positive Corwin Edwards cannot deny that under Robinson-Patman a very large proportion of FTC prosecutions involves small firms and that in general the act has had "no uniform effect of raising or lowering prices" (*The Price Discrimination Law* [Washington, D.C.: The Brookings Institution, 1959], Chapter 4).

what Robinson and Patman were trying to do in 1938. Moreover, since 1938 there has still been nothing remotely resembling a full-scale reconsideration of FTC legislation, despite barrages of criticism from all sides. An important antimerger amendment to Section 7, plus a vain effort to change basing-points practices in 1948–50, constitute the sum total of congressional effort.[39]

Law in the National Labor Relations Board has had quite a different history. From the beginning of collective bargaining/fair labor practices legislation in Section 7 of the National Industrial Recovery Act of 1933, through the National Labor Relations Act to Taft-Hartley and Landrum-Griffin, labor law has contained clearer standards of implementation. Although the NLRB was explicitly set up as an adjudicatory body to deal with the merits of individual cases—and although NLRB must certainly be guilty of its share of abuses—labor law has always been more heavily weighted toward rule-oriented bargaining. Its history is as a consequence superior to that of the FTC or ICC. There has been far more omnibus legislation and review in thirty years of the NLRB than in the entire fifty-five-year history of the FTC or forty-seven-year history of the ICC under its minimum-rate-making powers. And the end is not in sight.

Case 4 is of a different order. It has to do with the important hypothesis in the literature on the political process that there is a natural, secular decline in concern for law among administrative agencies and that, parallel to this, agencies ultimately become captured by their clienteles.[40] The analysis here suggests that age and nature have almost nothing to do with the decay of legal integrity, or, as the pluralist might put it, with the development of whirlpools or communities of interest or equilibrium. To Bernstein the maturity, that is, the onset of decline, of the ICC dates from 1920;[41] but that happens to be the year when the legal integrity of the agency was all but destroyed in a single stroke by the grant of minimum-rate-making powers, a factor Bernstein does not even mention. Rather, he pictures ICC decline as a long and natural process in which original support groups run out of steam, hostile groups make their peace, and the agency makes all this possible by learning how to espouse the business interest in the interest of peace, friendship, and equilibrium. In an earlier study Huntington speaks of "gradual withering away" and "marasmus" as though regulatory agencies were animal organisms. But in truth the

39. To push the point still further, basing-points policy got a full airing during that period precisely because FTC doctrine against the practice was known and rather consistently applied. For another example see Bork and Bowman, pp. 91–93, where they compare consequences of one antitrust provision with legal integrity to the more typical laws on price fixing and mergers, which have no legal integrity.

40. See Marver Bernstein, *Regulating Business by Independent Commission* (Princeton: Princeton University Press, 1955), Chapter 3; and Samuel P. Huntington, "The Marasmus of the ICC: The Commission, the Railroads, and the Public Interest," *Yale Law Journal* (April 1952). See also Harmon Ziegler, *Interest Groups in American Society* (Englewood Cliffs: Prentice-Hall, 1964), pp. 119–20, for an example of standard textbook treatment of this hypothesis.

41. Bernstein, p. 90.

agency is an agency operating under a statute. Again it is as though the statute is not a relevant political datum. The cases above, as is true of the entire argument of this book, militate against such notions of natural political tendency. Jaffe's critique of the pluralist thesis seems much more supportable, and provides a suitable summary: "Much of what the agencies do is the expectable consequence of their broad and ill-defined regulatory power."[42]

It is remarkable that the liberal leadership of the 1930s and 1960s could not see in well-known cases such as these the highly probable consequences of their way of using government. The fact is they did not, and they went on to establish, much in this manner, a national presence in virtually all aspects of American life.

Regulation in the 1970s:
The Sky Is No Longer the Limit

Were there ever to be a change in the direction of historical development, 1969 would have been the time for it. The Nixon Administration was unusually partisan; and partisan Republicans felt they differed most from partisan Democrats in precisely such matters as government intervention and state's rights. Republicans, as was documented in Chapter 4, could embrace the agriculture subsidies and the varieties of indulgences to all economic interests. But the regulatory arena is quite another matter. Controlling the conduct of corporations and the private affairs of individuals hit at the very core of the Republican concept of liberty.

However, the Republicans did not pick up their option after 1969. The celebration of federal government activism in the 1960s seemed virtually to become a binge in the 1970s. In a 1977 review article, William Lilley and James Miller document exhaustively for 1970–75 a "quiet explosion in the scope and pervasiveness of federal regulation."[43] During that six-year period they report that the number of pages published annually in the *Federal Register* more than tripled and the number of pages in the *Code of Federal Regulations* grew by 33 percent. To put that on a more work-a-day basis, in 1936 the *Federal Register* had a total of 2,400 pages. By 1970 it contained 20,000 pages. By 1976 it contained 60,000 pages. Moreover, the total budget of $4.7 billion for federal government regulatory activities is no indication of the true cost, because it does not reflect the costs of regulation borne by individuals and corporations in the economy. For example, the Environmental Protec-

42. Louis Jaffe, "The Effective Limits of the Administrative Process: A Reevaluation," *Harvard Law Review*, May 1959, p. 1134.

43. William Lilley and James C. Miller, "The New 'Social Regulation,' " *The Public Interest* (Spring 1977), p. 49.

tion Agency will, by 1984, cost $40 billion to implement. OSHA could cost as much as $18.5 billion, assuming that its most serious proposals are adopted and implemented. These are indeed remarkable figures and ought to be unsettling even to those who feel that the social benefits of regulation far exceed the costs. But regardless of increased federal regulation, and regardless of the growing concern for the quality and quantity of federal regulatory activities, the binge in new regulatory programs continued throughout the eight years of Republican control of the White House. Items could be added or subtracted from Table 5.2, depending upon one's definition of regulation; but no amount of quibbling over the items in the table would alter the impression of continued efforts by the federal government to keep itself involved in every nook and cranny of American society.

Two very reasonable responses to these data should be identified and evaluated. First, Republicans as well as many Democrats will insist that Republicans, especially in the 1970s, were far more concerned with sociocultural issues and were far more eager to intervene in questions of local law and order than in issues involving the economy. A second argument would demur on the question of continuity and then would argue that this was imposed upon Republicans by a Congress dominated by Democrats.

As to the first argument, I seriously question whether Nixon was all that much more committed than Johnson or Kennedy to law and order, to a national police force, or to social rather than economic interventions. It is true that Nixon had that reputation, and it is also true that his own personal record during the 1940s and 1950s marked him as a strong interventionist on matters of individual beliefs and values. However, it would have been very difficult for the Nixon Administration to go much further than the Democrats had already gone by the end of 1968. It was the Democrats who formulated and enacted the Safe Streets and Crime Control Act of 1967 and the Crime Control Act of 1968. These were the programs that made millions of dollars available to local law-enforcement agencies to beef up their police forces, to modernize their equipment, and to institute crime-prevention programs in schools and related local institutions. Indeed, it is true the Republicans would have gone further; but this is only a matter of degree. The Democrats also instituted most of the conspiracy trials against the leaders of dissenting movements in the 1960s. The Democrats are responsible for putting thousands of people under illegal surveillance. Democrats going back as far as Attorney General Robert Kennedy were responsible for drafting legislation that would legalize electronic surveillance under a variety of conditions. And in the 3½ years between August 1965 and December 31, 1968, there were 179 federal interventions using 184,133 federal troops, to combat racial disorders and civil rights demonstrations, menacing strikes, neighborhood riots, student marches, and the like.[44] It could be argued, of course, that this shoddy record was forced

44. For accounts of efforts by Democratic and Republican administrations to produce a national police force, see Victor Navasky, *Kennedy Justice* (New York: Atheneum, 1971); and

TABLE 5.2

Federal Regulatory Laws and Programs Enacted since 1970

YEAR ENACTED	TITLE OF STATUTE
1969–70	Child Protection and Toy Safety Act
	Clear Air Amendments
	Egg Products Inspection Act
	Economic Stabilization Act
	Fair Credit Reporting Act
	Occupational Safety and Health Act
	Poison Prevention Packaging Act
	Securities Investor Protection Act
1971	Economic Stabilization Act Amendments
	Federal Boat Safety Act
	Lead-Based Paint Elimination Act
	Wholesome Fish and Fisheries Act
1972	Consumer Product Safety Act
	Equal Employment Opportunity Act
	Federal Election Campaign Act
	Federal Environmental Pesticide Control Act
	Federal Water Pollution Control Act Amendments
	Motor Vehicle Information and Cost Savings Act
	Noise Control Act
	Ports and Waterways Safety Act
1973	Agriculture and Consumer Protection Act
	Economic Stabilization Act Amendments
	Emergency Petroleum Allocation Act
	Flood Disaster Protection Act
1974	Atomic Energy Act
	Commodity Futures Trading Commission Act
	Consumer Product Warranties/FTL Improvement Act
	Council on Wage and Price Stability Act
	Employee Retirement Income Security Act
	Federal Energy Administration Act
	Hazardous Materials Transportation Act
	Housing and Community Development Act
	Pension Reform Act
	Privacy Act
	Safe Drinking Water Act
1975	Energy Policy and Conservation Act
	Equal Credit Opportunity Act
1976	Consumer Leasing Act
	Medical Device Safety Act
	Toxic Substances Control Act

upon the Democrats during very stormy years, while Republicans like Richard Nixon actually advocate these kinds of policies. But I think a line of argument more consistent with all the years and administrations is that both political parties have been contributing to a new and positive national state and that each Administration has been drawn into doing whatever seems necessary in order to cope with that positive national state. The fact of the matter is that federal troops and federal regulators are drawn into local matters once the federal government becomes a party to more and more local transactions. That is inherent in the notion of establishing a national *presence*. Intervention is built into the logic of the situation. It is expected.

The second objection to the argument that Republicans merely continued the Democratic patterns is really more important to deal with because it is quite undeniably true that a strongly Democratic Congress often imposed its will on the Republican Administration. Few of the regulatory laws identified in the table were distinctive parts of President Nixon's program; and the most important enactment—wage and price controls—was passed despite President Nixon's grumbling that such authority was not needed and that he would not use it if it were handed over to him. Nonetheless, the Republicans did more than merely accept the domination of the Democrats during this period. There is ample evidence to support the argument that the continued expansion of the regulatory authority of the federal government is the direct consequence of a modern liberal state that had come to be accepted as much by Republicans as by Democrats. Democrats may stress the social benefits of regulation while Republicans may worry more about the costs. Criticisms from Democrats may focus upon improved efficiency of regulation while criticisms from Republicans may stress a shift in the burden of regulation. But as far as can be determined by their behavior, Republicans have become just as much as the Democrats committed to the contemporary liberal state and to the principles of liberal jurisprudence.

UNIVERSAL PROTECTION OF WORKERS AND CONSUMERS

OSHA and the Consumer Products Safety Commission (CPSC) are prime examples of the continuation and reinforcement of 1960s liberalism applied to public policy. OSHA was the first national effort to deal with all industry. And it was quite patently an effort by the federal government to take this vital function almost entirely away from the states.[45] CPSC was a consolidation of

Edward Jay Epstein, *Agency of Fear* (New York: Putnam, 1977). For an elaborate documentation of the involvement of federal troops in local disorders, see Adam Yarmolinsky, *The Military Establishment* (New York: Harper & Row, 1971), p. 154 and passim.

45. States receive only 50 percent federal assistance if they run their own programs of occupational safety and health, but are relieved of 100 percent of the burdens if they leave the job to OSHA. Of fifty-six jurisdictions entitled to submit plans to OSHA for federal support, only twenty-two have such plans, and the expectation is that the number will decline still further. For

several existing consumer-protection activities, but went far beyond the scope of preexisting federal law by attempting to cover virtually all sources of consumer risk from the purchase and use of commodities. In scope, jurisdiction, and purpose, these two pieces of legislation are open-ended, abstract, and universal beyond anything included in Table 5.1. The legislation creating OSHA covers every employer in the country (except public agencies) and seeks to provide a safe environment for employment by obliging the new agency to set standards the observance of which would produce the desired state of affairs. CPSC legislation seeks also to provide the safe environment for all consumers by having that agency set standards whose observance will create such an environment.

In neither piece of public policy did Congress attempt by law to identify a single specific evil that the regulatory agency was to seek to minimize or eliminate. In neither case did the statute attempt to identify a single cause of action against which aggrieved employees or consumers would have an easier day in court. Quite to the contrary, OSHA and CPSC laws provided only an expression of sentiments for the desired end result. The OSHA legislation took as its purpose "to assure so far as is possible every working man and woman in the nation safe and healthful working conditions and to preserve human resources" (Section 2B). The CPSC Act is, if possible, even more vague and universal, in that it ordains the commission to reduce unreasonable risk of injury from use of household products but does not identify a single risk, does not suggest what might be a reasonable undertaking of that risk, and definitely does not suggest how to make such risks reasonable. Instead, in both of these instances, Congress provided that the agency could set standards of behavior, respectively, for employers and for the producers of consumer products. Congress provided no standards whatsoever for employers or producers, nor did Congress provide any standards for the conduct of these two regulatory agencies. All Congress did was to assume that the agencies in their own wisdom would be able to provide such standards.

Where, indeed, were these standards to come from? The law is fairly explicit in both instances, and both instances provide almost pristine examples of interest-group-liberal resolutions of the problem of balancing power and interest against policy choice. Under OSHA, a standard is defined as any practice or method thought by the secretary of Labor or the agency to be appropriate to provide safe and healthful employment. There are two routes to such standards. The first is a standard for a given industry or sector of the economy which is developed within the department itself on the basis of work with an

example, four of the largest industrial states—New Jersey, New York, Illinois, and Wisconsin— have removed themselves from state occupational safety regulatory programs despite the fact that they have federally approved plans. See Nina W. Cornell et al., "Safety Regulation," in Henry Owen and Charles Schultze, eds., *Setting National Priorities: The Next 10 Years* (Washington, D.C.: The Brookings Institution, 1976), Chapter 11.

advisory committee appointed by the secretary consisting of fifteen members, including one or more drawn from HEW and the rest from experienced and qualified representatives of employers and employees, as well as one or more representatives of health and safety agencies of the states. The second route to such industry standards, and the route most frequently employed, is the adoption of what the law calls a "national consensus standard" which is defined in the law to mean any occupational safety standard that has already been adopted and promulgated by a "nationally recognized standards-producing organization under procedures where it can be determined by the Secretary that persons interested and affected by the scope or provisions of the standard have reached substantial agreement on its adoption" (Section 3(9)). The result basically has been that OSHA adopts the criteria of industrial safety prevailing in a given trade association at the time. These consensus standards are so closely tied to trade association standards that some manufacturing concerns have found themselves in a bind, because trade association practices change faster than the OSHA bureaucracy can keep up with.[46] These so-called consensus standards would appear to be indistinguishable from the practices under the old NRA codes that were declared unconstitutional in the 1930s. The difference is that in the 1970s they are not merely constitutional; there is so little suspicion as to their constitutionality that there is no particular urge to take these issues to court.

Regulation under CPSC is an example of a different, though related, extreme. Rather than look to industry to find existing industry standards to embrace, CPSC keeps its own counsel, not by adopting its own standards and regulations that can be expected to apply to a broad class of consumer items for a certain period of time, but by not making any advance rulings at all. It takes each case on its merits and moves toward consumer items and toward regulation of those items with a vigor that is matched only by its unpredictability. It can ban a product altogether. It can issue standards that regulate the design of a product. It can respond to consumer complaints about individual products, or it can take initiatives and pursue one consumer item or a broad category of consumer items; and it can do so by specific identification of an item as a risk or by a more general standard of the degree of riskiness of the product or products. It may, or it may not, take into account alternative ways of dealing with the riskiness of a product. In brief, the agency began with an almost unlimited mandate from Congress, and it can go on avoiding limits on itself by the simple expedient of not issuing rules of general legislative content. It can stick to specifications. This agency is an example of pure administrative power.[47]

46. Cornell et al., p. 495. See also James Anderson, *Public Policy-Making* (New York: Praeger, 1975), p. 105.
47. This treatment is guided by Steven Kelman, "Regulation by the Numbers—A Report on the Consumer Product Safety Commission," *The Public Interest* (Summer 1974), pp. 83–102.

Congress and the administrators seem to be perfectly well aware of the basic illegitimacy of what they are doing with CPSC. Having created a monster of unadulterated administrative power, Congress then turned around and granted the agency broad discretion to subsidize persons who would come in and speak for consumers in opposition to agency decisions. These people were called offerors and were expected to be professional standard developers from the private sector.[48] In 1976 Congress added still another provision to the original act authorizing the courts to award to plaintiffs the costs of the suit, including attorney fees and the fees of expert witnesses, in order "to enable interested persons who have rights under the CPSC to indicate those rights."[49] Since that was also not enough assurance that CPSC would have any claim to legitimacy, a move was already afloat at that time to create a Consumer Protection Agency that would perhaps more effectively speak for aggrieved persons. But no amount of after-the-fact tinkering with administrative or clientele arrangements will counterbalance the unhappy tendencies set in train by any piece of regulation as badly drafted as CPSC.[50]

Between the OSHA method of embracing current industrial standards and the CPSC method of arbitrarily pouncing without any administrative guidelines at all, it would be extremely difficult to choose a good method of administrative regulation. But why choose either? How many abuses of contemporary government do we need before we look beyond the practices to the basis of the liberal state itself? And the need for this is all the more pressing if Republican administrations embrace that same liberal state.

ENVIRONMENTAL PROTECTION: INTIMATIONS OF NIXON

Although President Nixon did cooperate with Congress in the drafting and the acceptance of the new and vast OSHA and CPSC regulatory programs, his own approaches and preferences can be seen more directly through the Environmental Protection Agency actions and through wage-price controls. EPA was established in 1970 by executive orders issued by President Nixon. Through these actions President Nixon sought to consolidate several major programs in a single agency. EPA was then to do its job in a manner already established by OSHA and CPSC—by "setting standards consistent with national environmental goals." In other words, "EPA would be charged with

48. Section 7(D)(2).
49. Consumer Products Safety Commission Improvements Act of 1976, section 10; House Report no. 1022, 94th Congress, 2d Session, 1976 (*Conference Report* accompanying Consumer Products Safety Commission Improvements Act of 1976).
50. For relevant and generally reinforcing evaluations of CPSC, see Lilley and Miller, "The New 'Social Regulation,' " and *Federal Regulation and Regulatory Reform*, Report by the Subcommittee on Oversight and Investigation of the Committee on Interstate and Foreign Commerce, House of Representatives (Washington, D.C.: U.S. Government Printing Office, October 1976).

protecting the environment by abating pollution."[51] Nixon's concept of the agency was typical of the liberal approach. EPA would "monitor the condition of the environment," "establish quantitative environmental base lines," and then "set and enforce standards for air and water quality and for individual pollutants."[52] To do this, EPA would take guidance from itself but could also encourage broader participation "through periodic meetings with those organizations and individuals interested in that regulatory package."[53]

The whole universe is covered by the EPA's jurisdiction. Since pollution can come from anywhere, we must naturally equip our agency with power to cover anything and everything. How can anyone be against clean air or water? And let us, indeed, have it by 1976; and if not, then by 1986; if not by then, at least let there be satisfaction that authority was exercised on behalf of the people. It is as though there were a trade-off between pollution and the number of regulations concerning pollution. Congress knew nothing in the beginning and admitted it by mandating clean air and water to administrators to pursue entirely as they saw fit. And neither Congress nor the president has reviewed the substance of the thousands of standards and regulations emanating from EPA in order to determine whether there is any relation at all among these regulations or between them and the original legislative enactments. It seems that Nixon's main preoccupation was to be sure that he had a hand in environmental protection regulation, not that he wanted to restrain or to regularize it, or to make it more explicit, or to impose upon it the sense of justice that a strict constructionist might have had. Our experience with the Democrats of the 1960s, including the Democratic-dominated Congress, would have led us to expect little more from them. But the important point here is that the Republican administration did nothing different.

WAGE AND PRICE CONTROLS: THE ESSENCE OF NIXON

The Republican approach to wage and price controls provides still more telling evidence of continuity from Democrats to Republicans in the concept and use of national authority. Too much can be made of the fact that President Nixon did not support the enactment of wage and price controls in 1970. Very shortly after Congress enacted the Economic Stabilization Act of 1970, recession and inflation, very much the legacy of Vietnam, joined hands in an unholy matrimony that seems to have convinced President Nixon, using the 1970 authority, to inaugurate a program of economic regulation unparalleled

51. From the full text of President Nixon's *Environmental Reorganization Plan of July 9, 1970*, reprinted from the Government Printing Office in *Congressional Quarterly Almanac* (1970), pp. 119a–120a.

52. Ibid, p. 119a.

53. Testimony of Russell E. Train, administrator, EPA, *Hearings before the Subcommittee on Oversight and Investigations on Interstate and Foreign Commerce, House of Representatives* (Washington, D.C.: U.S. Government Printing Office, 1976), vol. 5, p. 27.

in United States history, except in periods of total war. As Democrats joined Republicans in disillusionment with the Keynesian faith in the ability of fiscal and monetary policies to maintain a balance between employment and inflation, the Nixon Administration found itself joining the conclusion of the majority in Congress that a regulatory approach was the only answer. And since, as we shall see, Nixon accepted the administrative arrangements implicit in the enabling legislation, and since Nixon a year later requested continuation and extension of the 1970 authority, it is possible to view the entire program as a continuing one, spanning the two parties and the two administrations of the 1961–77 period.

Let us look first at the enabling legislation itself. It is the most extreme example of use of government power among the interest-group-liberal cases. Yet it is typical:

The President is authorized to issue such orders and regulations as he may deem appropriate to stabilize prices, rents, wages and salaries. . . . Such orders and regulations may provide for the making of such adjustments as may be necessary to prevent gross inequities. [Section 202] The President may delegate the performance of any function under this title to such officers, departments, and agencies of the United States as he may deem appropriate [Section 203].

In this enabling legislation Congress granted unconditionally to the president the authority to write the actual laws controlling all prices, wages, and other costs of doing business or making a living. (Control over interest rates and dividends was added, at Nixon's request, in 1971.) This extended presidential jurisdiction to all segments of the economy—to more than ten million business firms, ranging from General Motors to the corner market, to all employees from the AFL-CIO to the unorganized children working for McDonalds. But the act goes beyond this unconditional grant of authority to make war on inflation; the act also grants the president the authority to dispense exemptions to any rules and regulations he ultimately promulgates. And he may of course subdelegate any or all of this to any agency of his choice.

Nixon's choices in virtually all matters dealing with the concept and implementation of this authority were the same as the various choices made by the Democratic leadership during the 1960s. Nixon delegated primary administrative responsibility to a Cost of Living Council, which in effect was a domestic version of the National Security Council.[54] The council was responsible for designating those sectors of the economy to be subject to price control and for classifying units by size (an important distinction, since only the largest

54. The Cost of Living Council was composed of the secretaries of Treasury (chairman), Agriculture, Commerce, Labor, and HEW, along with the director of OMB, the chairman of the Council of Economic Advisors, the director of the Office of Emergency Preparedness, the special assistant to the president for consumer affairs, and "such others as the President may, from time to time, designate."

firms had to obtain prior approval for price adjustments). But the significant price and wage decisions were made by the Price Commission and the Pay Board. Finally, the enforcement responsibility was handed over to the Internal Revenue Service—which, in 1971, had approximately three thousand agents to police, in addition to their other duties, ten million enterprises.

The seven-member Price Commission, although composed entirely of public members, was in fact composed largely of members with substantial business experience. More to the point was its approach. The Price Commission set general price ceilings, with specific ceilings for each of the basic sectors of the economy—trade, manufacturing and services, public utilities, rental units, and health services—based on the more general decision to stabilize inflation at a rate of 2.5 percent by the end of 1972. Ceilings were set on the basis of estimated industry-wide trends in productivity applied to each firm; however, in their applications for price adjustments (these would be called variances in local zoning), individual firms were permitted by law to use *their own estimates*. This was an open invitation to bargain with the commission.[55]

The consensus among expert observers appears to be that the inflation rate did drop during the regulatory phase of Nixon's program ("Phase II"). However, three things are not part of that consensus: (1) whether prices would have stabilized without controls; (2) whether the control period would be followed by a spiral of increases frustrated during the control period; and (3) whether the average reduction of the rate of inflation during 1971–72 masked a large number of special exceptions rationalized as adjustments. The first two points of contention are likely to remain forever hypothetical; however, some data from the Pay Board can be brought to bear upon the third point.

The Pay Board was undoubtedly the most important part of the Nixon program because of the theory shared with Republicans by many Democrats that the basic problem was one of imposing some restraint upon big labor and its ability to push up wages despite the downward competitive pressure of surplus labor during a recession. Consequently the executive order provided for a Pay Board composed of fifteen members, five of whom were to be "public" along with five "labor representatives" and five "business representatives." Official references were made to labor and business representation as though these were organized and duly constituted functional communities.[56]

The consequences were inherent in the interest-group approach, and they unfolded as though they had been intended as a matter of policy. The problems of control and legitimacy had given us the tripartite board. The tripartite board made policy as any tripartite board would be expected to make policy. It

55. A good description of the setup will be found in Barry Bosworth, "Phase II: The U.S. Experience with an Incomes Policy," *Brookings Papers on Economic Activity*, no. 2 (1972), pp. 343–83.

56. Midway during the year of Phase II (March 22, 1972) four of the five labor members resigned, but due care was exercised to get labor's views thereafter. The reconstituted seven-member board included one representative each from labor and business; the rest were public.

set wage ceilings rigidly and rather impressively in line with the goal of 5.5 percent annual rate of inflation. Moreover, contemporaneous evaluations tend to confirm the administration's claim that the wage controls were on the average effective.[57] Nonetheless, there was lurking doubt whether the board was "equipped to enforce its own rules."[58] Behind those averages was a clear pattern of favoritism in the exceptions the board granted to the 5.5 percent ceiling. The pattern of favoritism was toward big unions and toward the noncompetitive, oligopolistic sectors of the economy. Aerospace Workers got 8 percent, down from a requested 12 percent, while Longshoremen asked for 20 percent and got 14 percent. United Transportation Workers got 10 percent of their 11 percent request. Organized miners got 12.9 percent increases, counting 1972 agreements plus the honoring of increases due in 1972 from earlier contracts.

These examples are all the more significant because most big, multiyear contracts had been signed in 1970–71, the highest contract increases had been implemented at that time, and 1972 was primarily a year for deferred increases—whose averages were around 6.1 percent. This, plus the fact that some sectors of the economy came in with wage hikes below the ceiling and well below the average, helped produce the favorable overall figure for Pay Board effectiveness. The walkout of four of labor's Pay Board representatives came after most important concessions had been made. In at least fifteen cases the Pay Board granted increases exceeding 8 percent, and all but one involved a major union. And the walkout did not necessarily change the pattern of dispensations. Nearly two months after labor's advance to the rear, Gulf and East Coast Longshoremen picked up exceptions of 9.8 to 12 percent.

Corporate interests on the Cost of Living Council, on the Price Commission, on the Pay Board, and in the economy at large, did not necessarily take these concessions lying down. But for at least four reasons there was little, if any, confrontation.

1. Business was not an organized opposition; quite the contrary, each corporation and sector was seeking its own concessions.

2. Since big unions are most often in the noncompetitive oligopolistic sectors, out-of-line wage concessions could more readily be passed along as higher prices by the employers—because according to explicit regulations of the Price Commission, increased costs (including 1971–72 increases in the costs of labor approved by the Pay Board) could be passed through without counting against cost calculations in relation to the price ceilings.

3. The Price Commission could be still more lenient whenever it wished, by falling back on another of its own regulations which provided that firms

<hr />

57. Michael E. Levy, "From Phase I to Phase III," *Conference Board Record* (June 1972), pp. 11–14; Barry Bosworth, especially pp. 364–65; and Michael Wachter, "The Current Wage Controls: An Evaluation of Phase II," *Wharton Quarterly* (Fall 1972), pp. 28–32.

58. Levy, p. 13; Wachter, p. 28.

receiving price increases must maintain a profit margin below the average of the highest two out of three fiscal years prior to the program. Since wage hikes pulled down profit margins, substantial price increases did not appear to be out-of-line with the Price Commission's ceilings.

4. Finally, the Price Commission allowed firms to use their own estimates of productivity improvement and anticipated sales in their requests for above-ceiling increases. Both of these concepts—productivity and anticipated sales—are capable of almost infinite manipulation, especially when it is in the interest of the calculator to do so. And the advantage goes to the larger firms because they have the staff to work up the credible data.

Liberal Jurisprudence in the 1970s: The End of the Rule of Law

These case histories involving the presence or absence of standards in legislative delegations and rules in administrative practice overwhelmingly support the simple proposition that *law begets law*. Agencies that begin in a context of statutes that associate guidance with power are agencies that begin with legal integrity and have histories of greater legal integrity. Agencies that begin with little or no legal integrity are very unlikely to develop any along the way.

An attack on the practice of delegation turns out actually to be a hopeful view. If the rise of delegation and the decline of law were the mere result of technical complexity it would be an irreversible process because technical complexity is the law of modernity. However, this review suggests that the real problem is one of abstraction rather than one of complexity.[59] It is from abstraction that uncontrolled discretion flows. Abstraction is reversible, with the increase of knowledge, *but only if the leadership desires to reverse it*. This is why a change of public values is so essential.

Liberal jurisprudence persists as the ideological support structure for interest-group liberal legislation because it still holds so many of the top legal minds in its thrall. The most important of these is Kenneth Culp Davis, whose writings through three decades have been carefully studied and widely cited. Davis's argument can be paraphrased as follows: The reason why Congress makes policy-without-law and commits full discretion to administrative agencies is simply that we had to have each program and no one was willing or able to make a clear decision or set any guidelines. Since we must

59. The case studies reported in this chapter undermine the proposition that complexity is the problem. Moreover, examples drawn from labor-management law (as already suggested), Social-Security law (see below, Chapter 8), civil-rights law (Chapters 7 and 9), and drug-control law, to name but a few, deal with extremely complex situations; yet, there is a great deal of legal integrity to be found in these areas, and there is strong rule-oriented bargaining in between frequent legislative phases.

have these programs, and since no one is able to say what the rule of law should be, we must throw ourselves upon the mercy of those given authority; then we must do whatever we can to be sure these officials are of good quality and that there are procedural safeguards against arbitrary use of government power.[60] No proof is offered, only an assertion that the "objective of requiring every delegation to be accompanied by meaningful statutory standards had to fail, should have failed, and did fail."[61] This offers a jurisprudential carte blanche for poor legislative drafting and at the same time sweeps away all concern for the consequences.

The decline of Congress, the decline of independence among regulatory agencies, the general decline of law as an instrument of control are all due far more than anything else to changes in the philosophy of law and the prevailing attitude toward laws. Admittedly the complexity of modern life forces Congress into vagueness and generality in drafting its statutes. Admittedly the political pressure of social unrest forces Congress and the president into premature formulations that make delegation of power inevitable. But to take these causes and effects as natural and good, and then to build the system around them, is to doom the system to its present slide toward its lowest common accomplishment. A government of statutes without standards may produce pluralism, but it is a pluralism of privilege and tight access, evidence of which is seen throughout this volume. A government of policies built on legal integrity will not destroy pluralism but will lift pluralism, and political discourse, to the highest levels of political responsibility where decisions on rules are supposed to be made.

From this formalist or constitutionalist standpoint, a bad program is worse than no program at all. If, from time to time, political pressure or the force of circumstance makes a standardless regulatory program necessary, it will always be better to admit the necessity than to pronounce it a good thing. If the empty enactment is seen as a necessary evil, there might then be something of an urge to give it, after a few years' experience, the standards and guidelines the legislators had been unable to give it the first round.

This does not represent so extreme or global a change in point of view, yet it could contribute substantially toward revitalization of Congress, toward the opening up, if not the complete severing, of agency-clientele relations, and toward some modest elevation of the level of political discourse. The effort to regulate, especially when it comes as late as in the United States federal system, immediately attaches a morality to government. When that morality is a criterion for the regulatory act, it is bound to have a characteristic influence of some sort on the political process. When the regulation is done permissively

60. Kenneth Culp Davis, "A New Approach to Delegation," *University of Chicago Law Review* (Summer 1969), pp. 713–25; and Davis, *Discretionary Justice: A Preliminary Inquiry* (Baton Rouge: Louisiana State University Press, 1969).
61. Davis, "A New Approach to Delegation," p. 719.

and in the deliberate absence of the morality implied in the very use of coercive language, the result can only be expected to be demoralizing, to the clientele, the agency, and the law itself. The group process is dynamic and cumulative when groups have an institutional structure against which to compete. Without that formal structure the group process is not truly pluralistic at all. It is merely co-optive. And it is ineffective. Worse, it converts mere ineffectiveness into illegitimacy.

Liberal sentiments remain, and, indeed, they may be the best sentiments. But the interest-group liberal method is as inappropriate for our time and for those sentiments as was the laissez-faire liberal method for 1929. The interest-group method was an ideal means of achieving a bit of equity. Its day is done, for equity is no longer enough. It has proven itself unequal to the tasks of planning and achieving justice. A grant of broad powers to administration is not a grant of power at all. It is an imposition of impotence.

Cases drawn from the 1970s show mainly that neither Congress nor the Executive Branch learned anything significant from the 1960s. Liberal jurisprudence—belief in the goodness of policy-without-law—seems to be as strong as ever, despite the growth and expansion of criticism of the way our national government is conducted. Unfortunately, that criticism has not turned fully enough to the real source of the problem. We are fast being done in by our national government, but not by its inefficiency or its corruption, its size or the irresponsibility of its senior officials. We are being done in by the very efficiency and zealousness with which officials pursue the public interest. It is not the officials who are corrupt, but their jurisprudence, which seems to render them incapable of making right decisions.

6

MAKING DEMOCRACY
SAFE FOR THE WORLD
On Fighting the Next War

Modern liberals cannot plan in domestic affairs because of their opposition to stating real goals in clear and authoritative language. They cannot plan in foreign affairs for almost the opposite reason, for here they seem to set enormously high store upon having rules—or at least programmatic rhetoric. However, the two apparently opposite tendencies have a common base. In both domestic and foreign politics interest-group liberals display too little trust in the formal institutions of democracy.

Put in its most elementary textbook fashion, democracies are supposed to operate between frequent elections through formally constituted institutions which are supposed to possess all the power necessary to carry out their responsibilities. Modern liberalism has so defined the problem that Congress now does its duty only when it seeks to alienate the power it truly possesses and to retain power which inherently it does not and cannot possess. In both cases there is only one guarantee, which is that power will not be very effectively used at all.

Vietnam is simply one, albeit a classic, illustration. Academically it has little significance beyond any of the cases to be dealt with here in detail. The war contributed to the liberal crisis in the United States. But most assuredly, liberal attitudes were instrumental in the escalation of the war to the crisis level. Liberals are not saber rattlers. In their revulsion against mere self-interest, many in fact turned to a form of pseudoisolationist withdrawal. The liberal contribution to the war was rather its support of a system of politics that is inappropriate for foreign-policy formulation by a major power. During the period of America's emergence to world leadership, the public philosophy interfered with the emergence of appropriately mature structures of foreign-policy-making and implementation.

At the end of World War II Americans were properly impressed with two facts. We had been opened up, we had become an international power despite ourselves. And we had prosecuted the war with incredible efficiency and impressively rational integration of strategy, production, and diplomacy. The most pressing problem toward the end of the war and afterward was somehow to perpetuate the organizational successes of the war in order to use our power properly to prosecute the peace. Harnessing an eighteenth-century constitution and institutions that were perfectly geared to peacetime irresponsibility into a force for consistency, continuity, restraint, and understanding—in short, for planning on an international scale—involved nearly the reverse of Woodrow Wilson's goal for World War I. We had somehow to make democracy safe for the world.

Success thus eluded America twice, for making democracy safe for the world has not proven altogether possible. Our peacetime efforts have lacked the one condition that made our wartime efforts successful. In the peace there is no longer the crisis of the war itself. In the United States this made a difficult task impossible. Crisis constitutes a very special condition in the workings of American foreign policy. Crises are fortunately not everyday occurrences; however, a crisis does tend to bring out the very best in Americans. Postwar examples of exemplary behavior in crisis include Greek-Turkish aid and the Truman Doctrine, the Berlin Airlift, the response to the Korean invasion, the Dienbienphu crisis of 1954, the Arab-Israeli intervention of 1956, the 1962 Cuban missile crisis, the 1967 and 1973 Arab-Israeli wars.[1] Due to our poorer record in foreign affairs when there are no crises, our capacities to deal with crises are consistently underestimated by potential enemies. This is a major reason why guerrilla warfare is such an effective anti-American weapon.

Crisis situations are special because they combine intensity of conflict with shortage of time. Politically this means a very narrow scope of participation and an extremely limited range for bargaining. The public and public-serving institutions are far removed. Decisions are made by an elite and are usually highly legitimate—if we may measure by the largely ceremonial and affirmative responses crisis decisions tend to receive.

At first glance these patterns seem to confirm C. Wright Mills's idea that the United States is run by a "power elite" when it comes to making the key decisions for the country: "Within the higher circles of the power elite, factions do exist. But more powerful than these divisions are the internal discipline and the community of interests that bind the power elite together."[2] On further inspection of crisis decisions, it would seem that Mills did not go

1. I will frequently make value judgments in this chapter. In all instances they will be grounded upon the following assumptions: (1) The United States has some vital and legitimate interests abroad. (2) The United States is acting rationally when it pursues these interests, especially if the results do not too palpably disturb international equilibrium. (3) Rational foreign policy is good foreign policy and irrational foreign policy is bad foreign policy.

2. C. Wright Mills, *The Power Elite* (New York: Oxford University Press, 1959), p. 283.

far enough. As is well known, Mills defined his power elite to include all holders of the top institutional positions in the military, the Executive Branch of the national government, and industry. Inspection of crisis decisions suggests that the real participants comprise an even smaller elite than the so-called power elite. Even when the crisis offers a small grace period, such as was true of Dienbienphu in 1954 and the British withdrawal from Greece in 1947, rarely has more than a small segment of the standard power elite been directly involved before the fact. Moreover, it was a very special segment whose reality is inconsistent with both the pluralist and the Mills model of the distribution of power. *Crisis decisions in foreign policy are made by an elite of formal officeholders.*

Rarely is there time to go further. Rarely is there need to go further unless the aftermath of the crisis is a longstanding commitment that itself becomes unpopular.

There is an obvious corollary to this first proposition, which is that in times of crisis the people who make the decisions are those who were elected and appointed to make those decisions. That is to say, *under crisis conditions our government has operated pretty much as it was supposed to operate,* all theories of the informal distribution of power to the contrary notwithstanding.

There is also a normative corollary. Since our record of response to crisis is good, then the men in official positions have been acting and are able to act rationally. If, when there is no crisis, officials and their policies appear to be less rational, then we must conclude that something is wrong with the structures and institutions within which they operate.

After World War II the effort of the United States to face the peace as a world leader took the form of great expansion of the instruments of foreign-policy formulation and implementation. New agencies were established, and old ones were greatly expanded. However, while there was so vast an expansion of the units there was no creation of a foreign-policy establishment, or as Europeans would call it, a foreign ministry. As in domestic government, each new foreign-policy commitment was set up in a new instrumentality, each was given separate but inevitably overlapping functions, and each was given a grant of legal independence from the others. Whether instinctively or according to the dictates of ideology, the founders of our international posture in peace were groping their way toward the maximization of rule by bargaining. From this fact about the liberal state emanate most of our foreign-policy problems.

The cases analyzed below were chosen because they involved the basic instruments and commitments for dealing with noncrisis foreign policy. They have a double value to the analyst. First, each is a history of decision-making through which we can assess the behavior of individuals and the values they apply to decisions. That is, each is a study in the political process. Second, each of these basic decisions led to the creation of a program or instrument which contributed, for better or worse, to the political process of later decisions.

Each case tells about the same political story with about the same moral. In the liberal state when there is time for planning there is time for disagreement. Since there is nothing in American culture to limit the course of disagreement, disagreement spreads. It spreads among all individuals who have the interest and the resources. It ultimately becomes public and involves all of the engines and motives of public politics, as well as all of the unpredictability of publicly made decisions. This natural tendency in American politics was, during the postwar years, exaggerated to dangerous extremes, with consequences dangerous to world order, by leaders who believed in the goodness of the liberal state and proceeded to construct the foreign-policy system around it.

Institutions: In Search of an Establishment

MARSHALL PLAN: HOW TO AVOID AN ESTABLISHMENT IN FOREIGN ECONOMIC POLICY

The story of the opening of America is the story of the Economic Cooperation Act (ECA), or Marshall Plan (European Recovery Plan). Its reputation as a proud moment in American history will not be attacked here because its economic timeliness and its accomplishments in Europe are not at issue.[3] Reassessment is necessary in order to identify the kind of politics it reflects and, after passage, contributed to.

Almost everything about the structure and operation of ECA reflected the effort to impose a bargaining frame of reference upon it. But the most compelling evidence can be found in the placement of the agency itself, for the price of our peacetime involvement in world affairs was the creation of a second State Department in the ECA. Everything else about it seems to follow from that fact.

The State Department draft of the European Recovery Plan called for an administrator "whose every function, especially those involving foreign policy, would be performed 'subject to direction and control of the Secretary of State.' "[4] Ultimate State Department control was something President Harry

3. For a detailed but quite readable account, see Joseph Jones, *The Fifteen Weeks* (New York: Viking, 1955).

4. Arthur H. Vandenberg, Jr., *The Private Papers of Senator Vandenberg* (Boston: Houghton-Mifflin, 1952), p. 388. See also President Truman's message to Congress, December 19, 1947: "The Administrator must be subject to the direction of the Secretary of State on decisions and actions affecting our foreign policy" (*State Department Bulletin* [December 28, 1947], p. 1,243).

Truman and General George C. Marshall had insisted upon. But Senator Arthur Vandenberg, with Congress behind him, was dissatisfied, even though he had earlier been aware of the problem of having dual responsibilities in foreign affairs.[5]

Bipartisanship, invented as a harness for Senator Vandenberg, became instead a whip by which Congress might influence the Executive and the overly liberal State Department. In the act, the administrator was given a fully independent agency and the authority and status of Cabinet rank. Since it would be bad form to have two secretaries of State, there would just have to be "successful liaison"[6] between the administrator and the secretary of State. Optimistically, section 105(b) of the Economic Cooperation Act provided that the administrator and secretary were to keep each other "fully and currently informed on matters, including prospective action . . . pertinent to the duties of the other." Somewhat more realistically and very much in point is section 105(b) (3), which provided that "if differences of view are not adjusted by consultation [between administrator and secretary], the matter shall be referred to the President for final decision."

If there had been any doubts about the likelihood of such an arrangement becoming a second State Department, all actions following passage should have dispelled them. Marshall's choice for administrator was his undersecretary of State Will Clayton. Vandenberg successfully opposed Clayton on the grounds that the "overriding Congressional desire [was] that the ERP Administrator come from the outside business world with strong industrial credentials and *not* via the State Department. . . . [T]his job as ERP Administrator stands out by itself—as demonstrated in all of the Congressional debates—as requiring particularly persuasive economic credentials unrelated to diplomacy."[7] On similar grounds, President Truman's initial proposal of Dean Acheson was also vetoed. Paul Hoffman suited the requirement of business experience to a T.

Hoffman's operational code for ECA was based upon a profoundly political decision to be nonpolitical: "I believed that in fighting communism in Europe, we would lose all our moorings if we adopted the Machiavellian philosophy that the ends justify the means. Therefore I insisted on confining ourselves to the recovery field. . . . I had a strong belief that no pattern imposed by a group of planners in Washington could possibly be effective. . . . Coming into this with a business background, I thought that if we in the ECA adopted a new role—as a kind of investment banker—that would be the right approach."[8]

5. On Marshall, see H. B. Price, *The Marshall Plan and Its Meaning* (Ithaca: Cornell University Press, 1955), p. 69; on Vandenberg, see *Private Papers*, p. 388.
6. Vandenberg, p. 393.
7. Ibid., p. 393. (Emphasis in original.)
8. Quoted in Price, pp. 73–74.

The statute also provided for a special representative to Europe, with rank of ambassador extraordinary and plenipotentiary (section 108). The special representative was to direct the special ECA missions, which were to be established in each country *independent from the regular diplomatic mission* (section 109). In any disputes with diplomatic missions, the chief of the ECA mission and the ambassador in each country were considered equal parties in consultation that could be carried up to the administrator and secretary of State (section 105(b)(3).

The staffing of ECA made it in reality the second State Department. Averell Harriman, appointed special representative, had been Truman's secretary of Commerce. He had served as an ambassador, but in his experience in foreign affairs he was more accustomed to dealing directly with the president. William C. Foster, named deputy special representative, had been undersecretary of Commerce. The deputy administrator was Howard Bruce, a Baltimore industrialist-financier and formerly director of materiel, Army Service Forces. Others in offices close to Hoffman included three professors of specialties important to ECA; two New York attorneys, one of whom was also president of Time, Inc.; a onetime president of the Export-Import Bank; the chief of foreign agricultural relations in the Department of Agriculture; and a couple of professional administrators. There was some experience in foreign affairs among them, *but there was not a single professional from the State Department in the entire company* (unless Harriman's very special experience is counted). The list contains several important departures from Hoffman's principle of business experience, but no departures from an unspoken rule of independence from the "other" State Department. Among the first chiefs of ECA missions were: Thomas K. Finletter, executive, attorney, air expert sent to the United Kingdom; David Bruce, assistant secretary of Commerce, 1947–48, sent to France; J. D. Zellerbach, San Francisco businessman, sent to Italy; and Roger Lapham, former mayor of San Francisco, sent to China. Only David Bruce had had State Department experience prior to his appointment to ECA, and that was as a vice-consul in Rome, 1926–28.

The initial expectation was that ECA would be a small agency whose staff would be essentially a few experts in agriculture, industry, and procurement.[9] But once in operation, ECA began to grow, not merely in obedience to some Parkinson's law of bureaucracy, but in a politically significant manner. The staff turned immediately to analysis of economic conditions in order to have independent means of assessing the plans of the Organization for European Economic Coordination (OEEC). Although the autonomy of OEEC and the

---

9. Price, p. 75; see also Truman's ECA message to Congress, p. 1,242. "I expect that the Economic Cooperation Administration will need only a small staff. No vast new agency or corporation is needed to perform functions for which government facilities now exist." The facts in this section are taken largely from Price, Vandenberg, and Robert Asher's *Grants, Loans and Local Currencies* (Washington, D.C.: The Brookings Institution, 1961); however, none of these authors would necessarily agree with my interpretations.

independence of the program were stressed from the very beginning (see Hoff-man's attitude above, for example), it is impossible to believe that the framers of the aid agency were naïve enough to think they could make the whole pro-cess self-executing and nonpolitical. If ECA was not going to accept OEEC plans as final, it was going to have to make value judgments. That is the implication of their analyses of economic conditions. If only to that extent, ECA had to become a second State Department.

A second aspect of this expansion of the political character of ECA was the early growth and elaboration of the special representative's office in Paris, despite the fact that it was expected to be a staff merely for the representative himself, "Never before had an overseas regional office been set up to play so large a part in a peacetime operation of the United States government."[10] This separated still further our economic aid from our central political arms, while at the same time it further guaranteed that political considerations would be involved in ECA's economic decisions. With complete lack of con-cern for the political dimension, the administrator also set up an Office of Labor Advisors for propagandizing European unions on the commitment of American labor to the democratic point of view.

ECA was a partial decision, inasmuch as Congress was saying, in effect, "You can have the money but you cannot use it as a means of realizing our interests abroad or as a means of unifying our far-flung foreign operations." Although Congress was not altogether at fault, the compulsion of many of its leading members to maintain Congress's access to foreign policy agencies fed the general confusion about how a democratic foreign policy ought to operate. Frequently domestic policy has been so partial that it is an empty ges-ture—or worse, a myth, or part of one. Sometimes it can be so partial as to be confusing beyond words (such as three or four different ways granted the presi-dent to control strikes). Policies can be so partial that they are self-destructive (as when one program is dedicated to getting people off farms while another serves to keep them on). This is called slack in the system, and through such means we buy time, displace conflict, avoid the costs of planning. Obviously this is expensive, and perhaps a rich country can afford partial decisions. We cannot, however, afford them in the international realm; but they occur, as in the Marshall Plan. When they occur here, they are evidence of a bargaining pattern and logrolling values.

The objection to the original presidential plan was not so much to the lodg-ing of such additional international power in the State Department. Perhaps that sentiment could be found among many leftover isolationists, but not among the new or the old internationalists. The stronger objection was to lodging so much power in a State Department *to regulate the domestic econ-omy* for purposes of manipulating international patterns. The isolationists

10. Price, p. 76.

disliked power because they did not want to shape the world. The new liberals did not want the power because they did not really want to shape the United States. Placed outside the State Department, pure economic aid could be seen as merely an expansion of trading domain, but that approach robbed the program of much of its value as an instrument of foreign affairs. However well ECA may have served Europe, its independence deprived the United States of a major opportunity to regulate and coordinate its own resources. Formulation of ECA, far from being a case of elite or of presidential power, is a reflection of the inability of officialdom during the postwar period to formulate effective policies. It was also one of their contributions to the decentralized and bargaining system of foreign policy that formulated undependable policies during the 1960s.

BUILDING A NONESTABLISHMENT IN DEFENSE

Following World War II, everyone seemed to desire unification, and it seemed not only possible but necessary. The success of that new invention, the Joint Chiefs of Staff, proved the possibility. Bipolarity proved the necessity by constantly pushing marginal issues toward high policy. Occupation policy and collective security proved the necessity because of their whole-country view of obligations and resources. Development and control of atomic power obviously proved the necessity. Yet, we did not get unification in 1947, and no very serious effort was ever made to get it. The malefactors in the first instance were Congress, in cooperation with military jealousies. The interest-group liberal approach to foreign policy can best be seen in how liberal leaders rationalized these patterns and then coped with this system in the later years.

The core of the new defense establishment was the National Security Council (NSC), which was set up in the Unification Act of 1947 as an ex officio body with very little in the way of arms and legs. It was a committee of the Cabinet with all the representativeness of a committee and none of the coherence of a working organization. Moreover, it came to mean the existence of a second Cabinet for defense by which disputants were given their choice of forum.[11] Except for the Central Intelligence Agency (CIA), the statute contemplated no organizational reality for NSC at all, for there was not even the mention of a Department of Defense. There was to be a small Office of the Secretary of Defense.[12]

The entire defense establishment was a confederation. There was even a "Tenth Amendment." Section 202 provided the secretary with some general powers but further provided that each of the respective military services "shall

11. See Paul Hammond, "The National Security Council as a Device for Interdepartmental Co-ordination," reprinted in Andrew Scott and Raymond H. Dawson, eds., *Readings in the Making of American Foreign Policy* (New York: Macmillan, 1965), p. 360.

12. The 1947 statute provided for only a "National Military Establishment, and the Secretary of Defense shall be head thereof" (section 201a).

be administered as individual executive departments . . . and all powers and duties relating to such departments not specifically conferred upon the Secretary of Defense by this Act shall be retained by each of their respective Secretaries." The powers left to the secretary of Defense were largely fiscal and, despite some change after 1958, remain the same today. The fact that so many secretaries have been out of Big Finance or Big Business seems more a reflection of the true function of the job than of the power eliteness of the incumbents. The narrowness of the secretary's powers is most clearly evidenced by the rights of the military branches, too well known to belabor here. Not only did the act totally brush aside the civilian secretaries of each service department, it went so far as to provide for no chairman of the Joint Chiefs but rather allowed them to "take rank among themselves according to their relative dates of appointment" (section 208b). The scheme favored by the president, the Collins Plan, called for a single chief of staff of the Armed Forces responsible to the secretary of Defense.[13] In Millis's judgment ten years later, this decentralization rendered the Joint Chiefs "almost constitutionally incapable of resolving the major problems which the National Security Act had confided to them"; but since no other unit in the establishment had power to do better, "there was something to be said for leaving them to an agency which, rather than resolve them wrongly, would not resolve them at all."[14]

At about the time of Millis's observations the Eisenhower Administration made some attempt to strengthen the center of the defense establishment. However, the opinions of students of the act suggest that the statutory effort was meek and unhelpful. While enlarging the Office of the Secretary and adding an undersecretary and some assistant secretaries to the Department of Defense created in 1949, the 1958 act continued to forbid the secretary to encroach upon the "combatant functions assigned to the military services" while also making it quite explicit that the new assistant secretaries "should not be in the direct line of administrative authority between [the Secretary] and the three military departments."[15]

If the position of the secretary of Defense was strengthened in the 1960s it was not due to conscious plans of the policy-making elite but rather to the chance and unpredictable factors of technology and personality.[16] As to the first, it is clear that new weapons and the expansion of research and development gave the center a stronger hand, because the assignment of new mis-

13. Paul Y. Hammond, *Organizing for Defense* (Princeton: Princeton University Press, 1961), pp. 213 ff.

14. Walter Millis and Harvey Mansfield, *Arms and the State* (New York: Twentieth Century Fund, 1958), p. 183.

15. Gene M. Lyons, "The New Civil-Military Relations," in Scott and Dawson, *Readings*, pp. 414–15.

16. In all of this I am indebted to Hammond, to Lyons, and to Millis and Mansfield; however, they would not necessarily agree with the interpretations I have put upon their research.

sions and functions is a powerful source of influence when used with the desire for influence clearly in mind. The second factor was strong personality and intellect—that is, Robert McNamara. Personal rationality coupled with special techniques of program budgeting and cost-benefit analysis gave the secretary and the Office of the Secretary an unusually strong hand. During the late 1950s and 1960s, as a consequence, the civilian service secretaries lost reputation and then power to the Defense Department undersecretaries and assistant secretaries. During the same period it seems clear that the Joint Chiefs also lost relative to the secretary. Their inability to centralize around a real chief and their consequent inability to reach and hold agreements gave McNamara and his predecessors some of their opportunities to exert influence.[17]

However, if one looks closely at these developments one cannot find any strong evidence that fundamental change took place. The modern secretary became a more powerful figure, but his enhanced power rested upon the subterfuges of budgetary controls—the allocation of moneys and missions—which suggests that real cohesion around the secretary and the president was not institutionalized. Any greater accountability was most probably due to bargaining advantages. Secretary McNamara's very strength contributed to the undoing of his successors. His initial assignments of roles used up many of the options of future secretaries. (Perhaps it is indicative that the Navy announced its decision not to use the F-111 shortly after McNamara's retirement.)

Much more could and should be said of the internal life of the Pentagon. But there is more to be learned by looking briefly outside the department to the relations between it and the other working parts of our total defense activity. Of those parts the most fascinating is atomic energy. No one any longer questions the proposition that the Atomic Energy Commission (AEC) and its successors have been very loosely connected to central political controls. Relations here were so loose as to make foreign governments wonder whether the United States had any national interests at all.

The powers originally granted the old AEC exceeded "those of any department of the government ever before established. The commission has, in effect, a plenary charter to do anything in the field of atomic energy that will promote the public safety and welfare."[18] Section 4 of the act of 1946, for instance, turned over to it all ownership of fissionable materials and control of all production facilities. Decisions on fissionable material to be released for research or as irrelevant to bomb production were left to the commission. The commission was set up deliberately and legally as a monopoly.

17. In Lyons's opinion this is the most important explanation for the increase of civilian authorty (p. 415).
18. James R. Newman and Byron S. Miller, *The Control of Atomic Energy* (New York: Whittlesey House, 1948), p. 27.

There was probably never any issue over whether atomic energy and its production would or would not be a government monopoly. The issues, rightfully in my opinion, revolved around how the monopoly would relate to the rest of the government. But the significant thing here is the alternative control features that were debated. In high-sounding tones the fate of atomic energy was defined as passing to civilian control or to military control. This simplified things for purposes of debate in Congress and in the press; and, better, this definition of the problem gave everyone a point of reference by fitting the perplexing atom into established (prewar) liberal-conservative alignments.[19] But obviously it had very little to do with the real problems of how to make the atom serve national interests. To the combatants, civilian control meant ease of access to atomic information and materials by universities and businesses, and military control meant access and control by the separate military services. It is clear from the debates that few on either side sought to vest control in neither of these sides. Almost none of the interested parties expected that control should rest in the hands of the political executives who would run the defense establishment. Robert Dahl and Ralph Brown were left to ask five years later whether the commission should or should not be placed within the Department of Defense. Since the overwhelming proportion of its work was in military and strategic uses, why, they asked, should the program be anything more than one part of the arms program?[20] The question should emphasize the fact that the separation of the AEC from the executive was almost a foregone conclusion, and that with its founding, the decentralized and bargaining system of foreign policy was institutionalized still further.

Thus the AEC became its own boss. It was made independent of State and of Defense, and, therefore, of the presidency. In security affairs, the AEC was made a coequal partner of Defense. AEC-Defense disputes, like ECA-State disputes, were settled, according to the act, by the president. At first this arrangement may appear to be a sound principle of insuring presidential involvement, but that would be mere rationalization. During the formative years, through 1951, only one dispute—over the custody of atomic weapons—was taken to the president, and that one would have gone up to him regardless of AEC location. More important is the fact that the president decided this one in favor of the AEC and, given the spirit of the act, that was really the only decision possible.[21] Monopoly of the secrets[22] along with vir-

19. Byron S. Miller, "The Atomic Energy Act of 1946," in Theodore J. Lowi, ed., *Legislative Politics U.S.A.* (Boston: Little, Brown, 1962, 1965), p. 267.

20. See Robert A. Dahl and Ralph S. Brown, *Domestic Control of Atomic Energy* (New York: Social Science Research Council, 1951), pp. 25–26.

21. Ibid., p. 24.

22. Section 10, in which the commission was given power to "control the dissemination of restricted data" and also to decide what were "restricted data." (Sec. 10[b][1] defined restricted data as all data having to do in any way with fissionable material for bombs or power, and then it left it to the commission to decide what data could be published.)

tual monopoly of the materials, provided the old AEC the advantage in bargaining with the president.

The secretary of Defense has mainly been the biggest customer of the AEC and its successors but with no statutory rights of direction. In stark contrast, Congress gave to itself an extremely strong statutory right to participate in, with the distinct possibility of controlling, atomic policy. This meant that all the arguments about the novelty and the unique significance and the international security importance of atomic energy were largely empty rhetoric. The setup was essentially like every other independent agency and public enterprise. During its first fifteen years, despite its youth and despite the military stature of President Eisenhower and despite the strategic importance of atomic development, the AEC remained an "independent commission";[23] and the legal theory of the independent commission made it an agent of Congress— giving the AEC an ability at least to play president and Congress off against each other and against any other agencies threatening to its independence. The Eisenhower years were characterized as "not congressional predominance in its simplest form" but rather an alliance between the AEC and the Joint Committee on Atomic Energy.[24] The change to President Kennedy and the restoration of common party majorities in both houses of Congress and in the presidency did not change the pattern very much. As contemporaneous observer H. L. Nieburg put it, Kennedy's AEC chairman, Glen Seaborg, has "not yielded to congressional direction, but through the graceful maneuvers of politics, his boss the President has."[25]

After the great 1973 energy crisis the best Congress could do was to cut the AEC into two separate agencies—the Energy Research and Development Agency (ERDA) and the Nuclear Regulatory Commission (NRC). This may have clarified authority and functions, but it hardly brought more unity to the conduct of foreign policy. Neither did the Department of Energy, created at President Carter's request. In fact, the new department, whose first secretary, James Schlesinger, was a strong man with experience as secretary of defense and CIA director, definitely contributes to the fragmentation of the foreign policy establishment.

When fragmentation and conflict are perpetuated in separate agencies, each with statutory integrity, none enjoying many rights to intervene against others, policy decisions are inevitably shaped by the momentary requirements of getting agreement, not the ultimate fact of realizing foreign objectives.[26] In that context, creating atoms agencies, a sacred separation among the services,

23. H. L. Nieburg, "The Eisenhower AEC and Congress," *Midwest Journal of Political Science* (May 1962), pp. 116–17.

24. Ibid., p. 116.

25. H. L. Nieburg, *Nuclear Secrecy and Foreign Policy* (Washington, D.C.: Public Affairs, 1964), p. 36.

26. Samuel P. Huntington, "Strategy Planning and the Political Process," *Foreign Affairs* 38 (January 1960): 291.

an independent NASA, a subterranean CIA, and so forth must have seriously impaired efforts to put any of these instruments to the service of political strategies. More academically, their separate existence should destroy any claim made by liberal analysts or leaders in the 1950s or 1960s that foreign policy formulation was a fundamentally different kind of system, or that it was in any considerable way insulated from domestic political forces.[27] These instruments were all partial decisions in themselves and their existence produced partial decisions in the everyday activities of the central political leaders. Let us look directly at how central leaders have responded to the diffuse liberal system created for them.[28]

Policies: Oversell, Not Overkill

International liberalism got the country committed to the international system, but the liberal system of organization interfered with fashioning this commitment into a self-serving force. The patterns observed above left the president and his foreign policy elite a hopeless task of making a ministry out of what can at best be a coalition. Despite the frequency with which this system was praised, and despite the valiant efforts since 1946 to make do with it, the behavior of the president and his elite reflected the real problems and the pathologies. Their behavior since World War II can be summarized as oversell: They have been forced to oversell every remedy for world ailments and to oversell each problem for which the remedy might be appropriate.

OVERSELLING THE REMEDY

Support for the United Nations was a policy the United States determined to fashion after World War II, if only as repayment for having helped destroy the League of Nations. Enormous care was taken to insure passage of the United Nations Charter as a treaty in the Senate—passage without crippling amendment or embarrassing debate. So well was the UN sold that when the

27. That these patterns are not ancient errors unlikely to be committed again can be seen in such decisions as having a second secretary of State in the White House (national security adviser) and creating a Department of Energy.

28. Kenneth Waltz has insisted that fragmentation exists in Britain and the USSR and that it does not constitute a special American problem of disunity. True, most advanced states are highly differentiated (*fragmentation* being reserved for differentiation one does not like). However, this becomes a special problem in the United States because it lacks the centripetal institutions possessed by the other countries. See Waltz's *Foreign Policy and Democratic Politics* (Boston: Little, Brown, 1967). For some stimulating observations on institutional disunity in American foreign policy, and some thoughts on how to gain some integration of foreign policy agencies, including Congress, see Arthur Schlesinger, *The Imperial Presidency* (New York: Popular Library Edition, 1974), Chapter 9.

Charter came before the Senate for advice and consent, almost no opposition remained. As Bertram Gross recorded it,

Since little defense of the Charter was needed, few senators planned to speak on its behalf and there was genuine danger that an impression of disinterest would be created. As a last-minute measure . . . Senator Connally . . . was seen walking around the floor with a pad of paper in one hand and a pencil in the other, button-holing one senator after another and beseeching them to speak on behalf of the United Nations.[29]

What seemed politically appropriate and successful for the occasion, however, proved to have been almost too heavy a price to pay, for many of the most attentive members of the public had become convinced that the UN would be a real instrument of our foreign policy. Thus, when the critical emergency of aid to Greece and Turkey arose, the possibility of a timely response by the United States ran into serious difficulty from unexpected sources. Once the news of direct United States action in Greece and Turkey became known,

the overwhelming attachment of the American public to the United Nations made itself felt in no uncertain terms, and many of the staunchest supporters of the President's policy, who were at the same time backers of the United Nations—including Walter Lippmann, Marquis Childs, Barnet Nover, and Anne O'Hare McCormick—were deploring the failure of the President to notify the United Nations and to adopt other procedures that would have brought his proposed action "within the spirit of the United Nations."[30]

Hands were burned but apparently no lessons were learned, for Administration leaders treated Greek-Turkish aid and the larger ideas created to package this aid as though it would be the last time Congress and the public would ever have to be faced. These programs were "proposed and accepted with panacean overtones"[31] for the quickie rebuilding of Europe, righting the wrongs in underdeveloped lands, and containing the Communists once and for all. So the original Policy Planning Staff memorandum prior to Marshall's Harvard speech stressed that "the program must contain reasonable assurance that if we support it, this will be the last such program we shall be asked to support in the foreseeable future."[32] President Truman stressed this get-it-over-with theme in his December 1947 special message on aid.

Two years later when the pressures for expansion of economic and military involvement were so great—note NSC 68 alone[33]—the Korean outbreak must have come as a considerable relief to those who had to face Congress, for

29. Bertram Gross, *The Legislative Struggle* (New York: McGraw-Hill, 1953), p. 368.
30. Jones, *The Fifteen Weeks*, p. 181.
31. Gabriel Almond, *The American People and Foreign Policy* (New York: Harcourt, Brace, 1950), p. 88.
32. Quoted in Jones, p. 250.
33. Millis and Mansfield, *Arms and the State*, p. 256. NSC 68 was a major policy paper dealing with the escalation of the cold war toward a period of "maximum danger" in 1952.

without the war, the totalism of the Marshall Plan would have made any reassessment look like badly broken pledges. One other important aspect of oversell in the aid programs was the stress the public was allowed to put upon the doctrines of (1) self-help and (2) anti-Communism. Soon after passage, the Administration got into hot water over the glaring inconsistencies of opposition to helping Spain (anti-Communist and ready to help herself) and eagerness to help Yugoslavia (Communist).

Examples of oversell can just as easily be found in noneconomic policies, and they serve even better as indices to the politics of the foreign policy establishment. The most interesting is the case of the Administration's perjury on American troop commitments under the NATO treaty. At the time of the treaty ratification, there was intense opposition in Congress to the degree of entanglement implied in NATO. To the treaty unanimously reported by the Foreign Relations Committee, Senator Kenneth Wherry, for himself, Robert Taft, and Arthur Watkins attempted to attach the reservation that none of the parties was committed "morally or legally to furnish or supply arms."[34] Due to unequivocal assurances made publicly and privately at that time, the reservation was withdrawn and the treaty was allowed to pass unamended. A year later, when we did become committed to stationing troops abroad, these early assurances hurt.

In April 1949, Senator Bourke B. Hickenlooper asked Secretary Dean Acheson, "Are we going to be expected to send substantial numbers of troops over there as a more or less permanent contribution to the development of these countries' capacity to resist?" Acheson's 1949 reply was, "The answer to that question, Senator, is a clear and absolute 'No.' "[35] In the 1951 hearings, Acheson, when reminded of 1949, attempted to get out of his embarrassment with labored definitions. He explained that if the "expected to" in the 1949 question meant that under the treaty we had undertaken a commitment, the answer was "No"; however, that did not mean an absolute "No" to a question whether we "intended to" send them.[36] His testimony was accompanied by an elaborate brief showing that the president, in his role as commander-in-chief, needed no congressional authorization for sending the troops, and that the treaty had not affected this power one way or the other.[37] No one questioned this, but many felt that such a brief would have been more appropriate in 1949.[38]

34. Quoted in Bradford Westerfield, *Foreign Policy and Party Politics* (New Haven: Yale University Press, 1955), p. 332. See also *Hearings*, cited in note 35, pp. 119–20.

35. Committee on Foreign Relations, *Hearings on the Assignment of Ground Forces of the United States to Duty in the European Area* (Washington, D.C.: U.S. Government Printing Office, 1951), p. 111. For further reference to "absolute assurance," see p. 120. These extraordinary hearings were held pursuant to the Wherry Resolution discussed below.

36. Ibid., p. 112.

37. Ibid., pp. 88 ff., 110. This contrasts with the Administration's 1949 assurance that the treaty would be resubmitted if troops were contemplated (p. 120).

38. Ibid., p. 120.

What is significant is that such misrepresentation was necessary. What is significant is that there could be no proper conspiracy among leaders in the pursuit of the national interests of the United States. Misrepresentation by the Administration in the presentation of the package to Congress is a strong example of oversell. Moreover, it was the sense of misrepresentation felt by Congress that had brought forth the 1951 Wherry Resolution in the first place. The Wherry Resolution declared that no troops would be stationed in Europe under NATO "pending the adoption of a policy with respect thereto by the Congress."[39] This incredible expression would have forcibly pried open the foreign policy establishment. The hearings pursuant to the Wherry Resolution achieved the following, according to Senator Richard B. Russell: "It is the first time, I suppose, in such a critical international situation that any great power has laid all of its cards on top of the table not only to be seen by our allies but by our potential enemies."[40] This is the reaction of a consumer who discovers he has been oversold.

Overselling of package doctrines was repeated over and over again in the years after the postwar period. Eisenhower's personal diplomacy ("I shall go to Korea," "spirit of Camp David"), John Foster Dulles's brinkmanship, and Charles E. Wilson's "bigger bang" were necessary parts of the task of selling the New Look—which in turn was marketing language for making the absolutely necessary downward budgetary adjustments in the post-Korean period. Since so much foreign policy between Korea and Sputnik involved implementation and amendment of basic instruments already in existence, naturally much of the process in these years landed in the fiscal area. Consequently, Congress enacted fiscal versions of the Wherry Resolution as a means of dispelling for itself the fog of oversell. In 1951, Congress enacted a requirement that military departments must "come into agreement" with the Armed Services Committees on virtually all transactions involving real estate for military installations.[41] Eight years later it was repealed through constitutional (attorney general) construction, and only after that by Congress. But it was immediately replaced by another "fiscal Wherry Resolution," the Russell Amendment. This stated, "No funds may be appropriated after December 31, 1960, to or for the use of any armed force of the United States for the procurement of aircraft, missiles, or naval vessels unless the appropriation of such funds *has been authorized by legislation enacted after such date.*[42]

It seems then that one special development in foreign policy since the for-

39. Ibid., pp. 38–39.
40. Ibid., p. 87.
41. See Raymond H. Dawson, "Innovation and Intervention in Defense Policy," in Robert L. Peabody and Nelson W. Polsby, eds., *New Perspectives on the House of Representatives* (Chicago: Rand-McNally, 1963), p. 283. This amendment was vetoed by Truman and then passed as a rider to another bill.
42. Ibid., p. 273. (Emphasis added.)

mative years has been the institutionalization of second thoughts in Congress. This is the mentality of "Stop the world, we want to get on" that has arisen out of the failure of leaders to find means of dealing with each other frankly yet confidentially. The Common Market was so far oversold to Congress as to imperil the 1962 Trade Act. The Alliance for Progress was packaged to sound like an attempt to revolutionize the hemisphere. The lack of coherence that makes oversell necessary caught Presidents Eisenhower and Johnson in outright lies on the U-2 incident and the Pueblo affair. It caught the more sophisticated Kennedy in one of the most disastrous adventures in the history of national prestige. The Bay of Pigs is the classic case of the partial decision: "You may go to war in Cuba but you may not have the support necessary to succeed." No wonder the president must propagandize his colleagues and the country if he is to avoid the partial decision.

No policy has escaped injury to itself and to national interests and international stability in the years since American statesmen have felt the need to oversell policies in order to avoid coming up with a partial decision. The war in Vietnam was just another instance of the point. The fighting in the south was not of our making. The crisis was. The escalation was. The involvement in Vietnam was sold by American image-makers as a case of unambiguous aggression and therefore of the need for military victory. Perhaps it was both of these things, but to sell it on the front pages that way in order to insure support at home left world diplomats, including our own, with almost no options. Under increasing popular pressure, magnified by congressmen who might rightly feel that they had not been properly informed, the extremes of oversell were exceeded over and over again. From domino theories we got the Rusk Doctrine of the total involvement of the credibility of the United States. From that we went to the myth of democratic election and popular support for the Ky and Thieu regimes. There was also the myth of eminent military victory, which was eventually replaced by the myths of Vietnamization and of peace with honor. Each seemed total at the time but was promptly enough replaced or moved over for another total myth as realities became too hard to rationalize.

When experiments must be sold as sure things and specialized sure things must be sold as cure-alls, frustration and failure are inevitable. An experiment may be partially successful; but after oversell partial success must be accepted as failure. Failure leads to distrust and frustration, which lead to more oversell and to further verbal excesses, as superlatives become ordinary through use. Since international politics is special in the amount of risk involved, these responses become especially intense. All of which leads to the worst possible abuse of oversell, the rhetoric of victory. The rhetoric of victory is constantly on the verge of gaining ascendancy. It is the last stage before the end of politics.

OVERSELLING THE THREAT

The second type of oversell is essentially the attempt to create the moral equivalent of war. It is the conversion of interactions into incidents, incidents into challenges, challenges into threats and threats into crises for the purpose of imposing temporary and aritificial cohesion upon the members of the foreign policy establishment. It is the escalation of meanings. When peace is in peril, all presidents have found it necessary to create that sense of self-restraint, self-sacrifice, and devotion to higher causes that seems to come about so naturally in war. For modern presidents, this tactic has become necessary, compelling, and regular whether there is a true crisis or not.

Typically, a Briton provided us with our most important concepts. In the vocabulary of oversell no doctrines have been as important as the cold war and iron curtain. (Also typically, the British proceeded to take it all less seriously than we.) There were, of course, varying amounts of truth underlying both terms. Perhaps there is a total but unseen war. Perhaps there has been a Communist devil who will "get you if you don't watch out." But the analytic value of the terms was lost to their hortatory value: We might get some cohesion in the policy-making elite if we can only attribute to our enemies a singleness of purpose and a perfection of rational means to achieve it. These two Churchillian themes proved to fill basic psychological and political needs in our system, and they have regularly been used to help oversell crises.

Containment, first seized upon to help provide a package for Greek-Turkish aid, was also found to be generally valuable. It became a significant American contribution to the more pervasive themes of cold war and iron curtain. It helped show that all local wars, guerrilla actions, and *coups d'état* were interrelated and cumulative.[43]

Along with these pervasive themes were the more specialized, *ad hoc* emotions. President Eisenhower had an important oversell mechanism in McCarthyism. Functionally, McCarthyism was the internal equivalent of con-

43. See Lippmann:

All the postwar Presidents have taken if for granted that they had to create the majority they needed [for unpopular foreign policies], and that, while some . . . might respond to argument, the others had to be scared into joining up. . . . As a result, it has become part of the established procedure of American foreign policy to invoke the threat of Communist takeover whenever American opinion is divided. As the practice has grown, the formula has been generalized. Now we are accepting the unique burden of resisting the advance of Communism everywhere.

Lippmann referred to this as the "all-purpose myth" despite the "essential fact" about disorders like Vietnam and the Dominican Republic that "they are at bottom indigenous to the countries where the social order is broken down, not originally, not essentially, conspiracies engineered from the centers of Communist power" (*Newsweek*, May 4, 1965, p. 23). He went on to argue that the myth would be used to "reassure our people that Mr. Johnson is not going to take part in an unending series of wars," because we can teach the "masterminds of a universal conspiracy" a lesson in only one or two encounters.

tainment, and it helped bring the Democratic, tea-sipping, and pro-Soviet State Department into line as well as to silence much independent opposition. Late in his Administration, Eisenhower found overselling of foreign crises increasingly valuable as his personal prestige declined. Dulles became famous for such talk as the "brink of war" and "massive retaliation." The latter phrase was particularly effective because it helped oversell the positive value of atomic over conventional arms, and at the same time helped create the sense of the seriousness and immediacy of the threat that made nuclear retaliation necessary. Dulles opposed containment as "negative, futile, and immoral" and implied its replacement with rhetoric that (especially for Europe) verged on preventive war. But he continued to sell all outbreaks the world over as interrelated and cumulative. Finally there was the use of Sputnik for a variety of issues in the arms race on into the 1960s.

Much of the activity in Kennedy's short term was of the same nature. In fact, Kennedy spent more of his time in the earlier months on creating a moral equivalent of war than on just about anything else. The "ask not" passage of his inaugural address appeared to be a suitable method of national mobilization. The idea of man-on-the-moon-by-1970 had all sorts of value besides the increasing of space appropriations. A race always implies a threat to virility. The Bay of Pigs, once survived, became an excellent means for creating a sense of unity, then some real unity, on a host of defense-related items. (It is hard to forget the Kennedy-MacArthur, Kennedy-Hoover, Kennedy-Truman, and so forth, unity pictures.) During the Dominican conflict, President Johnson added another major variant to the threat of Communist encirclement. His approach was almost like a parody of old Southern racial fears: a thirty-secondth fraction of Communist blood makes a local movement part of the "world Communist conspiracy."

Republican Foreign Policy:
The Legacy of Vietnam and the Democrats

Interest-group liberal values and institutions produced, among many problems, a special relationship between the president and the public. Carrying the domestic system over into foreign-policy-making tended to turn the foreign policy process on its head. Instead of an elite consensus guiding the nation, there developed an institutionally fragmented elite seeking a national consensus to be guided by. An old aphorism held, "He who mobilizes the elite mobilizes the public." In the 1960s the reverse came closer to the truth: "He who can mobilize the public may mobilize the elite." The 1970s, with Republicans in the White House, Democrats continuing to rule Congress, and Democrats or nonparty liberals still roosting widely among the senior civil servants, were almost certain to experience an exacerbation of institutionalized fragmentation which would make the presidency even more plebiscitary than it had already become.

Before examining microscopically several important case studies of the foreign policy establishment and its behavior in the 1970s, it might be well to look statistically at the plebiscitary relationship of the president to the public. This will give some sense of the everyday realities of Washington to which presidents have been reacting when they turned to oversell as a basic foreign policy strategy. In Table 6.1 are the results of questions asked a national sample concerning how they felt in general about the way the president was doing his job. This question is asked on each poll once every three weeks or every month. The poll is not timed according to national or international events and does not seek to get a referendum on any particular action. In each case shown here, a poll was chosen that had been taken immediately before the event and as soon as possible after the event. The results are extremely suggestive. A disaster, like the Bay of Pigs, tended to rally the people to the president regardless of their attitude toward the event itself. Even a low-pressure event like President Johnson's 1966 visit with former Premier Nguyen Cao Ky in the Pacific bolstered the president's faltering popularity. Of even greater interest are the 1962 data. Here one can see how clearly the public discriminates between a domestic and an international action. Immediately following the dispatching of federal troops to the University of Mississippi campus, President Kennedy's standing dropped. At the time of the next poll, the Cuban missile crisis had occurred and President Kennedy's standing had gone up significantly. In 1969 President Nixon brought his general rating up 15 points from 53 percent to 68 percent by his announcement of a plan to withdraw from Vietnam, even though it was not to be implemented for a long time. Less than a year later when withdrawal policy was drastically reversed by an advancement into Cambodia, President Nixon's approval rating went up from 53 percent to 59 percent. Five years later, as the South Vietnamese regime was collapsing and bringing down with it all our illusions about an honorable peace, President Ford brought his general rating up a whopping 11 percentage points from 40 percent to 51 percent when he ordered a forceful recapture of the U.S. freighter *Mayaguez* from the Cambodian military.

The logic of the situation is clear. If the president can revive his major resource, his public following, with almost any international act with which he can clearly associate himself, then he must always be under some pressure to prefer such actions. Yet such unambiguous acts are the worst enemy of international diplomacy. Inevitably an unambiguous act encourages other unambiguous acts, military rhetoric tends to displace political rhetoric, and eventually military functions replace diplomatic functions.

Because of this plebicitary relationship between the president and the

TABLE 6.1

THE PRESIDENT'S RELATION TO HIS PUBLIC*

"Do you approve of the way the
president is handling his job?"

		% YES
June 1950	Before Korean outbreak	37
July 1950	After U.S. entry	46
August 1956	Before Israeli, British, French attack on Suez	67
December 1956	After U.S. opposition to the attack	75
July 1958	Before Lebanon	52
August 1958	After U.S. marine landing	58
May 1960	Before U-2 incident	62
June 1960	U-2 debacle; collapse of Summit	68
March 1961	Before Bay of Pigs	73
April 1961	After Bay of Pigs	83
September 1962	Before troops to Mississippi	67
October 1962	After troops, eve of Cuban missile crisis	61
December 1962	After Cuban missile crisis	74
October 1966	Before tour of Pacific	44
November 1966	After tour of Pacific	48
June 1967	Before Glassboro conference	44
June 1967	After Glassboro conference	52
October 1969	Before announcement of Nixon withdrawal plan	53
November 1969	After announcement	68
March 1970	Before Cambodian incursion	53
May 1970	After Cambodian incursion	59
May 1975	Before *Mayaguez* incident	40
June 1975	After *Mayaguez* incident	51

* SOURCE: Press releases of the American Institute of Public Opinion (AIPO). See also Nelson
W. Polsby, *Congress and the Presidency* (Englewood Cliffs: Prentice-Hall, 1964), p.
26; and Waltz, *Foreign Policy and Democratic Politics*, Chapter 10.

public the public has not matured in its international conscience. It possesses
insufficient tolerance for ambiguity. The public did not become interna-
tionalist, it became neoisolationist. It seems satisfied only if the world is put to
rights. As Denis Brogan observed during the McCarthy period, there is an
"illusion of omnipotence" such that our power to put the world to rights is
thought by us to be limited only by stupidity or treason in high places. Years
later one looks at the polls and wonders whether progress has been made. For
example, in November of 1967 the polls showed that 23 percent of the people

approved and 53 percent rejected President Johnson's handling of the Vietnam War, but 63 percent were for stepping up rather than reducing the military effort. A great danger in oversell by a plebiscitary president is that even if a sense of crisis or cure is an appropriate setting for a timely policy decision, it can create misleading expectations and fears among allies and adversaries. Another danger is that the president's own flexibility may be further reduced at a later point when he would like the crisis to be over. He might, in other words, wish it on at will, but he cannot so easily wish it off. Given the regular use of oversell despite such obvious dangers, the need for it must be enormous. Four important cases from the 1970s go well beyond the public-opinion data to show the persistent connection between institutionalized fragmentation—multiple foreign ministries—and the apparent need for plebiscitary politics in foreign policy.

FOUR CASES FROM THE NIXON YEARS

Case 1. OPEC and the energy crisis • In October 1973 the Yom Kippur War ended just short of an invasion of Egypt. Henry Kissinger undertook a series of shuttles between the capitals of the Middle Eastern countries to work out some kind of settlement. Suddenly the United States was hit from the blind side by one of the very blows Kissinger was trying to avert—blackmail by the frustrated Arab countries. The Arab-dominated Organization of Petroleum Exporting Countries (OPEC) voted to impose an embargo on all shipments and to quadruple the price of crude oil once the shipments were resumed. That, in brief, was the basis of the energy crisis of 1973. The immediate effects of the energy crisis were managed surprisingly well; but the near- and long-range effects were another matter entirely. After a period of stalemate between Secretary of State Kissinger and Secretary of the Treasury William Simon, Richard Nixon proclaimed his response under the title "Project Independence." The term *energy crisis* was itself a very important part of the package, implying that we were suddenly at that point in the history of our body politic where we would either get well or die.

Here is another instance where in one breath the president of the United States oversold the nature of the threat and the character of the remedy. But it can be understood as a realistic effort to build consensus among the American people and some kind of unity within his Administration. One account of Project Independence reported that at least the following agencies had a rightful place in the policy process: eleven congressional committees or subcommittees; the Departments of State, Treasury, Commerce, Transportation, Interior, Justice, Defense, and Agriculture; the Federal Power Commission; the Interstate Commerce Commission; the Civil Aeronautics Board; and the Environmental Protection Agency. And, they report, each of these agencies asserted jurisdiction over some aspect of the problem.[44]

Despite all the inconvenience to millions of American automobile drivers, and despite all the hullabaloo in President Nixon's response, the Administration was unable to put together an energy package until 1975, and then Congress changed the bill in several important particulars in the process of passing it. Consequently, we not only failed to gain independence but also failed to achieve any noticeable conservation of energy or expansion of domestic production. As late as 1978, the United States was importing more oil than before the embargo of 1973. Nonetheless, we were paying for energy independence. One student of energy politics observed that the import quota system which was in effect between 1959 and 1973 gives some hint of the cost of energy independence: The taxpayer was being burdened with several billions of dollars a year in gas prices merely to get a slightly higher level of domestic production. In order to eliminate completely the need for imports, for energy independence, the price to the taxpayer would have to be astronomical, and only a small proportion of that was actually being provided for in the 1973–75 energy independence package. What *is* energy independence? And is that really what our policy should be? Indeed, is that really what our policy was after the energy crisis of 1973? We cannot really know, since all we got was a lot of rhetoric and a lot of flurry as regards the threat and the solutions.[45]

Case 2. Agriculture, agribusiness, and the depletion of reserves • During the 1970s, Secretary of Agriculture Earl Butz was the dominant force in international relations where food was concerned. His position was very strong within the Nixon Cabinet, as indicated alone by the fact that Butz was to become one of the four heads of superdepartments under the Nixon reorganization plan that was aborted by Watergate. Butz's position in international affairs was shored up by his close relationship with the enormous grain exporting companies whose activities were supposed to be supervised by the Agriculture Department. A scandal in 1975 revealed publicly the exploitation of access to Butz by the big grain exporters and the degree to which the obscure departmental inspectors of their activities were being bought off. Butz responded to this scandal first by denouncing it and demanding a vast establishment of public inspection officials and then eventually by adding a few federal supervisors to the corruption-ridden contract system of inspection.

Butz's great moment of power in international relations, however, had

44. Graham Allison and Peter Szanton, "Organizing for the Decade Ahead," in Henry Owen and Charles Schultze, eds., *Setting National Priorities: The Next 10 Years* (Washington, D.C.: The Brookings Institution, 1976), pp. 230–31.
45. David H. Davis, *Energy Politics* (New York: St. Martin's Press, 1974), pp. 1–5 and 196–97. See also John M. Blair, *The Control of Oil* (New York: Vintage Books, 1978).

come three years before, in the summer of 1972, when he almost single-handedly arranged for the unprecedented trade agreement whereby the United States would sell to the Soviet Union nearly a billion dollars worth of grain on the basis of low-interest credit and a highly subsidized per bushel price. By September, over a billion dollars of American grain had passed through the hands of a few USDA officials, representatives of the six largest grain exporters and a few Russian officials. (Two of the highest ranking members of the United States negotiating team were at that very time negotiating also with two of the big export companies for high-ranking jobs with them. They moved over to the private jobs with these companies before the ink on the Russian contracts was entirely dry.)

Butz, momentarily our secretary of State, praised the deal as a "major breakthrough for peaceful co-existence between Russia and the United States."[46] The diplomatic corps for the secretary of Agriculture, acting as secretary of State, was composed of the six grain exporters operating for the Department of Agriculture as mercenary diplomats.

The deal set between Butz and the Russians fixed the wheat price at about $1.67 per bushel. The price of wheat for that bumper crop, before public knowledge of the deal, was around $1.27 per bushel. After the the deal was announced, wheat went up toward $2.10 per bushel and above. In the first instance, the windfall went to the Russians because the contract had fixed their price at a very low level. In the second instance, the windfall went to the grain exporters because of the United States policy of subsidizing wheat exporters as a means of keeping domestic wheat prices competitive in world markets. Most of the exporters had bought a great deal of their wheat while the price was low. However, for the millions of bushels they bought after the price started going up, the USDA acted as an indemnifier. And the exporters had been assured from the beginning that they would be so indemnified. Thus, at the height of the exchange, with the price of wheat hovering at $2.10 per bushel of wheat, the subsidy amounted to a mind-boggling $.47 per bushel. As the cost of the subsidy began to mount at an alarming pace and to a startling figure, the director of the Office of Management and Budget made a crash investigation of the situation, confronted the Department of Agriculture with the results, and demanded that the subsidy be immediately suspended. In the end, the cost to the taxpayer was approximately $131.6 million. It was referred to as the Great American Grain Robbery.[47]

The wheat deal severely embarrassed Washington. The Russians beat us out on a straight capitalist bargain. A few large corporate combines had

46. Quoted in A. V. Krebs, "Of the Grain Trade, By the Grain Trade, and For the Grain Trade," in Catherine Lerza and Michael Jacobson, eds., *Food for People Not for Profit* (New York: Ballantine Books, 1975), p. 354. This article is also the best single source on the 1972 wheat deal.

47. A. V. Krebs, p. 364.

cheated the government and the farmers out of the reasonable profit to be expected from a major grain deal. And we had severely depleted the large stockpiles of grain that not only had had a stabilizing effect on the world food prices but was, like a standing army, an effective diplomatic weapon. Yet, in 1975 the Department of Agriculture was still the State Department on the international traffic in food. Another good grain crop in the United States coincided with another bad year for agriculture in Russia. Butz decided virtually unilaterally that the United States could sell ten million tons of grain immediately in the summer of 1975 with additional sales possible in September. He even ordered departmental officials to handle the sales quietly through the private grain companies and probably would have succeeded in keeping it quiet had it not been for the publicity given the projected sales by Federal Reserve Chairman Arthur Burns. A dispute with Secretary of State Henry Kissinger over the handling of the sales contributed to President Ford's decision to replace Kissinger with Butz as chairman of the White House Agricultural Policy Committee. Consequently, until nearly the end of Ford's tenure in office, when Butz embarrassed himself out of office with a scatological racial slur, Butz ran his own foreign policy and had his own diplomatic corps and his own independent representation at the White House.[48]

Case 3. Salvador Allende and the CIA as a foreign ministry • Earl Butz went to his political grave believing that "corn is helping to maintain peace in the world," and that food "kept the Russians on the sidelines" in 1975 while Secretary of State Kissinger was negotiating a Middle East peace agreement. There is a lot of truth in these contentions. Because of the world food situation, the United States Department of Agriculture is able to maintain its own foreign ministry. But on what basis does the CIA also maintain still another foreign ministry?

In 1970, Salvador Allende won the presidency of the Republic of Chile. Allende was the first avowed Marxist ever to win a free election in this hemisphere and he was watched hopefully by left-wing parties throughout the rest of the world and very apprehensively by the United States. During his electoral campaign, his opposition was in part financed by contributions made secretly by an American conglomerate, International Telephone and Telegraph (ITT). ITT eventually admitted having spent at least $350,000 in the campaign, and many will argue that the amount was closer to a million dollars. While these expenditures were not actually illegal under American or Chilean law, our own attitude toward such direct intervention was indicated by the pandemonium which arose in 1976 and 1977 over the Korean lobbying efforts in Washington.

Apparently the CIA had nothing to do with channeling the ITT funds into the Chilean elections. However, the CIA was drawn directly into Chilean

48. Details of the 1975 situation were drawn primarily from James Risser and George Anthan, "Why They Love Earl Butz," *New York Times Magazine*, June 13, 1976, p. 10 and pp. 48–54.

ereafter as part of President Nixon's decision to "destabilize" ernment. Nixon's efforts intensified after Allende nationalized dollars of United States investments and opened diplomatic ʻidel Castro. Part of our retaliation against Allende was open, ɪrough channels. Credit through American banks and the Export-Import bank was cut. An embargo was placed upon American aid and development programs. But a large part of our campaign against Allende was secret and outside the established channels of international relations. Secrecy was maintained not because our opposition to Allende or our various embargos required secrecy—and, indeed, they were not secret to the Chileans—but because our actions were distinctly at variance with accepted practices of diplomatic relationships and in violation of virtually every dimension of the code of international conduct we had been trying to establish and maintain since becoming a world power. Apparently all President Nixon needed to say was, "Get rough." This was enough to remove the conduct of our relations with Chile from the State Department and put them into an alternative foreign ministry, the CIA.

Ironically, the prevailing theory about Allende at the time was that his policies would probably bring down his regime because they were irrational, self-defeating, enormously inflationary, and shortsighted. But we were unwilling to test this theory. Like Lenin, we arranged for a vanguard to insure the inevitable. We will probably never know exactly what the CIA did in Chile, but public investigations and responsible scholars have well enough documented the fact that the CIA did not limit its activities to the collection of intelligence for use by senior policy-makers to improve peacefully the realization of our interests abroad.

The CIA was created in 1947 to centralize and coordinate the collection, analysis, and dissemination of foreign intelligence. It was an acute response to our failure in 1941 to accumulate the various bits of data coming in from different sources which, if assimilated, might have enabled us to predict the attack on Pearl Harbor. But two things happened to the CIA as it tried to make its place in the national scheme. First, existing intelligence units, including the FBI, refused to cooperate with the director of Central Intelligence (DCI). Consequently, thirty years later there were still over twenty agencies responsible for gathering and disseminating different kinds of international intelligence—three of which are separate agencies within the CIA itself. And since the CIA is only one of many intelligence gatherers, its data have been relegated for analysis mainly to working-level officials rather than to senior policy-makers.[49] The second development, equally early in the CIA's history, was the taking on of covert or clandestine activities along with the collection of international intelligence. The ability to engage in clandestine activities

49. Drawn from the final report of the Senate Intelligence Committee on the activities of the Central Intelligence Agency as reported verbatim in the *New York Times*, June 7, 1976, p. 24.

was considered absolutely vital during the height of the cold war. However, as the cold war became less frigid, the capacity for clandestine activity was not reduced, and there continued all through the 1960s to be instances of important clandestine activity by the CIA, though no one knows if the scale and frequency was as great as during the 1950s. What we do know is that it still holds the highest importance in the esteem of the officials in the CIA. For example, except for the brief period of James Schlesinger's directorship during the CIA's greatest crisis, all of the directors have been agency careerists recruited through the Clandestine Service within the CIA.[50]

Thus the CIA became the arm of American foreign relations in Chile, just as it had been the arm for John Kennedy in Cuba in 1961 and, jointly with the Marines, for Lyndon Johnson in the Dominican Republic in 1965. Apparently, whenever there is uncertainty about the outcome of a transaction—whether it is economic or political—the president and his foreign policy elite seem to look among their three or four foreign ministries and pick the most military approach to the problem. It is not always the CIA; it is not always the Marines or a combination of the CIA and Marines. Moreover, the military careerist is not always the most militaristic of our foreign policy analysts. Nonetheless, our multiple-ministry foreign policy establishment seems to have a heavy military bias. This preference and pattern existed long before Richard Nixon came to office.

Case 4. Treasury, another foreign ministry • On August 15, 1971, President Nixon announced his decision to terminate the convertibility of dollars into gold and to impose a surcharge of 10 percent on all imports. This was a drastically new international economic policy, and it shocked Americans as well as Europeans. The surprise itself was of course necessary, if the decision was to be made at all, because advance consultation, with the likelihood of leakage, would have resulted in a frenzy of international currency speculation. However, what is interesting about this decision is the background of participation in it. According to the best available reports, the action was taken after consultation between Nixon and a small group of his advisors meeting at Camp David on August 13–14. The group included the secretary and undersecretary of the Treasury, the president of the Federal Reserve Board, the director of the Office of Management and Budget, two members of the Council of Economic Advisors, and the head of the recently established Council on International Economic Policy. Conspicuously absent were Henry Kissinger, Secretary of State William Rogers, and any other representative of the State Department.[51]

The meeting was dominated by Secretary of the Treasury John Connally, who had joined the Cabinet about six months prior to that time and had

50. Ibid.

51. This account is drawn primarily from Wilfrid Kohl, "The Nixon-Kissinger Foreign Policy System and U.S.-European Relations," *World Politics* (October 1975), pp. 1–43.

become very close to President Nixon. Consultation had not spread beyond the aforementioned group; in fact the Council for International Economic Policy was not even used as a mechanism of consultation. For about three months following this announcement there was a great deal of activity among high policy-makers and middle-level bureaucrats in Washington, mainly aimed at heading off the decision and John Connally's influence on foreign policy. Here again, Secretary of State Rogers stayed out of the struggle. Those who joined the struggle were operating under great fear that the European position would harden into retaliation and that the whole international trade system would revert to old-fashioned mercantilism.

Eventually, the anti-Connally coalition managed to have an influence on Kissinger and Nixon, but not before Secretary Connally was able to succeed in negotiating the realignment of the currencies of all the industrial nations of the world in the Smithsonian Agreement of December 1971. A few days later President Nixon in a conciliatory gesture lifted the import surcharge.

The Treasury Department has held the dominant influence in international monetary policy for a long while. The secretary is an important figure; perhaps of even greater importance in everyday affairs are the undersecretary for monetary affairs and the assistant secretary for international affairs. This latter office has a staff of over two hundred professional economists plus access to economists in other Treasury bureaus.[52] With this kind of backing and his own peculiar kind of confidence, Secretary Connally accomplished an enormous innovation in American foreign policy, with the support of the entire elite of foreign policy-making, including the president. Although based on technical expertise and a large and prestigious bureaucracy, the influence of John Connally, and his predecessors in that office, was not technological nor limited to narrow and specialized areas. It was the tail that wagged the dog; it was possibly the tail that became the dog. Treasury rises and falls in influence, depending upon world economic conditions and upon the personality and commitments of the occupant of the secretary's office. But no one can doubt that within its very large domain, the Department of Treasury is one of America's important foreign ministries.

THE LEGACY OF THE DEMOCRATS

The foreign policy establishment identified by these four cases is the liberal legacy extending back at least to the end of World War II. This was the foreign policy establishment Richard Nixon inherited in 1969. The record will show that he coped with it better than the Democrats had but that ultimately it was his undoing.

All during the 1960s, the Department of State had continued its long-range

52. Stephen D. Cohen, *The Making of United States International Economic Policy* (New York: Praeger, 1977), p. 46.

decline toward a position as no more than one of the many foreign policy agencies. This is an incredible status for a department that houses the institutions of diplomacy. But that is precisely indicative of the development in the liberal state in the United States: fragmentation; the application of domestic political principles to the international realm; the effort to displace domestic problems onto the world.

Fragmentation, in the form of multiple foreign ministries, each with a legal right to conduct its own foreign policy and a legal right to be consulted in the definition of national interests, gave us Vietnam, among other things. Account after account has shown how we were drawn into that war, slice by slice, and, once in, how we converted it into a war to end all wars.[53] Each tactical failure became the basis for another strategic escalation, not because failure produces success but because failure was defined as success. Liberals had put such high value on hardheaded practicality that they held rigidly to the belief that we were really fighting China in Vietnam.

They were also hardheaded about the fragmented bureaucracies available to them for the conduct of foreign affairs. This was seen as an opportunity, and an opportunity that must be pursued vigorously after the Bay of Pigs fiasco had given the Kennedy Administration such an antagonistic distrust of several of these agencies. Kennedy beefed up the White House capacity to cope with the State Department's dispatches, including a capability to produce the White House's own intelligence. The White House staff grew; it became filled with distinguished, hardheaded, experienced foreign policy analysts— "the best and the brightest." Kennedy sought to become his own secretary of State, undermining still further the status of institutionalized diplomacy and the ideal of a dominant single foreign ministry in the State Department. Not only did he make fairly clear what his own role was expected to be, he chose as his special assistant for international security affairs McGeorge Bundy, a man who was not only closer to Camelot but had actually opposed the appointment of Dean Rusk as secretary of State. Kennedy also put Douglas Dillon, a man of much higher standing in the private international affairs community, at Treasury, another of the separate foreign ministries in the United States.

Perhaps of even greater significance was the structure and orientation of the Defense Department in the 1960s. The appointment of Robert MacNamara was part of a general effort to put the military in their place and, in fact, to impose some coordination over the services. MacNamara was not merely the image of the successful executive, manager, and planner. He was the incarnation of rational analysis. He had been in on the development of systems analy-

---

53. Two of the most devastating accounts, precisely because they are written on a human scale with considerable sympathy, are David Halberstam, *The Best and the Brightest* (New York: Random House, 1972), and Philip Caputo, *A Rumor of War* (New York: Holt, Rinehart & Winston, 1977).

sis and engineering, first in the university, then in the war, and then with his Whiz Kids at Ford Motor Company, where these new methods of management were given credit for having turned the company around. He was to reduce costs and to give the president a way to confront the experience and intuitions of the military with the hardheaded rationality of the new liberal civilians. Methods of rational analysis vary, but they all revolve around the use of hard data and computer technology to identify options, to lay the costs and gains of each option out on the table, and to present to the highest policymakers a set of weighted alternatives—not merely this plane against that, but this strategy against that, and, ultimately a diplomatic versus a military option, an economic versus a political option, and so on. There was no end to what such a systems analysis might help produce. But its immediate value was to reduce the stature of the old military leadership and to enable the president to cope with an otherwise impossibly fragmented system—without actually trying to unify it.

The trouble is that reduction of the influence of military personnel comes at a cost, or involves a trade-off. It actually meant further reliance upon private industry to develop the new weapons and weapons systems. The systems approach upgraded the younger and civilian components of the Defense Department, but it also upgraded the civilian components of research and development and the civilian components of foreign affairs. It was as though Eisenhower's farewell warning about the specter of the military-industrial complex were simply the ravings of an outmoded partisan.

Rational analysis implied that the entire, fragmented apparatus could be left intact and coped with from the center by management through appropriate calculation and manipulation based upon the information (which would now be called data) flowing in from those very agencies, the multiple foreign ministries, whose actions and decisions would ultimately have to be integrated.[54] And this would in no way be inconsistent with the great public campaigns of overselling remedies and overselling threats. With his mass public techniques, the president could on a few occasions wage his war to "unify the elite by unifying the masses." Rational analysis would be one more device for coping with fragmentation, the more appealing because liberals love rationality. No matter that dependable data on goals, costs, methods, truly comparable alternatives, and so forth, were needed before the analysis could work. No matter that this requirement led to "body counts" as our measure of the effectiveness of weapons and strategies in Vietnam. No matter that self-interest and cynicism led the military and lower-level officials to falsification of all the data necessary to carry out the continuing analysis. The "best and the brightest" were undone by a decision-making formula they had adopted precisely to produce automatic decisions and legitimate coordination. Rational

54. For a sober, and sobering, assessment of decision-making models, see Richard R. Nelson, *The Moon and the Ghetto* (New York: Norton, 1977).

analysis exacerbated rather than solved the unhappy tendencies inherent in multiple foreign ministries. And rational analysis added to the Democratic legacy, when subtraction is what was needed.

THE NIXON RESPONSE

Richard Nixon brought to the White House more foreign affairs experience than any Democrat in the twentieth century and almost as much as some of his Republican predecessors, such as Eisenhower, Hoover, and Taft. Moreover, Nixon demonstrated a decisiveness and adroitness that earned him the begrudging admiration of many of his most aggressive adversaries. Nonetheless, he had inherited a fragmented and, by 1969, demoralized foreign affairs establishment in which the White House had to fight it out among a dozen major contenders for foreign policy primacy.[55] Despite his tremendous ambition to establish a unique place for himself in foreign affairs, he went about coping with the foreign policy establishment in an old and familiar way. Just like John Kennedy in 1961, Richard Nixon sought to be his own secretary of State. Like Kennedy, he kept his foreign policy strength in the White House by choosing the immensely talented Henry Kissinger as his special assistant for national security affairs. A much weaker person, and close and loyal friend, William Rogers, was made secretary of State. To stake out the superiority of the White House in foreign affairs, Nixon expanded his foreign policy White House staff to fifty-two persons by 1972.[56] Nixon sought still further to gain coordination around himself by establishing a new agency for intelligence, the Foreign Intelligence Advisory Board, even while using the CIA

55. A few statistics may help indicate the extent of our foreign policy fragmentation and may help underscore the significance of the problem facing presidents when they want some kind of unified posture. As of the early 1970s, only 16.6 percent of all American employees working abroad were working for the State Department in diplomatic activities. Nearly 12.4 percent were State Department employees attached to other agencies. All the rest (71 percent) worked for such agencies as Defense (28.7 percent) or domestic departments with large international commitments, such as Treasury and Agriculture (15.4 percent). These figures are based upon total employees that do not include the CIA and the NSA. Take one other example. As of 1974, 3,656 officially accredited government delegates attended official international meetings, representing the United States. Less than half are State Department delegates. The first set of figures comes from I. M. Desler, *Presidents, Bureaucrats and Foreign Policy* (Princeton: Princeton University Press, 1972), pp. 10–11. Figures on delegates were drawn from Robert Keohane and Joseph Nye, *Power and Interdependence* (Boston: Little, Brown, 1978), p. 241. The conclusion Keohane and Nye draw from these kinds of figures is highly supportive of the picture I am trying to draw in this chapter, although the two of them take a more positive and optimistic attitude toward it: "Thus, miniature foreign offices, which have evolved in many United States domestic agencies, are not mere bureaucratic nuisances, but have a positive role in managing interdependence. They need to be sufficiently well controlled that they do not establish separate bureaucratic fiefdoms that form coalitions with counterpart agencies to thwart official government policies; but the transgovernmental policy coordination that they engage in is essential" (p. 241).

56. Compare that to the eleven White House foreign policy aides to Franklin D. Roosevelt during World War II. These figures are from Graham Allison and Peter Szanton, "Organizing for the Decade Ahead," p. 254.

more than his predecessors to provide intelligence for himself. In addition, by having such close personal and political associates as Melvin Laird at Defense and eventually John Connally at Treasury, Nixon tried to impose unification through his National Security Council, of which these Cabinet officials are the key members along with the secretary of State.

We are only now beginning to find out how much further Richard Nixon went to gain foreign policy unification through his effort to organize a national and international war on drugs. Whatever his motives, the Drug Enforcement Agency did hold out some promise to the president as a means of coordinating such agencies as the FBI, the CIA, the Bureau of Narcotics, and other agencies that are able to conduct their own foreign policies. It is indicative that many of the people he eventually used to keep his administration from crashing down—John Ehrlichman, Egil Krogh, Howard Hunt, Gordon Liddy, David Mardian, and John Dean—were people he had employed in his unified drug campaign.[57]

President Nixon's efforts to unify the foreign policy establishment were entirely consistent with the efforts of his Democratic predecessors, and were entirely rational, especially considering the situation he had inherited: He was, as president, personally responsible for setting the world to rights, but he had inherited a war not of his making, a deteriorating international situation, the distinct possibility of a real missile or technological gap, a deterioration of domestic legitimacy, the rising tide of domestic dissent, and the absolute need to face the world with a single national posture while being flanked by as many as a dozen agencies each with its own foreign policy. Consequently, tinkerings with the national security establishment were not going to be enough, and it was going to be too little as well as too late to try the even more substantial change of unifying State with White House by the appointment of Kissinger as secretary of State while retaining him as National Security Advisor in the White House. Nixon, therefore, had to resort to the same forms of authoritarianism and demagoguery to which his immediate predecessors had been led. He had to try, as they had, to unify his elite by unifying the masses.

His methods are well known, better so because of the investigations during the Watergate scandal, but they are far less appreciated as consistent with the methods of his predecessors. And they are consistent because all recent presidents have had to respond to the same structure, the same intractably fragmented foreign policy process. Nixon sold his escalation of the Vietnam War as a peace crusade. He claimed to be bombing the North Vietnamese to the armistice table when in fact his primary obstruction was the South Vietnamese and their holding out for assurances that their regime would be maintained no matter what.[58] He sought to unify the national security agencies by

57. Edward Jay Epstein, *Agency of Fear* (New York: Putnam, 1977).
58. See Walter La Feber, *America, Russia, and the Cold War—1945–75* (New York: Wiley, 1976), p. 277.

declaring a gigantic war against heroin. He needed that war against which to make a broad declaration and to raise American fears, and he needed it as a pretext to create his own national police force.[59] He and his special assistant, Henry Kissinger, used international travel, not only as a means of conducting direct diplomacy, but as a means of manipulating press coverage and the public opinion polls.[60] His international travels, and those of Henry Kissinger, became more frequent as the Watergate scandal began to undermine his administration.

These methods and others were altogether typical of the Democratic techniques of oversell. There was the gigantic oversell of the energy crisis. There was the oversell of the presidency itself and its need to engage in illegal conduct, as the only way we can extricate ourselves from international peril. And there was, of course, the oversell of the domestic threat to our role in foreign affairs. In fact, it is quite possible that demagoguery is inherently associated with the suppression of dissent. In any case, Nixon followed the lead of Johnson by making up artificially for the unity he could not get through his campaigns of oversell. His carefully selected, ex-CIA plumbers were employed to use illegal tactics to plug leaks inside officialdom. Large public agencies, such as the Army, the CIA, the FBI, and the Internal Revenue Service, were also assigned to find the real enemies and to put them under surveillance, no matter how many such persons there were. Mass illegal arrests were made. At least a hundred thousand civilians were eventually put under surveillance, illegally, by the United States Army. Untold additional thousands were put crudely under surveillance by other agencies—crudely because knowledge of being under surveillance has its own chilling effect, totally aside from any information that might be picked up. Watergate was itself a mere symptom of the politics of foreign policy in the contemporary United States. In that particular instance, America gained a great deal from the competition among the multiple foreign ministries; but it is easy to draw the wrong principle from this. The wrong principle would be that we should continue to have many foreign ministries so that their competition will give us counterpoise against an autocratic president. Despite the profit we gained from competition in the Watergate affair, the fact remains that many foreign ministries will simply produce many foreign policies and a tendency toward oversell, militarism, and overkill. Though there are no absolutes in foreign policy, we would be at least closer to a defensible moral position if we drew from this case the principle not that multiple foreign ministries are worthwhile, but simply that high-ranking officials have a moral obligation not to engage in patently illegal actions. If we could establish that principle, we could afford to rid ourselves of all of the independent agencies and to have a single and mature foreign ministry in the United States.

59. Edward Jay Epstein, *Agency of Fear*.
60. See the example in Table 6.1.

Leaders in Congress did not fail to recognize some of the basic flaws in the foreign policy establishment; they began to react to them even before the Johnson administration ended. But Congress's behavior was meek and floundering until the Nixon Administration gave the Democratic majority a solid focus. Congressional action did not become well organized and concerted until 1973, when the Watergate scandal began to reveal the extent of manipulation, lying, political suppression, and illegality. The reaction probably began in 1970 when Congress, with Nixon's cooperation, sought to reassemble some of the powers it had squandered on the president by the Gulf of Tonkin Resolution. But this was a fruitless gesture, as quickly indicated by President Nixon himself with his unilateral and unannounced invasion of Cambodia. The president's top legal advisors, William Rehnquist—whom President Nixon later appointed to the Supreme Court as a strict constructionist—testified before a congressional committee that the president's unilateral action was "a valid exercise of his constitutional authority as Commander-in-Chief to secure the safety of American forces." This claim to inherent power and prerogative guided Nixon throughout his Administration. But having rejected Tonkin, and then having its rejection rejected by the president, Congress took about three years to reassert itself along several very important fronts. Following is a list of congressional actions, all taken in 1973, which were aimed at restoring some kind of balance between the two branches:

1. Forced cancelation of Nixon's request to create a supercabinet of four major department heads who would also hold positions as special assistants to the president in the White House.

2. Enactment of the War Powers Resolution (over President Nixon's veto) which required the president to report to Congress within forty-eight hours any commitment of American military forces, and to obtain Congress's approval within sixty days.

3. Enactment of the congressional Budget and Impoundment Control Act, which provided an entirely new structure of congressional control over fiscal policy and the executive budget, and for some elaborate safeguards against presidential power to undermine congressional intent through impoundments and deferrals by requiring the president to submit proposed cuts or deferrals to Congress for approval within forty-five days.

4. Sought and got new congressional investigatory powers, validated by Supreme Court rejection of President Nixon's claim that executive privilege is absolute, including total control over the White House tapes.

5. Drove the president from office in anticipation of an almost certain impeachment and conviction.

But to what effect? Congressional reaction in 1973, rather than ending the interest-group-liberal pattern of foreign policy, reinforced it. There is hardly any question that Congress was more powerful and more assertive in relation to the president than it had been for many years prior to 1973. This is probably true despite the fact that Congress gave President Ford their *post hoc* approval for his discretionary and unilateral action invading Cambodian territory to rescue the American supply vessel the *Mayaguez*. But the key to the problem of American foreign policy on into the 1970s is to be found in the contrast between the very real reassertion of congressional power and the capitulation of Congress in face of the *Mayaguez* episode. As in the 1960s, Congress seems still to vacillate between meticulous meddling and slavish cooperation, probably depending upon whether the president can convince the public he is operating under conditions of emergency. And presidents have proved time after time that they can create and confirm the impression of a state of emergency by their own assertions coupled with temporary suppression of the data. This is certainly true of the *Mayaguez* episode, despite the fact that it came so soon after all of the Vietnam and Watergate embarrassments attributable to the suppression of information.

Congress's reentry into the arena of foreign-policy-making seems to have reinforced the fragmentation that has been the prevailing characterization of our foreign policy establishment. Congress tends to impose upon the foreign policy establishment the very domestic patterns of politics that have prevented the emergence of a separate and calm and integrated foreign ministry. Congress reinforces that fragmentation by becoming an additional agency of foreign policy. Recognition of that fact has drawn many a foreign lobbyist toward Congress rather than the State Department. (This was going on long before the "Koreagate" scandal.) Congress also tends to reinforce fragmentation by its tendency to convert foreign policy issues into constituency problems. Congressional committees tend to protect their favorite agencies— surely that is part of the secret of the ability of Agriculture, Labor, and Treasury to maintain their own foreign ministries.[61]

The record of the United States in world affairs since World War II probably compares favorably with the records of other major world powers during the same period, and, especially during other postwar periods prior to the time when we were one of the leaders. But that is hardly a sufficient judgment. In the first place, we do not stand up well when we judge ourselves by our own aspirations. Deliberate subversions of electoral processes or elected regimes— in Vietnam (1956), in the Dominican Republic (1965), and in Chile (1970–73)—go contrary to everything we were taught to hold dear. The same is true of foreign assassination plots (Castro) and the killing of nonbelligerents (in Vietnam, Cambodia, Laos, and the Dominican Republic). Support for to-

61. James Sundquist provides an ancient example with great contemporary relevance with a story told by Henry Stimson about the chairman of the old House Naval Affairs Committee shortly after World War I. Responding to the charge that the navy yard in his district was too small to accommodate the latest battleships, the chairman replied, "That is true, and that is the reason I have always been in favor of small ships" (Sundquist, "Congress and the President: Enemies or Partners?" in Owen and Schultze, eds., *Setting National Priorities*, p. 600).

talitarian dictatorships is also absolutely contrary to our values; yet we have not only supported them publicly in what might be required for normal diplomatic relationships but we have gone out of our way to support them with military and economic aid and with our cooperation in the suppression of their opposition parties or factions. Outright bribery of foreign elites and involvement in their electoral processes also cuts sharply into the quick of American values, whether the bribery involves Chilean legislators or oil potentates in the Middle East. Since the Watergate investigations and the publication of the Pentagon Papers, we are painfully aware of the frequency with which our leaders have kept secrets from the American public which the rest of the world already knew. This is indicative of the extent to which our actions have unnecessarily violated our norms.

In the second place, our comparatively good record is not good enough because we continually violate, even when we succeed, the standards of conduct appropriate for the world's most powerful nation: consistency, predictability, sobriety. We will never achieve those standards so long as we leave the entire responsibility for foreign affairs with the president whose task is complicated by having to cope with several separate and independent foreign ministries, a defensive Congress, and a plebiscitary relationship with a phantom public.

The Federative Power: Beginning of Maturity

Democracy is not safe for the world so long as it is not organized for consistently rational action. Without a capacity for real planning, allies cannot trust the system and enemies can too easily miscalculate.

As should by now be clear, the villain of the piece has never been the public, the foreign affairs agencies, Congress, its committees or leaders, the president, the military-industrial complex, or the peace agitators. The villain is the outmoded system itself and the outmoded beliefs that support it. It is the system itself that has so often made our international relations so inimical to our own best interests. Interest-group liberalism did not, of course, create this system, but interest-group liberalism perpetuates it by worshiping its virtues. The liberal system today is an anachronism in foreign affairs. The liberal presidency is a hopeless burden for the man and a dangerous responsibility for the country.

After thirty years of world leadership we must ask how a pluralistic democracy can adjust to the requirements of its world role. The interest-group-liberal, quasi-egalitarian requirement will never be conducive to modern foreign-policy-making. The autonomy of international agencies, the direct and intimate relationship of our plebiscitary president to his public, and the opportunities each has to influence the other, are as frightful for foreign policy as they would be attractive for domestic policy.

Adjustment will obviously not be easy, even if possible. A step in the proper direction might be taken, however, by appreciating the fact that democracy does have its problems. We could take the most productive step beyond that if we find, next war, some means of imposing the most severe requirements of self-restraint upon our leaders, in their relations with each other and with the public at large. Ultimately the solution will be found in restoring respect for formal institutions and for the roles assigned to them before the outbreak of a war. This involves returning to John Locke's *Second Treatise*. If we wish to salvage our eighteenth-century system we will have to take as an essential part of the Separation of Powers the separation of the "federative power," by which Locke meant, "what is to be done in reference to foreigners."

At first these proposals may seem to constitute an elitist view of a cure. But it is elitist only in the sense that democracy does have special elitist tendencies. The elite in a democracy is comprised of those persons directly responsible to the largest electorates. This elite was expected to have great powers—allowable because the elite could be peacefully cashiered—but great powers nonetheless.

This is actually a *formalistic* rather than an elitist view. And that returns us to a central concern of this book. Legitimacy is bound to suffer if the real veers too far away from the formal. There is bound to be great natural divergence, but why make a virtue of it? A legitimate democracy is a very formalistic system. Everything about it is an attempt to commit power to a regular and understandable exercise. Americans in particular have always been committed to these forms as though they had some bearing on realities. Even the greatest of informalisms, political parties, are subject to hundreds of pages and thousands of titles and sections of state laws. Voluntary associations operate by an iron law of formalism whereby after the first meeting they give themselves a name and elect officers, and after the second meeting write themselves a constitution.

Until recent years these preferences were called due process, and too much informality was called arbitrariness. In our times, stress on formalities is pejoratively called formalism, and informality is called flexibility, participatory democracy, creative federalism, or even due process. This is why the new liberal state suffers from illegitimacy despite its generosity. That is why it is weak at planning, domestic or foreign. That is also why the liberal state cannot achieve justice, an oft-repeated proposition which must now be tackled head on.

Part III

WHY LIBERAL GOVERNMENTS CANNOT ACHIEVE JUSTICE

"[W]e find ourselves on wide, filthy, hostile Fifth Avenue, facing that project which hangs over the avenue like a monument to the folly and the cowardice of good intentions. . . . The projects in Harlem are hated. They are hated almost as much as policemen, and this is saying a great deal. And they are hated for the same reason: both reveal, unbearably, the real attitude of the white world, no matter how many liberal speeches are made."

James Baldwin

7

CITIES
The American Tragedy

The United States has been an urban nation for several decades. Why now, when resources should be sufficient to meet basic needs, are cities continually demonstrating their inability to sustain themselves and their citizens? In the 1960s the liberal state seemed to have the answer. In fact it had several answers. Take, for example, the so-called Moynihan Report of 1965. It blamed the problems in the cities on the dissolution of black families and the black ghetto social structure. This conveniently proved that the struggle would be long and would ultimately rest more upon general improvement within the black community than upon any changes made by the majority community or through formal redress at law. A second presidential inquiry, following the Los Angeles riots in the Watts area, took a straight deterministic view, laying the blame upon economic deprivation. This conveniently proved that such national social programs as the War on Poverty were the best of all possible urban and civil-rights approaches. A third presidential inquiry, completed at the time of Martin Luther King's assassination, was brutally frank in its position that the blame lay with white bigotry. However, this only proved that the burden of revolution should fall upon the white lower classes.[1]

Presidential inquiries running all the way back to the Truman Committee on Civil Rights in the late 1940s have expressed strong sympathy for cities and their black citizens; yet, except for the Truman Committee, these reports have received a good deal less than enthusiastic reception among black leaders. And there may be very good reasons for their coolness. First, these inquiries in particular have implied that as cities became more black they also became more problematic. Second, though none of the inquiries show that conditions in the black ghettos today differ greatly from conditions prevailing when other ethnic groups were on the bottom, they do imply that the response of

---

1. The Moynihan Report was published first in a document entitled *The Negro Family—The Case for National Action* (Washington, D.C.: Office of Policy Planning and Research, U.S. Department of Labor, 1965). The second of these reports was *A Time to Listen . . . A Time to Act* (Washington, D.C.: U.S. Commission on Civil Rights, 1967). The third of these reports was the *Report of the Presidential Commission on Civil Disorders* (New York: Bantam, 1968).

blacks to those conditions has been more extreme. A socially deterministic explanation for conduct—which almost all applied social scientists assume—tends toward an uncomfortable conclusion that blacks made an inferior adjustment. The response to that kind of implication was a plea for greater black participation in the affairs of the society. This was a straight interest-group liberal sentiment, predicated upon the notion that lack of participation produced the problem and that more participation would give blacks the internal organization they needed as well as the morale or whatever it takes to become better and more obedient citizens.[2]

A third dimension of the coolness of black attitudes toward these presidential inquiries could be the absence of any reflections upon governmental structure itself. Government officials did admit that there was insufficient participation within government. Public commissions even admitted that police and other agents of government had occasionally been guilty of criminal misbehavior, as in the case of police rioting against the white rioters in Chicago during the 1968 Democratic National Convention and against the black rioters in Miami at the same time. But none of the self-critical official studies confronted the basic problem. It is the contention of this and the succeeding chapters that life is on the decline in our cities in large part because governmental structure has become incapable of dealing with modern social problems. This is a relatively new factor in American history and it is important enough to exacerbate the problems of any persons living in central cities. The analysis of this problem rests on three interrelated ideas:

1. Liberal ideologies foster and support a division of powers such that the real sources of the urban crisis of our time fall in a no-man's-land among duly constituted but politically impoverished governments inside the metropolitan regions.

2. Liberal ideology in the guise of local government reform has so structured the central city government and most of the local governments in the suburbs that they are increasingly incapable of using in a socially significant way the vast powers that do remain in their hands.

3. Urban areas have failed to get socially meaningful support from Washington because the presidency in the liberal state is incapable of dealing in a direct and discretionary and personally responsible way with urban life.

---

2. At the very same time, other studies were beginning to question the comfortable myths about the low level of indigenous organization and family structure inside the black community. See, for example, the important but obscure study of the National Health and Welfare Council (sponsored by the National Institute of Mental Health) which was published actually during the time most of these important presidential commissions were conducting their inquiries. Reported in the *New York Times*, February 20, 1966. See also a good review of the entire literature in Thomas F. Pettigrew, ed., *Racial Discrimination in the United States* (New York: Harper & Row, 1975).

Old Shame and New

Something indeed is new in urban America, but it will not be found by sifting through social and economic causes. It will be found in the governmental structure of the metropolis and in the structure of the major centers within each metropolis. The metropolis has become hopelessly fragmented while the cities within them have become overorganized, but in the wrong terms.

FRAGMENTING THE METROPOLITAN REGION: DIVIDING THE INDIVISIBLE

The city was never a melting pot. It has always been a boiling pot. Americans have reason to be proud of their social history because they have had so much to adjust to; but there was never a period free of problems with what we now euphemistically call intergroup relations. And violence has always been an important method of settling intergroup conflict in the United States. Although many problems, perhaps a majority of problems, have been settled peacefully, violence has always been an integral part of urban, nay social, life in the history of the United States. Moreover, a still greater number of our problems were probably solved neither by peaceful adjustment nor by violence: The pot simply boiled over. Many escaped to the West; most simply escaped to areas just beyond the city.

This is not a new pattern. Cities have always grown at their peripheries. Escape from the city is as old as the cities themselves. R. E. Park and E. W. Burgess plot out the fossil remains of outward movement in their concentric circle theory of Chicago.[3] Between 1910 and 1930, the old city of St. Louis along the Mississippi lost 50,000 inhabitants, while the greater city itself was growing. Then as now, the center spilled over into its periphery.

Closer examination of the makeup of the earlier population movements suggests that the reasons for growth through escape to the periphery were also about the same, even before the automobile age. The reasons are hate and fear. Yankees hated the Germans and the Irish, and escaped to whatever was a suburb at the time of the escape. The Germans and Irish hated and feared the Jews, Italians, Bohemians, Poles, and Greeks—and they, too, escaped. All of them hated and feared the varieties of "poor white trash" who inherited the third and fourth generations of central ruins in the wake of their escaping predecessors. Large parts of Harlem were Jewish before they were black. Common fear and hatred by whites of all nonwhites and off-whites is one more turn in the cycle, and it can hardly be the last turn. For example, black middle classes do not rest easy with white or black lower classes. As one

3. See Robert E. Park et al., *The City* (Chicago: University of Chicago Press, 1925).

Chicago comedian put it, "The black and white walk shoulder to shoulder against the lower classes."

If all of these patterns are about the same as before, then the original question becomes even more compelling: Why in the recent past have cities shown increasing signs of decline, disorder, and insolvency?

During the 1920s and 1930s, something much more important than northward immigration or the automobile began to happen to the cities. The residents of the outer periphery of virtually every city in the country began to erect political barriers to the development of the center. The suburban city fathers did the impossible: They divided the indivisible. Until the 1920s east of the Mississippi and more recently further west, the city as a political and governmental entity grew along with its population. Governmental jurisdiction tended to go wherever the escapees went, and the governmental city could remain nearly coextensive with the socioeconomic city. The legal city was about the same as the real city. City problems were not necessarily larger than city power or city resources.

Between the two World Wars, governmental jurisdiction became as selective as the escape pattern itself. In the real city—the metropolitan region— there emerged a large number of political jurisdictions where once there had been only one or a few. In short order each developed its own interests and sense of integrity, for in each case the city fathers knew what they wanted. Incorporation as a legal principality gave each suburb power to defend itself by zoning, taxation, the provision of services, and the manipulation of building codes. More generally, incorporation gave them power to enact and preserve their version of the American way of life. Obviously this gave an entirely new meaning to the old practice of escaping the center of the city.

The new pattern of political subdivision cut the central cities off from their best human and material resources. Cities have been the source of the great American dynamism. But even if this is changing, cities continue to specialize in another function absolutely vital to the societies: The cities specialize in immigrants, in the absorption of lower classes, in the induction of new peoples into the culture, and in the care of the elderly. That is to say, American cities specialize in the care of those in greatest need of attention and who have the least experience or ability to govern themselves. The city has replaced the family, the tribe, the neighborhood, or the internment camp as the collecting place for the dependent. *Yet, as each city incorporates more and more needy people, it becomes less and less successful in keeping up with its most successful residents.* They have escaped from Hyde Park to Glencoe, from Brooklyn to Scarsdale. That is distinctly not the same as the previous escape from Chicago's West Side down to Hyde Park or from Manhattan's East Side over to Brooklyn.

The curves of despair in Figure 7.1 show this strong but inverse relationship between city needs and city capacities. Diagram A shows how strongly the factor of age can kill a city. Among the thirty-five cities which, at the time of the study, had most recently surpassed 50,000 in population, over 20 percent of their population growth between 1950 and 1960 was attributable to annexation. This means that the pattern of escape did not have overwhelmingly negative value to these cities; it continued merely to be a shift of population. Note in contrast how the forty-nine oldest cities grew through annexation by an average of less than 5 percent. Diagram B adds a special note of desperation to Diagram A because educational composition is a strong index of the city's capacity to prosper and of the capacity of its citizens to prosper with a minimum of public service or assistance. Here we see that educational composition exacerbates the problem of city age. The city whose typical adult was badly educated was also a city with a poor record of keeping up, through annexation, with the escape of its best educated adults. Among the forty cities whose adults were largely high school and college graduates, nearly 25 percent of their population growth was attributable to annexation of territory. In contrast, among the thirty-six cities in which the typical citizen was a school dropout, population growth through annexation of suburbs accounted for less than 5 percent of total growth.

Diagram C makes abundantly clear that the socially significant pictures presented in the first two diagrams are not spurious. The factor of city size itself, which most discerning observers would assume is of great importance, played almost no role in explaining why the old cities and the poorer cities have had such bad luck in keeping up with their escaping middle classes. Cities of over 500,000 population did almost as well (or poorly) as cities of only 80,000 and actually better than cities of around 100,000. Suburbanites fear the social characteristics of city populations and the aging of central city facilities rather than the size or the absolute age of the city.

This general, national pattern is complicated by some important regional variations. Controlling for region, and using percentage territorial growth rather than percentage population growth, the curves of despair turn out primarily to be a phenomenon of the Northeast and the older Midwest. Cities in the Sunbelt are continuing to annex territory in significant amounts.[4] Moreover, in many instances state laws in the Sunbelt facilitate the annexation of territories by central cities. For example, the state of Texas has an extremely liberal home-rule constitution which provides power to cities to set their own boundaries for territories lying adjacent to themselves. In addition, the Texas constitution prevents the incorporation of suburbs within two miles of the corporate limits of cities of over 25,000. This effectively postpones the time when the cities in the Sunbelt will have to face an iron ring.

4. Data on the annexation of territories will be found in *Adjusting Municipal Boundaries* (New York: National League of Cities, December 1966) and *Municipal Yearbook* (Washington, D.C.: International City Management Association, serially). My thanks to Professor Richard Bensel for perceiving the need for this analysis and for participating in it.

A. Annexation and city age

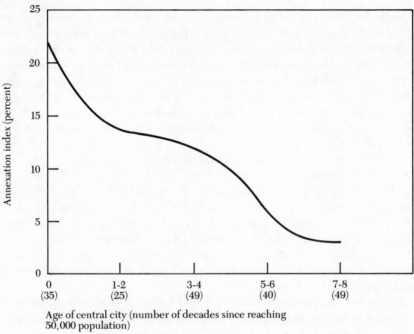

Age of central city (number of decades since reaching
50,000 population)

B. Annexation and level of education

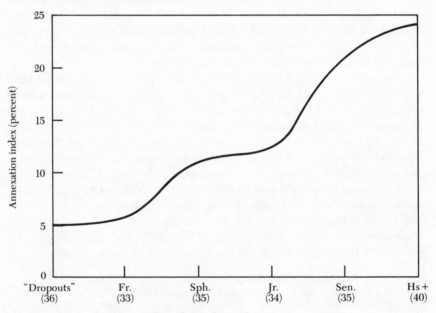

Median school years, all residents of central city

C. Annexation and size of city

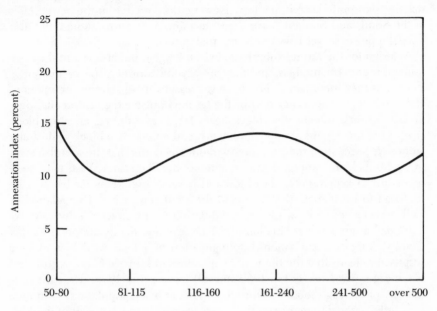

Size of central city (in thousands)

FIGURE 7.1 The Curves of Despair*

    * Data are drawn from the research of Professor Thomas R. Dye ("Urban Political Integration: Conditions Associated with Annexation in American Cities," *Midwest Political Science Quarterly* [November 1964], pp. 430–46), who does not necessarily agree with the conclusions here. Numbers in parenthesis represent the actual number of cities in each category. The total, 213, constitutes all of the Census Bureau's "urbanized areas" in 1960. The Annexation Index is a simple expression of the proportion of a city's growth of population between 1950 and 1960 which was attributable to annexation of new territory.

At first blush this Sunbelt pattern of continuing access of central cities to their immediate environs would seem to weaken the argument. However, a closer look will show that it actually strengthens the argument. Sunbelt cities are on the average newer, attract more capital, offer more employment opportunities, and are expanding at a rate that tends to soften class and racial conflict. Part of that expansion and part of that attractiveness to capital is attributable to the access of these cities to new territory without losing control over that territory. Annexation is in largest part controlled by state annexation laws, and these laws are very much a reflection of the preferences of powerful interests in a state. Thus, as in Texas, when cities are new and have everything economically going for them, they also have the ability to get or to maintain favorable annexation laws. Here is the original dilemma in another form. Cities most in need of reaching new territory and escaping middle classes lack the political power to get the necessary favorable state annexation laws; and the suburbs surrounding those same older cities have the power in state legislatures to keep it that way. Newer cities, or cities in the newer states of the South and Sunbelt, have access to more open surroundings and also have the power to get laws protecting that access.

As a sign for the future, suburbs do exist in large numbers even in the large Sunbelt metropolitan areas, and they are beyond control of the central cities as soon as they incorporate. For whatever reasons these suburbs incorporate, and to whatever extent they occupy the territory outside the central city, they in fact become an effective block against city growth, an effective block against the movement of city populations, and an effective block against city authority. Population statistics show without any doubt that the suburbs, even in the Sunbelt and among the newer cities of the Plains and West, have been successful in keeping out nonwhites and lower classes. Few readers will be surprised to learn that Washington in the 1970 census had a population of 72.1 percent nonwhite while the neighboring Montgomery County, Maryland, had a nonwhite population of 5.3 percent and the neighboring Fairfax County, Virginia, had a nonwhite population of 4.1 percent. Few may be surprised to learn that the nonwhite population in DuPage County, just west of Chicago, was 1 percent in 1960 and still 1 percent in 1970, while the central city of Chicago reported around 35 percent black population.[5] But note how little contrast there is with the newer metropolitan areas west of the Mississippi, despite the greater access of the central city to the open country beyond its borders; in 1970 there were just under 23 percent nonwhites in Kansas City, while in one neighboring county there were 18 percent, in another there were slightly over 1 percent, and in still another slightly under 1 percent. There were just under 13 percent nonwhites in Seattle in 1970, while in neighboring King County there were 7 percent and in neighboring Snohomish County there were under 2 percent. In the twin cities of San Francisco/Oakland there were, respectively, 28 percent and 41 percent nonwhites, while in the immediately neighboring counties there were 20 percent, 10 percent, 4 percent, and 8 percent nonwhites. Similar contrasts between central city and suburban counties will be found in the matter of median annual family income.[6]

These highly selective illustrations can be best generalized for the country

5. The figure of 1 percent does not do full justice to the situation in DuPage County. An NAACP study of 1967 revealed that there were only 589 blacks in DuPage County whose total population was 400,000. In a press release from Syd Finley to the Illinois Atomic Energy Commission, January 19, 1967, quoted in Theodore Lowi, Benjamin Ginsberg, et al., *Poliscide* (New York: Macmillan, 1976), p. 127. And, although Washington may not constitutionally annex territory, its suburbs are as selective and its center city problems are as pressing as are all the others.

6. Interestingly enough, among the few nonwhites who do reside in the suburbs, median annual family income is not appreciably higher than that of nonwhite families in the central cities. This suggests that a very high proportion of suburban black families earn their incomes from menial jobs and household services.

at large by drawing upon the disinterested observations of the *Municipal Year-book*:

The most striking feature of population change in the central cities continues to be the polarization of metropolitan populations resulting from a loss of white population and large increases in black population. . . . In suburban areas during 1960–70 the numbers of both blacks and whites grew by more than 25% (15 million whites and 800,000 blacks). The increase of whites in metropolitan areas took place entirely in the suburbs. The black population increased by 4 million in metropolitan areas, but only one-fifth of the increase was in suburban areas.[7]

This highly differential population growth is balkanizing all metropolitan areas, Northeast and elsewhere, and is everywhere producing the same kinds of problems, even though as yet to a slightly lesser degree west of the Mississippi. This is not altogether the result of racism as such; there is also the purely economic fact that lower income families require more local services. But regardless of the reason, suburbs everywhere resist the needs of the urban centers—as merely indicated by the discontinuity of population characteristics—and produce all of the conditions that lead principalities in the balkanized suburban areas to resist each other and to try to displace their costs upon each other. No matter how the problem is viewed, the tragedy appears about the same: Cities most in need are cities least able to provide.

Finally, differences between the Sunbelt and Northeast, such as those indicated by different annexation patterns and annexation laws, merely add complexity to an already highly variable phenomenon of the city in the United States. The federal system relegated the entire question of local government to the states; and most of the states, especially in the twentieth century, permitted localities much leeway in their own development. This variability alone renders virtually impossible any effort to produce a national urban policy that is at one and at the same time uniform, equal, equitable, fair, and clear. But that is far from all there is to the structural problem. Division of the metropolis into many principalities created or intensified the pressures of American urban life because of the artificiality of suburban government. Regardless of the variations in population movement and annexation patterns, and regardless of the many different motives that gave rise to separate suburban governments, suburbs are fictions, legal fictions. They are that part of the real city that chose, for whatever reasons, to stay apart and to perpetuate that apartness in the law. A suburb is ultimately an instrument by which the periphery can exploit the center, by which a single unit of the whole can exploit the rest. A suburb is a parasite whose residents can enjoy the benefits of scale and specialization without sharing in all of the attendant costs.

The true city, the socioeconomic city, is the entire metropolitan area, or

7. *Municipal Yearbook* (1975), p. 12. See also Anthony Downs, *Opening Up the Suburbs* (New Haven: Yale University Press, 1973).

some definable portion thereof. It is the entire six-county region of Chicago, or the entire fifteen-county region of New York; it may possibly be an even larger area if one could identify the actual flow of economic transactions and commuters. Fear found a means, *through government*, to divide the indivisible unit into an incapacitated marketplace of publics. There are now many publics, but there is no polity. Some years ago Robert Wood counted 1,400 governments in the "city" of New York.[8] A more recent count in the far smaller region of Chicago produced 1,060 governments, of which 995 were substantial enough to have the power to tax. In the country at large there has been a substantial reduction in the total number of local governments, but this is not true in the metropolitan areas. Between 1960 and 1972, the total number of local governments in the United States dropped from 91,236 to 78,218. During roughly the same period (1962–72), the number of municipalities in the standard metropolitan areas of the United States increased from 4,903 to 5,467. Moreover, the number of special districts in those same metropolitan areas increased from 6,153 to 8,054.[9]

There are no signs of a substantial decline in the number of general-purpose governments or of special-district governments in the metropolitan areas, because the incentives to incorporate remain strong, and the disincentives are not so strong. Moreover, the federal government has stepped in to reward incorporation into separate principalities by basing so many of its grant programs upon the local governments in metropolitan areas. The *Municipal Yearbook* reports that since the early 1960s, most metropolitan areas have experienced a mushrooming of single- and multipurpose area-wide districts supported by federal grants-in-aid. Over 4,000 geographic program areas have been recognized under 24 federal programs. Examples include: 481 Law Enforcement Planning Regions; 975 Community Action Agencies; 419 Cooperative Area Manpower Planning System Councils; 56 Local Development Districts; 247 Air Quality Regions. An important Federal Budget Circular (the famous A-95) issued many years ago and reaffirmed from time to time with amendments and clarifications, requires the multitudes of suburban governments to get together under some kind of metropolitan plan before they can qualify for many of the important federal grants-in-aid. However, the planning requirement is so permissive and so many kinds of useless procedures and phoney arrangements can qualify that the federal requirements do not impose any incentives for local governments to consolidate or any disincentives for them to continue their separate ways and form additional special dis-

8. Robert C. Wood, *1400 Governments: The Political Economy of the New York Metropolitan Region* (Cambridge, Mass.: Harvard University Press, 1961).

9. Data drawn from U.S. Bureau of the Census, *Census of Governments*, vol. 1 (Washington, D.C.: U.S. Government Printing Office, 1972). Actual compilations drawn from Marian L. Palley and Howard A. Palley, *Urban America and Public Policy* (Lexington, Mass.: Heath, 1977), p. 58, and John J. Harrigan, *Political Change in the Metropolis* (Boston: Little, Brown, 1976), p. 210.

tricts to get themselves out of financial burdens without having to consolidate with other general-purpose governments. Thus the federal government encourages metropolitan fragmentation or, at the least, refuses steadfastly to discourage it.[10]

FRAGMENTATION OF THE OLD CITY: EMERGENCE OF THE NEW MACHINES[11]

Even if the metropolitan city had not become hopelessly fragmented and divided against itself, the central cities were already developing their own structural incapacities for governing. Cities, and especially the large central cities like New York and Los Angeles, have modernized their governments and their managements in successive reform movements during the past forty or more years. However, when cities decided to eliminate their political machines, or to adopt measures to prevent their emergence, they did not necessarily become better governed cities.

Modernization has meant replacement of old machines with new machines. The new machines are the professionalized, administrative agencies that now run the cities. The career bureaucrats who head these agencies are the new bosses. They are more efficient, more honest, and more rational than the old amateur bosses. But they are no less political. If anything, the bureaucrats in their new machines are more political because of the enormously important decisions we entrust to them.

Sociologically, the old machine was a combination of rational goals and fraternal loyalty. The cement of the organization was trust and discipline created out of long years of service, probation and testing, slow promotion through the ranks, and centralized control over the means of reward. The power of the old machine in the community was based upon services rendered.

Sociologically, the new machine is almost exactly the same sort of organization. In any given city there are now many new machines where there used to be only one or two old machines. The base of their power is functional rather than geographic. They rely on formal authority rather than upon majority acquiescence. And they probably work with a minimum of graft and corruption. But these differences do not alter their definition; they only help to explain why the new machine is such a successful form of political organization.

The new machines are machines because they are relatively irresponsible

10. Data on federal programs that reinforce metropolitan fragmentation will be found in the *Municipal Yearbook* each year. The data used here were drawn from *Municipal Yearbook* of 1975, p. 13.

11. A longer treatment of this will be found in my Foreword to the revised edition of Harold F. Gosnell, *Machine Politics: Chicago Model* (Chicago: University of Chicago Press, 1968).

structures of political power. That is, each agency shapes important public policies, yet the leadership of each is relatively self-perpetuating and not readily subject to the control of any higher authority. Each must be contended with on its own terms. New machines are machines in that the power of each, while resting ultimately upon the services rendered to the community, depends upon its cohesiveness as a small minority in the midst of a vast dispersion of the multitude.

The modern city is well run but badly governed because it is comprised of *islands of functional power* before which the modern mayor stands impoverished.[12] No mayor of a modern city has predictable means of determining whether the bosses of the new machines—the bureau chiefs and the career commissioners—will be loyal to anything but their agency, its works, and the related professional norms. Our modern mayors have been turned into the likeness of a French Fourth Republic premier facing an array of intransigent parties in the National Assembly. But the plight of the mayor is worse; at least the premier can resign and yet have a reasonable probability of staying in the government. These modern American machines, more monolithic by far than their ancient brethren, are entrenched by law and supported by tradition, by the slavish loyalty of the newspapers, by the educated masses, by the dedicated civic groups, and, most of all, by legitimized clientele groups enjoying access to particular agencies under existing arrangements.

Reformers have not faced up to the potential inconsistencies between running a city and governing it because they tend to operate under the illusion of government by neutral specialist. This is the good-government equivalent to the rational man in law and the economic man in classical economics. The assumption is that if specialists know their own specialties well enough, they are capable of reasoning out solutions dispassionately to problems they share with specialists of equal but different technical competencies. That is a very shaky assumption, indeed, and Charles Frankel's analysis of such an assumption in Europe provides an appropriate setting for a closer look at it in the United States: "Different [technical] elites disagree with each other; the questions with which specialists deal spill over into areas where they are *not* specialists, and they must either hazard amateur opinions or ignore such larger issues, which is no better."[13]

This problem has not gone unrecognized among reformers and other leaders of government, but their efforts seem paltry against the years of development of these new machines into functional feudalities. For example, New York City tried to strengthen the office of mayor in its 1961 charter. But this

12. See Wallace Sayre and Herbert Kaufman, *Governing New York City* (New York: Russell Sage Foundation, 1960), pp. 710 ff., who coined the phrase but would not necessarily agree with my attitude toward the phenomenon.

13. Charles Frankel, "Bureaucracy and Democracy in the New Europe," *Daedalus* (Winter 1964), p. 487.

reform did not even address itself to the power of the local agencies that are not under mayoral jurisdiction—such as education—nor did it address itself to the power of all of the agencies that are defended by organized civil-service unions. Between 1966 and 1970, Mayor John Lindsay tried to centralize, or recentralize, power in the mayoralty by reorganizing the far-flung municipal bureaucracies into ten superagencies, each with a commissioner responsive to the mayor. But this provided the mayor of New York with no additional means of checking the runaway inflation of agency programs and budgets, despite concerted attacks by the mayor upon the power brokers (by which he meant the civil-service leadership and their union-leader supporters). Lindsay's successor, Mayor Abraham Beame, despite his long career as budget director and elected comptroller, was unable to keep New York from going into bankruptcy. It was a runaway city even though few, if any, of the individual agencies were unprofessional or poorly managed.

Although the mayor of New York is formally an extremely powerful chief executive, in practice the mayor of New York is not a great deal more potent than the mayor of Los Angeles and mayors of other cities where the separateness of the city agencies is enshrined in charter protections. The mayor of Los Angeles has no authority over the independently elected school board, the county-operated welfare program, the legally independent health department, or the housing and transit operations which are in independent authorities. The very large city of Oakland, California, reports that only about 1 percent of all federal spending was administered through city hall. The same is generally true of any of the cities upon which political scientists have recently focused attention.[14] All of this suggests that New York City, from which the following cases are drawn, is simply an advanced version of a typical urban government situation. And these are cases of fragmentation and immobilism in areas of public policy most vital to the life of the city:

1. Welfare problems always involve many large agencies, including health, welfare, and hospitals. Yet, during more than forty years, successive mayors of New York failed to reorient the Department of Health away from its regulatory public-health functions toward a more service-oriented concept of organization.[15] Consequently, many new areas of welfare have been set up in still newer agencies in order to be administered at all. New poverty programs were very slowly organized in New York and most other big cities—except in Chicago, where the last of the old machines exercised an impressive amount of central guidance, for its own reasons, in order to get these poverty programs into operation.[16] (It may be worth repeating here that only 1 percent of all federal spending in Oakland, California—including welfare spending—was

14. See John J. Harrigan, *Political Change*, pp. 139 ff. for a review of some of these cases of fragmentation.
15. Sayre and Kaufman, *Governing*, p. 274.
16. See below, Chapter 9.

administered through city hall.)

2. The control of environmental pollution in New York City has been within the province of at least six agencies—the Departments of Health, Parks, Public Works, Sanitation, Water Supply, and Air Pollution Control. The failure of cities like New York to work up effective programs of environmental-pollution regulation produced large but lame federal efforts. New York City cannot even control the pollution created by its own public facilities, including the millions of tons of sludge the city dumps into the sea each year. They cannot even dump it far enough out into the sea to avoid occasional sewage backups on the beaches of the south shores of Long Island.

3. Land-use patterns are influenced in one way or another by a great variety of city agencies, among which some of the most professionalized personnel are employed. Nevertheless, in New York the opening of Staten Island by the Verrazzano Narrows Bridge, creating a vast new urban frontier, found New York City with no plan whatsoever for the revolution in property values and land uses to take place in that borough. In most cities it has proved virtually impossible for one land-use agency to impose its criteria upon the others. Zoning agencies have little to do with construction-regulation agencies; public-health agencies cannot push either of those around, and public-works agencies can usually go their own ways as well. Probably the worst example of the results of governmental fragmentation in the land-use area is not in New York, but in St. Louis, where a public-housing project containing 2,762 apartments in 33 eleven-story buildings was newly occupied in 1954 and was demolished less than twenty years later. Whatever one can say of the attitudes and behaviors of low-income persons inhabiting those apartments, one must also recognize the severe lack of coordination and planning among the various agencies that would have built, maintained, or served that project. This kind of fragmentation is reflected in Washington and reinforced by Washington's responses to city agencies along the lines of the technical and professional personnel who communicate with each other. In September 1977, President Jimmy Carter and his secretary of Housing and Urban Development made a well-publicized tour of the South Bronx, one of the most deteriorated areas in New York City. He demanded the development of a plan for the rehabilitation of this area, only to discover later that such a report had been prepared three years before by a different New York City agency and sent to a different Washington agency.

4. Transportation is also the province of agencies too numerous to list, and the consequences fall naturally from their separateness. New York under Mayor Robert F. Wagner, Jr., pursued a vast off-street parking program at a cost of nearly $4,000 (in 1960 dollars) per parking space, at the very time a local rail line was going bankrupt. Meanwhile the Port Authority and the Robert Moses agencies were building access roads into the city totally out of proportion to any parking, on or off the streets, that the city could possibly

have prepared.[17] Mayors throughout the country have been unable to harness and control the separate tendencies of these agencies. Transportation and associated agencies are the ones most likely to have their separateness protected by state or interstate charters, making them public corporations with their own boards of directors and their own sources of finance. The Port of New York Authority is the classic case. The Port Authority literally put New York City on rubber tires; nevertheless, it could not control the activities of Robert Moses and the several agencies through whose control he became one of the great builders of parkways, tunnels, and bridges. In effect, Moses and the Port Authority worked out spheres of influence in the region, with the Port Authority sticking to the West Side and spilling over into New Jersey, and Moses on the East Side, spilling over onto Long Island. The best a succession of New York mayors has been able to do is to ratify their decisions; but perhaps it has been of some solace to these mayors to know that New York is not unique. There are transportation authorities all over the country; they do possess great power and great independence in their own domains; and yet, like the agencies in New York, neither they, the local mayors, nor local legislatures can directly bring their decisions into line with the decisions of other agencies.

5. The obligation to pursue and defend the civil rights of citizens is imposed upon all such agencies by virtue of federal, state, and local legislation. Yet, efforts to set up a public Police Review Board, and then a moderate City Council review process, were successfully opposed by the professional, organized police. One police commissioner resigned at the very suggestion that nonpolice authority would be imposed in any way on the department. From the beginning, in the mid-1960s, efforts to experiment with busing of school children to integrate the schools were successfully resisted. One contemporaneous education journalist observed, "Often . . . a policy proclaimed by the Board [of Education], without the advice and consent of the professional, is quickly turned into mere paper policy. . . . The veto power through passive resistance by professional administrators is virtually unbeatable." He was speaking of New York City, but it might as well have been Chicago, or Boston, or almost anywhere else. The only force strong enough to turn these local education agencies around has been a federal court order or a directive from the Department of Health, Education and Welfare threatening to take away federal funding (see Chapter 9).

This is not to argue that there are no local agencies responsive to central political control. Nor is it to say that bureaucrats are oligarchs or bigots. It is only to say that when there is a difference of views among agency chiefs or between them and the chief executive, bureaucrats are likely to consult their professional norms before consulting their civic conscience.

17. For an elaborate and an effective analysis of the adventures of Robert Moses and the many local agencies he almost completely controlled, see Robert Caro, *The Power Broker* (New York: Knopf, 1974).

The decentralization of city government toward the career bureaucracies has resulted in great efficiency for the activities around which each bureaucracy was organized. As a direct consequence, the city is indeed well run. But what of those activities around which bureaucracies are not organized, or those which fall between or among agency jurisdictions? For those, as suggested by the cases above, the cities are either suffering stalemate or elephantiasis—an affliction whereby a particular activity, say urban renewal, or parkway construction, gets pushed to its ultimate success totally without regard to its balance against the missions of other agencies. In these instances the cities are ungoverned.

Mayors have tried a variety of strategies to cope with these situations, but to little avail. The 1961 mayorality election in New York is probably the ultimate dramatization of their plight. This election will someday be seen as one of the most significant elections in American urban history. For New York it was the culmination of many long-run developments. For the country it may be the first of many to usher in the bureaucratic state.

In 1961 Mayor Robert F. Wagner, Jr., was running for mayor against his own Democratic leader of that era, Carmine DeSapio. Thanks to DeSapio, and the fact that Wagner was the son of a very famous New York politician of the 1930s and 1940s, a very young Wagner had been elected mayor in 1953 as the regular Democratic candidate. In 1957 he was overwhelmingly reelected on the same basis. During that period, however, the Democratic Party in New York was coming unstuck. Insurgents were ousting regular district leaders. DeSapio was himself on the way out. Business groups, ethnic groups, and unions were beginning to scramble for new ways of gaining or maintaining a piece of New York government. Mayor Wagner adapted to the emerging reform movement within the Democratic Party by turning against the party and attempting to establish a base of power within the reform movement and within the city bureaucracies themselves.

The basis of Mayor Wagner's new electoral organization is indicated by the following: His running mate for president of the City Council had been commissioner of sanitation, which had itself been the ultimate reward for a person who had spent virtually a lifetime career in the Department of Sanitation. He had an impressive following among the sanitation workers, who, it should be added, were organized along precinct lines. The mayor's running mate for comptroller had been for many years the city budget director (Abraham Beame, who later became a one-term mayor of New York). As a budget official he had survived several administrations and two vicious primaries pitting factions of the Democratic Party against one another. Before becoming director, he had served a number of years as a professional employee in the bureau. Leaders of the campaign organization included a very popular fire commissioner who retired from his commissionership to accept campaign leadership and was later to serve as deputy mayor. The campaign organization also included a former police commissioner who had enjoyed a strong following among professional cops as well as within the local reform movement. Added to this coalition was a new and vigorous political party, the Brotherhood Party, composed in large part of unions with broad bases of membership among city employees. This is not to mention the support of the Liberal Party, which also drew heavily upon union support. Before the end of the election most of the larger city bureaucracies had political representation in the inner core of the new administration.

For his 1961 reelection, Mayor Wagner had put his ticket and organization together just as the bosses of old had put theirs together. In the old days the problem was to mobilize all the clubhouses, districts, and counties in the city by putting together a balanced ticket about which all adherents could be enthusiastic. The same seems to have been true for 1961, except that by then the clubhouses and districts had been replaced almost completely by the new types of units of the new machine.

As a direct consequence of Wagner's dealings with the civil-service organizations, and as a direct consequence of his heavy political dependency upon their support, municipal expenditures began to increase at the unusually high rate of 8.9 percent per year, and the city's expense budget fell into the red for the first time since the Depression. New York City has not been able to stay out of deficits since 1961, nor was it able to reduce the rate of budgetary growth until the 1975 fiscal crisis that bankrupted New York in every respect except by legal definition.[18]

In 1965 reformers and antimachine Democrats abandoned Wagner, the civil service, and its unions, joining Republicans in a fusion movement to elect John Lindsay mayor of New York. Lindsay made an attack on the power brokers an essential part of his 1965 campaign, and he drew heavily upon nongovernmental reform groups and the newly emerging black groups in the city. However, this did not check the power, the independence, or the growth of the New York civil service, so that by the time the 1969 election approached, Lindsay had learned that he could not cope with the city without the support of these agencies and the largest of their supporting unions. He thus repeated 1961 by joining them, giving them virtually everything they asked for, and producing further spurts of budgetary expansion. He eventually lost control of the city.

Although neither Wagner nor Lindsay derserves the blame for the 1975 fiscal crisis, their strategies for political survival reflected and contributed to the runaway inflation of city government that brought the fiscal situation to a head. The runaway inflation was the direct result of the runaway separateness of agencies in New York City and the extent to which agencies feed upon as

18. For more on the crisis and on the New York pattern and its generalizability, see Martin Shefter, "New York City's Fiscal Crisis: The Politics of Inflation and Retrenchment," *The Public Interest* (Summer 1977), pp. 98–127.

well as feeding the demands of important constituencies in the city. The 1975 fiscal crisis merely confirmed the fact that city hall was not governing the city. The federal government extended emergency loans up to $250 million to meet pressing obligations, but set severe conditions on local reform and retrenchment. The state government in Albany also intervened in the nick of time by setting up a Municipal Assistance Corporation (MAC) which refinanced much of the city debt and removed fiscal control from the city. In the summer of 1978 Congress declared that since, in its opinion, New York had met the conditions set in 1975 it would authorize between $2 and $4 billion in loan guarantees—federal underwriting of city and MAC local-revenue bonds that enable them to be sold on the open market without exorbitant interest rates. This puts New York into a state of permanent receivership (see Chapter 10), and it is likely to last for a long time, if one can judge from the persistence of older patterns under Mayor Edward Koch, elected as a minority Democrat to succeed Mayor Beame in 1977.

Koch was one of the reform leaders who deposed Carmine DeSapio in the 1950s. In the intervening years Koch served in Congress and returned to city hall without a popular base independent of the city's bureaucracy. Many civil-service unions opposed him during the primary, but he was not long making peace with them. The 1978 wage settlement of 4 percent in each of the next two years was reported to Congress as less than the 5.5 percent being used as the standard for inflationary increases. The report neatly dodged the fact that the city employees were getting cost-of-living increases *in addition* to the 4 percent contract raises. Even more than his predecessors, Mayor Koch confronted his agencies from a position of weakness and needed to build his governing coalition upon them if he was not to become another frustrated, one-term mayor.

Destruction of the old machine and streamlining of city government did not, in New York or elsewhere, elevate the city into some sort of political heaven. Reform did not eliminate the need for political power; it simply altered what one had to do to get political power.

Local government reform is another part of the pluralist approach to government. Traditionally, the reform cry was populism, technocracy, and decentralization; but its results are pluralistic—with predictable consequences. Reform was based upon an assumption that the city needed to make no hard political choices but only to set up a process by which agencies and clientele would make the laws by arrangement. The public interest would emerge from interactions between elites of skill and elites of interest. The actual result has been little government at all.

The problems of cities seem to go beyond all the known arrangements for self-government. This is, however, less a cause for despair than for a moment for realizing that some city problems require substantive law, not procedural tinkering and marginal incrementalism. Unfortunately, all the tinkering of the past, however honest and efficient its administrative results, seems to have ended in an institutional incapacity to make law. Thanks to reform, cities no longer have serious problems of management. Their problems require fundamental moral choices, and morality is not a question of technology.

Why Federal Idols Broke

If there is anything new in the cities of the United States, it is the failure of political institutions. In the city there are many publics but no polity, therefore little law. In the central cities the polity has been carved up into rigid technocrized domains, so their functional power increases at the expense of substantive authority. The crisis in the cities has been one of governmental inefficacy and governmental illegitimacy. The black revolution merely showed it up for what it really was. The city began to fail its residents, black and white, as it fragmented itself. Cities can move mountains of earth and stone to build, but they seem no longer to possess the capacity to reach the bases of decay. Whether the issue is pollution, transportation, or integration, there can be no policy for the city without a *polity of the city*.

It would seem natural, then, that despite any advancements in technology or in general well-being, there is no advancement in the respect of American citizens for public objects; respect for public objects may have reached a new low among urban blacks. While rioting cannot be condoned, it at least can be properly understood in this context. Many of the urban disorders of the 1960s and 1970s possessed a strong element of randomness and desperation; but it is no coincidence that the riots of the 1960s tended to be literally triggered by minor involvement with the police. It is also no coincidence that when riots become focused on an attack, this attack seems to be against the police and firemen—not the "white devil" as such, but officialdom which happens to be white. When rioting becomes a concerted attack, it tends to move against authority and the symbols of authority. Phrases like "black power," "the power structure," "green power," and "black nationalism" constitute a political rhetoric because the source of the problem is political. And as the riots of the 1960s became the lootings of the 1970s, another aspect of the same phenomenon could be perceived. In the first place, there is something deeply wrong with legitimacy, with civic consciousness, and with civic training when hundreds of people will wantonly trespass and loot the innocent as soon as there is reasonable probability they will not be apprehended. But in the second place, it is even more indicative that the looting does not become a riot as long as the police make no effort to intervene. This is, in fact, the official analysis of the New York Police Department. According to the police commander (himself a black) of the North Brooklyn district where the worst looting occurred after the New York City blackout in the summer of 1977, the police would have been occupying, clearing, and cooling that area for weeks after the looting if they had fired a single shot over the heads of the looters.

WASHINGTON: RISE AND DECLINE

Cities, recognizing their own inadequacies, began to turn to Washington even before World War II. But the response in federal programs with special relevance to the cities was slow and sporadic until after 1957, following the Little Rock and Sputnik embarrassments, the urban-liberal takeover of Congress in 1958, and the return of the Democrats to the White House in 1961.

It would be impossible to construct an authoritative list of federal urban policies. Many of the most important federal programs in the cities are not, strictly speaking, urban but merely have special urban relevance. And some involve guarantees and insurance rather than actual transfers. Thus the list in Table 7.1 is selective, informal, and noncumulative. However, it does provide a good context for grasping the scale, the nature, and the problem of federal involvement in urban life.

It is clear from the table that the most recent federal policies are those that are directly and exclusively urban in nature. Primarily they are the housing, transportation, and health programs of the 1949–50 and 1958–62 periods, plus the new urban welfare programs of the late 1960s. These direct urban-oriented programs are not only the most recent, but they are governmentally weak in a way that prevents them from answering the real cries of the cities. Because of the weaknesses, they will continue to constitute an inadequate response, no matter how greatly they may be expanded or how sincerely and efficiently they may be implemented.

The older policies had two important features in common. In the first place, they were general, problem-oriented programs that simply had a special relevance to urban life. That is, they constituted an attack on the problems of industrial society as they were understood at the time. In the second place, these programs tended to be nondiscretionary or at least a good deal less discretionary than the later direct urban programs.[19] There are of course variations of degree; but it is nonetheless true that the older programs were clearer in their definition of the problem and were a great deal less discretionary in the manner in which they delegated implementation to administrative agencies. Moreover, the older programs that were discretionary share the weaknesses of the newer programs. The older programs—such as Social Security, public health, research, highway construction, and so on—sought to achieve their generality by defining a category and applying assistance to the entire universe

19. This is an application of criteria developed in Chapter 5. For further treatment of welfare within this context, see Chapter 8; for a look at their special impact on cities, see Chapter 9.

TABLE 7.1

FEDERAL PROGRAMS OF RELEVANCE TO URBAN LIFE*

	1976 (MILLIONS OF DOLLARS)
Department of Commerce	
Economic Development Administration and other planning assistance	823.4
Minority business development	49.8
Pollution control and abatement activities	61.4
Department of Agriculture	
School Milk and Lunch Program	1,403.2
Food Stamp Program	5,266.0
Pollution control and abatement activities	146.9
Department of Health, Education and Welfare	
Health	
Training and education	1,476.0
Construction	1,243.0
Health planning	256.0
Alcohol, Drug Abuse and Mental Health Administration	881.0
Education	
Aid to Impacted Areas Program	704.0
Elementary and secondary school aid	2,409.5
Higher education facilities construction, etc.	3,350.9
Vocational education and other problem teaching areas	799.2
Social and Rehabilitation Service (Welfare)	
Office for Civil Rights	24.6
Public assistance	17,240.9
Work incentives	400.0
Supplementary Security Income (SSI) Program	5,518.5
Human development (education and vocational education, social services)	1,702.3
Pollution control and abatement activities	43.7
Department of Housing and Urban Development	
Low Rent Public Housing Program	535.0
Urban transportation assistance	0.4
Rent Supplement Program	800.0
Community planning and development	2,082.3
Public assistance and other income supplements	36.2

* SOURCES: *Special Analyses: Budget of the United States Government*, Fiscal Year 1978; and *The Budget of the United States Government*, Fiscal Year 1978 (both Washington, D.C.: U.S. Government Printing Office.)

TABLE 7.1 (*continued*)

	1976 (MILLIONS OF DOLLARS)
Department of Housing and Urban Development (continued)	
New Communities Administration	8.4
Community development (annual contributions for assisted housing, contract authority)†	18,033.5
Department of Labor	
Employment and training assistance	2,916.8
Community service employment for older Americans	85.9
Temporary employment assistance	2,825.0
Federal unemployment benefits and allowances	410.0
Unemployment Trust Fund (training, employment, unemployment insurance)	16,213.5
Department of Transportation	
Urban mass transportation (contract authority included)	946.6
Federal Aviation Administration	547.0
Pollution control and abatement activities	75.3
Department of Treasury	
Payments to State and Local Government Fiscal Assistance Trust Fund	6,354.8
Independent Agencies	
ACTION—domestic programs	103.1
Community Services Administration (formerly OEO)	519.7
District of Columbia	465.5
Environmental Protection Agency (pollution abatement subsidies)	2,428.6
Insurance and Credit Programs ‡	
Direct Loans in 1976	5,250.0
VA	525.0
District of Columbia	266.0
Treasury, New York City seasonal financing	1,260.0
Guarantees of New York City issues	1,082.0
Value of Loans Guaranteed and Insured in 1976	
Low-rent public housing	454.0
FHA	2,338.0
GNMA	7,887.0
VA	6,133.0

† "Budget Authority usually takes the form of Appropriations, which permit obligations to be incurred and payments to be made. Some budget authority is in the form of *contract authority*, which permits obligations in advance of appropriations and therefore requires a subsequent appropriation or receipts to liquidate these obligations." SOURCE: *Budget of the United States Government*, Fiscal Year 1978, p. 229.

‡ Loans and guarantees should not be cumulated with budget outlays. See Chapter 10.

of persons, practices, resources, or symptoms within the category. Many of these are called categoric assistance for good reason. There was necessarily discretion within which the administrator could deal with unanticipated cases; however, there was also a considerable amount of statutory guidance that was either explicit or inherent in the definition of the category.[20]

The newer urban or urban-oriented programs try to achieve their generality by delegation rather than by definition or categorization. And they are general only by being vague, as to jurisdiction, methods, scope, objects, and any other dimension in which an administrator requires guidance. It should be clear from common sense as well as from the earlier discussion in this chapter that cities in the United States are too variable to be grouped into a single urban classification for purposes of making public policy. Once the policy category is defined as urban rather than in terms of some specific problem that may be particularly revelant to the urban situation, the argument for delegation becomes compelling and the need for delegation becomes unavoidable. Since it is true that each city is in many ways unique, and since it is true that each city has its own way of doing things, and since it is true that people on the scene know more about their own problems than do people in Washington, it then follows that the federal agency administrator and the chief executive must be left with almost complete discretion in dealing with local situations. But if we turned the situation back on its feet and held the federal government to policies for which they were able to define a particular problem, the arguments for delegation and for administrative and local discretion would be a good deal less compelling.

The election of Richard Nixon provided an opportunity to reintroduce some restraints and guidelines into national urban policies. Nixon owed cities and blacks less than any Democrat would have, and he did not hide his awareness of that. What better time to change the situation, at least to turn federal-urban relations into a great debate? What meaning can we give to the fact that this did not happen?

Nixon's Urban Policy

THE TWO-PARTY SYSTEM PROVES COMPATIBLE
WITH THE INTEREST-GROUP SYSTEM

One of Richard Nixon's leading campaign banners was the New Federalism, and another one was state's rights. Nixon declared war on the War on Pov-

---

20. Another good criticism of the liberal theory of delegation and its justification on the basis of how much more complex modern life is that there is more good law to be found in the social legislation that was new in the turbulent 1930s than in the urban legislation of the 1960s and 1970s, or in the more recent regulatory legislation discussed in Chapter 5.

erty, war on Washington, and war in particular upon the generosity of Democrats toward the cities. Early in his Administration, President Nixon denounced the "radical departure from the vision of Federal-State relations the nation's founders had in mind," and he sought to return "power to the people" not through local participation in federally sponsored programs but by returning to local governments the power and resources themselves. Quite clearly there were going to be fewer resources turned back to the local governments from Washington than the amounts spent by the Democrats for urban and urban-related programs during the 1960s. Many felt that the New Federalism was merely a mask for reduction and retrenchment against the cities. It could have been that, and it could have been more. It could have been a real rejection of the uses of government by the statist liberals of the 1960s—a turning toward a reduced national presence, a rejection of narrow and selfish definitions of interest, and an embrace of the community in a real resurgence of state's rights. As it turned out, the Nixon approach involved none of those possibilities. The Nixon approach involved a contrast from Democratic policies only in terms of scale; there was a reduction in the rate of increase of federal appropriations for urban programs. Except for that, Nixon's method and concepts were drawn from the interest-group liberal universe; and Nixon's approach actually reinforced interest-group liberalism, not only by continuing those methods but by proving that a real two-party system could operate within an interest-group liberal governmental system.

President Nixon's answer to the Democrats was revenue sharing. The concept can be traced back into the 1950s, but the actual Nixon proposals were developed by a Democrat, economist Walter Heller, in the early 1960s. Nonetheless, from the beginning, the idea seemed to get more support from Republicans than Democrats. Unions in particular had been fearful of the implications of revenue sharing. In 1968 the Republican platform had explicitly endorsed revenue sharing, while the Democratic platform waffled in quite vague terms about the same thing. And in 1969 President Nixon moved almost immediately to propose important revenue-sharing legislation. It was to be the featured policy in the Nixon urban plan—indeed, the featured policy in his entire domestic program. After nearly three years of prodigious and sincere effort, President Nixon got his revenue-sharing program through Congress.[21] So propitious a moment was it for President Nixon that he took the legislation—the State and Local Fiscal Assistance Act of 1972—to Philadelphia for an outdoor signing ceremony at Independence Hall. In the presence of many national, state, and local dignitaries, President Nixon expressed his

21. Detailed accounts of this important legislative decision will be found in Richard P. Nathan and Susannah E. Calkins, "The Story of Revenue Sharing," in Robert L. Peabody, ed., *Cases in American Politics* (New York: Praeger, 1976), pp. 11–43; and Joseph Penbera, "A Test of the Lowi Arenas of Power Policy Approach: The Case of the State and Local Fiscal Assistance Act of 1972" (Ph.D. dissertation, American University, 1974).

hope that the ties to the American federal system, created two hundred years earlier in Philadelphia, would be strengthened. After the signing, as the dignitaries were either congratulating one another or scrambling for position with President Nixon, the meeting was adjourned, the crowd was dispersed, and the document was left unattended on the signing table: "[A]fter the great ceremony of signing under the shadow of Independence Hall, nobody picked up the bill. And after everybody else had left, it was still sitting there. One of the policemen picked it up and asked: 'Does anybody want this?' "[22]

That is a good introduction to the legislation itself. There was so little law in this legislation that, beyond the authorization itself, nothing in it meant very much. At least we can give the president credit for explicitly seeking to keep the guidelines to a minimum. He succeeded. For example, general revenue funds were to be limited to "priority expenditures." However, the list of priority expenditures was so long and open-ended that it turned out to be no limitation whatsoever upon the ability of local governments to use the revenue-sharing funds or to divert other funds freed because of the revenue-sharing windfall. Another general limitation was the prohibition on the use of revenue-sharing funds as matching funds by state or local governments on the basis of which additional federal categoric or special revenue-sharing monies might be obtained. This, too, was an ineffectual guideline, for at least two reasons. First, it could not control the diversion of other funds to match additional federal grants. Second, especially because revenue-sharing dollars became indistinguishable from other monies in the local or state budgets, it would be impossible for a few federal agents to monitor the uses of monies by thirty-nine thousand state, county, township, and municipal treasuries.

Another of the important guidelines in the revenue-sharing legislation was the allocation formula. This had been a serious matter to members of Congress, and each chamber sought to direct the Administration in its eventual distribution of billions of dollars from the federal treasury. The House version of the bill provided for a formula that was biased in favor of populated and industrial states. The Senate provisions favored low-income states with more heavily rural populations. In the end, "the Conference Committee resolved its dilemma with a Solomon-like compromise. Each state would have its entitlement determined under both the House and Senate formulas; it would then receive its allocation under whichever formula would give it the higher amount."[23]

To be sure that no additional liens or restrictions were put on these funds,

22. Attributed to Senator Howard Baker (R-Tenn), quoted in Dennis R. Judd and Francis Kopel, "The Search for National Urban Policy: From Kennedy to Carter," in Theodore Lowi and Alan Stone, eds., *The Nationalization of Government: Public Policies in America* (Santa Monica: Sage, 1979).

23. Nathan and Calkins, "The Story of Revenue Sharing," pp. 40–41. Since this approach would allocate more than the full amount, Congress improvised a way out by reducing all state allocations proportionately to conform to the available funds.

the law provided that two-thirds of the state allocation would go directly to the local governments with only one-third retained by the states for distribution by the states under conditions they might set. Thus the only effective limitation in any part of this large and important piece of legislation was the nondiscrimination provision (section 122), which was an application of the general restriction on all federal programs that no person shall be excluded from participation or benefits on the basis of race or sex.[24] As glaring proof of the effectiveness of legislative restrictions on administrative action, we will see in Chapter 9 the dramatic effects of the nondiscrimination provisions in federal law.

Although the total amount of revenue-sharing monies made available by the federal government seems large—over $30 billion during the first five years—the actual amounts reaching local governments constitute a small component of their budgets. For example, in 1974, when the apportionment to local governments amounted to $4.5 billion, revenue sharing accounted for only 3.1 percent of local government revenues.[25] Without any clear federal guidelines, and with such a modest proportion of a windfall, local governments made their own decisions and kept their own counsel with regard to the local allocation of those funds. And as it turns out, the substantial proportion of their funds went to police and fire protection services. Smaller principalities reported having spent 33 percent of their revenue-sharing funds on public safety, while larger cities spent more than 44 percent on public safety. The nation's fifty-five largest cities spent 59 percent of their revenue-sharing funds on public safety.[26] An unnoticed and unappreciated aspect of this, however, is the extent to which these revenue-sharing funds freed other local revenues for other purposes. During the very period when revenue sharing became an important proposal and was eventually adopted, cities were getting into more and more trouble in their ability to raise funds through borrowing and were spending more and more of their annual operating budgets on service to the debt they had already accumulated. For many of the largest cities in the United States, debt service had become the third most important budgetary outlay, following only those outlays for education and welfare. In an important sense, therefore, revenue sharing became an indirect subsidy to the private finance capital market, because the increased ability of cities to meet their debt extended for still another few years the ability of the private capital market to buy local revenue bonds at more or less reasonable rates of interest. The New York City fiscal crisis of 1975 proved that revenue sharing

24. It is interesting that section 122 does not include religion as one of the characteristics. However, that is probably not a significant oversight because of the general application of the Civil Rights Act of 1964 and other legislative, administrative, and judicial rulings since that time.
25. Judd and Kopel, "The Search for National Urban Policy," p. 31.
26. Ibid.

was not enough, but it, for the moment, has sufficed to avert bankruptcy in many other cities.[27]

Another very important implication of revenue sharing and the additional discretion it has given cities over federal funds is the shrinkage of local government expenditures on local human resources programs. In 1972, the last year before revenue sharing, human resources accounted for 69 percent of all grants-in-aid outlays by the federal government. Primarily as a result of the diversion of at least 11 percent of federal outlays through revenue sharing from the categoric programs, the human resources categories of the federal grants-in-aid outlays dropped by 14 percentage points immediately the next year.[28] Local governments could continue, if they so chose, to maintain their accustomed outlays in these human-resources categories. But with the increased discretion over the monies that were coming from the federal government, most local governments chose to divert still additional outlays from these human-resources programs. Thus many local governments gave up welfare for General Sherman tanks and computers.

Partially to placate the Democrats, who worried that general revenue sharing would simply be adopted at the direct expense of existing urban programs, but partly out of a sincere effort to simplify national administration and to free local governments, Nixon had tried to consolidate the many existing national categoric grants. Within little more than a year of his general revenue-sharing proposals, President Nixon proposed seven types of special revenue sharing, each of which would consolidate several existing state and local grant programs. If enacted, these programs would have amounted to more than twice as much as general revenue sharing itself.

These proposals for special revenue sharing were not welcomed by the Democratic majority in Congress, but eventually two of them were adopted. These were the Comprehensive Education and Manpower Act of 1973 and the Housing and Community Development Act of 1974. The first of these collapsed the existing 10,000 federal manpower contracts into 50 state and 350 large city block grants. Most of the discretion was put into the hands of the mayors of these cities. The Housing and Community Development Act, which took effect on January 1, 1975, replaced seven major categoric grant programs with a single block grant. Examples of existing categoric grant programs that were consolidated under the CD block grant authorization were grants for water and sewage systems, grants for neighborhood facilities and

27. Thomas Boast, "A Political Economy of Urban Capital Finance" (Ph.D. dissertation, Cornell University, 1977).

28. Judd and Kopel, p. 33. Richard P. Nathan et al., *Monitoring Revenue Sharing* (Washington, D.C. The Brookings Institution, 1975), observe that the older, larger, and more hardpressed cities tended to use the largest proportions of their revenue-sharing funds on maintenance of programs, while smaller and more affluent jurisdictions used theirs for new services (p. 230).

land-acquisition programs, grants for code enforcement and neighborhood development, grants for urban renewal, and grants for the Model Cities program. Here again, the major portion of discretion was expected to be lodged in city hall.[29]

The significance of these Nixon proposals and the eventual legislation does not lie in the comparative generosity of Republicans and Democrats; nor does the significance lie in the details of implementation. The significance lies in the fact that the Republican approach to the problems of the cities is exactly in line with that of the Democrats. It was one more step, and a large one, precisely in the established direction. Through revenue sharing and block grants, President Nixon took the already highly discretionary policy area of national government aid to state and local governments and made it still more discretionary. Before Nixon, urban policies at least embodied a minimum of instruction, if only through the fact that each was a categoric grant. Each grant category was fairly small; and there were many such categories. Everything within the category may have been left to the discretion of the administrator and the local government. Indeed, that was true of most categoric aid programs all along, all the more true after the Democrats established the War on Poverty. Nevertheless, there was an outer limit; it was inherent in the definition of the category itself. A grant for uban renewal could not be spent for a General Sherman tank. A grant for adult education could not be diverted to street cleaning or to payments on the local debt. President Nixon, through revenue sharing and the block grants, eliminated what remained of guidelines in the categories. After 1973 there was no structure or form at all in these urban programs. Nixon could have been a great deal more generous. Ford, in the end, did loosen up a bit on the purse strings. But until the structure was changed, the nature of urban policy and the nature of liberal government was not going to change. Comparative generosity had little to do with it.

After Nixon, as before Nixon, cities were left to their own devices. Revenue sharing may have given them a longer leash but not a new lease. Cities were left to confront their suburbs. Suburbs were left to confront each other and the central cities. And all local areas were left to compete, catch as catch can, for the inflated yet shrinking dollars in the private capital market. Probably most important of all, local governments were made victims of the largest interest groups that had a special or exclusive stake in city affairs. Revenue sharing had reduced to a minimum beyond that which could have been conceived in the 1960s the capacity of cities to deal advantageously with the bankers, the insurance companies, the investment brokers, and the large, locally based unions. On the one side, for example, revenue sharing was virtually a subsidy to the private capital market—at least it was an assurance that

29. Good treatments will be found in Judd and Kopel, pp. 37–46, and in Owen and Schultze, *Setting National Priorities: The Next 10 Years* (Washington, D.C.: The Brookings Institution, 1976), pp. 359 ff.

they could continue to buy and sell tax-free local bonds without fear of bankruptcy. On the other side, revenue sharing, like the War on Poverty, had reaffirmed home rule and therefore had left most cities without allies in the state capitols and without the ability to play some interests off against others. Cities could lobby for more money, especially in Washington. In fact, during the decade between 1965 and 1975, the United States Conference of Mayors became one of the most active Washington lobbies. This group was part of what one expert has called "the urban interest network," composed of the whole variety of urban-based interest groups whose purpose was largely to flank the problems of the cities by more effectively drawing upon national largesse.[30] In addition to the National Conference of Mayors, the 1960s and 1970s saw the emergence of the National Housing Conference, the National League of Cities, the National Association of Housing and Redevelopment Officials, and a host of other national conferences and associations of urban interest. There were also the individual lobbyists for specific cities, who were competing vigorously against other cities. Yet with all of that interest and all of that organizational effectiveness, those same cities were unable to confront their own organized bureaucracies and related private unions, because these interests, with their exclusively local base, had the superiority of bargaining power, sticking power, and the power of embarrassment that would tend to level even the most ambitious and powerful of local officials.

Why Effective Urban Policies
Cannot Be Made in Washington

The delegation of discretion in urban subsidy and assistance programs is a fact of modern life, justified, as is the delegation of discretion in regulatory programs, by the speed and complexity of modern life. National legislation attempts to generalize its applicability to all cities, but it achieves that generality only through vagueness. Chapters 8 and 9 will give additional illustrations of these programs and of the consequences of broad and vague delegations of power. But in anticipation of those additional cases and evaluations, it is worth showing first in general why a discretionary approach by the federal government to the cities almost inevitably converts federal assistance into a product hazardous to our health.

In the first place, since the national government is precisely a national government, and since each city is special, a federal policy oriented toward cities as such can be general only if it is vague. But if these programs make federal funds available without any criteria they are merely an open invitation to

30. Suzanne Farkas, *Urban Lobbying: Mayors in the Federal Arena* (New York: New York University Press, 1971), Chapter 2.

scramble, forcing cities to become vigorous lobbyists and forcing federal administrators to become purely bargaining politicians without any goals whatsoever. As we shall see, under these circumstances federal aid merely enables
local elites to reinforce local patterns and practices.[31]

In the second place, vague enabling legislation renders the national government politically incapable of applying broad national goals even if the president should have some. The delegation of discretion to the president may involve an increase of power for the president and for those to whom the
implementing power is subdelegated. However, discretion also involves a
commensurate increase in personal responsibility. All presidents have a heavy
stake in urban America; and, even though Democrats tend to be more sensi-
tive to central cities than Republicans, no president in our age is going to be
willing to take personal responsibility for favoring some cities or suburbs over
others or for inconveniencing cities unduly by insisting on special placement
of public housing or by rejecting an elaborate redevelopment or demon-
stration plan. To the liberals, the special sensitivity of presidents to the urban
situation has been one of the appeals of the Executive Branch over Congress.
But the new urban and urban-oriented programs alter the meaning of that
relationship almost completely. Who is to be responsible for the decision that
adversely affects a local situation?[32] The fact that Gerald Ford did as well in
the urban-industrial states of the West as Jimmy Carter did in the urban-industrial states of the East, and the fact that Ford did fairly well even in some of
the Eastern industrial states he ended up losing, cannot be lost on any Republican president.

In the third place, an urban-policy orientation tends to destroy the clarity of
other federal programs once they are brought into the urban orbit. To be quite
specific, the urban-policy orientation of the 1960s took most of the civil rights
out of civil rights. In order to reach a level of generality above the morass of
individual cities, Presidents Kennedy and Johnson redefined the problem of
urban living as economic. Civil-rights laws had defined the general problem
of American life in the 1960s and 1970s, just as welfare and labor laws defined
the problems of the 1930s. Civil-rights laws are not urban legislation; in fact,
the original civil-rights laws were enacted with distinctly nonurban—
Southern—practices in mind. When the social revolution of our time became black and shifted North, the civil-rights acts became overshadowed, first

31. For a thorough study of the conditions and extent of urban lobbying since 1961, see
Suzanne Farkas, *Urban Lobbying*.

32. In 1965, for example, the Office of Education decided to withhold around $30 million
from Chicago's Board of Education pending an investigation of charges of *de facto* violation of
civil-rights laws. A combination of Mayor Richard Daley's special access to the White House and
his control over the Chicago congressional delegation proved too much for the combined strength
of the Office of Education and the presidency of the United States. The prostration of the mighty
Washington before a scrappy mayor is merely suggestive of the problem; and it is one to which the
Republicans are not immune.

by Kennedy's efforts to solve urban problems economically through fiscal policy and then through Johnson's efforts to transform the Northern cities through the War on Poverty. Due largely to the political foundation of the presidency and the turn of the liberals toward the urban orientation, the federal government was virtually forced to react to the cries of the cities with cash. *Federal policy became a matter of indemnifying damages rather than righting wrongs.*

8

INTEREST-GROUP
LIBERALISM AND POVERTY
The End of the Welfare State

Poverty is all relativity. The cutting line for the poor can be drawn anywhere, depending only upon one's propensity to sympathize. When Marie Antoinette said, "Let them eat cake," she probably assumed most of the poor were well enough off to buy cake when there was no bread to be had. On the other hand, the line can be drawn harshly at the level of actual physical survival, as Ricardo and the gloomy nineteenth-century liberals tended to do. But even this is arbitrary, for subsistence changes with medical advances and according to prevailing definitions of survival. For example, the leadership of the 1960s chose to draw the line at around $3,000 of family income per year. Such a criterion had important policy implications, because it defined as poverty-stricken and in need of public assistance nearly one-fifth of the population of the United States. There are many technical objections to this criterion, especially to basing it upon money income.[1] But there is nonetheless no principle by which one can object to the high cutting point as such. This generosity was somewhat exhilarating, especially given the tardiness with which Americans agreed to discuss the issue in public at all.

Almost from the dawn of the Industrial Revolution poverty was recognized as one of the new problems. There had always been poor people, but never before industrialization had there been a permanent stratum of propertyless, dependent paupers (that is, dependent persons outside almshouses and other institutions).[2] The mechanism by which industrial poverty was created may not have been the poor redistribution of Henry George's "unearned increment" on land; nor need it have been deliberately created by capitalists to instill the will to work. But undeniably poverty did not disappear with progress.

1. See the excellent remarks of Professor Margaret C. Reid before the Poverty Subcommittee of the House Committee on Education and Labor, April 24, 1964, pp. 1427 ff. Reprinted in *Poverty American Style*, Herman P. Miller, ed. (Belmont, Calif.: Wadsworth, 1966), pp. 231 ff.

2. For an excellent treatment of the relation of poverty and pauperism to industrialization, see Karl Polanyi, *The Great Transformation* (Boston: Beacon Press, 1957), Chapters 7–9.

As industrial states became industrial democracies poverty became an intolerable condition rather than merely an established fact. At first, industrial poverty in the United States was taken care of—haphazardly but rather well in relation to contemporary attitudes—by personal, family, and local resources. Organized philanthropies, neighborhood and fraternal organizations, settlement houses, and other more or less formal organizations were soon to join in. Only at the end of the nineteenth century were state and local governments to begin picking up a significant share of the costs. State and city departments of charities were soon set up to dispense aid directly and to participate indirectly through grants in support of existing private institutions. Once the pattern was established, growth was probably inevitable. A public aid lobby developed under the leadership of such visionaries as Frances Perkins in New York and Edwin Witte in Wisconsin. Public aid appropriations expanded. Methods of administration were invented. Concepts, definitions, and means tests were invented. A whole new profession of welfare administration emerged. In 1928, at the height of prosperity on the eve of the Depression, 11.6 percent of all relief granted in fifteen large cities came from public funds.[3] A meager proportion by present standards, but by that time the basis for the welfare revolution had been established. Even the meaning of being poor had been redefined, as suggested by the almost universal change of local administrative designation from "Department of Charities" to "Department of Public Aid," then to "Department of Welfare," and, most recently to "Department of Human Resources."

The rudimentary welfare systems of the early part of the century were probably adequate for their times, just as private methods may have been sufficient for the early periods of industrialization. While they met only a fraction of the need, by any definition, these agencies worked among people who expected far less (whole populations were poor according to present definitions), who could return to the family farm, and/or who lived amid a self-conscious ethnic or regional group. It is hardly necessary to report that the 1929 Depression changed all this. The scale of industrial failure made nationalization of welfare necessary. The degree to which it rendered poor many thousands who had never known poverty before also meant that all lingering notions about individual guilt for poverty would be forever eliminated. The Depression revealed that capitalistic poverty is systematic. Obviously this meant that something systematic should be done about it.

However, recognition of national responsibility for poverty is only half of the problem, perhaps the simpler half. How one proceeds to discharge that responsibility is quite another matter. America's initial response was the Social Security system of the 1930s—by 1965 this was old welfare. Once it established itself as a basic part of the American way of life its inadequacies

3. From a WPA study by Anne E. Geddes, reported in Merle Fainsod et al., *Government and the American Economy* (New York: Norton, 1959), p. 769.

came to be stressed. Since no amount of revising categories of aid or liberalizing benefits could meet all criticisms, a search for an entirely new concept of welfare was initiated in the early 1960s. The conclusion of this search was the new welfare. Old welfare was a creation of old liberalism, which took capitalism for what it was and sought to treat the poor as the inevitable, least fortunate among the proletariat. It was a good system and was endangered only because of efforts to make welfare policy do more than it could possibly do. New welfare is a creation of new liberalism, interest-group liberalism. While new welfare defines poverty in simple economic terms, it rejects the notion of poverty as a natural and inevitable sector of economic life. It seeks to humanize poverty. It seeks to organize poverty as though it were a human characteristic comparable to any other "interest" around which interest groups form. The results, for the poor and for the society at large, are far from what liberalism in any form could possibly desire. New welfare is self-defeating because it has sought to apply notions like welfare and poverty to entirely alien phenomena. The real poverty problem of the 1960s could have been dealt with entirely by mere liberalization of old welfare. The new problem since the 1960s, for which new welfare has been a total misapplication, is the problem of justice. The interest-group liberal approach has proven useless for that.

The Old Welfare System, 1935

The federal Social Security system was framed in a context of fear. There was fear for the economy, and there was fear that even if prosperity returned it would never wipe out large-scale dependency. There was fear of the repercussions of unrest left too long unattended. Huey Long was only one of many popular figures with a crackpot scheme. Frances Perkins reported how she was cornered in a hall at the White House by her friend Adolph Berle, in the spring of 1933, and was urged by Berle to leave Washington before summer if she possibly could. Berle feared widespread violence in Washington and New York.[4] Fear had made a welfare program of some sort necessary; fear had also made it politically possible. As Miss Perkins put it, "We would not have had Social Security without the crisis of the Depression."[5]

BUREAUCRATIZATION OF ROUTINE FUNCTIONS

Out of these conditions emerged a clear view of the problem. First, it became supremely clear that poverty was national, because the economic system that made poverty the sort of problem it had become was national. Sec-

4. From conversations between Miss Perkins, the author, Laurence Pierce, and Michael Schwartz, Cornell University, April 14, 1965.
    5. Ibid.

ond, it became clear that in addition to age, unemployment, injury, and disability were the key causes of poverty, and obviously these were conditions into which people fall most often through no fault of their own. In our day these conditions had become the normal "cost of doing business."[6] Through the heat of depression and the fear of insurrection, we had changed our ideology so fundamentally that we were now prepared to see poverty as a social rather than a personal condition. The Depression destroyed once and for all the old puritanical concept of poverty as the wages of sin, sloth, and stupidity. Grinding poverty had hit thousands of temperate and sturdy workers in 1930 and was not showing much of a tendency to lift by 1934. Industrial poverty could hit anyone, and industrial society poorly equipped its finest specimens for its own occasional lapses. After the third and fourth generation of industrialization, industrial workers had no skills for producing a whole product; neither had they an original homestead and would not know how to farm it if they had one. Industrial poverty was now seen as random as well as inexorable. The poor in 1934 were not a select group. The poor were all those people whose jobs and abilities were affected by the market. Industrial poverty was indeed a random harvest. It was an objective socioeconomic fact that required an objective politicoeconomic solution.

In 1935 Congress marked the passing of the old order with the Social Security Act. It was the result of a year of careful research and drafting, done primarily by academic and government technicians in the Executive Branch. One or two important changes in the original version were made in the House Committee on Ways and Means, but these were ratifications of compromises made between Treasury Secretary Henry Morgenthau and Labor Secretary Perkins. After very unspectacular debate the House voted 371 to 33 and the Senate 77 to 6 for passage. The act that virtually ushered in the welfare state had been prepared, drafted and passed with incredible calmness as well as speed. To be sure, several serious issues were settled only after protracted controversy. However, the controversies were contained within the President's Committee on Economic Security (headed by Frances Perkins) and its Technical Board (headed by Professor Edwin Witte). Congress's major contributions were (1) reduction of the degree to which the act would redistribute wealth by holding out for Secretary Morgenthau's scheme for joint contribution by employee and employer in old-age and survivors insurance, and (2) holding out for a federal-state rather than a national scheme of implementation.[7]

In the more than forty years since its passage, the act has held up well. It

---

6. Frances Perkins, *The Roosevelt I Knew* (New York: Viking, 1946), p. 290.

7. No book-length study of the important act exists. The best sources are: Perkins, *Roosevelt*; Edwin E. Witte, *The Development of the Social Security Act* (Madison: University of Wisconsin Press, 1962); and Paul H. Douglas, *Social Security in the U.S.* (New York: Whittlesey House, 1936).

has been expanded; its systems have become more intricate. But its assumptions and its basic structures remain unchanged. [8] Social Security was what is called an omnibus act. The statute contains eleven titles; seven titles deal with separate but strongly related programs. However, Social Security is an omnibus act in a very special sense. Each of the titles is carefully defined in relation to the others, and the several parts were to be interrelated and to add up to something of a relatively comprehensive package of welfare. In this sense it is better to call Social Security categoric than omnibus.

The primary distinction in the act is between two groups of beneficiaries—those who contribute and those who do not. The first is the base for an insurance system, from which payments are received as a matter of right by virtue of contributions made during one's income-earning life. The other is the base for a system from which payments are made to all needy persons after determination of the actual degree of individual need. The former, the contributory or insurance scheme, is probably what most people have in mind when they refer to Social Security. The latter is generally known as public assistance. Both were set up in the original act. (See the outline in Table 8.1.)

Within each of these groups of beneficiaries there are categories of welfare activity. Each category is designed to deal with a primary type of dependency, whether of disability or of reduced income. Take first the insurance group, because it was expected to become the overwhelmingly predominant group after prosperity returned. The act set up two categories for treatment by insurance: (1) aged persons and their survivors, and (2) temporarily unemployed persons. Insurance is actually a misnomer, for it implies an ideal of actuarial soundness—meaning that sufficient funds should be collected from all beneficiaries to cover, after interest is added, the payments drawn out of it as they come due. Indeed, an Old-Age and Survivors Trust Fund was created to receive all federal employment tax revenues, and this implied actuarial soundness (Title II, Sec. 201 of the act). But the rates were never set high enough to guarantee such soundness. As the population grew older and benefits and coverage were increased, especially after 1958, the subsidy to the Trust Fund from general revenues began to increase even though Social Security taxes were increased. However, the actuarial soundness of the system is not the issue. A good argument can even be made against rigid adherence to sound financial principles for social insurance, because a sound fiscal system for the whole economy must be able to take into account the total flow of cash between government and the public. It is safer to call the retirement and the unemployment systems contributory rather than real insurance plans. [9]

8. See Gilbert Y. Steiner, *Social Insecurity: The Politics of Welfare* (Chicago: Rand McNally, 1966), p. 6.

9. James M. Buchanan, *The Public Finances* (Homewood, Ill.: Irwin, 1960), pp. 321 ff. The act also established an Unemployment Trust Fund (Sec. 904, Title IX), but no such actuarial expectations seemed to be applied to it.

The second group of beneficiaries comes under the general rubric of non-contributory welfare, but within that the law specified at least six distinct categories of welfare. The latter three (II. D., E., and F.) are service activities, involving no payments but only services that are available to all but primarily focused upon the poor. The first three comprise the public assistance categories of the act. The act achieved something of a guarantee of state public

TABLE 8.1

PROGRAMS UNDER SOCIAL SECURITY ACT OF 1935

I. CONTRIBUTORY (INSURANCE) SYSTEM

    A. OLD AGE AND SURVIVORS—TITLE II. National system financed by taxes on employer and employee, plus subsidy from general revenue.

    B. UNEMPLOYMENT—TITLE III. State systems, National Trust Fund with state accounts. Financed by tax on employers of eight or more persons, 90% of which is credited against contributions to an approved state program (Secs. 903 and 902, Title IX).

II. NONCONTRIBUTORY SYSTEM (PUBLIC ASSISTANCE)

    A. OLD-AGE ASSISTANCE—TITLE I. Grants to states for one-half of all payments of up to $30 per month to individuals of 65 or over, if state program is approved by Social Security board.*

    B. AID TO DEPENDENT CHILDREN—TITLE IV. Grants to states for one-third of payments of up to $18 per month for first child and $12 for each additional child.†

    C. AID TO THE BLIND—TITLE X. Grants to states for one-half of payments of up to $30 per month, subject to approval by Social Security board.

    D. MATERNAL AND CHILD WELFARE—TITLE V. Nonmonetary welfare. Payments based on number of births and financial need to states providing hospital, nursing, and public-health services under plans. By secretary of Labor and children's bureau, up to one-half of cost of services.

    E. VOCATIONAL REHABILITATION—TITLE V. Extension of act of 1920. Nonmonetary welfare.

    F. PUBLIC HEALTH—TITLE VI. Nonmonetary welfare. Grants to states for improved services, personnel, or sanitation.

* Federal grants were made quarterly and could be stopped at any time violations of federal standards were discovered. The ceiling and the rates have changed many times since 1935, but the basic structure remains the same. As of 1977, the federal share of old-age assistance is 31/37 (about 84%) up to the first $38. The total federal share can be no less than 50% and no more than 65%. SOURCE: 42 *U.S. Code Annotated* s. 303(a), 1301(a).

† In 1977 the federal share of AFDC was determined by a two-part formula. The first part awards five-sixths of the first $18 of the average payment per recipient made by the state multiplied by the number of recipients. The second part provides from 50–65% of the next $14 of the average payment multiplied by the number of recipients. SOURCE: U.S. Department of Health, Education and Welfare, *Social Security Bulletin* (October 1977), p. 19.

assistance by provision of matching grants for states whose welfare programs were designed according to the categories defined in the federal law.

The three noncontributory programs plus the two contributory programs include within federal-state responsibility virtually every type of honest dependency known to man: age, disability, unemployment, abandonment, desertion, and blindness. These programs are seldom administered to the full satisfaction of anyone, and there is grave doubt that payments are realistic. However, even from this brief review it is possible to support the following propositions: (1) Poverty was not discovered in 1964: "The poor" have been recognized wards of the federal government for at least forty years. (2) Charges of bureaucratization are hurled against these programs constantly—charges that there is delay, waste, formality, and irresponsibility. However, it seems clear that the greater flaw is insufficient bureaucratization, because the perfect bureaucracy (see Chapter 2) would minimize delay and waste, and the perfect bureaucracy would be formal in order to maximize services to real clients, eliminate service to the ineligible, and minimize errors and irresponsible behavior toward needy clients. (3) Programs, especially the three based on means tests, are criticized for being unduly harsh. But that is only a sign that the local administrators are obeying laws clear enough in intent to require obedience. It is the laws that are unsympathetic, not the intrinsic character of the programs of old welfare. Such laws can be made less harsh without changing the character of the system itself.

THE INTEGRITY OF OLD WELFARE

Charges of inadequacy, bureaucratization, and arbitrariness are hurled by the ignorant at those flaws of the welfare system that mere reform could have remedied. Even a formal review of old welfare reveals its basic integrity. Despite its lack of actuarial soundness—or perhaps because of it—old welfare has fiscal integrity. It builds up very large, anti-inflationary funds without being rigidly deflationary. The system of contributions is regressive, but that is a minor point on which disagreements can never be settled. It has fiscal integrity from the standpoint of the economy as a whole. Not only has the system relieved much of the suffering of the poor, it is the key variable in counter-cyclical compensatory policy. Its outlays are automatically cranked up as private mechanisms run down. The increase of buying power automatically effected by federal social transfer payments during economic decline regularly makes up a large proportion of the decrease of buying power due to layoffs and cutbacks in the private sector. This aspect of the system is not only fundamental to the modern consumer economy, it cannot work at all unless it is highly bureaucratized.

Despite abuses, the organizational integrity of the system is also clear. The categories of poverty are clearly identified. A person is either old or not, blind or not, unemployed or not, dependent or not, and so on. Each condition is a standardized source of poverty and can be routinely met with food, shelter, clothing, or the guidance and wherewithal to secure them. Any function that can be dealt with routinely ought to be administered; it must be bureaucratized as much as possible. Charges against the system, like red tape, are usually the result of insufficient bureaucratization.

Finally, old welfare has a very notable legal integrity. The Social Security Act is a distinctly modern piece of legislation in that it operates through broad delegations of power—in this case to state legislatures and, thence, to state administrative agencies. But legal integrity is achieved by specification of standards very much lacking in regulatory policy (Chapter 5). The first, and principal, standards to guide the administrators can be found in the categoric structure of the act itself. While the act left to the states the discretion to be as generous as they wished, they were clearly prevented from (1) going below certain minimum payments and (2) establishing any types of aid or conditions to aid as they saw fit. The act identified basic sources of objective poverty and saw to some provision for each.

Relatively clear standards also accompany each category or title within the act. The age of sixty-five was set for eligibility under old-age assistance. The act also set citizenship and residence requirements, as well as procedures for settling the inevitable disputes that arise over questions involving eligibility. It set down several principles for financing and administering the programs, and clear guidelines for investment of trust funds by the federal Treasury. One of the harsher standards was that of limiting eligibility for annuities strictly to those who had ceased to be employed (Sec. 202 d). However, it is a clear policy choice and can be changed in the same manner.

Public policy in the act was also careful with jurisdictional and procedural standards in the unemployment title. While it was silent on the duration of unemployment necessary for eligibility (in most states the waiting period is a week), the act was more than clear on other features of the category. For example, persons were required to take new work if available, but not if the job offered were vacant due to a strike or other labor dispute, not if the wages, hours, and conditions were substantially less than the going rate, and not if the condition of employment included the obligation to join a company union or to refrain from joining a bona fide union (Sec. 903). Standards for state administrative procedure were set, as were procedures for review of decisions involving denial of compensation. States were free to determine the length and size of benefits but not to change the minimum conditions of eligibility.

The aid-to-dependent-children title (ADC, later known as Aid to Families of Dependent Children, AFDC) attempts to establish a category of assistance more difficult to identify than old age, unemployment, blindness, and so on. However, the category is defined in terms quite elaborate enough to begin the task of guiding administration. *Dependent child* is defined (by Sec. 406) as "a child under the age of 16 who has been deprived of parental support or care by reason of the death, continued absence from the home, or physical or mental incapacity of a parent, and who is living with his father, mother, grandfather, grandmother, brother, sister, stepfather, stepmother, stepbrother, stepsister, uncle, or aunt, in a place of residence maintained by one or more of such relations as his or their own home." The title, although somewhat shorter than those preceding, also established a series of important administrative obligations for the state to uphold, including the requirements that there be a single responsible state agency and that the state program be uniformly in effect in all subdivisions of the state (Title IV). These were particularly important in the days when few states had any modern machinery by which to process or serve needy clients.[10] There were also in the title strict eligibility rules. The purpose of the title was to help keep the family together following loss of the primary breadwinner or some other disabling blow.

Though meager in support and harsh in eligibility, these titles, and the others not singled out for treatment here, are undeniable statements of public policy. They are not mere expressions of general public sentiment. And there is still more to the legal integrity of old welfare. The existence of fairly clear rules, standards, and definitions in the organic act gave rise to considerable administrative rule-making (in this case, state rule-making) down the' line. This means that the highest line agency—in this case the state legislature— was forced to enter into the spirit of the act by passing further rules, standards, and definitions. State welfare law as a consequence may be a thicket to the uninitiated and a nuisance to the operating case worker, but it is, for all that, an effective guide to administrative conduct. It makes a reality out of the myth of the neutral administrator acting "in accordance with law." And as usual law begets law. The wide latitude left to the states was ultimately narrowed by the states because there were clear legal issues to begin with. New York State welfare law, for example, is nearly six hundred pages in length, yet covers only the public assistance categories. Two pages—sixteen subsections—are devoted to the definition of *child, dependent,* and other features of the ADC category (Sec. 371). Still further specification of the category is provided in Section 349, in which parent eligibility is dealt with. This hardly exhausts the guidelines.

Some have objected that no full-scale reexamination of the system took place between 1935 and 1962.[11] That is not exactly true. At the federal level there was no basic revision because until the 1960s, during war, postwar, reaction, and recession, there were neither financial resources nor political support for it. But meanwhile serious changes in the law were taking place frequently in every state. When that reexamination did come, the eventual at-

10. See Douglas, *Social Security,* pp. 185–96.
11. See Steiner, *Social Insecurity,* p. 34, for example.

tack was on the very legal and organizational integrity of the welfare system it-self. The interest-group liberal leadership chose to improve and then to sup-plement the welfare system with nonlaw—discretion and bargaining. The onset of decline of the welfare state can be dated by those efforts.

New Welfare

John F. Kennedy ran into poverty for the first time in his privileged life only as he was preparing to run the country. To him it was a real discovery, and he carried it to Washington as part of that virgin territory, the New Frontier. His entire Administration was imbued with dedication to service, inspired by a glowing sense of their own efficacy, and infinitely confident of the great American system. They set themselves the heroic task, among many others, of eliminating poverty. Alleviation was for sissies.

Getting down to political realities, alleviation was also costing too much. Worse yet, too much of it was going to the wrong people. Still worse, the size of the welfare portion of public expenditure did not seem to show any down-ward responsiveness to prosperity. A closer look at these realities helps explain why the established welfare system came in for a serious reexamination in the 1960s.[12] However, it should be made clear before reviewing these factors that they do not explain the particular response the New Frontier and the Great Society finally formulated. Only the new public philosophy can explain that.

NEW FACTS ABOUT OLD WELFARE

The first politically relevant fact about the old welfare system was that after thirty years the several noncontributory, public assistance categories had not even begun to "wither away."[13] From the beginning, most experts and politi-cal leaders were confident that as the insurance features expanded the public assistance features would contract. After fifteen years of operation, this expec-tation was still expressed, although surely by this time it was totally mythologi-cal. At the time of a significant expansion of old-age-insurance benefits Presi-dent Truman could say, "The basic purpose of public assistance . . . is and has always been to supplement our social-insurance system. Our aim has been to expand coverage of social insurance and gradually reduce the need for supplementary public assistance programs."[14] Through the Eisenhower Ad-ministration the same theme was expressed, by enthusiasts outside and by the

---

12. In this I am most indebted to the excellent research of Gilbert Steiner and Sar Levitan, nei-ther of whom probably would agree entirely with the conclusions I draw.

13. Steiner, Chapter 2.

14. Quoted in Steiner, pp. 21–22.

hesitant inheritors within the Administration, who on this faith incorporated disability insurance into the old-age insurance system and significantly expanded its coverage.[15] Rather than wither away, public assistance payments have gone rather steadily upward. And, since the federal share of the payments also increased, the actual federal outlay increased significantly, while that of the states remained constant, but at a high level.

The second relevant political fact is that the composition of the public assistance rolls shifted toward the least influential and least admired of humanity. By the time John Kennedy took office, assistance to the aged, the most popular of the categories, actually declined, relatively speaking, as a proportion of the increasing number of older persons in the population.[16] The culprit, aid to dependent children (ADC), had grown steadily in cost and coverage since 1946. The plain and simple truth was that the typical ADC recipient had become a black woman with one or more children; one out of every five children on ADC was illegitimate; and double that many were children of broken homes and estranged parents.[17] At that time just below half of all ADC children (1,112,106) were black and half of them were sufficiently concentrated in our largest cities to constitute three-quarters of the ADC recipients there.[18] This is the backdrop of the New Frontier's social program.

The first response of President Kennedy to the problem of poverty was the result of his own apparent preference for government manipulation of aggregate demand, and this was reinforced by the conditions of mild recession and gold outflow which surrounded his election. However, his success seemed only to underscore the fact that prosperity is no antidote for poverty. If the bulk of public assistance is for unemployables, neither it nor the poor will be eradicated by an economy heated up even to 98 percent of full employment.

Given these unmistakable tendencies in the development of old welfare public assistance categories, the initial attack by the New Frontier is incredible. President Kennedy, HEW Secretary Abraham Ribicoff, and most of their welfare advisers produced the 1962 amendments to Social Security, which were the culmination of a massive reexamination. These were hailed as "landmarks"—"the most far-reaching revision of our public-welfare program since it was enacted in 1935." This bold revision amounted to nothing more than the provision of matching grants (up to one-fourth of state costs) as an incentive for the states to undertake rehabilitation programs in conjunction with ADC casework. How this was more bold than the Eisenhower self-help effort

15. Ibid., pp. 21–23. Mrs. Oveta Culp Hobby, secretary of Health, Education and Welfare, testified, "It really happens much faster than you think, as the federal old-age and survivors' insurance really begins to do its job, the need for public assistance would deteriorate."

16. Steiner, p. 23.

17. In Miller, *Poverty American Style*, p. 170. See also Steiner, pp. 26 ff.

18. Daniel P. Moynihan, "Employment, Income and the Ordeal of the Negro Family," *Daedalus* (Fall 1965), p. 762.

TABLE 8.2

WELFARE EXPENDITURES, 1929–76*

	Public Assistance			Social Insurance			Other Welfare Services†		
	TOTAL (IN MILLIONS OF DOLLARS)	FEDERAL PERCENTAGE	STATE AND LOCAL PERCENTAGE	TOTAL (IN MILLIONS OF DOLLARS)	FEDERAL PERCENTAGE	STATE AND LOCAL PERCENTAGE	TOTAL (IN MILLIONS OF DOLLARS)	FEDERAL PERCENTAGE	STATE AND LOCAL PERCENTAGE
1929	500	1	99	340	21	79	76	2	98
1935	2,998	79	21	384	26	74	99	2	98
1940	3,599	63	37	1,216	29	71	116	9	91
1945	1,031	41	59	1,388	53	47	198	33	67
1950	1,496	44	56	4,911	42	58	448	39	61
1955	3,003	50	50	9,845	65	35	619	41	59
1960	4,101	52	48	19,292	74	26	1,139	37	63
1965	6,283	57	43	28,090	78	22	2,062	39	61
1970	16,488	59	41	54,691	83	17	4,145	54	46
1971	21,262	61	39	66,369	81	19	4,983	55	45
1972	26,078	62	38	74,809	82	18	5,364	59	41
1973	28,691	63	37	86,165	84	16	5,698	62	38
1974	31,520	65	35	98,953	84	16	6,721	58	42
1975	40,709	67	33	122,947	81	19	7,532	57	43
1976	48,946	68	32	146,592	82	18	8,076	56	44

* SOURCE: *Health, Education and Welfare Trends*, 1966–67, Part I, National Trends (Washington, D.C.: U.S. Government Printing Office); *Social Security Bulletin* (January 1977), p. 7.

† Includes vocational rehabilitation, medical services, surplus food for institutions, child-welfare services under the Social Security Act, the Community Services Administration (formerly OEO), and ACTION. Columns 1 and 3 are a fair approximation of new welfare, column 2 of old welfare.

is hard to imagine.[19] It is significant only because it is a tip-off to the interest-group liberal approach to welfare that matured only three years later. The 1962 effort was an attempt to solve the real problems of ADC, a nondiscretionary program, merely by making it discretionary. ADC was in need of serious reform. But the means chosen in 1962 were the worst possible ones: simply to state a general national goal of getting people off the welfare rolls (a goal ardently shared by the Republicans) and to delegate the achievement of this goal to the state ADC programs and the public-assistance caseworkers.

The liberal solution thus seemed to be the incantation of some bold new words and the allocation of funds to provide incentives for each state to give real substance to the words. *Administrators far down the line were being told to make law. Further, local personnel were being assigned the personal responsibility for making federal law.* The fact that these increasingly strike-prone caseworkers were already overworked even without these new functions, that they were in no way professionally equipped to carry out the new rehabilitation and family-service work anticipated in the amendments, that by the very definition of their local status they could never make laws only shows how impossible the entire situation was.

The choice made by the president, his advisers, and Congress in 1962, after due consideration of impressive technical services, was to make no choice. All they did was to create a new function and a new set of powers, and then to set the political process going round them. Increments of change in the state ADC agency resulting from interactions among the agency, the interests, and the clientele would, it was hoped, ultimately result in a new program. This explains the 1962 amendments and the *modus operandi* of interest-group liberalism in the entire field of welfare. The "bold" 1962 package of amendments constitutes only a warm-up. The new welfare of interest-group liberalism came into full maturity in 1964 with the War on Poverty.

THE WAR ON POVERTY: UNDERLYING ASSUMPTIONS

Despite publicly expressed faith that the 1962 amendments constituted a "new spirit" and a "completely new philosophy . . . in welfare," actions inside the Kennedy Administration by mid-1963 indicated an entirely different private attitude. Kennedy had already used the phrase "war on poverty" in his 1960 campaign, and as it became increasingly clear that neither prosperity nor rehabilitation were going to wipe out his memory of and his promises to West Virginia, he ordered further "basic soul-searching" by the Council of Economic Advisers (CEA).[20] Soul-searching led to a flow of technical papers

19. For evaluations, see Steiner, pp. 34 ff. Steiner is himself critical but provides an excellent list of sources for those who would try to defend the 1962 amendments.
20. Facts on the prehistory of the War on Poverty are taken from John Bibby and Roger Davidson, *On Capitol Hill* (New York: Hotl,Rinehart and Winston, 1967), Chapter 7; Brian Henry Smith, unpublished master's thesis, Columbia University, 1966; and Isaac Balbus, unpublished master's thesis, University of Chicago, 1966.

by Council, Budget Bureau, and White House personnel, but without inspiration. In early November, Council Chairman Walter Heller issued a formal request to all the heads of domestic departments and major independent agencies to examine their existing programs as a means of generating new program suggestions.

The response to Heller's request was overwhelming, and probably not a little distressing. More than a hundred distinct proposals were made. However, each agency tended to see a new war waged by expansion of its own programs. All the CEA could do at this point was to seek the president's encouragement to plan toward a statement for one of the January messages to Congress.

One of President Johnson's earliest decisions upon taking office was to press for an antipoverty program: "That's my kind of program. It will help people." But the gnawing problem was that there had already been an unbelievable proliferation of uncoordinated programs "helping people." Each was in justifiable need of expansion because each was, indeed, already an attack on poverty. The Bureau of the Budget was called in to help process and evaluate the proposals in a manner not unlike its normal budget review. Unfortunately, however, this was neither normal budget review nor normal legislative clearance of individual agency proposals for legislation. It was full-scale program development—planning and policy-making at its highest level. The question here then becomes, how do interest-group liberal policy-makers go about their jobs when there is a large substantive (one is tempted to say *critical*) issue rather than several discrete, *incremental* issues? The answer is, *incrementally just the same, which means they make no substantive decision at all.* How can those who discover incrementalism at the top accept it as the reality of politics and not see it for what it really is—the implementation of an ideology?

It is not always easy to make a decision that is not a decision, but in the fall of 1963 such a solution was discovered. It was then that the Bureau of the Budget hit upon the notion of the "Community Action Program." Since there was to be a mere $500 million above existing program commitments for this antipoverty war, each agency feared loss of important roles in the war. One would think that under the circumstances a way would have to be found to make hard choices from an actual priority listing of public activities. But this is not only extremely difficult to do, according to prevailing public philosophy it is positively undersirable. The Community Action Program idea provided just the right tactic for avoidance. Priorities would be found not at first but at last.

The Community Action idea had been developed in the 1950s by Ford Foundation teams in "gray areas" of cities as a means of extending civic education. President Kennedy's juvenile delinquency program had made use of the same self-help idea in a small series of experimental efforts. The purpose of Community Action in the far larger War on Poverty was to provide a coordinated and comprehensive approach to poverty without basically altering existing federal patterns. It seemed to have dual virtues. It could involve the clientele and thus be self-educative as well as self-executing. And it would provide a method of substantially coordinating existing programs out in the field; that is, it provided a means of blasting loose a generation of professionally supported incrementalism at the bottom without bothering the top at all.

But why is coordination good at the local level and not good among the parent agencies at the center? Why do power structures need shaking up in Washington State but not in Washington, D.C.? Why was there talk of substantive policy in the cities and not in the federal government? A close look at the statute suggests that there was no perceived inconsistency between the two. The framers sought no revolt against the separated and stalemated power structure in Washington, D.C., not because they lacked the courage but *because their ideology blinded them to the need.*

The new welfare, perhaps more than any federal activity, was a systematic expression of interest-group liberalism. It was a classic example of provision of official routes to official recognition of private decisions reached by a process dimly specified in the statute. It was an ultimate in efforts to deliberately fulfill the pluralist conditions of groups-with-countervailing-groups. It was a paragon of policy-without-law.

New welfare was not only hostile to law. In implementation it was antithetical to rational and responsible administration, because the principle of representation is antithetical to the principle of administration. The further down the line one delegates power, the further into the administrative process one is forced to provide representation. While much of this is unavoidable, formalizing the fusion of administration and representation is a way of discrediting both. The worst results of interest-group liberalism in general and new welfare in particular follow from this. Let us look more closely at these tendencies.

NEW WELFARE IN LAW: ULTIMATE
INTEREST-GROUP LIBERALISM

The Economic Opportunity Act of 1964 was an omnibus act composed of seven titles and approximately ten programs—approximately because the number can shift according to the definition of a program. Some programs were new and distinct, like Job Corps, work-study, and Volunteers in Service to America (VISTA). Others involved expansion of existing programs—work-training, adult education, work-experience,[21] business incentives, and rural assistance (a tripartite feature of Title III). The total number depends especially upon how one counts the Community Action title (II) and the Office of

21. This was a small boost for the almost-forgotten "bold new philosophy" public welfare amendments of 1962.

Economic Opportunity (OEO, Title VI), because in these no programs were created but important powers were conferred.

Delegation of power is the order of the day in this statute. Operative standards are almost impossible to find anywhere in it. In contrast to the Social Security statute, this act reflects care to avoid the identification and definition of categories and to avoid cumulation of these into some kind of interrelated package. The most important sources of standards in old welfare—definitions, lists of examples, exceptions, exclusions, prerequisites—are almost absent here. In its place one find a grab bag. This was to be a war ending in the total elimination of poverty. The partisans praised it by condemning old welfare for dealing only with symptoms and not with causes. Yet, strangely enough, it was a war in which neither the enemy nor the methods were positively determined. It was a campaign waged without placing any strong imperatives to action upon the front line, the administrators. The act is a catchall of job-creating, job-training, and money-providing programs aimed largely at making lower-class life a bit more comfortable for the existing lower classes. Some object that it would have been paternalistic to have a program in which administrators had clear goals which they were obliged to seek. But nothing is more paternalistic than Job Corps, VISTA, and training for manual and semiskilled labor, however benevolent and permissive they may appear. Worse, and more directly to the point here, the absence of central direction and guidance simply deprived the disappointed of something to shoot against.[22] This is a paternalism that demoralizes.

Within each category, the statutory directives are almost completely end-oriented, but only in the sense that they express sentiments. Examples of ends that constitute sentiments rather than standards abound in the act. The director (of OEO) is empowered to arrange for the "education" and "training" of enrollees and to provide programs of "useful work experience." The VISTA volunteers are directed to "combat poverty"—with the consent of the governor, another completely undefined role. The climax of the legislation came in the formulation of community action, the real work component of the program, the core that was to draw the otherwise unrelated programs into a unity. The Community Action Program was defined as one:

1. which mobilizes and utilizes resources, public or private, of any urban or rural, or combined urban and rural, geographical area (referred to in this part as a "community"), including but not limited to a state, metropolitan area, county, city, town, multicity unit, or multi-county unit in an attack on poverty;
2. which provides services, assistance, and other activities of sufficient scope and size

22. In a perverse way, the case of the South and civil rights makes the same point. The fact that Southern states had actual laws governing racial privileges made it easier for civil-rights movements to get under way and helped bring about quicker changes. The Northern situation, in which power over race relations is delegated to public and private agencies, is more subtle, more permissive, less paternalistic only on the surface, and far more demoralizing. One need only note the failure of Martin Luther King's movement in Chicago.

to give promise of progress toward elimination of poverty or a cause or causes of poverty through developing employment opportunities, improving human performance, motivation, and productivity, or bettering the conditions under which people live, learn, and work;

3. which is developed, conducted, and administered with the maximum feasible participation of residents of the area and members of the groups served; and

4. which is conducted, administered, or coordinated by a public or private nonprofit agency (referred to in this title as a "community action organization") which is broadly representative of the community.[23]

Paragraph (1) defines location, which could be anything, and it is certainly *not* limited to all of the principalities and combinations of principalities known in the United States today. Paragraph (2) defines jurisdiction, which, other than limiting the focus to poverty, could be anything, and certainly is *not* limited to all of the sources of poverty and all of the ways of improving conditions known in the world today. Paragraph (3), of which more in a moment, defines one special condition regarding how poverty policy should be made. However, paragraph (4) makes clear that (3) is inclusive rather than exclusive by requiring the participation of any and every other relevant group besides the immediate clientele groups.

These features reveal the meaning of the Great Society's poverty program in no uncertain terms. The act is, especially in its most important and most novel titles, completely process-oriented nonlaw. It speaks of reaching the causes of poverty, but this is almost entirely rhetorical, for there is nothing in these clauses of the statute and official records that even the most legal-minded bureaucrat had to feel guided by. There is no guidance because all the apparent guidance is suggestive and permissive. Categories are open-ended; they are lists always introduced with "not limited to" or "such as." The following example is Sargent Shriver's important initial elaboration of the Community Action Program and how it would unify the effort to eliminate poverty:

The local organization applying for a community action program grant must satisfy only one basic criterion: it must be broadly representative of the interests of the community. It may be a public agency. . . . *Or it may be* a private nonprofit agency which has the support of *the relevant elements* of community government. . . .

Communities will have wide discretion in determining what program activities should be undertaken. . . . It *is likely* that community action programs will include activities *such as* the following, all focused on the problems of poor people:

1. Services and activities to develop new employment opportunities;
2. Strengthening the teaching of basic education skills, especially reading, writing and mathematics;

23. U.S. Congress, House, *To Mobilize the Human and Financial Resources of the Nation to Combat Poverty in the United States*, 88th Cong., 2d Sess., 1964, H.R. 10440, pp. 17–18.

3. Providing comprehensive academic counseling and guidance services and school social work services;
4. Providing after-school study centers, after-school tutoring, and summer, weekend, and after-school academic classes;
5. Establishing programs for the benefit of preschool children;
6. Reducing adult illiteracy;
7. Developing and carrying out special education or other programs for migrant or transient families;
8. Improving the living conditions of the elderly;
9. Arranging for or providing health examinations and health education for school children;
10. Rehabilitation and retraining of physically or mentally handicapped persons;
11. Providing health, rehabilitation, employment, educational, and related services to young men not qualified for military service;
12. Providing community child-care centers and youth activity centers;
13. Improving housing and living facilities and home management skills;
14. Providing services to enable families from rural areas to meet problems of urban living; *or*
15. Providing recreation and physical fitness services and facilities.[24]

Compare the language of the Social Security Act with the extremely informal and inclusive language of the Economic Opportunity Act, bearing in mind that the great bulk of Social Security law is in state-implementing statutes. In new welfare, the Economic Opportunity Act, including implementing documents such as Shriver's, *is all the law there was to be.*[25] Old welfare obviously works through law, new welfare through delegation.

Finally the poverty program got at causes no more, or no better than, the Social Security Act. In both, the assumption is that the cause of poverty is being poor. The difference is that the Social Security Act recognized that and went after it as a matter of law and appropriate bureaucratization. In contrast, the poverty program assumed, rightly, that something else is behind being poor. But rather than identify what it is, the act simply delegated to public and private groups the task of finding it out; and the causes were expected to vary from one city to another. Granted, the War on Poverty anticipated a wider array of palliatives than Social Security could. But if there were causes of poverty untouched by old welfare, why were the framers of new welfare so reluctant to identify them?

This question points to the primary features of the War on Poverty and how these are the direct and necessary expression of interest-group liberalism: (1) It is better not to state hard policy but only to start a process. (2) Everything is

24. *The War on Poverty*, Senate Document No. 86, Committee on Labor and Public Welfare, 88th Cong., 2d Sess. (Italics added.)
25. In the OEO's *Community Action Program Guide* and in various official statements, the OEO people have been extremely reluctant to specify standards even about the process itself. See, e.g., Barbara Carter, "Sargent Shriver and the Role of the Poor," *Reporter*, May 5, 1966, p. 18.

good to do. Make everything available and the bargaining process will provide the appropriate mix. (3) It is not desirable to distinguish too clearly between public and private agencies. Authority hampers the bargaining process. (4) The distinction between public and private is in general undesirable because it interferes with delegation of power by specifying goals and responsibilities; and you cannot have a real policy-making process without broad delegation of power. These sound familiar because this is the logic of interest-group liberalism whenever and wherever it operates as a guide to the public function.

Interest-group liberalism has produced two important consequences in new welfare. First, new welfare misses the new causes of poverty more than almost any conceivable program could. Second, new welfare demoralized the civil-rights movement and would demoralize any mass effort to redress injustices. Interest-group liberalism has thus produced two major antilibertarian consequences far more surely than if these consequences had been heartfelt intentions. These consequences were produced because of the refusal of interest-group liberalism to make moral choices and set clear legislative standards. Prosperity is its own kind of problem: When everything is good to do nothing seems compelling.

The End of New Welfare

Well before the Democrats were ousted from the White House in 1969, the consequences of new welfare could be clearly seen by those willing to study the legislation and then to look objectively at the situation in the field. A few cases during the first three years of new welfare will provide insights into discretionary welfare, and will provide the setting for the Republican succession.

Hardly eighteen months after the War on Poverty was declared, its most important ally and influential lobby, the Citizens Crusade Against Poverty (CCAP), held its national conference in Washington. Already on record for maximum feasible participation (its executive director is credited with the invention of that famous phrase), its purpose in holding the national conference was to whip up support for maximum participation and against government interference. Suddenly the CCAP found itself swept by a storm from within. During a speech by OEO Director Sargent Shriver, in which he was praising the revolutionary aspects of the program, the meeting fell into an uproar. Shriver hastily departed, and the floor was seized by angry militants who expressed their hatreds, one after the other, for one aspect of the program after another. One speaker was inconsistent with another, and it seemed to make no difference that their attack was upon an organization whose goals they themselves espoused.

The message seemed to be clear.[26] Hope had curdled into indignation. Such expressions characterized outbursts in many meetings all over the country, because frustrated hope is sewn into the War on Poverty. Early returns from several cities tended to bear this out.[27].

THREE YEARS OF COMMUNITY ACTION

New York City represents one extreme of experience with new welfare, an extreme in the degree of real, maximum participation. Many participating groups already existed; others were created with government assistance. Developments in New York from the beginning revolved mainly around fights for recognition among groups and leaders. The results: maximum participation and minimum appropriations of actual funds to the poor and their projects. The Harlem program, upon which so many hopes were pinned precisely because the makings of a good group process were available, was something of a disaster. Not a tenth of originally expected federal and local funds became available, and for a time new money was stopped and leadership was totally in abeyance while the executive director took a leave to trace the whereabouts of an unaccounted-for $400,000. One leader and one element of the black community, in Harlem and elsewhere in New York, was set off against another, culminating in strenuous battles to create peace. A real culture of poverty was in the making.

Chicago represents the other extreme. Here the experience was minimum feasible participation and maximum appropriation of funds to the poor. In New York the sense of futility come from stalemate. In Chicago it came from paternalism. Mayor Richard Daley's immense success in getting poverty funds seemed equaled only by his ability to use them in support of (or without hurting) the Democratic organization of Cook County. On paper his CAP organization scheme looks like an ideal design for such a program. But all the directors are handpicked and the local CAP representatives are appointed with all due political care. The mayor appoints the executive director, and the executive director appoints the directors of the neighborhood urban progress centers, who appoint the neighborhood advisory committees—whose chairmen are appointed by the executive director. In New York City, politics is fragmented; new welfare reinforced the fragmentation. In Chicago, politics is tightly controlled by a political machine; new welfare reinforced the machine.

26. See Morton Kondracke, Chicago *Sun-Times*, April 17, 1966.

27. I am grateful in particular for the research of Paul E. Peterson, whose doctoral dissertation so thoroughly covered CAPs in New York, Philadelphia, and Chicago ("City Politics and Community Action," University of Chicago, 1967). Unless otherwise cited, my source is very likely this. Much of Peterson's research was incorporated into J. David Greenstone and Paul E. Peterson, *Race and Authority in Urban Politics* (New York: Russell Sage Foundation, 1973). Later research by Greenstone, Peterson, and associates, cited below, tends to confirm my assessments here.

The situation in Philadelphia located itself somewhere between the two extremes, but it also seemed to have combined the worst features of both Chicago and New York. There was evidence of some appropriation of funds and a modicum of real participation; however, upon a closer look, the appropriation of funds was used to co-opt the support of the leading participants.[28] Thus, Philadelphia's program encouraged direct participation but managed to involve, during its first two years, less than 3 percent of the residents of the neighborhoods served. Here again the sense of futility, not only because participation and influence were necessarily so slight but because there was evidence that much of Philadelphia OEO appropriation served mainly the representatives and their families and friends. This is an aspect of job creation that was probably not anticipated. Nepotistic patronage can be just as demoralizing as party patronage.

Los Angeles was on par with New York. There was in fact even less success in getting OEO funds down into the neighborhoods, as outright gifts or as continuing programs. After the Watts riots the appropriations and programs increased, but this was a rather corrosive form of representation. It was a bit like chasing one's tail. After the crisis, the increase of federal funds appeared as blood money. The spontaneity of the programs was lost, or had never existed. Federal involvement became a case of "damned if you do and damned if you don't."

Lest it be thought that rioting before the program began made Los Angeles special, there was the case of Detroit. Here was another city relatively faithful to the process principles of the Economic Opportunity Act. Here there was no preliminary riot. Yet here it was "damned if they did." Detroit was as participatory as New York and as successful in getting federal funds as Chicago—it had one of the best records in the country. Yet at the very same time Mayor Jerome Cavanagh's stock with the ghetto blacks, a vital factor in Cavanagh's own mayoral election, was declining precipitously. When rioting came to Detroit, it was especially severe. Opening up such functional representation had served only to intensify awareness that blacks had only one representative on Detroit's nine-man, reformed, nonpartisan Common Council. Likewise for another riot-torn city—Newark—where city hall had been so conscientious as to let itself be frozen out almost altogether in the formation of maximum participation in the rawest extreme.[29]

The Syracuse program brings all these various tendencies best into focus. Here OEO took maximum participation seriously enough to grant $483,000

28. See Paul E. Peterson, "Strategies for Educational Reform: The War on Poverty Experience," paper presented to the 1967 Convention of the American Orthopsychiatric Association. In Philadelphia, "formal representation of the poor, by and large, scarcely altered community action proposals" (p. 10).

29. See accounts in the New York Times Magazine, August 27, 1967, p. 51; in Carter, "Sargent Shriver"; and Jules Witcover and Erwin Knoll, "Politics and the Poor: Shriver's Second Thoughts," Reporter, December 30, 1965, p. 24.

to help organize the official poverty agency (Crusade for Opportunity) and then to grant $314,000 to a joint university-Saul Alinsky group (the Syracuse Community Development Association—SCDA) to organize the poor independently for purposes of representation on the Crusade. An early effort, Syracuse was also an early case study in the results of adding the element of broad discretion to welfare. Such discretion, coupled with organizations deliberately set up to exploit it, led to creation of inconsistencies between the poor and the government that did not necessarily exist before. It created the myth of a unitary power structure despite the fact that most large cities are plagued with multiple rather than single power structures. It created a conflict in the mayor's mind about how he should work. In fact, *it made him look at the federal poverty funds as co-optative resources whether he wanted to or not.*[30]

Did the cities gain anything in return? Even as measured by standards relevant to the spirit of the act—turnout in the CAP neighborhood elections— these efforts tend to discredit new welfare: the turnout in Philadelphia for the 1965 elections for CAP representatives was less than 3 percent. Is this a measure of failure to involve the residents of the affected areas? Other cities would tend to suggest at least that the program was not working to the best pluralist expectations. In mid-February 1966, 5 percent (8,287) of Kansas City's eligible adults turned out for a poverty election. This followed efforts by 276 candidates and 4,000 volunteer canvassers, and an official get-out-the-vote campaign contribution of $50,000. Later in the same month, the turnout in Cleveland amounted to 4.2 percent despite thousands of man-hours of campaigning, generous newspaper appeals, and babysitting services. Fewer than 1 percent turned out in Los Angeles. If an outsider can empathize at all he must inevitably share a sense of futility and embarrassment in the midst of the incredible paternalism and the goody-goody character of the organizing efforts.

End of the War: Armistice or Surrender?

In no area of government was there greater opportunity for policy change in 1969 than in the area of social welfare. The War on Poverty was being lost in the urban quagmire. Although many of its specific programs enjoyed strong support, overall support for OEO itself was not enough to prevent dismemberment and discontinuation. Yet, the sinking of new welfare did not yield political or economic benefits for old welfare. Unprecedented generosity—as measured by transfers, cash grants, and assistance-in-kind—had not made much

30. See Witcover and Knoll; see also, by same authors, "Organizing the Poor," in Miller, *Poverty American Style*, pp. 247 ff.

of a dent in the poverty, dependency, delinquency, or despair against which the 1964 war had been declared. There may always be controversy about the true extent of our generosity and the true extent of our success or failure during the decade following that declaration of war. But few would disagree with the contention that the poverty gap remained wide and that if it had been narrowed at all, the narrowing was not commensurate to the decade's expenditure of effort and money. Indeed, there would probably be universal agreement that the impact of the War on Poverty had fallen far short of the claims of its designers. Already by 1969 a reaction had set in, among Democrats as well as Republicans, and it was going to affect old welfare as well as new welfare.

ENDING THE WAR, SPOILING THE SPOILS

My evaluation of the War on Poverty in 1967–68, after a mere three years of experience, relied heavily upon the argument that weaknesses inherent in such a program would prevent it from fulfilling its mission. It is appropriate to compare those original estimates with careful evaluations of over ten years of experience with actual Community Action Programs throughout the country: "[The] goal of better service coordination proved so unfeasible from the beginning that both OEO and local Community Action Agency (CAA) officials devoted few resources to achieving it, and had almost no success."[31] However, as anyone with knowledge of bureaucratic politics should have expected, this abandonment of original mission did not lead to the abandonment of the program but rather to the search for a new mission. As these authors put it, Community Action "became an attack on political poverty."[32] In other words, instead of attempting to make use of citizen action to increase the amount of assistance to the poor and to direct the type of assistance to the poor, the program shifted the definition of the term *poverty* and diverted its own efforts toward creating the participation that pluralism had assumed was already there.

This is not to deny that the poor, including the black poor, made some economic progress during the decade after 1964. We can agree that progress was made, while leaving the assessment of the actual extent of progress to the experts. Yet, many of the experts who will argue that progress was made will also argue that the relationship of this progress to the War on Poverty was largely coincidental. One very important evaluation puts it this way:

31. Paul E. Peterson and J. David Greenstone, "Racial Change and Citizen Participation: The Mobilization of Low-Income Communities through Community Action," in Robert H. Haveman, ed., *A Decade of Federal Antipoverty Programs* (Madison, Wisc.: Institute for Research on Poverty, 1977), p. 241.
32. Ibid., p. 241.

It would be more accurate to say that while planned antipoverty policies have been responsible for some increase in the productivity and earnings of the poor, other changes also contributed to poverty reduction. Many of these latter changes were neither designed nor coordinated as part of the War on Poverty and, in many cases, were unanticipated and, on occasion, opposed by policy planners.[33]

The only sure and certain direct economic contribution of the War on Poverty to the poor in the urban ghettos was the jobs provided for certain residents of these areas in the Community Action programs themselves. Since these jobs were quite visible and paid better than the average ghetto jobs, and since blacks were given preference in program hiring, the effect of OEO in the ghettos was symbolically extremely strong and economically measurable. But was this to be claimed as a key strategy in a total War on Poverty? If that is the case, then clearly a War on Poverty is not nearly as good as a WPA. Since there were no restraints on the local Community Action leaders except the very general one that they should encourage "maximum feasible participation," they were freed to use the available Community Action jobs as patronage in the oldest American sense of the term. Leaving aside instances of crass nepotism, a key consideration in the disposition of jobs within the Community Action Programs was the building of agency support in the communities and for purposes of political clout back in Washington. Thus at least a proportion of the economic impact of the War on Poverty was incidental to (academically, a "latent function" of) the struggle of the program to create a constituency for itself. Claiming this as a success for the program would be akin to a claim by Japanese after World War II that they had gone to war against the United States in order to modernize their political system.

The most important direct economic benefit coming out of the entire War on Poverty is probably the single contribution of the Office of Legal Services. Going far beyond the expected provision of legal services for divorces, credit disputes, arguments over leases or installment buying, the young and dedicated lawyers in the agency counseled thousands of poor people on their rights and opportunities within the Social Security programs of old welfare. The striking increases in the numbers of persons covered by Social Security programs, especially Aid to Families of Dependent Children (AFDC or ADC), during the 1960s and early 1970s was to a large extent due to the success of the Legal Services program. And, even though the Legal Services program was housed in the Community Action agencies of local communities, this was not the happy relationship that was implied by the War on Poverty plans; in fact, almost immediately after the founding of Community Action programs, the

33. Robert H. Haveman, in ibid., p. 9. Relevant to this point is the essay by Henry Levin in the same volume, Chapter 4. All the essays in this volume are by independent scholars and each bears in its own way on these issues. See also Robert D. Plotnick and Felicity Skidmore, *Progress Against Poverty—A Review of the 1964–1974 Decade* (New York: Academic Press, 1975).

Legal Services office began efforts to escape OEO altogether. And finally, the very success of Legal Services in bringing real economic benefit to increasing numbers of poor people undermined the political position of the Office of Legal Services itself. By 1975 it had been fully reorganized as the Legal Services Corporation operating under new legislation that restricted rather severely some of the most radical propoor activities for which the Office of Legal Services had been noted.[34]

Other advances in the condition of the poor in the United States might well be attributed either to the direct action of War on Poverty agencies or at least to the preoccupation with poverty and hunger which the War on Poverty legislation reflected and also helped to engender. However, probably a much larger share of any modest progress made in improving the condition of the poor during this decade should be attributed to general improvements in the economy quite independent of the War on Poverty itself.[35]

The search for an impact and a meaning for the War on Poverty will therefore have to concentrate upon the political rather than the economic side. And it may well be the consensus of those who have studied the War on Poverty in actual communities that there was a marked increase in the participation of the poor and of minorities during the decade or so following the enactment of the War on Poverty legislation. In addition to the jobs made directly available by the implanting of War on Poverty agencies in urban centers, it is fairly clear that other federal and federally funded programs also opened up new opportunities for blacks and minorities. One distinguished black political scientist who was often critical of government programs conceded nevertheless that "the public sector [is] a steadily increasing source of employment for blacks and poor people."[36] And many would agree that this extended beyond the favorable hiring practices of new federal programs into the hiring practices of local governments themselves.

But still, the nagging question is whether or to what extent these advances were attributable to the War on Poverty agencies and their Community Action programs at local levels. A case might be made both ways, but any case favoring the record of the War on Poverty would have to explain away the existence and expansion of the civil-rights movement itself that both preceded and extended through the period of the War on Poverty. The War on Poverty was in large part a response to the civil-rights movement, and it is fairly certain that the civil-rights movement would have continued to move into Northern cities and to agitate for an expansion of minority rights whether the

34. A full account of the successes and the struggles of the Office of Legal Services will be found in Ellen Jane Hollingsworth, "Ten Years of Legal Services for the Poor," in Robert Haveman, Chapter 7.

35. Efforts to evaluate the extent of improvement and to identify the causes of that improvement will be found in Haveman, Chapters 1 and 3; and also Robert Plotnick and Felicity Skidmore.

36. Charles V. Hamilton, quoted in Peterson and Greenstone, "Racial Change," p. 271.

War on Poverty had existed or not. Not everyone will agree with my earlier argument that the War on Poverty actually reduced the effectiveness of the civil-rights movement by converting its clear moral authority based upon rights to a purely political interest-group pattern without any great moral advantage once the definition of the problem was transformed from the issue of civil rights to the issue of economic rights. But whatever the case, no one would really wish to deny the tremendous effectiveness of such local groups as Chicago's Operation PUSH and of the pressures of federal civil-rights programs upon the hiring practices of private corporations. All of this is to say that blacks had begun to participate in the political process in very large numbers and most probably would have begun to have political successes on a broad front regardless of the efforts of War on Poverty agencies.

The main influence of the War on Poverty on political participation seems to have been on the form rather than the amount of the increase. Community Action agencies invited thousands of members of minority groups to sit on their city-wide and district boards, to become paid, part-time, and voluntary members of their staffs, and to participate in the campaigns of CAA-sponsored elections or to attend meetings where CAA policies were formulated to help determine the mix of federal services. Community Action agencies also provided funds and other support for many independently organized neighborhood associations and in effect became the sponsor of many such associations and federations of these associations. This was the way they fulfilled their goals of "maximum feasible participation," and at the same time helped create a supportive constituency for the agency itself.[37] Surely this participatory ferment encouraged the Community Action agencies to spread beyond agency-sponsored activity and added participants to many political processes totally independent of agency activities. But this would have to be considered a small part of the larger ferment produced by the civil-rights movement and by the simple coming of age of blacks in Northern cities. Appraisal of the exact nature of the impact of the War on Poverty on political participation will have to be found within the agencies' activities themselves rather than in the general political situation in cities, where it is only one of many more important contributors.

The most probable influence of the War on Poverty on political participation is the increase of participation within federal government activities themselves, most particularly those activities that came within the administrative control of the local Community Action program. That is to say, political participation engendered by the War on Poverty was largely sponsored participation. It was participation within the agency activities, with or without expectation of immediate personal gain. It was participation that may have provided gains for the participants but at the same time would certainly have

37. More details will be found in Peterson and Greenstone.

provided support for the agency. It is a form of participation that would rise and fall proportionately to the political fortunes of the sponsoring agency. And it is the form of participation that was anticipated within the interest-group liberal model spelled out in this volume.

A second aspect of the influence of Community Action programs upon participation was that it was heavily middle class in bias. This is not only an evaluation made by some of its critics but also by many of the most ardent friends of sponsored community participation. For example, Milton Kotler, who, in the 1960s, wrote a very eloquent book on the virtues of neighborhood government, concedes that the so-called mobilization of the poor under OEO amounted to the mobilization of the black middle class. He simply goes on to say that the advancement of the interests of the black middle class did not come at the direct expense of the black poor and that the successes of the black middle class encouraged the emergence of still other movements for full inclusion in the body politic. What measure of success is it to say simply that the advancement of the black middle classes did not come at the direct expense of the black poor? As Kotler himself concedes, the result of all this was simply the inclusion of one or more new interest to the cast of characters in the American pluralistic system.[38]

Third and finally, the increased participation and influence directly attributable to the War on Poverty and its Community Action programs has been highly specialized. In most instances this influence simply does not extend beyond the federally sponsored programs themselves, and that tends to mean only those federally sponsored programs within the original War on Poverty. For example, a very careful and friendly study of the Community Action program in Providence, Rhode Island, concluded as follows:

Without the conditions of client participation attached to these programs by Federal authorities, it is improbable that these currents would have taken hold. The importance of such participation requirements is suggested by the history of the Model Cities program in Providence. . . . Blacks and other minorities have not been nearly as successful in building political power through Model Cities as they were with the CAP.[39]

This tendency toward the specialization of the influence is particularly troubling because it confirms the broader argument made earlier in this chapter that War on Poverty programs, because of their stress on economics and bargaining and plural-group representation, were likely to blunt the civil-rights movement and the moral authority of their absolute claim to increased recognition and representation all across the board. We now see it taking the form of the ability of minorities to capture programs designed for them and the inability in most cities to spread that influence through one set of pro-

38. Cited in Haveman, A Decade, pp. 281–83. Kotler's 1960s book is Neighborhood Government: The Local Foundations of Political Life (New York: Bobbs-Merrill, 1969).

39. John A. Perrotta, "Machine Influence on a Community Action Program: The Case of Providence, Rhode Island," Polity (Summer 1977), p. 502.

grams toward a variety of other programs. This calls to mind once again the proposition that blacks and other minorities have gained whatever general influence in the cities they have through the rise of general political leadership in these minority communities and their claim through confrontation and through the electoral process upon the governmental structures and processes in these cities. In fact, in many instances the specialized influence of the War on Poverty agencies can be a barrier to the spread of the political influence of minorities. At the end of his book-length evaluation of the Community Action program in Pittsburgh, Neil Gilbert concluded that the Community Action program was not a good "platform from which to launch a citizen's movement for deep-seated social reform." A study of five California cities came to a reinforcing conclusion, that, "if one . . . seeks to determine the cumulative influences [of various participatory techniques] on redirecting the focus and content of any part of the social service system, one finds relatively little change in the basic orientation of health, education, and welfare agencies." And, in a book the author chose to entitle *The Betrayal of the Poor* after having studied a sample of twenty cities drawn from a universe of all cities over 50,000 in population, Stephen Rose reported that only 3 percent of the Community Action programs had any general institutional change orientation at all. Another study of a sample of fifty-one cities by Jeannette Hopkins and Kenneth Clark reported a basic agreement with the contention that the influence as well as the orientation of these Community Action programs was extremely limited or specialized.[40]

Although there may be many specific exceptions to the patterns reported here, the net experience with the politics of the War on Poverty confirms the general proposition that interest-group-liberal policies are basically conservative, co-optive, demoralizing, and contrary to the very best sentiments and goals expressed by the liberals themselves. We do not, however, have to go as far as Piven and Cloward who argue that the co-optive and demoralizing results of Community Action were put in the legislation as part of a conspiracy among Democratic Party officials to finesse the discontent that was being expressed and organized in the minority sections of the city.[41]

Although it is true that the Community Action aspects of the legislation had not been the cause of some large pressure group, and although the drafting of this legislation occurred in virtually a public-opinion vacuum, the record does not show that the legislative leadership was any more aware of the need to placate discontent during the drafting of the War on Poverty than it was during the drafting of the civil-rights legislation, the various old welfare amendments, the other unrelated urban legislation, and many other pieces of

40. These and other studies are reviewed with considerable care in Peterson and Greenstone, "Racial Change," pp. 256–74.

41. Frances Fox Piven and Richard A. Cloward, *Regulating the Poor* (New York: Pantheon, 1971), pp. 256–82.

legislation before, during, and after that period in which no arrangements at all were made for "maximum feasible participation." It seems much closer to the actual sentiments of that time to say that the participatory phrasing was simply one more aspect of a general and sincere sentiment that we could have our positive state, reorient our services toward the poor, and at the same time avoid the appearance of governmental coercion by making money and processes available and leaving the ultimate choices up for grabs. That is to say, the ideology of interest-group liberalism was fully in the ascendancy and was taking a more positive posture by intervening to encourage the formation of interest groups where they did not yet exist. The results tended to be very much the ones Piven and Cloward had expected. But no conspiracy theory is needed. The results were a direct function of the interest-group-liberal policy structure. The Community Action policy within the War on Poverty offers a pure case of the extent to which policy can shape politics.

NEW WELFARE, OLD WELFARE, AND BEYOND

Republicans may generally be caught in a dilemma: They can support the expansion of welfare benefits and alienate their own constituencies, or they can oppose the expansion of welfare benefits and risk losing their access to the larger constituency that can give them majorities in Congress and in the Electoral College. But in 1969 there was enough criticism from Democrats as well as Republicans to reduce political risk to a minimum. There was in fact a pressure for fundamental reform that was going to be very difficult to evade. Nixon's explicit war against the War on Poverty was not actually declared until his budget message of 1973, following his great reelection victory. But his most fundamental efforts at welfare reform and social services came during his first term and were in old rather than new welfare.

By 1969, virtually everyone agreed not only that something was rotten in the state of welfare, but they tended also to agree on what was rotten. Benefits to the needy were too variable from one region to another and from one state to another. Benefits might be discouraging honest employment. The whole system was too costly. People were using it as a guaranteed annual income rather than as a source of emergency and temporary assistance. At the same time, only a small proportion of the total welfare outlay was actually reaching the poor. We had discovered that the cost of eliminating a poverty gap was far in excess of the poverty gap itself. For, if payments improved conditions for the poor by bringing them up toward a subsistence level, many low-wage workers would discover it was just as profitable to take the welfare as to continue working. As one observer put it, "Once adopted, the no-poverty target would recede, and the cost of reaching it would grow."[42]

42. Vincent J. Burke and Vee Burke, *Nixon's Good Deed* (New York: Columbia University Press, 1974), p. 13.

TABLE 8.3

FEDERAL SOCIAL WELFARE EXPENDITURES*
(IN MILLIONS OF DOLLARS)

	FISCAL YEAR 1965	FISCAL YEAR 1970	FISCAL YEAR 1976
Social insurance	21,806	42,245	120,809
Public aid	3,593	9,648	33,244
Health and medical programs	2,780	4,775	9,353
Veterans programs	6,010	8,901	18,790
Education	2,469	5,875	9,168
Housing	238	581	2,427
Other social welfare (Vocational rehabilitation, child nutrition, OEO, and ACTION)	812	2,258	4,534
TOTAL	37,708	77,433	196,325

* SOURCE: *Social Security Bulletin* (Washington, D.C.: U.S. Government Printing Office, January 1977), pp. 5–7. For a more discriminating statement of federal social welfare expenditures, see Lawrence A. Lynn, "A Decade of Policy Developments in the Income Maintenance System," in Robert Haveman, A *Decade of Federal Antipoverty Programs*.

Table 8.3 adds a few details to Table 8.2 (p. 209) and also presents a close approximation of the actual extent of federal involvement in our security.[43] To paraphrase an old cigarette commercial, we were spending more and enjoying it less.

Almost immediately upon assuming office, President Nixon proposed a bold Family Assistance Plan to replace AFDC (ADC), which had become more burdensome and more controversial than ever. In brief, the Family Assistance Plan (FAP) would have replaced AFDC with a basic federal payment of $1,600 a year for a family of four. Though this sounds paltry, it would have increased welfare benefits above current levels in eighteen states. The remaining states would have been required to maintain their current levels by supplementing the federal minimum, with the federal government paying at least a percentage of that supplement. FAP also provided, for the first time, benefit eligibility for the working poor. Under FAP the unemployed were required to take job training or lose their portion of the family benefit.

Nixon did not get his FAP. Although it passed the House of Representatives once in 1970 and again in 1971, it was killed in the Senate by an unusual alliance of liberals, who found FAP too severe in the level of support and in its work requirements, and conservatives, who opposed FAP because it was to

43. Estimates of actual welfare effort will vary from expert to expert, but the figures in Table 8.3 are sufficient to convey the appropriate impression.

them the beginning of a guaranteed annual income.[44] Although Nixon did not get his FAP, he did succeed in a less spectacular but still quite fundamental reform—the consolidation of the three other important programs of Social Security into a single national income maintenance program. Enacted into law late in 1972, to take effect at the start of 1974, Supplemental Security Income took the elderly, the blind, and the disabled and gave them a minimum income as a *matter of right*. This was in addition to any social insurance that they might carry. If judged needy under federal provisions, these three categories were eligible for a supplemental check each month regardless of whether they had ever paid any Social Security payroll taxes. But this very important advancement in social welfare skirted the major problem, the very problem Nixon had sought to confront with his FAP. As the Burkes put it, "That daring dream of radicals, the right to a minimum income from the United States Treasury, has come true for all but one group of those Americans who society feels should not be obliged to work."[45] Children had proven to be the most difficult to reach of the four categories of people who were not expected to work in our society. But that does not mean that children were eliminated. It simply means that they were left with the AFDC program as it had stood roughly since 1961. Moreover, as we shall see, even under the FAP, certain essential features of it would not have changed. That is to say, FAP and AFDC confronted the central problem of social welfare in the United States with almost exactly the same set of attitudes: extend the coverage and broaden the discretion.

The Democrats in 1961 had already changed the original Aid to Dependent Children (ADC) along these lines. It had become AFDC in order to get behind the sources of dependency and poverty among children, and this change had not only converted elements of old welfare into new welfare but also provided the basis for the tremendous expansion and coverage that we witnessed for over a decade following 1961. That legislation had also broadened coverage through AFDC-U to cover certain unemployed parents in two-parent families, in order to respond to the charge that AFDC was encouraging families to disintegrate. Aid to Dependent Children had been one of the lesser titles in the 1935 Social Security Act, extending assistance to "children deprived of parental support or care by reason of death, continued absence from home, or physical or mental incapacity of a parent." We have already seen how this was converted, especially after 1961, from aid-to-children to a discretionary aid-to-families-by-federal-grants-for-states-to-undertake-rehabilitation. All during the 1960s discretion was creating anomalies. Benefits varied greatly. Eligibility varied. Even as late as the mid-1970s only twenty-six of the states, plus the District of Columbia, had AFDC-U at all, with twenty-four of the states continuing to deny AFDC benefits to most two-parent families.

44. Lengthy accounts of FAP will be found in Burke and Burke, and in Daniel Patrick Moynihan, *The Politics of a Guaranteed Income* (New York: Random House, 1973).
45. Burke and Burke, p. 188.

In 1967 Congress liberalized the work disincentive aspects of AFDC by providing that federal case workers could ignore a portion of the earnings that welfare recipients could make from low-paid or part-time jobs so that an increase of $1 from the job did not amount to a 100 percent tax by a reduction of welfare benefits by $1. At first blush this sounds like a clear and unmistakable provision in the 1967 reforms; however, the structure of the entire AFDC is so loose that the actual calculation of total benefits in relation to earned income is done by at least eight different formulas.[46] Further discretion in the 1967 reforms will be found in the provision for the Work Incentive Program. First called WIP, this was changed to WIN because of the implications of its requirements that fathers and mothers, and in some cases older children in AFDC families, must register for work with the state employment service and be engaged in active job searches or training programs.

By the mid-1970s, AFDC had become a guaranteed income for female-headed households, despite every effort by the federal government and its case workers to control eligibility. Official figures for 1966 showed that more than a third of the eligible were not receiving AFDC benefits, while by 1971 this proportion had fallen below a tenth.[47] Nevertheless, access in all respects was left to the discretion of federal case workers and state legislatures, and therefore was left to vary from state to state. AFDC is indeed a guaranteed income, but it is also a very minimum income and one that is subject to whim, circumstance, and geography. And it is also one that does not necessarily reach the children toward whom it is aimed. Even the Nixon FAP would not have changed the coverage, the sub-subsistence minimum, or the discretion of the case workers, because eligibility would still have been based upon parents and upon their willingness, in the judgment of the case workers, to take the job or the job training. Under FAP, as under AFDC before and after FAP was proposed, there was to be no direct aid to children regardless of the condition of the parents.

Having abandoned FAP, the president and Congress had left AFDC as it had become already by 1969—one of the three largest programs of public assistance outside social insurance. The other two are food stamps and Medicaid. Food stamps and Medicaid differ from AFDC inasmuch as the two of them provide assistance-in-kind rather than direct monetary grants. Food stamps are a form of cash, but they are tied to specified purchases of food. Medicaid provides each welfare recipient with a Medicaid card which can be presented at a hospital in lieu of payment. What is more significant is the fact that neither of these is unconditional but is tied to the AFDC system. Issuance of food stamps is probably more discretionary than AFDC itself because the law provided that any household would be eligible for food stamps if its income "is determined to be a substantially limiting factor in the attain-

46. Frederick Doolittle et al., "The Mirage of Welfare Reform," *The Public Interest* (Spring 1977), p. 65.
47. Doolittle et al., p. 66.

ment of a nutritionally adequate diet." This meant that the program was not to be limited strictly to public welfare recipients. The question of adequacy would be left to the state and local welfare agencies. The agency was also given discretion to determine the household's normal food budget and to decide the value of the stamps that would be necessary to bring it up to an adequate amount.

Discretion was also left to the lower federal agents and the state and local agencies to determine if food-stamp applicants had met the AFDC requirement that, if unemployed, they were registering for work and accepting available employment; and, as with AFDC, increases in earned income were calculated as reduced food-stamp benefits. Once the federal expenditures for food stamps began to move up from $70 million in 1966 to $5.6 billion in 1976, many began to appreciate the food-stamp program as a "mininegative income tax."[48]

Medicaid is far more complicated, but its main lines and meanings can be rather easily set forth. Passed in 1965 as Title 19 of the Social Security Act, Medicaid was designed to reach all of the poor who were not old enough to be covered by Medicare. But unlike Medicare, and more like AFDC, few standards were provided in the act, and the basic decisions were left to the Social Security agency, and, primarily, to the states. Although provisions vary widely from state to state, all but one state (Arizona) had a Medicaid program as of the middle 1970s, and all of the states geared their eligibility to AFDC and AFDC-U. Some states extended their coverage to include some people who were not on AFDC but who fell far enough below a state-established threshold to be considered "medically indigent." Medicare is a discretionary program in a still more important, and characteristic, way: Except for the question of eligibility and employability, discretion has been turned over to the medical profession and to the hospitals. Once a Medicaid card has been issued to the AFDC beneficiary or to the others who have qualified as medically indigent, that card is presented to the hospital and doctor in lieu of charges. It is left to the doctor in the hospital to judge the appropriateness and amount of service and to determine the amounts to charge. The federal government simply acts with the states as the third party to the transaction without passing any further judgments upon the nature of service or the amount charged.

It would seem fairly certain that the tying of Medicaid to AFDC contributed to the increasing attractiveness, and expansion, of AFDC as a regular source of livelihood rather than as an emergency recourse. It is even more clear that Medicaid has encouraged people to stay on AFDC rather than to

48. Attributed to Richard Nathan. A concise treatment of the possible meaning of the food-stamp program will be found in Doolittle et al., pp. 66–67. Doolittle and associates observed that if the net value of food stamps was counted as income, the official count of the number of people in poverty would be reduced by as much as one-sixth.

take a job or expand the number of hours per month on the job, because in most cases Medicaid is discontinued when the person leaves the AFDC rolls. But Medicaid is significant in still another way, and this points to something relatively new and quite fundamental in the liberal state: The federal government is the third party in a very special sense. It does not intervene between the beneficiary and the physician or hospital; rather it *underwrites* the costs of that relationship. The doctor and patient enter into their usual cash nexus. The federal government simply guarantees that the payment will be made once the service has been performed to the doctor's satisfaction. This is not the same as a direct cash payment program from which an AFDC mother could divert any amount she wished for medical services. Nor is it like a food-stamp program where the beneficiary might be given supervalued dollars on condition they be spent for medical services.[49] Instead, Medicaid is a substantial part of what can now be called the *state of permanent receivership*. Through the technique of underwriting a relationship or a transaction, the government can influence without intervening; it can influence conduct without issuing rules and regulations determining that conduct but by manipulating the value of resources between alternative endeavors, some of which are underwritten and some of which are not. Underwriting is a fiscal or monetary technique, but it can be used in a far more discretionary manner than the traditional, fiscal and monetary policies, such as the tax structure or the Federal Reserve discount rate. Much more will be said of underwriting and of the state of permanent receivership in Chapter 10, but it is important to note here the fact that it has become an important feature of social welfare in the United States.

The political characteristics of underwriting go far to explain why the medical profession could have been lulled into quiescence, if not downright support for Medicaid after having opposed its passage so strenuously as socialized medicine. Underwriting is a constitutional way of delegating governmental power to private agencies, groups, corporations, and individuals. It gives producers and consumers within a sector a control over their environments that they would not have without government assistance, and yet this can be provided without changing any statuses. Underwriting perpetuates existing structures and relationships by reducing the risk of individual ventures, and through that it stabilizes the entire sector. From the perspective of the doctor and the hospital, underwriting works doubly well in the medical services sector because it provides no incentive to the consumer to exercise rational economic behavior—that is, to seek to restrain the producer by checking prices or by considering alternative services or alternative uses of the available re-

49. The idea of a medical-stamp equivalent to a food stamp has not, to my knowledge, been considered. But it could very well be a substantial alternative to Medicaid and other governmentally supported medical service programs, in that the doctor-patient relationship could be left alone but patients could play a greater role in deciding how much of their income should be diverted for medical service.

sources. For the patient, Medicaid is wasted if not used, and at the same time it enables the doctor and the hospital to universalize their services without risk and without a ceiling on cost. Even if standards are eventually enacted to regulate charges for particular medical services, there will still be no effective ceiling on the cost of Medicaid because of the discretion available to the doctor and the hospital to gouge the government through the provision of unnecessary services, especially services that are most profitable with least expenditure of time. To bring it down to its barest essentials, Medicaid policy has been emptied of law and therefore develops a political process accordingly. It is that same political process we have noted all through the analysis of interest-group liberalism—the decline of a public awareness, the decline of democratic conflict, the reduction of government to the preferences of the agencies and the clientele most concerned with a particular program.

Thus the verdict on new welfare presented earlier in the chapter is supported by the tendencies of four presidential Administrations: When governmental authority is delegated in programs to administrators without clear guidelines as to the purpose and limits of the programs—that is, when governments make policies-without-law—the resulting relationship between the agencies and citizens will tend not to be to the liking of the very persons who had supported the programs in the first place.

OLD WELFARE VERSUS NEW WELFARE

Welfare is a politicoeconomic conception appropriate to a special economic problem. *That problem is the problem of scarcity and of inefficient distribution of wealth under capitalism.* Old welfare was a successful effort to come to grips with poverty caused by capitalist technology and capitalist methods of production and distribution. The purpose of old welfare was and is to make the march to the grave a bit more comfortable. Capitalist poverty is an objective thing; it is a random harvest. Therefore it possesses the virtue of being susceptible to treatment by general rules and by bureaucratization of their implementation. Nothing is wrong with old welfare that cannot be reformed by merely increasing redistribution or revising categories as capitalist organization changes. The criticism that old welfare must perpetuate poverty is an absurdity. The welfare dole is no more demeaning than the socioeconomic conditions that made it necessary. Old welfare was and is an immensely successful means of tending to the human exhaust of capitalism.

New welfare is based upon a most meaningful, deliberate ignorance. Its creators sought to combat the poverty of their age as though poverty is poverty is poverty. But this is not true, and they would be incredibly obtuse to believe that it is. The phenomenon being called poverty today is not capitalistic poverty. The phenomenon we fight today is not a random thing, not a natural consequence of the objective weakness of economic or environmental forces.

The phenomenon we fight today is in fact not poverty at all. The phenomenon is the injustice that has made poverty a nonrandom, nonobjective category. Poverty in this case is the merest epiphenomenon, and there is nothing at this level that old welfare could not and cannot do better than new welfare.

The real task of our time was to attack injustice and to change social rules and conduct in order that poverty become and remain a random thing, an objective category. The interest-group-liberal approach—defining the effort as economic, attaching it to the welfare system, and making it almost totally discretionary—was not merely superfluous and redundant; it produced a whole array of unhappy consequences. These consequences were unintended, but they are not paradoxical. They arise out of features of the War on Poverty that were deliberately sought by the interest-group liberals. All but one of the consequences fit as various headings under the general rubric *conservatism*. I choose the word deliberately, despite Chapter 3, because it best evokes a sense of the very things to which traditional liberalism claimed to be most antagonistic. The last of the types of consequences is better termed *radical*; but that only confirms the character of the other consequences, because radicalism always tends to follow militancy against change.

Dulling the edge of civil rights • In general the War on Poverty blocked change by falsely focusing the attentions of responsible persons sincerely committed to social change. In particular, it is astonishing how many black leaders were taken in by the appeals of Community Action and the paltry extra sums of money forthcoming. The demand for civil rights declined as the demand for poverty money increased. The one cause was deserted for the other. Civil rights was for the South. Social injustice in the North was not to be rectified but only indemnified. For the South there was morality, for the North equity.

The "Peachum factor" • The effects of the War on Poverty were also conservative in their pattern of implementation. Delegation of the program to private groups requires official recognition of groups and representatives. In the first round we may be impressed by emergence of new groups—and at least impressed by the amount of effort expended to bring new groups about. However, once the situation is stabilized by official recognition of groups and representatives, the situation tends to militate against emergence of still newer groups. Official recognition is a very conservative force; at the neighborhood level, federal recognition becomes a valuable resource with which some groups can demoralize others. In South Chicago a gang called the Blackstone Rangers maintained its monopoly position through intimidation: "You belong to our gang or I'll knock your head off." Government recognition can work the same way: "Now we are official. If you don't join us you won't have any access." Official recognition tends to congeal social relationships. The latter instance differs from the Blackstone Rangers case only in the subtlety of the intimidation. And, as Peachum and MacHeath teach in "The Three-penny Opera," the poor are the easiest of all to intimidate, especially with symbols of authority.

The pseudo-Marxian factor • In order to overcome one kind of false consciousness, the War on Poverty sought to instill another; and it, too, militated against change. As the experience in Syracuse illustrated, Community Action organizing can create a conflict between the poor and the powerful that is neither natural nor inevitable. There is no necessary conflict of economic interest between the poor and the powerful. It depends on who the powerful are. Trying to give the poor, especially the black poor, a correct consciousness tends only to produce alliances between the rich and the powerful that may or may not have existed in the recent history of a given city. Behaving as though there is a single power structure helps create one and converts economic or racial issues into fights for the survival of the regime. The War on Poverty tended to reunite social, economic, and political elites in the cities.

The conservatism of narrowed vision • Paul Peterson provides another insight into the conservative tendencies of Community Action in his research on OEO and education:

> Even where the OEO achieved considerable success, as in East Harlem, the organizations newly organized had such narrow constitutencies that their demands were usually narrow and neighborhood-oriented rather than calls for broad reform which would improve education for all those in their class or ethnic group. . . . The East Harlem leaders sought neighborhood control, but neighborhood control, if applied equally throughout the city, would scarcely increase school integration. The East Harlem leaders sought a Negro or Puerto Rican principal for their school rather than insisting on changes in the general recruitment patterns for administrative positions that had effectively excluded minority groups. Even the compromise proposal sought quality improvements through a special arrangement with a university for a few East Harlem schools rather than a far-reaching program to improve quality of education in low-income areas throughout the city. The narrow constituency of the neighborhood organization made it an unsatisfactory vehicle for the articulation of broad demands necessary for major educational reform.[50]

The War on Poverty would never have integrated the city, racially or culturally. Narrowed perspectives are created by and reinforced by the neighborhood concept. The call for decentralization is a sound of great joy to liberals. But decentralization is an absurdity at the beginning of a program whose major goal is (or ought to be) reeducation toward new social values. Decentralization in this case was abdication.

The wasting of moral leverage • Even as it diverted attention from civil rights, so also did the War on Poverty militate against change by laying waste the real resources of the civil-rights movement. The War on Poverty, with its

---

50. Peterson, "Strategies," pp. 14–15. See also Grant McConnell, *Private Power and American Democracy* (New York: Knopf, 1966), for a general thesis on the effects of smaller versus larger constituencies.

emphasis on access and cash, was literally demoralizing. And it redefined the problem away from its most toward its least advantageous aspects. The political resources that impressed most blacks—numbers, organization, and "green power"—are admittedly important. But resources are not power; they must be exchanged for power, and the exchange is most effective where the moral claim is strong. The War on Poverty seriously weakened black political power by applying to it the pluralist notion that one set of ends is about the same as another. Everything is interests. The War on Poverty took the heat off. Given the strength of the black's moral position and the guilt feelings of the white Northern community, the revolution sold out cheap for a War on Poverty.

Tilting the recruitment process • Organizing poverty groups in and for the ghetto, and making money and recognition available as systematic rewards, tends to reinforce the ghetto in a most systematic way. The rewards tend strongly to tip the balance arbitrarily toward those prospective leaders who are most strongly proghetto, economics-oriented, and separatist. In a very important sense, the War on Poverty and especially Community Action helped bring on black separatism and anti-integrationism by making black separatism the trait most favored in recruitment and promotion into leadership. Federal programs under new welfare did not cause the attitude itself, but they did encourage certain types of key spokesmen and leaders.

Radicalism • No one can attend a conference or rally of community activists without being impressed with the simultaneous expressions of hope and frustration. New access has often led to disgust. The War on Poverty contributed to these waves of sentiment by encouraging cynicism. Moreover, direct sponsorship by government attached to personal cynicism a sense of the illegitimacy of public objects and their lack of efficacy in good causes. Government always depends heavily upon the accidental strength of the congressional delegation, the role of the city in the upcoming election, whom you know, how charismatic your spokesman is. However, when these political tendencies are elevated to officially prescribed criteria for making governments work, their meaning changes. The War on Poverty removed hope that federal power offers another route. Radicalism is an expression of lost hope for the existing order. Radicalism is usually what conservatism is put to rest by.

WHO SHALL BE POOR?

Old welfare was an enormously successful, even if belated, act of social responsibility. New welfare was an enormous misapplication of social responsibility resulting from derangement of liberal ideology. New welfare was sincere humanitarianism gone cockeyed. A full generation after 1935, the crux of the crisis was human rights and the fact that the existing rules were maintaining poverty as a nonrandom, unnatural category. No War on Poverty can be won by eliminating the poor—that is irresponsible rhetoric. It can be won only by changing the rules that determine who shall be poor. This required hard choices and much social adjustment. Economic incrementalism and pluralism cannot change rules. On the contrary, they operate on the assumption that the rules will not be changed.

There is a rather large gulf between indemnifying damages and righting wrongs. We are seeing this gap filled, first by disappointment and disbelief, then by cynicism, ultimately by militancy. New welfare sought merely to create a "culture of poverty" rather than an orderly process of lawful integration, and in so doing must have contributed to the decaying political relationships in the nation. New welfare stripped the black revolution of its moral superiority. It is one of the tragedies of our time that so many black leaders themselves took the War on Poverty as their own. For their people they chose comfort and mobility when they should have known that discomfort and immobility for them were mere symptoms that would pass away for most of them in a just society.

There will always be a stratum of discomfort. The yeast of revolt is not the discomfort but the declining propensity of members of that stratum to accept it as just. When the stratum is escapable, individuals will escape. When the stratum becomes to them unjust, they revolt, even if escape is made easier. Blacks had their black revolution. The only question was what they would do with it. Brought to leadership in an age of interest-group liberalism, they could not have chosen worse.

9

FEDERAL URBAN POLICY:
What Not to Do and What To Do
About Apartheid

The War on Poverty is not a special case. It is only an extreme case of the way in which the liberal state typically responds to power centers and social crises in the United States. The arrangements worked out for the War on Poverty differ only superficially from those in the first large federal endeavor—housing. Public housing, urban renewal, and the FHA-VA mortgage programs are, like new welfare, enabling legislation. Public housing and urban renewal have enabled cities to remove blacks and other undesirable lower classes from desirable locations. Public housing, with the help of urban renewal, has enabled the cities to relocate and to sift the lower classes into appropriate ghettos. Federally backed credit has then guaranteed to potential escapees from the city the right to a clean, single-family home—provided they are able to buy and the sellers are willing to sell the property. The framers of these programs almost certainly did not intend them to be used in this manner. But that is the most damning possible commentary short of evil intent itself. Such results make it absolutely impossible to continue supporting a public philosophy that makes a virtue of government by delegation at the center and government by bureaucratic lawmaking and interest-group privilege in the field.

A close look at the actual impact of these federal urban policies makes one wonder how there is any federal political legitimacy left. Washington is over one hundred years away from apartheid policy, but after years of serious federal urban involvement, the social state of American cities could be only a little worse if all the federal agencies had been staffed all those years with white secret agents from South Africa. The first part of this chapter is a simple case study of the implementation of federal urban programs inside Iron City. In its perverse way, the case illustrates the effectiveness of planning when governments do define their goals clearly. If only good plans were formulated half as well as this city planned apartheid. The second part of the chapter is a revisit to Iron City after it came under the authority of the federal courts in the application of explicit rules of law drawn from earlier civil-rights cases and the Civil Rights Act of 1964. This leads to some reflections on the logic of school integration as the policy for a stable and just multiracial society.

Housing Policy in Iron City: Have a Plan When You Plan

Iron City is an urban-industrial area whose corporate boundary surrounds nearly 60,000 residents and whose true metropolitan area includes about 100,000. The name of the city has been fictionalized to avoid embarrassing the local officials. They are guilty as charged but no more so than thousands of mayors, councilmen, planners, realtors, and builders all over the country. Iron City presents a single well-documented case. The case situation itself is extreme and unrepresentative, but it will soon be clear that that is precisely why it offers an ideal laboratory for discovering the nature and limitations of modern federal enabling legislation. Iron City is a Southern city, and its official development plan promulgates a set of explicit racial goals. In so doing, however, Iron City officials only stated, as the innocent child in Hans Christian Andersen's "The Emperor's New Clothes," the awful truth about the land-use goals of cities all over the country. The explicitness of Iron City simply documents beyond doubt the extraordinary permissiveness of federal urban policy; for these official development plans provided the local facts and proposals upon which the federal allocations were based.

INTERLARDED NEIGHBORHOODS: STATUS QUO ANTE

In 1950, over 20 percent of Iron City's population was black. But there was something peculiar about these blacks, peculiar at least to those acquainted only with Northern cities. In 1950 they did not live in a ghetto. The largest concentration was in the north-central section, "across the tracks." (Note the shadings on the map in Figure 9.1.) There was another large neighborhood in the south-central section. However, there were neighborhoods of blacks in virtually every section of town. There was a narrow strip along The River, and several strips in the west-central and western sections, in easy walking distance from the steel and textile mills.

This was the typical black residential pattern in Southern cities, especially stable, middle-sized cities. Beginning in the 1920s, relatively slow growth of the city and slow but steady immigration of blacks from outlying rural areas contributed to a patchwork pattern. Rather than a single black section, there were interlarded neighborhoods of black and white.[1] This pattern was sup-

---

1. Iron City extends to the east beyond The River as well as to the north. And black neighborhoods are interlarded with white ones in those sections as well. However, they need not enter significantly into the case here.

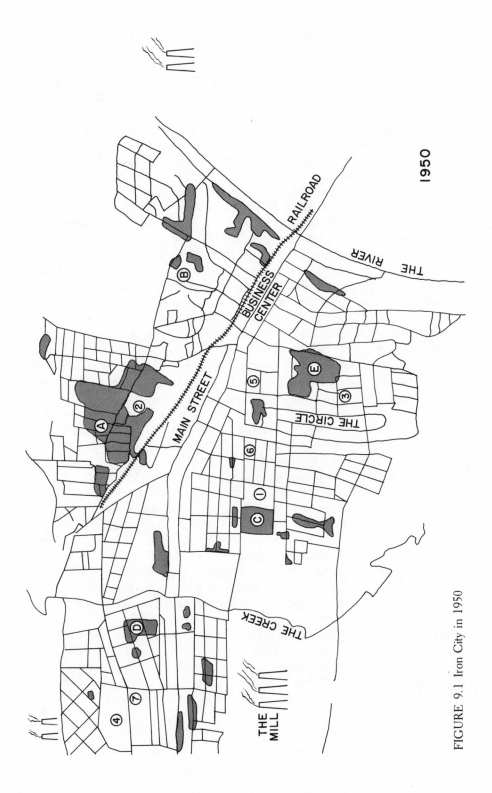

FIGURE 9.1 Iron City in 1950

ported by the needs of the wealthier whites for domestic servants. "Close quarters" was literally the predominant feature. For example, the black neighborhoods east and north of The Circle were surrounded on three sides by the wealthiest homes in Iron City.

Although the residents of Iron City tolerated the proximity of the races, in fact encouraged it in many ways, they could in no way be accused of living in an integrated community. There was of course no Harlem. The very word and its implications suggest the recency as well as the non-Southern origin of systematic housing discrimination. On the other hand, each black neighborhood was pure. There were no black-white-black-white house patterns (although there were a number of instances where several black families lived directly across the street from or "alley to alley" with a larger number of white families). In good urban fashion, blacks and whites learned to ignore each other, yet to profit from the proximity wherever possible. Blacks accepted their back-of-the-bus status. And indeed they received certain privileges unavailable to whites. Merchants and newsboys were more permissive in granting or extending petty credit. Crimes committed within the race were not as a rule investigated or prosecuted with utmost vigor. The raising of a pig or a goat was usually allowed, in violation of public-health regulations. Black bootleggers (legal sale of liquor was until the early 1970s forbidden in the county) had freer rein—and were often patronized by the insatiably thirsty white middle class. And the rents tended to run considerably lower.

This was the dispersed and highly status-bound social situation as recently as 1950. At that time most Southerners could see a racial crisis approaching, and for them the problems inherent in the residential pattern were immediately clear. In almost no direction away from the major public schools could one walk without encountering at least a strip of black housing and a collection of school-age children. Central High School received all white children in grades 9 to 12 who lived east of The Creek (in the map, Figure 9.1). Rebel High (No. 4) was for all white children in grades 9 to 12 who lived west of The Creek, including some areas not shown on the map. Washington High School (No. 2) was exclusively for the black children in grades 7 to 12 from the entire city and surrounding county. Note how perilously close were black families, with eligible children, to both of the white high schools, most particularly to Central, where virtually all of the children of upper-middle- and middle-class families attended. Note also how far a good half the black children commuted to Washington High and also how many of them actually crossed the paths of Rebel and Central in the course of commuting. The same problem obtained for the junior highs (No. 3 and 7) and elementary schools (No. 5, 6, 7). Another junior high and elementary complex was similarly situated in an unmapped area east of The River.

THE PLAN

Into this situation stepped the Iron City Planning Commission in 1951. The Commission's first step was a thorough analysis of housing, land use, economic facilities, and deterioration. In 1952 they produced a handsome and useful master plan, the emphasis of which was upon the need for measures "for arresting beginning blight and correcting advanced blight." On the basis of the master plan, a more intensive investigation was ordered, toward ultimate production of a rehabilitation plan to guide actual implementation and financing. The result was a careful study published in a very professional three-color, glossy-paper, fully illustrated booklet, *Iron City Redevelopment*. This plan centered upon three areas in which blight had made urban redevelopment necessary. On the map these are designated A, B, and E. Area E the plan identified as "occupied by Negroes, but the number is too few to justify provision of proper recreational, school, and social facilities. . . . The opportunity to reconstitute the area as a residential district in harmony with its surroundings was the main reason for its selection as the number one redevelopment site." The second area on the map, B, was chosen because "a relatively small amount of housing—standard and substandard—exists there"; therefore it would serve "as a companion project to . . . [Area E] . . . thus affording home sites for those occupants of [Area E] who are not eligible for relocation in public housing or who, for reasons of their own, prefer single-family or duplex dwellings." Area A, as shown by the intensive survey and the maps published with the plan, contained as much dilapidated and blighted housing as Area E; but Area A was not designated an urban redevelopment area in the plan. Although "blighted and depreciating," it was the "center part of the area . . . growing as the focal point of Negro life." Along the Main Street of this area, extending into Area B, the plan proposed the building of an auditorium, a playfield, and other public facilities "to serve [Iron City's] Negro community." Sites were inserted for the three black churches to be removed by the redevelopment of Area E.

The plan was clearly a black removal plan. All of the projects proposed in the plan are explicit on this point, as the selection of quotes from the document clearly demonstrates. The underlying intent of the plan can be further identified, if need be, in the inconsistencies between the design for Area E and that for Area A. The latter possessed as much blighted housing as Area E, and yet the standard of blighting was not applied to it. There the plan called for intensification of use rather than renewal.

THE PLAN IS IMPLEMENTED

Even before the completion of *Iron City Redevelopment*, implementation projects had begun in Iron City. These were expanded as financing allowed.

The first steps, quite rationally, were toward expansion of housing replacements for those families to be displaced by renewal. Consistent with the types of people to be most affected by the plan, those first steps were the construction of public housing. There had been some public housing construction under Depression legislation, but it is of no concern here. Iron City built four public-housing projects under the Housing Act of 1949. In Figures 9.1 and 9.2 they are the actual letters A, B, C, and D, and these designations have been placed as close as possible to their actual locations within each area.

Each public-housing project was placed carefully. Project A was built in the middle of the largest black area. Project B was built in a sparse area, about 50 percent black, but marked out in the plan as the area for future expansion of the black community. (In the plan, the proposed sites for the three new "colored churches" and the "colored auditorium" were strung along the area around Project B.) Project C, an exclusively white project, was built literally on top of the black area around it. While it is the smallest of the projects, as

TABLE 9.1

PUBLIC-HOUSING PROJECTS IN IRON CITY

PROJECT	SIZE (NO. OF UNITS)	PERCENT NEGROES IN PROJECT	COMPOSITION OF ORIGINAL AREA	DEVELOPMENT COST (DOLLARS)
A	160	100	Negro	1,491,000
B	224	100	Mixed	2,491,000
C	146	0	Negro	1,595,000
D	220	0	Negro	2,300,000

measured by the number of housing units, the structures were so designed to be spread over the entire eight-square-block area. It was, according to the executive director of the Greater Iron City Housing Authority, "a rather unique design, known in the architectural trade as a crankshaft design; thus providing both front and rear courtyards." This project was cited professionally as an outstanding example of good design and utility. And no wonder. Its maximum utilization of space, although it was a low-rent project, made it a combination of public housing and slum (and black) removal project par excellence. Project D was also built on top of a blighted black neighborhood. However, although it is a relatively large project it did not alone eliminate every black in the area.

By 1955 the public-housing projects had been completed and were occupied. From the start there was never any controversy over the racial distribution. The plan was being implemented smoothly and in every respect. Projects A and B were 100 percent black; Projects C and D were 100 percent white. Meanwhile, but at a slower pace, renewal of the central city had

begun. It was not until 1956 that implementation projects were fully designed. Two areas were marked out in the plan for intensive renewal, the shaded
areas around B and E. The important one was Area E, a fifty-six-acre area relatively tightly packed with rickety frame houses, outside toilets, corn and po-
tato plots, and blacks. In the official plan proposals, Area E included the un-
connected black neighborhood just north of The Circle as well as the entire
shaded area due east of The Circle. Area B, as noted before, was relatively
sparse. A few shacks needed removing, and in some of those shacks were
white unemployables.

Within three years the two urban renewal projects were declared 100 percent accomplished. In the official report to the Urban Renewal Administration (HUD) the results were as shown in the following table:

TABLE 9.2

ACCOMPLISHMENT	ACTIVITY	FOR AREA E	FOR AREA B
100%	Land acquisition, no. of parcels acquired	168	39
100%	No. of families relocated	176	24
100%	No. of structures demolished (site clearance)	236	33

In Area E, every trace of black life was removed. As the executive director of
the Greater Iron City Housing Authority put it, "In this project, all of the
then existing streets were vacated and a new land-use map was developed."
One entirely new street was put in, several of the narrow lanes (for instance,
"St. James's Alley") were covered over, and through connectors were built for
a dead-end street or two. By this time, as seen on Figure 9.2, almost all the
shaded areas had been removed, except Area A, which had, of course, expanded correspondingly.

All of Area E became prime property. Most of the area was zoned for
single-family residences, and the boom in construction of houses in the
$25,000–$40,000 range in the area continued through the 1960s. One large
supermarket and several neighborhood businesses were established on renewal land purchased from the Authority. A 95 percent white elementary
school, with lighted ballfield and large playground, occupied most of the eastern section. It was a consolidation of elementary schools No. 5 and No. 6,
which no longer existed. With the 95 percent white junior-high (No. 3), an
impressive campus resulted.

Area B also received a new elementary school, with fieldhouse, lighted
ballfield, tennis court, and playground. The city built a swimming pool in
this area as well, but it and the original municipal pool on The River closed
for several years to avoid integration of public facilities. As mentioned earlier,

three of the redevelopment sites in Area B were set aside for the three churches demolished in the redevelopment of Area E. Each of the churches ultimately chose locations elsewhere in the black community. Except for the 224 units of public housing, most of the relocating blacks chose the more densely populated and blighted Area A. Area B remained underutilized. The major part of Area B extended north of Project B toward the mountain, where although "some of the terrain is steep," reported *Iron City Redevelopment*, "much of it is gently rolling and well drained. . . . In most Southern cities there is a scarcity of vacant land located close to schools and churches and shopping districts and served by city utilities and transportation, land that is suitable and desirable for expansion of Negro neighborhoods or creation of new ones. [Area B] is such an area." But apparently the blacks did not agree, and most of the area remained a graded but raw expanse of red Southern earth on the side of the mountain. This is the one part of the plan that went wrong; this was the voluntary part of the plan, *the part unfinanced by federal agencies.*

The result, despite frustrated expectations in the north part of Area B, was overwhelming success for the plan (Figure 9.2). Well before the 1960 Census the large black area in Area E had been reduced to 5.1 percent of the entire census tract, and this was comprised of a few shanties behind the bottling works and the western edge of the area along The River. In Area C, the removal process immediately around Central High was complete with Public-Housing Project C. After 1960 some 10 percent of the area was still nonwhite, but other families continued to move out. Removal from Area D was approaching totality. By 1964, removal from all areas west of The Creek was given further assistance by the completion of one federally supported arterial running east-west through the city, and the inauguration of Iron City's portion of the new north-south interstate highway. That brought the nonwhite proportion in the western sectors of the city down to about 3 percent.

By the end of 1967, west of The Creek and north of Main Street (all around Area D), there remained six black families. When a nearby textile mill had closed down some years before, they, as employees, had been given the right to buy their houses, and they chose to remain. West of The Creek and south of Main Street (the area including The Mill) fewer than 5 percent of the housing units were occupied by blacks. Virtually every one of these houses was located in isolated and sparse sections along The Creek and behind The Mill, where one could still plant a plot of sorghum, catch a catfish, and, undisturbed, let a 1948 Chevrolet corrode into dust. East of The Creek and south of Main Street, closer to the center of things, the 1960 distribution of blacks was further reduced. Every last shack was gone from Area E and the entire central area of the white city. Three small pockets remained in the western portion near Area C, and that was all that remained in all of the white city. The last remaining black neighborhood of any size, a group of shanties

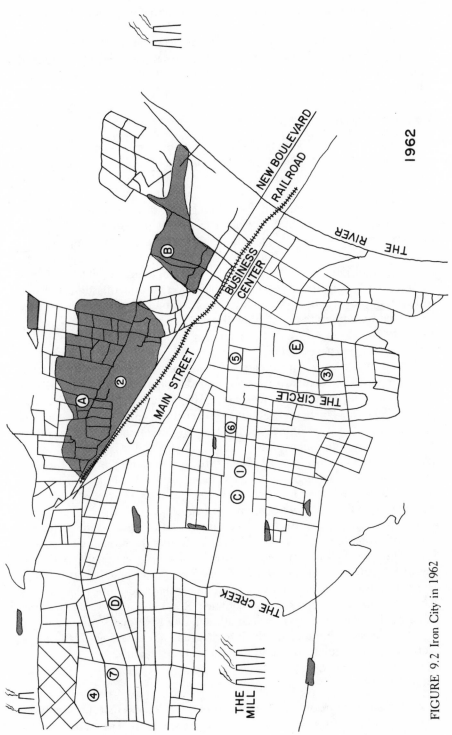

FIGURE 9.2 Iron City in 1962

running along The River south of Main Street, was removed by the construction of a city-hall–police-department–YMCA complex. Area B remained completely nonwhite and underdeveloped. Area A filled the entire triangle pointing north. It was a ghetto.

THE SECRET OF SUCCESS

The plan enjoyed strong consensus among officials and white citizens. It enjoyed at least the acquiescence and tacit consent of the blacks, who were, in any case, tenants whose landlords were white. But the plan would have had little chance of success, consensus or not, without outside financial assistance. The assistance came from federal programs. It was allocated, and continued in 1967 to be allocated, by federal agencies whose personnel could and did have access to the renewal plan, the master plan, and all the project plans. Nothing was kept a secret in Iron City. What we have seen here is an honest, straightforward job of physical and social planning. And despite Iron City's open approach to apartheid, federal assistance was never in question. Relative to Iron City's size, and especially the size of its annual public sector budget, federal aid was quite substantial. And the results were dramatic. Perhaps only New Haven, Connecticut, a town famous for redevelopment, has had a higher per capita success ratio.

Federal assistance was the secret of the plan's success. For the decade beginning in 1954 federal assistance for Iron City public housing amounted to at least $300,000 annually, increasing to $700,000 annually during the peak years of 1957–62. The figures cannot be broken down among the four projects because the aid was computed on the basis of development costs (given in Table 9.1 above) and granted as a lump sum. Federal assistance for urban renewal in Iron City between 1957 and 1961, by which time most of this part of the plan was a success, amounted to about $400,000 per annum. These federal grants to carry out Iron City's apartheid plan *came to almost exactly 20 percent of Iron City's annual government budget.*

To this should of course be added an undetermined amount of federal highway assistance which helped remove blacks from the western edge of Iron City. There were also FHA and VA, which helped provide financing for the lovely homes built in Area E. It was not possible to determine how much federal community facilities funds helped remove the blacks from The River, where now stands the new city hall complex. It was also not possible to determine whether the local banks balked at extending FHA and VA homeowner credit to blacks for building on the mountainside north of Area B. But these facts would affect the meaning of the case only marginally.

IMPLICATIONS

First, the case bears out the contentions of three decades that slum removal means black removal. It supports the even more severe contention that the ultimate effects of federal urban policies have been strongly supportive of the status quo, so much so as to vitiate hopes for positive programs of integration through alteration of the physical layout of cities.

Second, it supports the general thesis of this book, that policies without a rule of law will ultimately come to ends profoundly different from those intended by their most humanitarian framers. It supports, still further, the contention of the book that some of the most cherished instruments of the positive state may be positively evil, and that the variable by which this evil outcome can be predicted is absence of public and explicit legislative standards by which to guide administrative conduct.

Third, the case supports, especially by virtue of the explicitness of the racial policy, the main contentions of Part III, showing precisely how and why federal policy is ill-equipped to govern the cities directly and confirming beyond doubt the contention that the present disorder in the cities is properly explained by the failure of government and politics rather than by the inferiority of black adjustment. The case shows how national legitimacy can be tarnished to the degree that it is loaned to the cities for discretionary use, and how a crisis of public authority was inevitable as long as the virtue made of an untutored political process ended in the abuses cataloged in Iron City. In sum, it helps show why liberal governments cannot achieve justice.

Every black in Iron City knew what was happening. Blacks in Chicago and New York and Cleveland and Detroit know the same about their cities too, but since these Northern blacks are not so docile, does that leave any possibility that federal imperium was used completely differently outside the South? True, planning authorities would never so deliberately pursue racial planning. True, few social plans could be as extensive or as successful as Iron City's. Nonetheless, misuse of federal programs in ways indistinguishable in principle from Iron City has been widespread and undeniable.

Martin Anderson, for example, estimated in 1964 that about two-thirds of all people displaced from urban renewal homes were blacks, Puerto Ricans, or members of some other minority group.[2] In public housing the record is even more somber, first, because the pattern is even clearer, and second, because these projects stand as ever-present symbols of the acts of discrimination by which they were created.[3] As of 1965, only three of New York City's sixty-nine public-housing projects were officially listed as all nonwhite or all white in occupancy, but ten of Philadelphia's forty projects were all nonwhite, and twenty-one of Chicago's fifty-three, five of Detroit's twelve, four of Cleveland's fourteen, and all of Dallas's ten projects were listed as either all nonwhite or all white.[4] The rest of reality is hidden, because the Public Housing (since renamed Housing Assistance) Administration defines

2. Martin Anderson, *The Federal Bulldozer* (Cambridge, Mass.: M.I.T. Press, 1964), pp. 6–8.

3. See James Baldwin's observations, quoted at the beginning of Part III.

4. Source: Public Housing Administration (HUD), *Low-Rent Project Directory* (Washington, D.C.: U.S. Government Printing Office, December 31, 1965).

an integrated project as one in which there are "whites and more than one nonwhite, including at least one Negro family."[5] Not only is it impossible to determine the real number of truly integrated projects, this system of reporting, as permissive as the law itself, was ideally suited for local racial policies and local individual racial prejudices.[6] Until July 1967, the agency even followed a rule of "free choice" allowing eligible tenants to wait indefinitely for an apartment, which allowed them also to decline a vacancy on racial grounds. Thus, while the whole story cannot be told from official statistics, every urban black knows it.

The Civil Rights Act of 1965 was supposed to have put an end to such practices, but there is little evidence of improvement in public housing in particular or city housing in general. It was not even until July 1967 that the rule of "free choice" was replaced with a "rule of three" plan whereby an applicant must take one of the first three available units or be dropped to the bottom of the eligible list. All this produced was undeniable testimony that the practices all along had constituted a "separate but equal" system of federally supported housing. As of June 1967, therefore, following three years under the 1964 civil-rights sections and following more strenuous efforts by the Johnson Administration, two of Detroit's five segregated projects became "integrated," by virtue of the fact that in each case exactly one white family had moved into a totally black project. At the same time, at least eleven of New York's projects were classified as "integrated" when in fact fewer than 15 percent of the units were occupied by families of some race other than the 85 percent majority in that project.[7]

A month after the belated 1967 directive on public housing, the Federal Housing Administration (FHA) instituted a pilot program to increase FHA support for housing finance in "economically unsound" areas. This was an official confession that for thirty-three years FHA had insured over $110 billion of mortgages to help whites escape the city rather than build it. However, this step and others like it cannot erase the stigma of second-class citizenship placed upon the residents of federal housing programs nor remove the culpability of federal power in the American local government policy of apartheid. These remedial steps came five years after President Kennedy's famous "stroke of the pen" decision aimed at preventing discrimination in publicly supported housing, and three years after the first applicable civil-rights act. But all of the efforts surely suggest that mere remedy is never enough for bad organic laws, because bad organic laws literally possess congenital defects.

5. Ibid., p. v.
6. See a study by Bernard Weissbrourd which concluded: "Most cities have followed a deliberate program of segregation in public housing." *Segregation, Subsidies and Megalopolis* (Santa Barbara: Center for the Study of Democratic Institutions, 1964), p. 3.
7. Source: Computer printouts provided by the Housing Assistance Administration.

Better not to have had the housing at all than to have it on the Iron City pattern and at the expense of national legitimacy. Some would argue that the problem was actually one of mere timidity and that the answer is a proper expansion of public housing.[8] Judging from the patterns reviewed here, more could hardly have been better. Other writers and officials, including highly placed officials, have proposed solutions ranging from semipublic[9] to private[10] financing of public, low-cost housing. These proposals focus on the mere details of financing and offer further examples of the ignorance liberals have of the implications of forms of law and administration for the achievement of simple, ordinary justice. Regardless of the means of financing, these programs will produce no lasting social benefit without a rule of law that states unmistakably what is to be achieved and what is to be forbidden. That is the moral of the first part of the Iron City story.

Iron City Revisited

By 1962, Iron City could consider its master plan a complete success. Iron City no longer looked like a Southern city at all, but like a typical Northern, segregated city. Apartheid policy had, with federal aid, worked for housing in Iron City and was reinforcing racial segregation in the public schools. By 1968—thirteen years after the Supreme Court had ordered desegregation with "all deliberate speed"—there was only the slightest trace of intermingling of the races in the Iron City school system. Of twenty-six schools in the system, only one, an elementary school, could be said to be truly integrated (Table 9.3). For all the rest, if there was an intermingling at all, it was pure tokenism.

Even the tokenism was causing anguish. White parents saw the slightest trace of intermingling as the beginning of the end of a way of life. Black parents were not entirely happy either. Those who had boldly sent their children to previously all-white schools complained about two things. First there was the anticipated problem of the isolation of the few black children who first entered the all-white classroom. Second and unexpected was the discovery by black parents that some of the most desirable features of education in the white schools were financed by special assessments which few black families could afford. Consequently, some of the original pioneering black families decided in those early days to return their children to all-black schools. A critical mass had not been reached. Tokenism would not work, even if all but a few black families were willing to accept it.

8. See Michael Harrington, *The Other America* (New York: Macmillan, 1962), pp. 139 ff.
9. President Lyndon Johnson, for example.
10. Senators Charles Percy and Robert Kennedy, for example.

TABLE 9.3

IRON CITY FROM SEGREGATION TO INTEGRATION: 1968–73

	NUMBER OF SCHOOLS	1968	1970	1973
Elementary schools	Of 19:	12: completely segregated 4: 95% of one color 2: 89–93% white 1: integrated (62% white)	7: completely segregated 7: 95% of one color 3: 82–86% white 2: 46–54% white	15: integrated 2: closed 2: all white (but "out in the country" and of little interest to blacks)
Junior high schools	Of 4:	1: 96% white 2: 92% white 1: all black	3: integrated (77, 72, & 69% white) 1: closed	3: integrated (71, 77, & 46% white)
High schools	Of 3:	1: 97% white 1: 91% white 1: all black	2: integrated (85 & 82% white) 1: all black	2: integrated (83 & 47% white) 1: closed, formerly all black)

At least one black family was unwilling to accept the situation and in 1967 filed a complaint against the Iron City Board of Education, based upon two clear principles of law: the holding in *Brown* v. *Board of Education of Topeka* and Title IV and Title VI of the Civil Rights Act of 1964. The Supreme Court had ruled in the *Brown* case that separate school facilities based upon racial discrimination were "inherently unequal" and therefore unconstitutional.[11] Title IV of the Civil Rights Act of 1964 authorized the attorney general of the United States to file suit for the desegregation of public schools and colleges upon receipt of a signed complaint that he has reason to believe is meritorious. Title IV put all public schools on notice that they were progressively vulnerable to suits, and Title VI of the same act was intended to provide the

---

11. *Brown* v. *Board of Education of Topeka*, 347 U.S. 483. In the second *Brown* case a year later, after reargument, the Court handed down its famous order implementing the decision of the previous year. What the Court actually did was to remand these segregation cases to the lower courts and ordered the lower courts to work out equitable means to eliminate obstacles to the admission of black children "to the public schools on a racially non-discriminatory basis with all deliberate speed." *Brown* v. *Board of Education of Topeka*, 349 U.S. 294. The cases are often referred to as *Brown I* and *Brown II*. For an engrossing and enlightening account of these cases and of the behind-the-scenes considerations in the crafting of the 1955 order, see Richard Kluger, *Simple Justice* (New York: Knopf, 1976), especially Chapters 25 and 26.

coup de grace to school segregation by directing each federal agency to withhold financial assistance from any local program or activity that was discriminating on the basis of race. In the decade following enactment of the Civil Rights Act of 1964, the Justice Department brought legal actions against more than five hundred school districts and the Department of Health, Education and Welfare filed actions against six hundred school districts to suspend federal aid to education.[12]

Despite the federal activity against school discrimination, which was entirely focused upon the South during that first decade, school systems like Iron City's could remain almost completely segregated because of the manner in which district courts and federal agencies were stating their orders and decisions. The Iron City case is a good example. In response to the complaint by the mother of the black pupil who was plaintiff in the case against the Iron City Board of Education, the federal district court judge handed down the following decree: First the Iron City Board of Education "shall take affirmative action to disestablish all school segregation and to eliminate the effects of the dual system." However, for an indefinite period of time, commencing with the 1967–68 school year, desegregation was to take place through the "exercise of choice"; that is, students above ninth grade or over fifteen years of age could exercise their own choice of school; students below that age or grade level would have their choice made for them by their parents. The court even drafted a letter to be sent by the Board of Education to all parents and students to inform them of their annual duty—and indeed it was.to be a duty to make a choice of schools: "All students, both white and Negro, shall be required to exercise a free choice of schools annually." The decree also mandated to the board the obligation to provide for adequate transportation. And the decree also provided some protection for black teachers: "Race or color shall not be a factor in the hiring, assignment, reassignment, promotion, demotion, or dismissal of teachers . . . except that race may be taken into account for the purpose of counteracting or correcting the effect of the segregated assignment of faculty and staff in the dual system." Enforcement of the decree provided for annual reports to the judge, "tabulating by race the number of choice applications and the number of choices and transfers granted and the number of denials in each grade of each school. The report shall also state the reasons relied upon in denying choice and shall tabulate . . . the number of choices and transfers denied for each such reason."

Unfortunately, although it did reverse the legal relationship between blacks and the board, the decree did not advance much beyond the 1955 Supreme Court order for "all deliberate speed." As long as discretion was left to the board and the court to determine in each case an adequate progress toward

12. Kluger, p. 759. During the same decade, Kluger reports that more than four hundred antidiscrimination suits were filed against hotels, restaurants, taverns, gas stations, and other "public facilities."

desegregation, there was going to be an incessant bargaining process among all parties involved. A few additional black students were going to enter the white schools of Iron City under this decree, but most everyone was going to have to await the appeals, the first reports, the tightening of the decree, and the assessment of first- and second-round ramifications.

Consequently, the plaintiff filed another suit against the board following its reports for 1967–68 and 1968–69 school years. And in response the board filed "an amended plan of desegregation" based upon assistance provided it by the Office of Education (HEW). The district court accepted the board's plan and incorporated implementation of that plan as its order of September 1969. The board was given sixty days to report "the results of the adoption of the plan"; the very salutary results are reported on Table 9.3 for 1970. The report showed that modest progress had been made in the elementary schools and that quite substantial progress had been made in the junior high and senior high schools. The three remaining junior high schools were all integrated and the fourth, an all-black junior high school, had been closed. Two of the high schools were integrated, but the all-black high school, though declining in population, remained all black.[13]

All during the period after the first court order the Iron City Board of Education had been working with representatives of the Department of Health, Education and Welfare. Regular trips were made to the regional federal office in Atlanta. And all along HEW had been providing money and guidance toward a "long-range" plan for Iron City. This plan provided for construction of three "mini-parks" for elementary schools, placed strategically in three different parts of the city; the plan also provided in the interim for a redrawing of certain boundaries to provide further progress toward desegregation, especially of the elementary schools. In 1972 a third complaint was filed in the federal district court by the original plaintiff objecting not so much to the long-range plan but to the districting and to any further delays in complete desegregation. The question of speed should have been settled once and for all by an additional landmark decision in October 1969, when the Supreme Court finally decided that " 'all deliberate speed' in desegregation is no longer constitutionally permissible. . . . The obligation of every school district is to terminate dual school systems at once."[14] Nevertheless, the federal district court overruled the objections of the plaintiff, accepted the long-range plan, and in a sense relinquished Iron City from the grip of federal court control after over five years. The figures show that integration had become an accomplished fact in Iron City (Table 9.3 for 1973). Moreover there did not seem to be any

13. Integration is used here for shorthand only, since this is entirely a matter of each observer's definition. To help make that assessment, it might be useful to report that during 1969–70 the black school population in Iron City was 33 percent in the elementary schools, 27 percent in the junior high schools, and 25 percent in the senior high schools.

14. *Alexander v. Holmes County Board of Education*, 396 U.S. 19 (1969), p. 20.

massive emigration by white pupils and their parents from Iron City and its school system. The percentage of black pupils in the school system had gone up ever so slightly, but nothing like enough to indicate a serious withdrawal of white pupils.[15]

The integration of the Iron City schools is unusual only in the extent to which the federal court was involved. Most of the Southern school integration took place in response to HEW thrust and HEW guidance under Title VI authority.[16] And even in Iron City HEW tutelage was ever-present after the 1969 court order had set the process in train. The federal government provided almost unrefusable incentives as a sanction for the policy as set down in legislation. Unlike most of the legislation in modern times, the Civil Rights Act of 1964 was good law. It identified the goals in fairly clear language, it identified the evils against which sanctions would be employed, it provided the sanctions, and it defined administrative jurisdictions in these terms.

Many critics of the Civil Rights Act felt that the sanctions were not strong enough in relation to the goals sought and that at many points in the act deliberate delays in the enforcement process were introduced. The critics were quite correct; these weaknesses in the act were compromises self-consciously made with the opposition in Congress in order to get some kind of civil-rights bill enacted. But here we must identify two fundamentally different kinds of compromise, one of which is typical of interest-group liberal ideology and the other not, making the Civil Rights Act of 1964 an exception during the 1960s. In the case of the Civil Rights Act, the pro-civil-rights forces accommodated to the opposition by keeping legislative goals clear and by agreeing to soften the timing and the intensity of the sanctions. The result is good law, albeit not as strong as the proponents might have wished, but clear in rule, purpose, and sanction. In contrast, most liberal legislation of the 1960s and 1970s was drafted to meet the opposition not in the manner of the Civil Rights Act, but by successively obfuscating the goals sought by the proponents to such a point that every faction could go away feeling itself the victor. This is bad law, made worse by the fact that it is treated as good law by modern liberalism. The

15. The 1973 school census shows an actual drop of 1 percentage point to 32 percent for blacks in the elementary schools, an increase of 3 percentage points, to 30 percent, in the junior high schools, and an increase of 1 percentage point to 26 percent for the high school population. By 1978 the situation in the two high schools was as follows: The one with 83 percent whites in 1973 was integrated 65 percent/35 percent (694 white, 397 black students); the one with 47 percent whites in 1973 was integrated 70 percent/30 percent (717 white, 322 black students). Another high school in the eastern part of Iron City had meanwhile been established. In 1978 it was 58 percent/42 percent integrated (385 white, 280 black students). The number of white students had dropped slightly, but part, if not all, of this is attributable to declining birth rates in the 1960s.

16. Although the U.S. Civil Rights Commission is critical of HEW's role in a number of respects, it nevertheless admits that "HEW's vigorous use of the fund termination provided by Title VI was responsible, in large measure, for the dismantling of a number of dual elementary and secondary school systems in the south." *The Federal Civil Rights Commission Effort*, Report of the U.S. Civil Rights Commission (Washington, D.C.: U.S. Government Printing Office, 1974), pp. 127–28.

results of bad law—that is, law without legal integrity, policy-without-law— can be seen in case after case throughout this volume. The application of civil-rights law to Iron City is a good case of the results of good law. The principles of law were clear and eventually the community yielded. They gave up their school system temporarily to federal authority and then got it back with a slightly altered charter. Basic respect for law plus a fear of a loss of resources had brought the community around. Many were unhappy and remained unhappy, but their public demeanor was changed in a fundamental and permanent way. The dignity of Iron City blacks rose accordingly.[17]

The Iron City story is only one small part of a vast American problem whose final chapter has not yet been written. It is the problem of multiracial society and how it has come to its most critical point of development in public education. This is as we should have expected because we are a country built not upon the quest for order but upon the quest for opportunity. Education in the United States is literally organized as a channel of social mobility for groups as well as individuals. But even more compelling is the fact that education is the most important channel for creating and maintaining a single political culture in a country where the political culture seems constantly on the verge of coming unstuck. From the standpoint of the society at large, education is a duty. It is on this basis that we can compel people to go to school—to be educated is to be able to earn one's own way and to be able to participate in the defense of the country. The federal courts have appropriately included education as part of the "equal protection of the laws." Thus, from the standpoint of constitutional definition and the place and function of education in our society, access to education and educational facilities must be treated in absolute terms—as a matter of right and duty not of convenience or circumstance.

Yet, as criteria these characteristics of American public education seem to be increasingly disregarded outside the South. Few school systems are desegregating, and those that have officially desegregated now contain 75 to 100 percent nonwhite student populations. Within the corporate cities of the North there are no longer enough white children in the public schools to integrate with. As Saul Alinsky observed, in the Northern cities integration can be defined as that moment in history just after a school was all white and just before it is all black.

This vitiates the purpose of equal education in at least two ways. First, all-black and all-nonwhite inner-city schools are in fact not equal. Second, com-

17. Individual values as well as public demeanor probably changed drastically as well, as would be indicated by the following incident. Shortly after the integration of the Iron City schools was completed, the board unceremoniously fired the superintendent who had presided over the entire integration process and who symbolized Southern cooperation with the federal authorities and the civil-rights forces. Within two weeks of the firing, there was such a clamor of criticism that the board met hastily in a special session and reversed itself, imploring the superintendent to remain on the job. He did so until his retirement in 1975.

pletely racially segregated schools do not produce a single political culture—
to the contrary, they are continuing to give us the racial version of Two Nations.

Wherever rights are involved, there must be remedies. The federal courts
have recognized since the late 1960s that whenever racial segregation exists as
a result of housing segregation (as in Iron City after the success of their master
plan), interdistrict busing has to be provided within that corporate city. The
first case in which the Supreme Court laid down the guidelines to desegregation in the Northern cities was a case involving a Southern metropolitan
school district (Charlotte-Mecklenburg, North Carolina), but the guidelines
were clearly for Northern practices. Chief Justice Warren Burger, speaking for
a unanimous court, affirmed that school busing was a legitimate remedy for a
segregated school system.[18] The opinion, however, did set a definite limit
upon the power of courts to use busing or any other methods to desegregate
school systems—the requirement that cities be guilty of de jure segregation.
This turned out to be a very severe limitation because of the extreme difficulty
of proving anything more than de facto school segregation in Northern metropolitan areas. Some cities, such as Denver and Boston, fell within the range
of Chief Justice Burger's definition and were ordered by federal courts to
desegregate by busing and pairing. However, in 1974, as some of the implications of the Charlotte-Mecklenburg decision were being felt, the Supreme
Court, again led by Chief Justice Burger, handed down a decision on the Detroit case that would, if left standing, operate as an almost insurmountable
barrier to significant desegregation in the future. For the majority, Chief Justice Burger repeated the requirement of de jure segregation and even admitted
that it probably existed in the single corporate area of Detroit. However, he
went on to deny to the federal government the power to try to solve the
problem of Detroit by reaching beyond the Detroit corporate limits themselves to impose a multidistrict "affirmative action plan." In unmistakable
language Burger argued, "Without an interdistrict violation and an inderdis-
trict effect, there is no constitutional wrong calling for an interdistrict remedy."[19]

Fortunately for the future of metropolitan desegregation, the Milliken case
divided the court five to four and produced several strenuous dissents. The
one black justice on the Supreme Court, Thurgood Marshall, argued that the
court's decision would allow the state "to profit from its own wrong," would
accelerate white flight to the suburbs, and would "perpetuate for years to
come the separation of the races," into two cities, one black and one white.
But perhaps the most significant and most promising dissent came from Justice Byron White, who has been known as the moderate "swing vote" on the
Supreme Court. Why, he asked, did the court stop at district lines in ordering

18. Swan v. Charlotte-Mecklenburg Board of Education, 402 U.S. 1 (1971).
19. Milliken v. Bradley 418 U.S. 717 (1974).

remedies in a school segregation case? The Fourteenth Amendment commands the states, not the cities or their suburbs, to provide equal protection to all citizens. Since racial separation had been included as part of the equal protection exactly twenty years before in *Brown I*, the definition of equality and its remedies had to be at the level of state rather than locality. He argued that the courts "must be free to devise workable remedies against the political entity with the effective power to determine local choice"—and in this case the relevant political entity was the State of Michigan.

The Milliken case still stands; but how long it can withstand arguments like those of Byron White is a serious question. The equal protection clause of the Fourteenth Amendment combined with any understanding whatever of the place of the states in our Federal System, combined with any awareness of the actualities of racial segregation in the United States will ultimately produce a compelling brief in favor of converting White's dissent into a court majority.[20]

Busing is widely misunderstood in the United States. In the first place, few have explained with any care the relationship between busing and the requirement that for every right there must be a remedy. In the second place, busing has been implemented by officials as though they wanted to undermine not only busing but racial integration as well. Busing is merely a means drawn from the available technology to overcome racial barriers in one particular area. A much more integrated society could be achieved if racial barriers to the choice of residence were abolished; busing children to school is a far less drastic approach to providing remedies for rights. It is especially ironic to hear objections to busing on the ground that it is a drastic extension of government power. Not only is it not an extension of that power; it is a rather modest means of dealing with some of the consequences of earlier abuses of government power, such as the instance presented in this chapter in which local and federal power was used to segregate a previously unsegregated city.[21]

BUSING INTO THE FUTURE

Few would ever have thought that the ugly, yellow school bus would replace the covered wagon and the iron locomotive as the symbol of the great American venture. The school bus may become a more positive symbol when everyone has studied the views of conservative Chief Justice Burger speaking for a moderate to conservative Supreme Court: "The remedy for such segregation may be administratively awkward, inconvenient, and even bizarre in some situations and may impose burdens on some; but all awkwardness and

20. Justice White's dissent is quite similar to the argument presented in the first edition of this book, an argument that is extended and updated in this edition.

21. For confirmation of this view of busing, see Gary Orfield, *Must We Bus? Segregated Schools and National Policy* (Washington, D.C.: The Brookings Institution, 1978).

inconvenience cannot be avoided . . . when remedial adjustments are being made to eliminate the dual school systems."[22] In brief, busing is an appropriate technique, one of many techniques, and sometimes the only technique available to meet the problems flowing from governmentally produced residential segregation.

In context, busing is a rather modest approach, inasmuch as it leaves all property values and other rights in place and lays a claim only upon a very public dimension of our lives—education and the rights and obligations of all people to be educated. The only distinctive quality of busing is that it is a policy adopted by a higher government to be applied against a lower government, a power exerted by a larger government upon a smaller government. The logic of the situation cries out for a movement to declare unconstitutional the existing legal barriers to free movement of population—county and suburban governments—and to start all over again with reasonable state laws governing proper land-use policies, proper conditions of incorporation, proper employment of eminent-domain powers, proper and reasonable zoning codes, and proper distribution of students and of school districts for purposes of education. This argument will be expanded at the end of the chapter. At the moment it serves only to stress the modesty of busing as an approach to central-city and metropolitan desegregation.

We have wasted a great deal of the twenty-five years since the first *Brown* case; but we may still have a future if we resolve to make a serious and substantial beginning without further delay. One good start is to recognize the mistakes we have already made in the adoption and implementation of desegregation through busing. The first mistake we made was to try to integrate the schools within the corporate city alone. With few exceptions this continues to be the way we are trying, and it continues to be about the only way the Supreme Court will allow us to try it. But busing will never work except on a metropolitan scale. The distances involved in busing were proven irrelevant many years ago by millions of farm children who spent as much as an hour each way commuting to grammar school. And we never hesitated busing black children across white districts to all-black schools. The cost of busing is indeed a factor, but federal subsidies for busing to implement well-designed metropolitan integration plans would be small in comparison to many federal subsidy programs of far less importance to the nation's future.

The second mistake was the attempt to bus children in both directions. The schools in one direction are superior, the schools in the other direction are inferior, often in fact, still more often in symbol. Moreover, the many white families who possess the ability to flee from desegregation are much less likely to take that option if they are only the hosts of a busing scheme. This is a compromise toward white political power that could be made acceptable to

22. From *Swan* v. *Charlotte-Mecklenburg*, quoted by Judge W. Arthur Garrity in the controversial Boston busing case, *Morgan* v. *Hennigan*, 379 F. Supp. 483 (1974).

blacks. However, it should be repeated that integration is an obligation and not merely a matter of convenience or preference for black families as well as white.

The third mistake was that of basing so many integration decisions upon the assumption that black children would get a better education in a school with a white majority. This is a very pernicious misapplication of the findings of the Coleman Report of 1966. The data in this famous and influential study do confirm the hypothesis that blacks tend to get a better education in racially integrated schools.[23] But in the hands of many well-meaning persons, these findings came to mean that public-school officials need not be forced to integrate if they could somehow show that there would be little measurable increase in Standard Achievement Test (SAT) scores or some other measure of educational achievement. This has put the burden of proof right back upon the most disadvantaged groups, and it has been an impossible burden especially when added to the Supreme Court's requirement that *de jure* segregation must be proven. But totally aside from the problem of proof, arguments based upon the utility or efficacy of integration have blinded us to the real point, which is that the society is obliged to integrate for reasons deriving from the Constitution and citizenship rather than for reasons of specific educational prudence. We would be obliged to integrate even if studies showed a net loss of educational achievement, because the issue is one of citizenship and the rights and duties of citizens.

This leads directly to the fourth mistake, which was to try to integrate incrementally. Since fear of the decline of quality and safety in the schools would have a serious effect on even the most favorably predisposed whites, a single step toward integration became also a first step toward resegregation. But if, at a single stroke, all the schools in a reasonably defined region, regardless of corporate boundaries, had been included, parents would have confronted the need to adjust, rather than to escape.

Toward an Integrated Society, Through Law

Racial integration of the schools combines a concern for equality with a concern for legality, without extending government authority beyond clearly established and widely accepted domains. Moreover, integration as a policy may be seen as practicable as well as compelling when compared to alternative approaches to policy for a stable and just multiracial society.

What must first be rejected, if the foregoing analysis has any value at all, is the federal approach to an integrated society through economics and public-

23. James Coleman et al., *Equality of Educational Opportunity* (Washington, D.C.: U.S. Government Printing Office, 1966).

works policies. Without this rejection there will be no chance to regain the moral posture with which the revolution was begun several decades ago. If proper standards of administration had been applied from the beginning—to everything from integrated transportation to integrated races, from clean air and water to safe streets, from who shall pay taxes to who shall be poor—there might have been some hope. But after more than thirty years of permissiveness and misuse, no mere salvage operation on public housing, urban redevelopment, and new welfare will work. Elimination of practically all of the economics-public-works approaches, and limiting what is left to a role of implementing socially significant policies, would cut out a great deal of federal activity. However, a moral posture toward the revolution requires less activity and more authority. And more money would be left to ease the pains of integration.

Policies and proposals involving structural reform must also be rejected. The various commonplaces that parade under the banner of metropolitan government are weakest of all. Metropolitan government based on a confederal principle—where all existing governments in a metropolis maintain their identities and are given representation in some larger council—simply institutionalizes the social stalemate that already exists in the region. If, on the other hand, metropolitan government were seriously tried on a unitary principle—where all autonomy within the region is eliminated—the new government would indeed then have reach and resource commensurate with its problems. But any state or central city with power to achieve that would then not need to, because there would already be sufficient power without bothering with the new level at all. Thus the confederal principle is feasible but ineffective; the unitary principle is quite effective but almost completely unfeasible. A third popular structural reform, more or less opposed to both of the others, is decentralization toward smaller and smaller units of self-government within the metropolis. The renewed and intensified cries for decentralization in the past two decades—this time by the sentimental left rather than the right—provide further testimony to growing distrust of duly constituted authorities. But they provide no constructive direction for new uses of authority or new structures of authority. A time when national standards and local realities are almost completely out of joint is hardly a time for decentralization—or else Iron City is completely unique. Some day, when accepted moralities are enacted into law, decentralization of their implementation will be both possible and desirable. But until that time decentralization is only a carte blanche for vested interests. What was true in the South when the social revolution of our time was initiated in 1954 remains true in all its ramifications in all parts of the country during the third decade of the revolution.

Another effort, open-housing legislation, must also be rejected, although it warrants close attention for the future. Even though this type of law has been accepted by the courts as constitutional, it is not good legislation at this time, for several reasons. First, the law will not work. Its claim to obedience is too weak for the behavior it seeks to alter, and the requirements for enforcement are too complex unless there is a manifold increase in the federal police. Upon matters of ownership of personal property, government at all levels in the United States has its weakest claims, because ownership of personal property is historically remote from the obligations of individual citizenship. Exchange of personal property more frequently involves clear citizen obligations, but nonetheless the strong property tradition in this country will render such legislation as nugatory as liquor prohibition laws. This alone does not mean the laws should not be tried, but they run an enormous risk of inflating hopes that cannot be satisfied. Other approaches should be exhausted first.

A second argument against open-housing legislation is that, insofar as it is seriously implemented, it is a rather drastic measure to take before less drastic measures have been exhausted. This type of legislation involves a drastic change in the relations of citizens to government for which Americans have not been sufficiently educated. The social revolution of our time already involves the gigantic task of reeducation toward the universalization of the values concerning the human relations of Americans. In certain realms citizens already know they are obliged to be universalistic and may already feel guilty they are not. These realms are numerous and ripe for vigorous application of law. Public authority should prove successful there before turning to realms where citizens are still almost certain to feel that they have the right to be particularistic in their associations.

Third, open-housing legislation will not work, or will work only as a war of attrition, because it will have to be applied almost exclusively against the white lower classes. The framers of this legislation succeeded in redistributing responsibilities where they failed to redistribute rights or wealth, for open-housing legislation must necessarily apply in those neighborhoods in which black families can afford to take advantage of the law. True, blacks ought to be able to buy or rent where they can afford. But why deliberately seek to pursue the revolution through the white lower classes? If we truly seek to bring about a revolution through law, we should at least exhaust first of all the possibilities of pursuing it through those people in the community most likely to respect the law, to obey the law, and perhaps ultimately to come to see the actual necessity of eliminating all differences in human relationships due solely to indefensible and outmoded social criteria.

Also to be rejected are the prospective and seemingly bold proposals for what might be called new new welfare—that is, schemes for guaranteed incomes, including the negative income tax. If the method of guarantee is a nondiscretionary negative-income-tax scheme, like the first and most famous proposed by Professor Milton Friedman, it constitutes simply a bit of reform of old welfare. If the scheme is built on a discretionary distribution system it merely constitutes a large expansion of new welfare.[24] But either way, these are welfare and antipoverty plans and they do not get at the question of who shall be poor any better than old or new welfare. *Welfare approaches are simply not appropriate for the revolution of our time.*

REDISCOVERY OF THE CITY

A fresh approach to an integrated multiracial society will therefore stake its claim primarily upon the schools; it will base its claim upon citizenship; and it will tear away some old and outmoded political structures without threatening any fundamental social values. The federal approach to integration can, in sum, be implemented by rediscovery of the city.

Rediscovery is required on two levels. One level is socioeconomic. The other level is philosophic and constitutional. Both operate as powerful guides to good public policy.

Socioeconomically, the city is obviously something far larger than the corporate city. Only policies that deal with this true city will be effective in guiding the revolution. Sometimes only the federal government is extensive enough to produce effective policy for the true socioeconomic city, but that option is limited, as already suggested, by the awesome problem of regional variation. The other level is the state, although at this stage of the game use of this level may require the holding of the nose. But there are no other alternatives in the United States. No law is worthy of the name unless applied by a sovereign, and federal and state governments are our only sovereigns. We may dream of the central city getting together with its satellites, or we may dream of good will bringing about uniform remedial action throughout the metropolis. But if there is no polity there will not be any policy. No local government has the jurisdiction for the revolution. It is not sovereign. The corporate city is an anachronism, and it has been for forty years.

Since that which we conventionally designate the city really does not exist, we must define a new city. This is the philosophic dimension. The city is citizens. The city is the public character or the public dimension of people. In a democratic system citizenship is the only thing people absolutely, involuntarily, and perpetually have in common. And it is in regard to this public dimension of people and things that government has its really effective claim. Through schemes of corporatism, syndicalism, interest-group representation, and participatory democracy, liberals, in the name of liberalism, have sought to obliterate the distinction between public and private. The concept of citizenship restores that distinction and defines clearly where are the best opportunities to guide the revolution.

24. For an excellent brief analysis of the problems, see Sar Levitan, "The Pitfalls of a Guaranteed Income," *Reporter*, May 18, 1967.

This definition goes to the core of a vital and practical constitutional point. In the United States there are two kinds of citizenship. There is national citizenship—that bundle of immunities and obligations relative to federal power. And there is state citizenship—one's public character created by the constitutional grant of power to each state. This is one more type of citizenship than is found in most countries, but what is significant here is that there are only two and not three. *There is no city citizenship. Constitutionally, therefore, there is no corporate city.* The city is citizens. It is the state, or the federal government, in relation to people. The corporate city is an aggregation of people which the state saw fit to render into an administrative structure. The corporate city is merely a creature of the state. The corporate city may have traditions and may enjoy the (ever-weakening) loyalty of its residents. The corporate city may indeed perform vital functions in the core and at the fringes of metropolis. But the corporate city as a public entity with absolute claims upon citizenship need not exist *except at the convenience of the state,* notwithstanding any law or state constitution to the contrary. And the corporate city is no longer a convenience.

The fiction of a third citizenship residing in the corporate city, as though it were a city-state, has been cultivated in the United States for three-quarters of a century. Home rule it is called, and it was allowed to convey the totally erroneous impression that a corporate city could be made into a sovereign body. Thus home rule is not only inconvenient, it is unconstitutional, because it permanently delegates (therefore alienates) state powers to some part within the state. Home rule may have been a practical necessity in the early days of urban growth when the physical and social city was so far out of joint with the rest of the state. However, as the physical and economic distinctions between rural and urban disappear, the political distinction of a conventional city from the rest of the state becomes meaningless. And as the country at large comes to espouse certain values without regard to region or rural-urban differences, the political distinction of a city from the rest of the state becomes an unadulterated evil. The grant of home rule was once a grant of autonomy. Now it is simply a barrier to the peaceful resolution of revolutionary forces.

Rediscovery of the city therefore means rediscovery of the state role as well as clarification of the federal role. It is difficult to ponder the state as the key to the future, but the desirability of the state increases as other approaches are tried and found wanting. Some object on the mere practical grounds that state social policy is politically unrealistic, that states are remote and corrupt, that states have insufficient power or responsibility for such important tasks, and that state policy constitutes only an imposition upon local efforts. These objections, as well as others, all sound hauntingly familiar to anyone who lived through the period prior to the enactment of the first federal civil-rights bills, when Southern leaders pleaded so eloquently the same cases against Washington.

By simple use of grant-in-aid and tax-rebate powers the federal government could put starch in the character of state politics. A properly moral and legal attitude toward power could render the federal government capable of overcoming rural conservatism and suburban reactionism and fear in the state legislatures. After that, literally with the stroke of a pen states could proceed in the one single action the present revolution begs for: *the destruction of the corporate city*. This would simplify immensely the expansion of the rights of the individual in the United States.

Old welfare and the revisit to Iron City are clear enough illustrations of the power of federal resources when used to attain legal and clearly defined purposes—just as new welfare, urban renewal, and public housing represent the weakness of federal power when used diffusely and without clear legal focus. States must be offered the choice, in other words, of maintaining or not maintaining membership in the industrial prosperity club, the key to which is the federal revenue system. No aids of any sort would ever again be forthcoming without actual proof, before the fact, that state programs deal with the rights of citizens. The technique itself is not new; it is only being put to new purposes. Such was intended in parts of the 1964 and 1965 civil-rights acts, but for several important reasons they have only just begun to work, as illustrated in Iron City. One of those reasons is lack of will, but there are other hindrances even when the will exists. Most important is the fact that much of the substantive legislation to which the civil-rights acts would apply is not sufficiently clear, and most of the precedent is weighted toward continuing to enable cities to carry out their local policies. Next, even if the purpose in the federal legislation is spelled out clearly and an effort is made to apply antidiscrimination standards to it, the implementation of real social goals in cities will be hopeless as long as the city is defined as the corporate city. A federal law that requires corporate central cities to solve important problems involving human rights is requiring the impossible of those cities and at the same time is reinforcing the irresponsibility of the satellite cities. Therefore the federal government has no choice but to establish destruction of city boundaries as a clear goal, and the states must implement the goals with all the fervor of revival, because the future of state government, as well as the health of the society after the revolution, depends heavily upon the severing of these shackles. There are obviously other areas in need of federal action, and there are methods of action other than grant-in-aid, tax-rebate, and other fiscal devices. However, a good legal purpose enforced by fiscal power has the advantage of keeping involvement of federal sovereignty safely remote from tarnishing and unsavory relationships with local governments, without in fact destroying all hope of some regional and local variation.

BREAKING THE CYCLE: THE CASE OF EDUCATION

Education serves as the best single area for practical application of these principles. Education alone might break the cycle of dual status even if all other reforms failed to take place.

The public schools are clearly public property. They can be possessed by no one but the state (or federal) system. They cannot be the property, therefore, of the corporate cities or of the local school districts. They cannot be the property of, or subject to proprietary control by, any individuals or organizations, for individuals have no relation to the schools except in the capacity of their citizenship. Even a child of five is a citizen in the degree to which he or she must be educated—and these obligations do not change if the child is in what is called a private school. In any case, neither the children, nor the neighborhood, the races, the PTAs, the unions, nor, indeed, the professional educators can sustain any proprietary claim. All these traits, while admirable to be sure, are totally irrelevant to school life, school districting, school eligibility, school organization, school purposes. Their claim, far from being proprietary, is no stronger a claim than that of the bricks or slates that comprise the physical school. If educational reform is to come, if education is to be made the key instrument in the revolution, the corporate school district with vested neighborhood rights must fall along with the rest of the old trappings of corporate cityhood. Real equality in education will die inside the conventional city and its conventional school-district boundaries.

A school district is a useful administrative convenience. But if it is composed of citizens it can be of any shape, any size, any character. It can obviously be designed without regard to preexisting corporate boundaries. Why does one fiction have to recognize another? Federal legislation must provide simply the incentives for states to create socially meaningful districts. This is the concrete and practical way by which the federal system can break down an important barrier to justice.

The private schools and academies must also be included. Whether these existed before an integration order or were set up specifically to flank integration, private schools exist primarily to fulfill the obligation of citizens of a state to be educated, and they must not be used to evade this basic public policy. Those who feel that the quality of the cultural or religious training of their children is suffering in integrated schools continue to have the right to provide for additional instruction outside the school. That is the way it has been for most and should have been for all. The state should not have the right to compel students to take any courses beyond those that can be shown to be absolutely essential to the requirements of citizenship—the three R's. Most of the rest of the school curriculum is probably not within the right of the schools to offer, much less to require.

Note on the accompanying map of Metropolitan Chicago (Figure 9.3) how easily a few oval-shaped, relatively compact school districts could accommodate the black ghetto population. On the corporate Chicago part of the map, at the center near the lake, the key black ghettos are sketched out roughly. An oval reaching upward through Evanston and Kenilworth toward Glencoe in the north could easily accommodate a large proportion of the northernmost ghetto and the northern part of the next ghetto. A northeasterly and somewhat larger oval-shaped school district running toward Morton Grove and Glenview could easily accommodate the remainder of the second ghetto. Another just to the south and west of that one, running toward Des Plaines, could accommodate a large part of the school population of the West Side ghetto. A goodly proportion of the remainder of the schoolchildren of the West Side ghetto could be spread and shared among school districts running due west and slightly north and south of due west. Parents in the largest ghetto, the

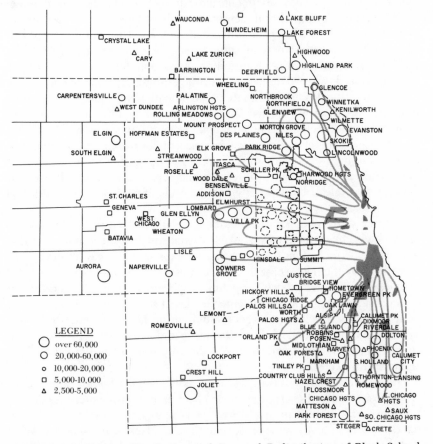

FIGURE 9.3 Chicago: Distribution and Proposed Redistribution of Black Schoolchildren

South Side ghetto, could be required to send their children to one of several school districts flanking outward toward the south quadrant of the map.

No child would have to spend more than thirty to forty minutes commuting each way in order to reach the outer fringes of each school district. And that is hardly any distance at all compared to the distances children had to travel in the days of the old consolidated county school districts and in the days before school buses. A mere twenty-mile commute from the northern black sections could reach Glencoe and environs. A mere twenty-mile commute from the West Side ghetto reaches Glenellyn. A mere twenty-mile commute from the very center of the South Side ghetto could reach any one of several prosperous and desirable South Side suburbs. Once corporate boundaries are disregarded the choices become amazingly easy.

Many, possibly a majority, of whites object even to modest busing experiments. But their practical arguments are extremely weak, and their claim to constitutionally vested rights in their present school situations has been shown to be illusory. Many black parents also fear such a system, but they must balance their fears against present educational opportunities that doom their child far more certainly than commuting. As long as the majority culture is a white-produced, white-dominated industrial culture, separate schools will be inherently unequal. Ghetto schools are perpetuating the separate culture that second-class citizenship created, and the cycle can be broken only by abandonment of those schools. The only real problem is whether the black community itself is as yet mature enough to accept positive discrimination. The hope is that they are already so accustomed to being singled out that a little more, especially if benign instead of malicious, will not hurt. It must be done, if the cycle of black poverty and the cycle of white fear and guilt shall ever be broken.

Another source of opposition that has been and may again be influential is black power, black nationalism, black separatism. One may indeed sympathize with the frustration these movements express. One may almost justifiably patronize them by seeing there an expression of new-found identity. But their expressions have no status as policy. Their suffering gives them cause but does not define rights or specify remedies. Legal support for their separatism, in any form, is as evil as was legal prohibition of their integration. Both run against the very fiber and fabric of citizenship and statehood. Separatists are in effect demanding two legal systems at the very time when the nation is in agony trying to create one.

One of the subsidiary advantages to an educational scheme cutting across all existing boundaries is its immediate effect upon housing pressures. White homeowners in Cicero are less likely to feel the urge to move or fear a potential decline in property values in face of the first black neighbor if they know that the school situation will not change appreciably. Hidebound school districts and residential requirements leave frightened residents almost no choice but to remove themselves totally from the area, even at the risk of great financial loss. Hidebound school districts are surefire ways of making certain that the main burden of revolution will be borne by the lower- and lower-middle-class whites. To spread that burden into the school systems all over the area is to extend to these frightened city residents the right to remain where they are. This is bound to stabilize neighborhoods.

CITIZENSHIP: PUBLIC MORALITY

However, the strongest argument of all is that integration policies put some kind of meaningful morality into the relationship between government and citizen. Despite what social science may say, politics is morality. Politics is the making of choices between good and bad, choices of priorities among competing good things. Democracy appeals because its emphasis on method keeps private moralities in check. But that does not mean that moral choice is not involved. Pretending that it is not may have been the beginning of the rise of cynicism and the decline of legitimacy. Marx believed that the seeds of revolution were implanted the moment when a "cash nexus" was established between persons, their employers, and their product. In the modern state, alienation may have begun with the establishment of a cash nexus between citizens and their government.

Public morality is a behavioral fact. Its basis is citizenship, and its influence and its limits can be studied like any other political phenomenon. Only time will test out the most important hypotheses, but certain of the tendencies of this cash nexus can be perceived now. At the most general level, the absence of public morality or citizenship will almost certainly yield Two Nations. All industrial states successfully met this problem when it manifested itself in the polarization of economic classes. The United States is one of the first to face the problem in racial and ethnic terms. The policy choices may be more agonizing this time because popular majorities do not fall easily on the side of change. But the obligations of citizenship and the results of not obeying them are about the same.

The suburbs, legally separating themselves from American life, represent a failure of citizenship. Blacks who prefer to remain apart in the ghetto represent an escape from citizenship. Congress, in spreading the obligations of citizenship to uncertain realms before successfully exhausting federal powers over certain realms, is deranging citizenship. The president, in calling forth these obligations when he cannot forcefully implement his own, is demoralizing citizenship. Programs erasing the obligations by buying off demands that they be fulfilled are destroying citizenship.

If the revolution is to be directed away from the Two Nations, the notion of citizenship must be restored and the strongest and most authoritative of laws must be applied to it. An easy and effective place to begin is with complete

destruction of the fiction of local citizenship and the sanctity of local corporate boundaries. Long ago the Supreme Court ruled that parties "cannot
remove their transactions from the reach of dominant constitutional power by
making contracts about them."[25] A corporate charter is merely a contract,
and no contract is protected from state power, especially when it involves
practices that are illegal or contrary to public policy. It is clear that the corporate city is contrary to public policy. Its destruction may be the first step
toward real progress in the North, just as destruction of state segregation laws
was the first step toward liberation of the South. Citizenship simply puts an
end to segregation in all its forms. The policies of interest-group liberalism
only serve to make segregation a little easier to abide.

25. Chief Justice Hughes in *Norman* v. *Baltimore and Ohio Railroad Co.*, 294 U.S. 240
(1935).

Part IV

BEYOND

LIBERALISM

"The law detains both man and woman
Who steal the goose from off the common
But lets the greater felon loose
Who steals the common from the goose."

Anon.

10

THE SECOND REPUBLIC OF THE UNITED STATES

The State of Permanent Receivership

During the decade of the 1960s the United States had a crisis of public authority and died.[1] A Second Republic was left standing in its place. We had held no constituent assembly and had written no second Constitution. Yet at some point, beginning in the 1930s and culminating in the 1960s, cumulative changes in national power, national institutions, and in ideology altered our relationship to the Constitution of 1787, making the Second Republic a reality, not a metaphor.

The term *Second Republic* has a peculiar ring to it only because changes of regime are not recognized and enumerated in the United States. Many Americans believe there have been no basic regime changes, and others fear that recognition of such changes might bring them about. Yet there have been regime changes worthy of recognition as a change of republic. Had there been a tradition of recognizing and enumerating such changes in the United States, our new republic of the 1970s might now be known as the Third or Fourth Republic. The republic under the Articles of Confederation would have been the First. It lasted thirteen years, which almost exactly equals the average life of a French republic since 1789. If that makes government under the Constitution of 1787 the Second Republic, what then of the republic after the Civil War? The change that has occurred in our own time is called the Second Republic only because previous changes were not given their due. This chapter is about that change, its character and its implications.

The Second Republic is not the end of liberalism but its triumph. The end of liberalism is still in sight because ultimately the modern, interest-group variant of liberalism is self-defeating. But interest-group liberalism must first have its era as the philosophic and jurisprudential basis of its own regime. What I attempted to describe in the 1960s as our *de facto* practices of policy

1. "Ideology, Policy, and the Crisis of Public Authority" was the subtitle of the first edition of *The End of Liberalism*.

and politics became, by the 1970s, the *de jure* regime of the United States. What might have been premature to define in 1969 was already too late to head off by 1974.

Every regime develops a politics characteristic of itself, consonant with its own claims to legitimacy and congruent with its own particular uses of government. Once the Second Republic is clearly distinguished along these lines, it will be relatively easy to show why and in what respects the Second Republic is not only a distinctive but a bad republic and why it will ultimately undermine itself.

The First Republic: Its Characteristics, Its Demise

The traditional American republic—that is, the republic or republics since 1787—can be defined by a few commonplace characteristics, bearing in mind that commonplaces are most likely to point to the bases of authority. The first and most important of these commonplaces was its federal structure, with a weak national government and strong peripheral governments which the Constitution deliberately called *states* precisely in order to indicate where most authority in the system was expected to reside.

The system was federal in practice as well as theory, in power as well as authority. One of the commonplaces least understood in contemporary America is the central role of the states under the traditional republic. The fact is that the states did almost all the governing. A glance at the annual session laws of Congress during the nineteenth century will reveal not only that the national government had very little to do, but that about 99 percent of what it did do was what we nowadays call subsidy or patronage policies; for example, land grants to settlers, land grants to railroad companies, tariffs to infant industries, subsidies to the merchant marines, and so on. Until very recently, all the rest of the governing was being done by the states. The states made all the property laws, family laws and estate laws, public health and safety laws, labor laws, occupations and professions laws, credit and exchange laws, banking and insurance laws, the laws of corporations, most of the criminal laws, and most of the other fundamental laws that provide the governmental and legal basis of modern life. These fundamental policies of the states were part and parcel of the exercise of police powers, which our constitutional theory had reserved primarily to the states and which were in practice being exercised almost exclusively by the states.

A national government producing mainly subsidy and patronage policies was a government ideally suited for legislative domination; and national government under the First Republic was very clearly a Congress-centered government. Woodrow Wilson's basic text on American national politics, published in 1888, was quite appropriately entitled *Congressional Government*.

And as Wilson put it, congressional government was primarily a committee government. Strong presidents were the exception; not all the others were literally weak presidents, but at best they were reactive presidents. The national bureaucracy was small in size and in force. For each major agency there was a parallel standing committee in the House and in the Senate.

The Emergence of the Second Republic

THE ROOSEVELT REVOLUTION: CHANGING
THE FUNCTIONS OF GOVERNMENT

The transition to the Second Republic began in earnest during the 1930s. A Second Republic might well have come into being during the Roosevelt period if domestic developments had not been cut off by World War II. The best-known but least significant characteristic of the New Deal period was the increasing size of the national government, measured in budgetary terms. Although it is true that federal domestic expenditure increased from .8 percent of GNP in 1929 to 4.9 percent in 1939, the factor of far greater significance is the change during the New Deal in the *functions* of the federal government. Subsidy policies continued to be enacted by Congress and implemented by the executive; in fact, growth in subsidies accounts for a large portion of the budgetary growth, and many of the new agencies were set up to administer subsidy programs. However, the federal government was adopting two entirely new kinds of functions, new at least for the federal government in the United States. These functions were *regulation* and *redistribution*. In adopting a large number of regulatory policies, the federal government had discovered that there was national as well as state police power. As for redistribution, conventional labels refer to fiscal and monetary policies, but these bland labels mask the true significance and the novelty for the federal government of the redistributive function.

Although regulatory and redistributive policies are quite different from each other, they share one very important characteristic which also distinguishes the two of them from almost everything the federal government was doing prior to the 1930s: These two new functions involved the federal government in direct and coercive use of power over citizens. Washington policy-makers could no longer hide from themselves the fact that *policy* and *police* had common roots. There were, of course, precedents for both of these new functions, ranging back to such significant examples of regulatory policy as the Interstate Commerce Act of 1887 and the Sherman Antitrust Act of 1890, and to such important redistributive policies as the early income-tax laws and the adoption of the Federal Reserve System. However, the New Deal is distinguishable because of the number of such policies adopted and because of the establishment of the constitutional right of federal government to exercise police power and to manipulate the economy.

These additions of function were accompanied by equally fundamental changes in institutional relationships and in public philosophy. In fact, the changes in function would probably not have lasted if there had not been some important adjustments in institutions and in public philosophy. In any event, it was during the New Deal that we began the probably irreversible change from a Congress-centered government to an executive-centered government. That development is in turn highly correlated, in cause and effect, to another commonplace feature of the New Deal, the rise of *delegated* power. The federal government literally grew by delegation. Although Congress continued to possess the lawmaking authority, it delegated that authority increasingly in statute after statute to an agency in the Executive Branch or to the president, who had the power to subdelegate to an agency. At first this delegation of power was rationalized as merely "filling in the details" of congressional intent and therefore consistent with even the most orthodox definition of the separation of powers. But ultimately, delegation was recognized for what it really was—administrative legislation. A whole new jurisprudence was developed in order to justify it, and the federal judiciary adjusted itself accordingly.

These very significant changes attributable to the New Deal should nevertheless be treated as transitional rather than final. There were many other characteristics of the New Deal period, and only the passage of time would tell which would take hold. The Second Republic emerges out of the pronouncement and validation of a few of these New Deal characteristics. The return of the Democrats to power in 1961 really signaled the beginning of the Second Republic. The return of the Democrats was accompanied by an entirely new attitude, and it is the attitude which selected out the particular New Deal characteristics that would ultimately become the basis of the new regime, of the Second Republic. This attitude at its most general level can be described as an eagerness to establish and maintain a national government presence in all aspects of social and economic life. If the 1930s had established a strong national state as politically feasible and constitutionally acceptable, the 1960s made the strong national state a positive virtue, desirable for its own sake. This was the major contrast between the 1930s and the 1960s. What had been done in the 1930s as a necessary evil justified by emergency became in the 1960s an obligation, a positive imperative.

THE 1960S: CHANGING THE INSTITUTIONS
AND JURISPRUDENCE

Two events in 1962 make that year a kind of turning point in the practice and theory of state in the Second Republic. The first of these was the *Eco-*

nomic Report of the President in January 1962. The second was President John Kennedy's Yale Commencement Address of the following summer. In his 1962 *Economic Report*, President Kennedy requested from Congress delegation of vast discretionary power over all public works and over the entire income-tax structure of the federal government. In effect, President Kennedy was asking for (1) personal discretion to make the laws controlling budget deficits and surpluses, (2) personal discretion over the laws determining the level of public capital investment, (3) personal discretion to manipulate the levels and rates that determine individual and corporate tax liability, and through that, the level of economic activity. Although President Kennedy did not get what he requested, he did establish beyond any remaining doubt the legitimacy of requests for unlimited delegation of discretion to the president. Eventually Congress would cooperate, not begrudgingly but eagerly.[2]

In his Yale Commencement Address in June 1962, President Kennedy argued that "old sweeping issues have largely disappeared. The central domestic problems of our times are more subtle and less simple. They relate not to basic clashes of philosophy or ideology, but to ways and means of reaching common goals—to research for sophisticated solutions to complex and obstinate issues." Thus on the very eve of one of the most ideological periods in American history, President Kennedy had accepted the "end of ideology" thesis. He had replaced it with a general theory that the solution to our problems rested with the presidency and a professionalized bureaucracy.

This was only part of the general reordering of public philosophy and governmental practice. The new public philosophy embraced the shift from Congress-centered to executive-centered government, going still further to encourage and to embrace the change from executive-centered to White House-centered government. Institutional and policy changes were reinforced by the general belief of the sixties that a strong national government was basically in harmony with all the interests in society. The new public philosophy went so far as to redefine majority rule, making the president, not Congress, its true manifestation. Congress was redefined as a useful collection of minorities and then belittled still further by the idea that Congress was only one part of a long policy-making process within which organized minorities had rightful access for purposes of informal and formal participation. And once the presidency was redefined as the true representative of the real major-

2. One outstanding example given earlier in the book warrants repetition here, not only because it is a delegation of unlimited discretion but also because it was not a delegation of power sought at the time (1970) by the president:

> The President is authorized to issue such orders and regulations as he deems appropriate to stabilize prices, rents, wages and salaries. . . . Such orders and regulations may provide for the making of such adjustments as may be necessary to prevent gross inequities. . . . The President may delegate the performance of any function under this Title to such officers, departments and agencies of the United States as he may deem appropriate.

Economic Stabilization Act of 1970, Sections 202 and 203.

ity, the overwhelming inclination was to embrace the principle of embodying maximum *legislative* powers in the presidency. That ties the package together: new functions, new institutional relationships, and a public philosophy which not only justified those developments but identified a presidency and a professional bureaucracy uniquely capable of leadership as well as implementation.

Emphasis should be put upon the fact that these were not merely changes in the locus of power but more fundamentally changes in the sources of legitimate authority. The language of laws under the Second Republic is virtually a language of the Bible, expressing broad and noble sentiments, giving almost no direction at all but imploring executive power, administrative expertise, and interest-group wisdom to set the world to rights. Whether the field is wage and price control, environmental pollution, unemployment, or inflation, congressional actions now amount to little more than an invocation, even though it is still called lawmaking and legislative drafting. In effect, "whereas all Americans have a right to a job, and whereas the economy might provide jobs for everyone if there were planning, now therefore let there come to pass plans, programs, rules and regulations from the President who shall in his wisdom . . . etcetera."[3]

Well before the end of the Democratic era of the 1960s we had established a full-scale, modern national state in the United States. A national presence had been established in all areas of social and economic endeavor. The national presence extended not only to matters pertinent to large corporations and their treatment of employees; it had also gone far beyond intervention into the affairs of state governments and their local units. The national presence had for the first time extended even into the streets. Police power had been nationalized in the fullest sense of the word. During the 1960s more federal troops were called up to deal with more local disorders than during the entire nineteenth century. President George Washington sent nearly 13,000 troops to meet the Whiskey Rebellion; afterward call-ups were small and infrequent. In contrast, in the twenty years between September 1945 and August 1965, federal intervention by use of National Guard and other military troops became a regular occurrence with 83 call-ups involving 44,000 troops. In the three and a half years between August 1965 and December 1968, there were 179 call-ups involving 184,000 troops.[4] During those same turbulent 1960s, at least 100,000 civilians were placed under surveillance by the army—despite the fact that this was an illegal and impeachable act. Between 1966 and 1976, court records show that the FBI in Chicago alone paid

3. This imaginary passage is, unfortunately, a fairly loyal translation of the Equal Opportunity and Full Employment Bill, otherwise known as the Humphrey-Hawkins Bill, which was around Congress for years before its passage in 1978 and continues to be advertised as a "giant step toward humanistic capitalism."

4. Adam Yarmolinsky, *The Military Establishment* (New York: Harper & Row, 1971) p. 154 and pp. 162–63.

$2.5 million to recruit more than 5,000 spies to inform on Chicago area residents and organizations. The FBI files themselves reveal that the Trotskyist Socialist Workers Party, although composed of only 2,500 members by the FBI's own generous count, had been infiltrated by over 300 paid informants at a cost of over $1.6 million; this does not count other possible informants placed by the CIA and other agencies in the same political party. Such political intervention is not limited to conservative Republicans. During the 1960s and 1970s virtually all the conspiracy trials undertaken by the Justice Department were taken under Johnson and his liberal attorney general, Ramsey Clark. Shoring up all crime-fighting units of local governments became a major program of the Johnson Administration.

One response to these data might be that the 1960s were very special years and that statistics on national involvements with local disorders are misleading. But out of special times come precedents that bind normal times, if indeed there are ever normal times in the United States. The fact seems to be that we had nationalized local disorders, just as we had nationalized commerce. All of the peripheries of this country now felt the glow of national presence.

THE 1970S: VALIDATION BY SUCCESSION

All of this gave the Republican Party an almost unique opportunity in 1969. The uncertain struggle for national supremacy had discredited the Democrats in almost every way, from the war in Vietnam to the War on Poverty. And Richard Nixon was one of the most partisan of Republicans.

Some Republican choices were a distinct departure from Democratic patterns. Nixon's Supreme Court appointments were distinctively different. The Office of Economic Opportunity (OEO), the organizational superstructure of the War on Poverty, was to be phased out. The Department of Health, Education and Welfare was going to be severely constrained in its ability to use federal aid for school desegregation. Many social programs were going to be cut back in favor of broad grants for local law enforcement, local government maintenance, and paying the interest of the local public debt. In most areas of government, very different interest groups were going to gain access.

However, only a superficial review of the Republican choices covered in this volume will be sufficient to show that the similarities between the Republican and Democratic Administrations greatly outnumbered and outweighed the differences. Some similarities were programmatic; Republicans were comfortable with many Democratic programs and in any event did not choose to fight too many battles at one time. But the more important similarity was in the manner in which government was being used. The best example was revenue sharing. It was the largest single domestic action Nixon took. Essentially it eliminated what little legal structure there had been in the domestic programs of the Democrats and left with the Administration a range and breadth of discretion over grants-in-aid that had never existed even in the days of grave domestic emergency. Wage and price control, agriculture, energy, commerce, industrial and consumer safety, and the environment are all areas in which the Republicans reinforced the Democratic practice of seeking broad discretion coupled with various degrees of sponsored-interest representation.

The governmental system of interest-group liberalism was, thereby, institutionalized. The test of institutionalization is succession. If successors repeat and imitate the practices of their predecessors, the patterns are being reinforced in the habits and thoughts of the successors. This is the sort of thing Richard Neustadt undoubtedly had in mind when he observed in the mid-1950s that the practice of having a president's program had been institutionalized through the repetition of the elaborate agency request procedure during the early years of the Eisenhower Administration, despite the misgivings of Republicans at that time about "creeping socialism."[5] The situation has gone still further when these practices are not only repeated but are treated as the right way to do things. Then the practices have been fully institutionalized.

The institutionalized politics of what is now the Second Republic can be summarized as a simple two-part model: (1) The national government by some formal action monopolizes a given area of private activity. This can be done by direct financial domination, as in the case of defense, space, hospitals, highways; or it can be done by declaring illegal all participation in a certain sector unless granted government permission (licensing), as in the case of communications, corporate merger, commercial aviation, or wage increases; or the domination can be through the underwriting of risk, as will be seen immediately below. (2) Following that, a program is authorized and an administrative agency is put into operation to work without legal guidelines through an elaborate, sponsored bargaining process in which the broad area monopolized by the government is given back piece by piece as a privilege to specific individuals or groups on a case-by-case basis (often called "on the merits").

That pattern was sufficiently mature as early as the mid-1960s to allow description of its character and consequences. Now the pattern has been elevated into a fixed institution. Privileges in the form of money or license or underwriting are granted to established interests, largely in order to keep them established, and largely done in the name of maintaining public order and avoiding disequilibrium. The state grows, but the opportunities for sponsorship and privilege grow proportionately. Power goes up, but in the form of personal plunder rather than public choice. It would not be accurate to evaluate this model as "socialism for the rich and capitalism for the poor," because many thousands of low-income persons and groups have profited within the

5. Richard E. Neustadt, "Presidency and Legislation: Planning the President's Program," *American Political Science Review* 49 (1955): 980–1021.

system. The more accurate characterization might be "socialism for the organized, capitalism for the unorganized."

The Character of the Second Republic:
The State of Permanent Receivership

What is the Second Republic? How shall we speak of it? What kind of a regime is it? Capitalist democracy? Social democracy? Postindustrial capitalism? A corporate state? A mature capitalist state? A stagnating industrial state? An overdeveloped postindustrial society?

Each of these labels captures something but does not do full justice to our Second Republic. Yet we need to conceptualize it, because concepts move political discourse away from news about political behavior toward the state (or system) within which that behavior takes place and from which political activity draws its meaning. Given the shortcomings of each of the conventional characterizations, discourse might best be served by an entirely new concept: the *state of permanent receivership*.

The state of permanent receivership is a logical, though not inevitable outgrowth of the expanding, positive liberal state. *Receivership* refers to the method of maintaining social order during a crisis involving the bankruptcy of an individual or enterprise. When any holder of wealth, individual or corporation, is on the verge of dissolution because it cannot possibly meet its debts, the public takes an interest in it for the obvious reason that the various creditors might fight over the remaining assets. A court appoints an officer to receive the properties of the bankrupt, to administer them during an interim period, and to make an orderly disposal of the assets in as equitable a manner as possible. Private property becomes public property as soon as it fails to maintain itself; receivership is a process by which order in the community is maintained until the bankrupt property is redistributed at a lower level of valuation.

Permanent receivership would simply involve public or joint public-private maintenance of the assets in their prebankrupt form and never disposing of them at all, regardless of inequities, inefficiencies, or costs of maintenance. This is quite conceivable as long as a government or a larger private enterprise assures all the creditors that they would be better off allowing the original enterprise to continue operations than if they liquidated it and took their ten cents on the dollar.

The concept of permanent receivership can be extended to include businesses that are not actually on the brink of bankruptcy but are in a sector of the economy where bankruptcies or reorganizations are likely unless there is some kind of a preventive measure. This could be called *anticipatory receiver-*

ship suggesting that the policy measures appropriate for the concept give the government a very special capacity to plan. Permanent receivership can also be extended outward to include organizations that are not businesses. If there are public policies which are inspired by or can be understood in terms of this expanded definition, then we have all of the elements of a *state of permanent receivership*.

The state of permanent receivership is a state whose government maintains a steadfast position that any institution large enough to be a significant factor in the community may have its stability underwritten. It is a system of policies that sets a general floor under risk, either by attempting to eliminate risk or to reduce or share the costs of failure. The stress here is on organizational stability, not upon the stabilization of a particular class or power elite. It is biased not so much in favor of the rich as in favor of the established and the organized. Permanent receivership is an answer to permanent crisis to the extent that this notion properly describes the situation of Western industrial states. The state of permanent receivership is reassuring for interest groups of any sort. It is also consistent with the goals of large state bureaucracies, because in concept and in practice permanent receivership is deeply conservative. It respects all skills and all existing social contrivances; above all it respects the established jurisdictions of government agencies and the established territories of private corporations and groups.

RECEIVERSHIP BY REGULATION

Some federal regulation is actually aimed at protecting individuals and the public from harmful products or practices. But a considerable proportion of federal regulation, regardless of its own claim to consumer protection, has the systematic effect of constituting and maintaining a sector of the economy or the society. These are the policies of receivership by regulation.

An immense number of examples of such policies have already been provided in this volume. Commercial air transportation policy is a good example to reiterate here. It is illegal to engage in any commercial air service without a "certificate of convenience and necessity" from the Civil Aeronautics Board, and no such certificate for the entry of a new company or the expanded services of an existing company will be granted without due consideration of the profit margins of all of the members. In mid-January of 1978, the CAB was up in arms against President Jimmy Carter for his decision to go against the CAB and grant Braniff Airlines a new, potentially lucrative route from Dallas-Fort Worth to London. By law the president has the power to displace the CAB with his own judgment in the granting of licenses between any American city and a foreign city, but the CAB was up in arms against the president because they had recommended Pan Am for that route. There was no compelling virtue on either side, but the reason for the CAB displeasure was that

Pan Am had just begun to earn a profit again after years of heavy losses. The CAB believed that it could not stand any more competition at this time and that the role of the government was to protect Pam Am from such competition. Although the CAB permitted some competition in 1978, this is still their prime posture. And virtually the same analysis can be made at any point in time for so many of the areas of public policy dealt with in previous chapters.

Many such regulatory policies are explicit and self-conscious receivership policies because they concern themselves with a total sector and attempt to maintain the stability and well-being of that sector by keeping limits on entry, limits on expansion, and limits on the type and degree of competition. There are, in addition to these, a number of regulatory policies that have a systematic receivership effect even though they are not set up self-consciously to maintain a particular sector. One example of this intermediate level of receivership regulation is trade regulation within the Federal Trade Commission. Alan Stone meticulously catalogues and assesses the long tradition of trade regulations in which the FTC has tried to outlaw in the name of "fair competition" those vigorous methods of competition most likely to be used by smaller firms hoping to capture a larger share of the market.[6]

Going beyond these specific policies, the basic argument of this book has been that any and all discretionary policies will tend to give us a receivership effect because discretionary policies develop a particular kind of politics which is supportive of the clientele it seeks to deal with. The only explicit departure from this general thesis is that certain important regulatory policies explicitly, self-consciously, and systematically intend to produce this result.

RECEIVERSHIP BY DISCRETIONARY FISCAL POLICY: PLANNING IN THE SECOND REPUBLIC

To look at regulatory policy as receivership policy is mainly to summarize and synthesize earlier findings in order to bring them from the context of interest-group liberalism into the context of the Second Republic. But one important component of policy is missing, and it was missing from the original analysis. It would have been only an additional documentation to the analysis of interest-group liberalism, but it is vital to the analysis of the Second Republic of interest-group liberalism because it gives meaning to the regime in

6. Alan Stone, *Economic Regulation and the Public Interest—The Federal Trade Commission in Theory and Practice* (Ithaca: Cornell University Press, 1977). Douglas Jaenicke's study of the power of the FTC to issue "cease and desist orders" reveals that it, too, is a type of receivership policy. The FTC is not obliged to stop or punish all restraints of trade but only those that in its opinion are against the public interest. This means that the FTC can permit large corporations to experiment with certain monopolistic practices and can then issue a cease and desist order returning that corporation to its prerestraint phase without any further punishment. Douglas Jaenicke, "Ideology and Public Policy in the Progressive Era: A Reinterpretation of the FTC Act," *Political Science Quarterly* (Winter 1978).

theory; and in practice it provides the Second Republic with a capacity to plan that is consonant with interest-group liberal values. This component is discretionary fiscal policy, and its underlying technique of control is *underwriting*.

To underwrite is to subscribe to somebody else's venture in order to help assure its success by accepting some of the risk. Underwriting implies insurance, but insurance in the broad sense that underwriters seek to support or guarantee a proposed action by their willingness to subscribe, literally to sign on the bottom line, in order to indicate willingness to accept part of the risk. Underwriting may involve agreement to buy a portion of the shares of stock if these have not been applied for by the public. Underwriting may mean an agreement to contribute an amount of money under specified conditions or to buy stock at a certain price. But generically, underwriting is an effort to support or to guarantee by sponsorship or subscription.

For these reasons certain regulatory policies can be appreciated as functionally a form of underwriting. An easy example was the felt obligation of the CAB to consider the profit margin of each of the airlines before expanding the schedules. But underwriting can be seen in its clearest and most classical sense in discretionary fiscal policy—to be specific, in policies that provide agencies with discretion to issue investment guarantees.

The Lockheed loan of 1971 will be a good introduction to permanent receivership through discretionary fiscal policy precisely because it was not a loan although widely understood to be one. Lockheed, on the brink of actual bankruptcy, was neither allowed to dissolve nor saved by direct government subsidy. The government took positive steps, but it spent no money, granted no loan, made no direct transfers of any kind. The government action was merely a signature of a representative of the Emergency Loan Guarantee Board on a document which stated that the federal government would guarantee up to $250 million that Lockheed could borrow from private sources. With that guarantee—and it was no more than a signature by a public official on a slip of paper—Lockheed could go to private banks and get money at relatively low interest rates or money that was not otherwise forthcoming at all. The authority of the Board established by statute in 1970 was as follows: "The Board, on such terms and conditions as it deems appropriate, may guarantee, or make commitments to guarantee, lenders against loss of principal or interest on loans that meet the requirements of this act."

The requirements simply were that the Board must find that "the loan is needed to enable the borrower to continue to furnish goods and services and failure to meet that need would adversely and seriously affect the economy or employment in the nation or any region thereof." This grant of authority empowered the Board to manipulate the system of credit in the United States for a specific outcome favorable to this particular corporation.[7]

7. The quotations are from Sections 3 and 4 of the Emergency Loan Guarantee Act.

As with regulation, not all fiscal and monetary policies are receivership policies. One of the largest of these exceptions is the Federal Deposit Insurance Corporation (FDIC) which insures unconditionally all deposits up to $40,000 in all banks which are members of the Federal Reserve System. Although the figures will vary according to the total amount deposited in member banks, the total amount insured under FDIC at the beginning of 1975 was $520,300,000,000. An additional $278,774,000,000 of deposits are insured unconditionally by the Federal Savings and Loan Insurance Corporation (FSLIC). But the key to the distinction here is the fact that these programs operate unconditionally, on a nondiscretionary basis. Permanent receivership fiscal policies are discretionary fiscal policies.

An important and well-known example is the discretionary investment guarantee authority of the Veterans Administration. In fiscal 1975 the VA guaranteed over $8 billion in new housing loans and held at the same time guarantees on the total of $115.4 billion worth of housing mortgages. The total of loans guaranteed by the VA was expected to drop in 1978 toward $78 billion. But whether one looks at the larger or the smaller of the two aggregate figures, VA activity in discretionary fiscal policy represents a very large sector of economic activity, especially considering that all of the decisions made by the VA are outside the United States budget and do not show up anywhere in the budgetary accounts.

The other important examples of discretionary investment guarantee and insurance authority are listed on Table 10.1. Each of these agencies works within a ceiling or total authorization set by legislation. But they rarely reach their ceilings because of lapses, defaults, and repayments, and the actual commitments from year to year vary according to the demands of the private sector. The gross amount of new commitments for investment guarantees for 1976 was $53.46 billion. The total of new commitments estimated for 1978 was over $80 billion. Figure 10.1 provides a clear enough impression of the amplitude and growth of investment guarantee activity since 1960. It is definitely a growth sector of the federal government, especially when viewed in comparison to direct government loan activity during the same two decades shown on Figure 10.1.

The degree of discretion each agency enjoys over its power to issue investment guarantees does vary. For some agencies the discretion is virtually complete, within the ceiling set by law. No real limit, for example, was put upon the Emergency Loan Guarantee Board in its decision to extend the loan guarantees to the Lockheed Corporation. It is difficult to find any meaningful limitations upon the thousands of decisions made by the VA and FHA officials on home mortgages. On the other hand, decisions to insure the liabilities for damages for corporations expanding nuclear plants are tied to the authority of the Nuclear Regulatory Commission to issue the original licenses to build and operate those plants. This means that the guarantees of insurance for damages

TABLE 10.1

DISCRETIONARY FISCAL POLICY:
FEDERAL INVESTMENT GUARANTEE ACTIVITY, 1976*

PROGRAM	NEW GUARANTEES (IN MILLIONS OF DOLLARS)	TOTAL GUARANTEES OUTSTANDING (IN MILLIONS OF DOLLARS)
International	1,412	2,502
Farmers Home Administration	4,391	17,847
Rural Electrification Administration	860	1,114
Maritime Administration	1,169	3,431
Economic Development Assistance	1	160
Defense-Tanker charters		180
HEW		
Health	215	1,061
Education	1,397	6,849
HUD		
Low Rent	7,660	13,607
FHA	8,316	88,988
Communities	210	2,799
GNMA	8,999	25,610
Other credit	0	549
Interior		
Indian Programs	29	29
Transportation		
Railroads	264	670
WMATA (DC Transit)	0	997
Aircraft	78	100
Treasury	1,260	0
General Services Administration	24	956
Veterans Administration—Housing	10,250	64,116
Emergency Loan Guarantee Board (Lockheed)	0	185
Export-Import Bank	5,147	5,273
FDIC	0	1,144
Small Business Administration	1,768	4,979
Other agencies	13	68
TOTAL	53,463	243,213†

* SOURCE: *Special Analyses, Budget of the United States,* Fiscal Year 1978, Sec. E. (Washington, D.C.: U.S. Government Printing Office, 1978).

† Several agencies, including the Government National Mortgage Association (GNMA), the Federal Financing Bank (FFB) and several federally sponsored private enterprises, including the Federal National Mortgage Association (FNMA), formerly a public agency, actually buy up many guaranteed loans from the banks, converting them essentially into direct government loans. In 1976, $25 billion, nearly half, of the loan guarantees were so converted; and enough conversions take place to reduce the accumulated figure from the $243.2 billion in the table to $169.8 billion. Budgetary policy at the Office of Management and Budget prefers the lower figures, arguing that otherwise there is double counting. But I prefer the larger figure because (1) it indicates the scale of this activity and (2) because all of it, converted or not, is discretionary and "off-budget." These intermediary or secondary institutions are a form of "backdoor" credit.

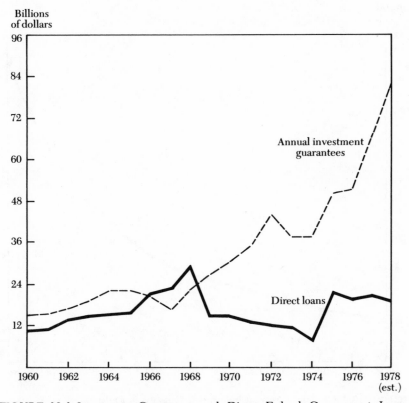

FIGURE 10.1 Investment Guarantees and Direct Federal Government Loans, Annually, 1960–78*

* SOURCE: *Special Analyses, Budget of the United States,* Sec. E, 1969–78. See note to Table 10.1.

tend to follow directly from the licensing decision, so that the discretion of the agency is tied to the licensing decision rather than to the guarantees on the loans or the damages. Yet, within this kind of variety the gross amount of discretion is very large, and the operating flexibility of these agencies can be all the more appreciated by the fact that their investment-guarantee and insurance activities do not appear anywhere in the federal budget.

The true size and significance of this sector might best be appreciated by pondering the value of all outstanding federally guaranteed investments. Table 10.1, column 2, sets the accumulated guarantees outstanding in 1976 at just over $243 billion, moving toward $323 billion in 1978. (Revised mid-year estimates for 1978 put that figure at $368 billion.) Figure 10.2 places these figures in a twenty-year time series showing the phenomenal growth of this activity since 1956. Note well that this does not include any of the totally nondiscretionary forms of insurance such as FDIC, FSLIC, Social Security

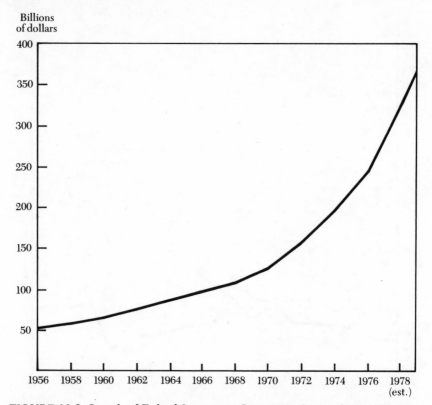

FIGURE 10.2 Growth of Federal Investment Guarantees Outstanding, 1956–78*

* SOURCE: *Special Analyses, Budget of the United States*, Sec. E, 1967–78. See note to Table 10.1.

insurance programs, and so on (see above, p. 283). If those were included, the actual insurance sector would be gigantic. Table 10.1 and Figure 10.2 also do not include government-sponsored credit enterprises such as the Student Loan Marketing Association (SLMA), the Federal National Mortgage Association (FNMA), the Farm Credit System, and the Federal Home Loan Bank System (see Table 10.2). These agencies, which are indeed highly discretionary, made a total of $36.2 billion credit commitments in 1976, but they are not counted here because they are not exactly government agencies. Although they are chartered by the federal government and are subject to some kinds of federal supervision, and although they consult the Treasury Department in planning their activities, these agencies are privately owned and managed. They are absolutely clear and definitive examples of interest-group liberal policies in that they are federally sponsored and enjoy special preferences and exemptions; but their relationship to the discretionary fiscal-policy

TABLE 10.2

LOAN COMMITMENTS AND DISBURSEMENTS OF FEDERALLY SPONSORED
CREDIT INTERMEDIARIES, 1976 (IN MILLIONS OF DOLLARS)

	COMMITMENTS	DISBURSEMENTS
Student Loan Marketing Association		
(SLMA)	227	227
Federal National Marketing Association		
(FNMA)	6,419	4,274
Farm Credit		
Banks for cooperatives	10,012	10,012
Federal intermediate credit banks	6,475	6,475
Federal land banks	4,439	4,438
Federal Home Loan Bank System	7,547	7,091
Federal Home Loan Mortgage		
Corporation	1,154	1,184
TOTAL	36,273	33,701

SOURCE: *Special Analyses, Budget of the United States*, Fiscal Year 1978, p. 106.

sector that makes up the state of permanent receivership is supportive and
facilitative rather than direct.

What remains is a narrower but more dependable definition of agencies actually engaging in the investment-guarantee activity that comprises the permanent receivership dimension of fiscal policy. And as Table 10.1 shows,
these programs extend throughout the entire range of public and private activity in the United States, from foreign and space matters to international trade
and domestic large and small business. The most important agencies, as indicated by their cumulative obligations are housing agencies; but energy, transportation, and international trade are beginning to grow in their dependence
upon government investment guarantees. For example, the Export-Import
Bank has loan guarantee and insurance authority; yet the national government saw fit in the 1960s to expand these activities, first through AID and
then through a separate Overseas Private Investment Corporation (OPIC).
The purpose of this agency is to provide incentives to invest in developing nations by underwriting a large proportion of the risk. A good 80 percent of all
OPIC's investment guarantees·have been extended to the large multinational
corporations with interests in developing countries. In early 1978, reports
were emanating from Washington suggesting that OPIC's authority to write
investment guarantees might not be renewed. Interestingly enough it got into
trouble when the House of Representatives adopted an amendment requiring
OPIC to earmark 50 percent of its investment guarantees for small companies.

Table 10.3 shows that the investment guarantee sector pictured in Figure

TABLE 10.3

THE FEDERAL INVESTMENT GUARANTEE SECTOR IN RELATION TO GROSS
PRIVATE INVESTMENT AND GROSS NATIONAL PRODUCT*

	1	2	3	4
		OUTSTANDING VALUE		
	GROSS PRIVATE	OF INVESTMENT	COL. 2	COL. 2
	DOMESTIC INVESTMENT	GUARANTEES	AS % OF	AS % OF
	(BILLIONS OF DOLLARS)	(BILLIONS OF DOLLARS)	COL. 1	GNP
1956	71	51.1	72	12.4
1958	62	58.5	94	13.2
1960	76	65.7	86	13.2
1962	85	77.0	91	14.1
1964	97	85.6	88	13.9
1966	124	99.2	80	13.8
1968	132	108.1	82	13.0
1970	141	125.1	89	13.0
1972	188	158.9	85	14.3
1974	215	197.2	92	14.5
1976	243	243.2	100.1	15.0
1978	320 (est.)	323.5 (est.)†	101.1	15.8 (est.)

* Figures are in current dollars. Sources for Columns 1 and 4: U.S. Bureau of Economic
Analysis, *The National Income and Product Accounts of the United States* (Washington, D.C.:
U.S. Government Printing Office, 1976), pp. 158–59; *Survey of Current Business* (June 1978),
p. 11. Source for Column 2: *Special Analyses, Budget of the United States*, Fiscal Year 1978.
    † During the Senate debate in August 1968 over the New York City loan guarantee bill the
1978 estimate was reported to be $368 billion.

10.2 is not merely an artifact of inflation. Between 1966 and 1976 the outstanding value of private investments guaranteed by federal underwriting programs moved up until they almost exactly equaled the yearly rate of private investment in the United States. The figures in column 1, gross private
domestic investment, are of course annual figures, while those for investment
guarantees depicted in column 3 are the cumulative total of outstanding
guaranteed investments regardless of the year they were made. However, it is
significant nevertheless that the cumulative amount of guarantees now equals
the yearly private investment rate. This is almost as though the investment
guarantees sector were operating as a kind of counterbalance. Estimates for
1978 indicate that more counterbalancing is being sought, and all indications
point to their being granted. In mid-1978, Congress approved a $12.5 billion
guarantee for New York City bonds, establishing for the first time a federal responsibility for the solvency of cities. This came at the very moment when
California and other states were setting constitutional limitations on local tax-
ing power, which made it likely that other cities would not be long in lobbying to follow New York City's claim for bond guarantees. At that time as well,

President Carter approved loan guarantees to farmers of up to $4 billion and authorization for the Commerce Department to guarantee up to $500 million in loans to modernize and install pollution equipment at financially troubled steel mills. And still more troubled American Motors made a bid to follow Lockheed for $100 million in loan guarantees to help redesign its automobiles.

Even the impressive data in Tables 10.1, 10.2, and 10.3 and Figures 10.1 and 10.2 are insufficient to convey a full sense of the importance of this activity in the economy. A true measure would have to show somehow the trillions of dollars in private investment decisions that were probably influenced, albeit indirectly, by these investment guarantees. Just as economists know there is a multiplier effect from actual deposits to total investment activities, so there must be some kind of equivalent multiplier effect as between the total dollars of investment guaranteed and the total amount of investment in the sectors enjoying such guarantees. Surely it affects investors to know that a sector has been stabilized by federal investment-guarantee commitments. And surely the capacity of the government to shape the economy through this technique is worthy of consideration as an emerging system of planning. In this manner we find ourselves moving from a collection of permanent receivership policies toward a state of permanent receivership.

In order to plan, a government must control at least some of the strategic resources and networks in the economy. Some nations have sought planning capacity by socializing production—one or more basic industries. Some may try planning by the socialization of natural resources, while others may socialize the delivery of central services. Some may socialize banks while others may seek to socialize the distribution of goods. The United States has so far skirted all of these alternatives in favor of the socialization of its most valuable resource: *risk*. Our state of permanent receivership works through the socialization of risk.

Permanent Receivership: The End of Capitalism?

Permanent receivership offers a number of distinct advantages to an activist party in a positive state. First and above all, it enables the government to influence without directly intervening. The government can manipulate the economy by manipulating the environment of conduct rather than by having to attempt to control conduct itself. This is a general capacity of fiscal policy, but discretionary fiscal policy is more attractive because the government official is able to break down the increments of decision further and further and is also able to avoid articulating the rules of discrimination. Large chunks of the economy can be manipulated through very small increments of privilege.

A second salient advantage of permanent receivership is that such policies involve no immediate transfer of funds, therefore no Treasury or congressional or budgetary clearances. The political advantages are clear. Agencies can plan without near-run or nearsighted political interference. Present commitments may require later congressional or presidential clearance when defaults have to be liquidated (the United States is the largest single owner of urban property). But this comes later, long after the initial commitment, when it can be treated as a mandated or involuntary cost. A loan guarantee is *off-budget* (an official term) at the beginning and is mandatory by the time it is in-budget.

A third advantage of receivership is its conservatism. Permanent receivership is a form of negative planning inasmuch as its primary power is the power of conserving that which already exists. As observed before, this conservatism is favorable to established organizations rather than to riches as such, but there is nevertheless a conservative bias, as is generally true of the policies of interest-group liberalism.

These advantages alone make permanent receivership attractive to most major organizations, including unions as well as businesses, universities, and professional organizations as well as chambers of commerce. Even the traditional antigovernment American Medical Association is susceptible. Medicare and Medicaid are less discretionary than many forms of government insurance, but they are receivership policies nevertheless. Medicare and Medicaid work through the underwriting of payments to doctors. The government does not intervene with cash to patients or with imperatives or restraints placed upon doctors; the government simply makes medical services accessible to the poor by guaranteeing that the payments to doctors will be made. This exposes another whole set of political advantages: Neither Medicare nor Medicaid nor any other policy of permanent receivership is explicitly socialistic since no corporations or resources need to pass to or through the hands of government or the dominant party. Permanent receivership is not as interventionistic as direct nationalization of industries; nay, it is not even as interventionistic as many of our standard regulatory policies. In an important sense, permanent receivership is quite voluntaristic. The issuance of investment guarantees is centralized in Washington but does not result in a centralization of power or knowledge. Any impression of advancing centralization in the state of permanent receivership is not really a matter of central coordination of the economy but a continuous effort in the economy to *coordinate itself* in terms of the resources, privileges, and inclinations perceived to exist at the center. Corporations can have as much of this kind of centralization as they want and in turn can allow the center as much opportunity for central coordination as seems desirable at any point in time by corporate boards. The potential for coordination through permanent receivership is bound to be discovered and utilized by the White House.

Ultimately I think it will be clear that the disadvantages outweigh the advantages. Conservatism is not in itself a disadvantage, but the particular kind of conservatism represented by permanent receivership goes contrary to, in fact undermines, many of the values of traditional liberalism. In the state of permanent receivership there is a tremendous pro-organization, pro-establishment, anti-innovation bias. Like tariffs and other mercantilist policies, receivership policies permit and encourage economically irrational uses of resources by encouraging expansion beyond demand or by encouraging the retention of inefficient firms or processes. Worse yet, as discretionary policies, they are most likely to partake of all the political tendencies already ascribed to other discretionary policies: They work in a public-opinion vacuum; they encourage and favor access by established organizations; they enable agencies and congressional committees or subcommittees to create highly stable and autonomous clienteles and autonomous clientele relationships; they favor professionals over amateurs; they encourage cynicism on the part of the favored as well as the disfavored; and they provide no civic education whatsoever because they do not provide any opportunities at all for discourse about the priorities or moralities in back of public choice.

Is permanent receivership really planning at all? At present it is mainly makeshift without accountability, a fieldday for professionals because there is no reckoning day. But if, as is likely, permanent receivership were discovered and brought into the White House, it could, and almost certainly will, become our planning apparatus. Well before that comes to pass, we can already say that even if an economic case could be made for permanent receivership the political case is virtually entirely negative.

Does American capitalism really need a state of permanent receivership? If the answer were yes, we should have entitled this work "The End of Capitalism." Up to this point the assumption had been that interest-group liberalism was an ersatz and passing phase of liberalism that would fade away as capitalism recuperated from depression and war and as the self-defeating tendency of the ideology had been appropriately revealed. But now that interest-group liberalism has developed its own state, its own jurisprudence, and its own capacities for artificial perpetuation, the ideology may have proven itself to be a more fundamental expression of the inherent weaknesses of mature capitalism and of the inabilities of capitalism to survive without massive, systematic, and authoritative efforts to shore it up.

Yet, if the state of permanent receivership should persist long enough, it is quite likely to produce its own revolutionary solution. Apparently revolutionary movements, including socialism, have not developed in the United States for at least two reasons: historically, the absence of a feudal order to overthrow; and related but more contemporaneous, the absence of a state apparatus whose presence validates Marx's analysis and provides the focus for revolutionary theory. But if emergence of the state of permanent receivership should validate the analysis, it could galvanize the movement. While we wait for this to develop, it may be worthwhile considering alternatives which, although radical, are within instead of outside the existing constitutional framework. One such alternative is *neo-laissez-faire*, which is beginning to appeal more to the new left as it is being abandoned by the old left and the right.

AN ALTERNATIVE SOLUTION: NEO-LAISSEZ-FAIRE

There are distinct human, political, and technical limits to the abilities of government to influence its economy and society. These limits exist whether the political system is liberal, socialist, or otherwise. In contrast, there are probably fewer limits on the amount of existing governmental controls that can be given up. Yet, one could radicalize economy and society quite directly by a deflation or abnegation of government power. A deregulation of airlines or communications or energy would completely radicalize those industries. Multinational and other giant corporations could probably be jolted back into more actual price competition if the hundreds of protections of industry and finance lodged in our public policy were suddenly eliminated.

A total deflation-of-power approach to government could be supported only by a return to all of the assumptions made by nineteeth-century liberals. However, neo-laissez-faire may be another matter entirely. It anticipates the coupling of a substantial deflation of government in general with a strengthening of certain aspects of government in particular.

This could be accomplished in three moves, preferably taken simultaneously. The precise means for making these moves, and some of the broader political desirabilities for doing so will be laid out in Chapter 11. Here it will suffice simply to sketch the map itself. The first move would be to abolish as many large discretionary economic programs as possible. The second would be to strengthen the original nondiscretionary fiscal policies—often referred to as the automatic stabilizers. The third would involve an expansion of certain federal police powers to replace a limited few of all those discretionary regulatory policies that would be abolished. A comment on each of these moves will suffice.

The first, abolition, would definitely implicate a tremendous proportion of the so-called pork barrel and subsidy programs. It would also implicate most of the discretionary regulatory programs and virtually all of the discretionary fiscal apparatus identified in this chapter. Retention of any such programs would have to rest upon a justification by its supporters that an activity absolutely essential to the economy or the society would disappear if it were not served by subsidies or supportive regulations. The difficulty of providing such justification is proven by its extreme scarcity in the past fifty years.

Second, nondiscretionary fiscal policies need strengthening because they provide much of the basic framework within which modern economic activity takes place. They are *prima facie* indispensable and are only weakened by the addition of discretionary fiscal policies. Basic and traditional fiscal policies are nondiscretionary. They have required very little administrative apparatus; they have been almost self-executing. They are literally the structure to which industrial managers and others can adjust themselves. Moreover, nondiscretionary fiscal policies possess a considerable capacity for redistribution of wealth, if those who want to accomplish such redistribution have the courage and clarity of vision to construct them with such a purpose.

The third move may be truly the *neo* part of neo-laissez-faire. But it should be emphasized once again that regulation of bad conduct does not mean the formulation of regulatory programs in terms of the broad sentiments we have observed in this volume, such as "fair competition" or "clean air." These are grants of authority, not guidelines for government action or guides and limits on private conduct. If there is conduct in the economy or society that contributes to an unacceptable distribution of income, to irrational use of resources, or to unwanted secondary effects such as water or air pollution or racial inequality, then politicians, planners, scientists, and technicians, even legislators, ought to be able to identify rather precisely what that conduct is. In the event the specific conduct cannot be identified, the program should not be adopted until it can. This criterion poses a very effective barrier against most existing and proposed regulatory programs, and we shall see at length in the next chapter the profound political desirability for such a criterion. At this point only the practical and everyday economic desirability of such a criterion is being considered. Many will answer that modern economies are too complicated for any precision in the definition of regulatory legislation. But if that is the case, then planning itself is impossible, and everything that is said against precision in regulatory laws applies with even greater cogency to the still more complicated and interdependent activity that makes up planning. All the economy or society really needs is a specification of bad conduct whose consequences justify restriction or elimination. These bad behaviors could range from particular instances of unfair competition all the way across to particular types of racial discrimination. *But they can be specified.*

The attack throughout this volume against the existing state as supportive of organized capitalism, and the anticipation here of a large though altered state apparatus, will inevitably invite the response, why not take the logical next step, to socialism? Indeed, on the basis of the critique in this volume, one could properly argue that the United States is already a socialist system, but only a bad one.

My first response is that if there were in the United States the consensus and the political party capable of bringing about the remaining transformation to socialism, there would also be sufficient power and consensus to deal with capitalism within the existing constitutional scheme. And the advantages would be that civil liberties would not have to be sacrificed during or after the transformation. Anyone who imagines that an industrial economy as large and complex as that of the United States could be transformed into true socialism without the interim sacrifice of civil liberties is engaging in pure political rhetoric or indulging in creative fantasy.

This does not mean that neo-laissez-faire is a solution without problems. As a liberal statist approach, neo-laissez-faire is, in fact, caught on a profound contradiction: Stress on civil liberties is always likely to work to the benefit of those who already have the wealth and power to defend their liberties as well as their luxuries. The contradiction between civil liberties and economic privilege is a true contradiction, not merely one in the mind of the analyst. Moreover, a socialist solution does indeed provide a way out of liberal contradictions. Yet it does so by encouraging contradictions of another kind. A socialist government may never be able to solve for itself the problem of restoring civil liberties once they have been suspended. Moreover a socialist government will not be able to cope with the problems of bureaucracy if it proceeds after the revolution to grant each administrative agency the same professional discretion that our present bureaucracies receive. Nothing in the contemporary experience of existing socialist governments suggests that socialism is immune to the problems of professional expertise, administrative discretion, and the close political relationships that emerge in that kind of state context. If socialist governments attempt to maintain a semblance of civil liberties through participation, they risk undermining the organizational capacity and professional ability to plan for the rationality and equality they seek. If on the other hand, participation is so restricted as to be no threat to the planning apparatus, then the concession to participation is a more grievous affront to civil liberties than no participation at all. Socialism as well as liberalism is caught on its own inherent contradictions.

The opportunity to choose between systems of government is a rare moment in history and often passes before it can be seized. More frequent may be the opportunity to choose among alternative contradictions. Within the context of our troubled times, which contradictions are we best able to abide?

11

TOWARD JURIDICAL DEMOCRACY
Notes on the Third Republic

During the twentieth century, the United States became a united state. Given the world and national history of our troubled century, this was probably inevitable, and there is surely no turning back, assuming anyone remains who wants to turn back. But, the particular way we adjusted to historical forces was almost certainly not predetermined, and if we got to our present state by deliberate choices, we can get out of it the same way. If the corruption of modern democratic government began with the emergence of interest-group liberalism, reforms must be oriented toward the influences of that point of view. These influences can now be summarized as a four-count indictment, an indictment for which the middle eight chapters of this volume are documentation.

The End of Liberalism: A Four-Count Indictment

1. *Interest-group liberalism as public philosophy corrupts democratic government because it deranges and confuses expectations about democratic institutions.* Liberalism promotes popular decision-making but undermines popular decisions by misapplying the notion to the implementation as well as the formulation of policy. It derogates democratic rights by assuming they are being exercised when more people have merely been given access. Liberal practices reveal a basic disrespect for democracy. Liberal leaders do not wield the authority of democratic governments with the resoluteness born of confidence in the legitimacy of their positions, the integrity of their institutions, or the justness of the programs they serve. Quite the contrary, their approach betrays their convictions.

2. *Interest-group liberalism renders government impotent.* Liberals are co-

pious in plans but irresolute in planning. Nineteenth-century liberalism had standards without plans—an anachronism even in its own time. But twentieth-century liberalism turned out to have plans without standards. Delegation of power was widely advertised as a counsel of strength but turned out to be a formula for weakness—an alienation of public domain, a gift of sovereignty to private satrapies. Because delegation of power turns out to be an imposition of impotence, it should render anachronistic the larger rationalization of interest-group liberalism. But doctrines are not organisms. They die only in combat, and no doctrine yet exists capable of doing the job.

3. *Interest-group liberalism demoralizes government, because liberal governments cannot achieve justice.* The question of justice has engaged the best minds for almost as long as there have been notions of state and politics, and since that time philosophers have been unable to agree on what justice is. But outside the ideal, in the realms of actual government and citizenship, the problem is simpler. In order to weigh and assess the quality of justice in our government, it is not necessary to define justice, because there is something about liberalism that prevents us from raising the question of justice at all. No matter what definition of justice is used, liberal governments cannot achieve justice because their policies lack the *sine qua non* of justice—that quality without which a consideration of justice cannot even be initiated. Considerations of the justice in, or achieved by, an action cannot be made unless a deliberate and conscious attempt was made to derive the action from a preexisting general rule or moral principle governing such a class of actions. Therefore, any governing regime that makes a virtue of avoiding such rules puts itself outside the context of justice.

Suppose there is a bull in the china shop. Suppose the shop is filled with objects that are so ugly that the bull could give us great pleasure by smashing the place to bits. Yet, though we may be pleased, we cannot judge the action of the bull. We can only like or dislike the consequences. The consequences are haphazard; the bull could not have intended them. Therefore they bear no relation to any esthetic principle. We cannot judge the bull. We can only celebrate our good fortune. Without the general rule, the bull could reenact his destructive scene daily and still not be capable of achieving, in this case, esthetic justice. Without the rule, the whole idea of justice is absurd.[1] A government without good rules, and without acts carefully derived therefrom, is merely a big bull in an immense china shop.

4. *Interest-group liberalism corrupts democratic government in the degree to*

---

1. Because the ideal of representative democracy is valuable in the United States, the general rule ought to be a legislative rule. However, this is an extrinsic feature of the rule. As argued in Chapter 5, there is a high probability that efforts to make clear rules will lead to the legislature. But in the present context, all that counts is the rule itself. And, contrary to the fears of many pluralists, a good rule can produce more flexibility and more competition than the avoidance of the rule. These tendencies are further developed under proposals for reform.

which it weakens the capacity of those governments to live by democratic formalisms. Liberalism weakens democratic institutions by opposing formal procedure with informal bargaining. "Playing it by the book" is a role often unpopular in American war and sports literature precisely because it can be used to dramatize personal rigidity and the plight of the individual in collective situations. Because of the impersonality of formal procedures, there is inevitably a gap between form and reality. But this is something that can be seen in two directions, only one of which has been stressed in the literature on war, sports, and politics. The gap between form and reality gives rise to cynicism, for informality means that some will escape their fate better than others. There has, as a consequence, always been cynicism toward public institutions in the United States; and this, too, is a good thing, since a little cynicism is the parent of healthy sophistication. However, when the informal is elevated to a positive virtue, and when the gap between the formal and the informal grows wider, and when the hard-won access of individuals and groups becomes a share of official authority, cynicism unavoidably curdles into distrust. Legitimacy can be defined as the distance between form and reality. How much spread can a democratic system tolerate and remain both democratic and legitimate?

Another homely parable may help. In the good old days, everyone in the big city knew that traffic tickets could be fixed. Not everybody could get their tickets fixed, but those who honestly paid their fines suffered to some degree a dual indignity—loss of money and loss of self-esteem for having so little access. Cynicism was widespread, and violations were normal; but perhaps it did not matter, for there were so few automobiles. Suppose then that as the automobile population increased, a certain city faced a traffic crisis and the system of ticket-fixing came into ill-repute. Suppose a mayor, victorious on the Traffic Ticket, decided that, rather than eliminate fixing by universalizing enforcement, City Hall would instead reform the system by universalizing the privilege of ticket-fixing. Equality would prevail, because everyone could be made almost equally free to bargain with the ticket administrators. But it is difficult to imagine how this would make total city government more legitimate. Meanwhile, the purpose of the ticket would soon have been destroyed.

Interest-group liberalism possesses the mentality of a world universalized ticket-fixing. Destroy privilege by universalizing it. Reduce conflict by yielding to it. Redistribute power by the maxim of each according to his claim. Purchase support for the regime by reserving an official place for every major structure of power.

In the process, liberalism has promoted concentration of democratic authority but deconcentration of democratic power. Liberalism has opposed privilege in policy formulation only to foster it quite systematically in the implementation of policy. Liberalism has consistently failed to recognize, in brief, that in a democracy forms are important. In a medieval monarchy all formalisms were at court or manor. Democracy proves, for better or worse, that the masses like that sort of thing, too. And this is not a superficial preference.

Juridical Democracy: Modest Proposals for Radical Reform

These concluding comments are written for a time when political leaders have begun to see that the Second Republic, the regime of interest-group liberalism, is finished. At this time they persist in their search for distant explanations for the American distress, and usually the victims or the society get all the blame. But ultimately they must come to see that they, the leaders, are the problem, their belief system is the source of the pathology, and their policies will not succeed except at great economic and political cost. As this moment approaches, there will be an opportunity for fundamental changes. But these changes will have to be guided by a new public philosophy, and a new public philosophy does not come out of a package. It will emerge from a kind of political discourse in which few of us have engaged during the false consensus of our generation. As a contribution to this discourse, I offer *juridical democracy*.

In our everyday lives we speak of civility and propriety without defining them, because we have some reasonable expectation we will be understood. The need to define juridical democracy is to me a measure of the decline of law and of legitimate government in the United States. Juridical democracy is rule of law operating in institutions. Juridical democracy is a public philosophy which rejects informality as a criterion, accepting it only as a measure of the distance between reality and the ideal situation. Juridical democracy rejects realism; when reality and forms diverge, it is the reality that must first be attacked.

Juridical is not the same as judicial. In fact, many judicial rulings would not qualify as juridical because they have left the rule unclear and have thereby perpetuated dependence upon judges for resolution of future conflicts—until a clear leading rule is handed down. The juridical principle would build a public philosophy around the state, including the judiciary, and would concern itself with how and why the state must limit itself in the use of its powers of coercion. The juridical principle therefore speaks to the powerless as well as the powerful. *The juridical principle is the only dependable defense the powerless have against the powerful.* In many cases the powerful would be immobilized if they had to articulate what they were going to do before they did it. On the other side, the juridical principle could relieve governments of many of their heaviest contemporary burdens. A delegation of

power to the president or to agencies is in reality a delegation of personal responsibility for which there is almost never commensurate real power or consensus. Much of the deceit we now associate with American politicians and
officials—all the way up to the White House—is attributable to the impossible expectations policies-without-law impose upon them. The juridical principle puts the burden upon the law itself; and the law, when clear, would
displace vague public expectation as the criterion by which the performance
of governments and government officials would be judged. According to the
juridical principle, a bad program is worse than no program at all. And when
the rule of law is clear and the program nevertheless fails, we would then have
a basis for changing the law rather than vilifying the responsible individuals as
though they were guilty of malfeasance and bad faith. Moreover, the juridical
principle would provide a basis for collective responsibility; the president or a
specific agency would no longer be alone but would share responsibility with
all those who supported the program from start to finish.

Juridical democracy is, however, two words; and each helps define the
other. While the juridical stresses form and the real impact of form, democracy stresses particular forms and particular contents. Taken by itself, the
juridical principle appears to be comfortable with, say, segregation as well as
integration laws, as long as the laws possess legal integrity. But within the context of democracy, especially if one lived by the juridical principle, it would
simply not be possible to support segregation in any form, because a democracy cannot abide two systems of law, two criteria for the provision of governmental services—in brief, unequal protection of the laws. On a host of issues,
therefore, juridical democracy has very clear and profound substantive implications; it is not merely a procedural matter. On the other hand, there are
many substantive issues upon which juridical democracy as a public philosophy would be silent, because no particular outcome would threaten to violate
democratic notions of citizenship and equal treatment. In such cases, perhaps
a majority of all cases, the only concern would be for the juridical—that is,
the institutions of government ought to say what they are going to do to us
before they do it; and if they cannot say they cannot act.

If a mature public philosophy should have a detailed design for its own at-
tainment, juridical democracy has not yet come of age. However, it is possible to provide a few planks in the platform of an incipient movement. All of
the proposals are in some sense radical, because each attempts to get at the
roots of the Second Republic. Each proposal is deceptively simple, each
would be enormously effective, and to that very extent, each would be politically difficult to accomplish. There is an inverse relationship between effectiveness and feasibility. Consequently, these proposals are offered with no
hope of adoption but rather as a way of rounding out the analysis for those
who are continuing to wonder where it is leading. And then at some point in
the near future when the political leadership of the country has become more

desperate with the failure of their efforts to salvage the Second Republic, these proposals may then appear very modest.

THE JURIDICAL PRINCIPLE THROUGH JUDICIAL ACTION

Since all the proposals revolve around the effort to restore and expand the rule of law, it is natural to begin the design for a movement with proposals for judicial action. But the reader should not be misled by this ordering to the idea that all our problems can or will be resolved by proper judicial action. With that in mind, it is clear that the first and most important step toward juridical democracy would involve revival of the still valid but universally disregarded rule in the Schechter case, where the Supreme Court declared the National Industrial Recovery Act void on the grounds that it had delegated legislative powers to the president without sufficiently defining the policy or criteria to guide the administrator. In other words, no rule of law, no agency.[2] To accommodate interest-group liberal programs the Supreme Court created modern jurisprudence by giving full faith and credit to any expression that could get a majority vote in Congress. The Court's rule must once again become one of declaring invalid and unconstitutional any delegation of power to an administrative agency or to the president that is not accompanied by clear standards of implementation.

Restoration of the Schechter rule would be dramatic because it would mean an occasional confrontation between the Supreme Court and Congress. But there is no reason to fear judicial usurpation. Under present conditions, when Congress delegates without a shred of guidance, the courts usually end up rewriting many of the statutes in the course of construction. Since the Court's present procedure is always to find an acceptable meaning of a statute in order to avoid invalidating it, the Court is constantly legislating. In contrast, a blanket invalidation under the Schechter rule is tantamount to a court order for Congress to do its own work. Therefore the rule of law is a restraint upon rather than an expansion of judicial function.

Just as there is no reason to fear the decline of Congress under the Schechter rule, there is also no reason to fear contraction of modern government toward some nineteenth-century ideal. Contemporary liberals have not studied rule of law and its implications because they defined rule of law as a goal of nineteenth-century liberals and therefore of twentieth-century conservative and vested interests.[3] Rule of law, especially statute law, is the essence of positive government. The bureaucracy in the service of the strong and clear statute is

2. Citation of the case and discussion of the issues in the case will be found in Chapter 5.

3. For example, F. A. Hayek's classic *Road to Serfdom* (Chicago: University of Chicago Press, 1944) was defined as a reactionary book. See especially his superb essay in that book, "The Rule of Law." It is a mystery how this could have been considered a tract in favor of the vested interests.

more effective than ever. Granted, rule of law requirements are likely to make far more difficult the framing and passage of some policies. But why indeed should any program be acceptable if the partisans cannot fairly clearly state its purpose and means? We ask such justification even of children. Although a juridical government might be smaller, it would certainly be more effective.

THE JURIDICAL PRINCIPLE BY PRESIDENTIAL ACTION

The first six presidents of the United States tended to use constitutional arguments to justify their vetoes of congressional bills. Andrew Jackson was the first president who vetoed bills simply because he considered them objectionable. But Jackson only vetoed twelve bills in his entire eight years as president, and as recently as President Grover Cleveland, constitutional arguments still tended to be preferred. Thus, even though modern presidents have disregarded constitutional arguments in their vetoes, there is ample precedent for a president's claim to a share of constitutional authority. Andrew Jackson put it eloquently, despite his own preference for not using constitutional arguments:

The Congress, the Executive, and the Court must each for itself be guided by its own opinion of the Constitution. Each public officer who takes an oath to support the Constitution swears that he will support it as he understands it, and not as it is understood by others. It is as much the duty of the House of Representatives, of the Senate, and of the President to decide upon the constitutionality of any bill or resolution which may be presented to them for passage or approval as it is of the supreme judges when it may be brought before them for judicial decision. The opinion of the judges has no more authority over Congress than the opinion of Congress has over the judges, and on that point the President is independent of both.[4]

Although there are some profound problems with such a point of view, and although the preeminence of the Court in constitutional matters is now an established constitutional fact, Jackson's point is extremely well taken at least with regard to the basis of presidential vetoes of congressional acts. This is not to take away from the president the right to veto bills for political reasons. It is simply to say that presidents have every right to base their decisions on their own interpretation of constitutional obligations.

The area where such a position is especially relevant is the president's obligation to see that the laws are faithfully executed. It would seem to me that the president is virtually obliged to veto a congressional enactment whenever Congress has not been clear enough about what should be executed, and how. The veto of a congressional enactment on the grounds that it said nothing would have the same effect as the Supreme Court's action under the

4. Quoted in Alfred H. Kelly and Winfred A. Harbison, *The American Constitution—Its Origins and Development* (New York: Norton, 1976), p. 317.

Schechter rule. But there are additional advantages—vital ones: The Congress would have been told to go back and do its job properly. The public would be to that extent better informed about what Congress intends and what is expected of citizens. The level of debate and general political discourse would have been raised toward the question of congressional intentions.

Finally, the president would be contributing, for that particular bill once it is reenacted and accepted, to a situation of collective responsibility. Virtually every expert on the presidency agrees that there is no collective responsibility in American national government. We do not have a responsible party system, and the Cabinet is not a collective institution but rather a collection of individually appointed Cabinet heads who are sometimes expert advisers. Politically and legally, presidents are alone in their responsibility for the faithful execution of the laws and are, increasingly, alone in their responsibility for setting the entire world to rights. The veto of an important legislative enactment would contribute to collective responsibility in at least two ways: (1) clarification of what is expected of the president; therefore, a clarification of the criteria by which presidential and administrative action can be judged; and (2) identification of that group in Congress who, by virtue of their vote on a clearly stated bill, ought to share with the president responsibility for the success or failure of the authorized program. Presidents, for their own sake as well as ours, ought to insist upon that kind of sharing of responsibility. And once that is done for practical reasons, we have also reached the still more important goal of improving the legal integrity of the legislation. Thereby we have taken one more step toward juridical democracy.

RULE OF LAW BY ADMINISTRATIVE FORMALITY

Schechter rules and presidential vetoes, even when forcefully applied in good faith, could never eliminate all the vagueness in legislative enactments and could never eliminate the need for delegation of power to administrative agencies. Ignorance of changing social conditions is important, although it is much overused as an alibi for malfeasance in legislative drafting. Social pressure for some kind of quick action also interferes with drafting of a proper rule, even though this too is a much overused alibi. Nevertheless, even if it would often be impossible for Congress to live by the juridical principle despite sincere efforts to do so, there are at least two ways to compensate for that slippage and to bring these necessarily vague legislative formulations back to a much closer approximation of the juridical principle. The first of these is administrative formality. The second, to be taken up in the next section, is codification.

Administrative formality would simply be a requirement for early and frequent administrative rule-making.[5] When an agency formulates a general rule it is without any question committing a legislative act. But in so doing, the agency is simply carrying out the responsibility delegated to it by Congress in the enabling statute for that agency, and is also carrying out the general intent of Congress as spelled out in the Administrative Procedure Act.[6] This power to promulgate general rules has been validated by the Supreme Court. But the trouble is, few agencies do this, and even fewer like to do it. Most of the administrative rhetoric in recent years espouses the interest-group ideal of administration by favoring the norms of flexibility and decision by bargaining. Pluralism applied to administration usually takes the practical form of an attempt to deal with each case on its merits. But the ideal of case-by-case administration is in most instances a myth. Few persons affected by a decision have an opportunity to be heard. And each agency, regulatory or not, disposes of the largest proportion of its cases without any procedure at all, least of all by formal adversary processes. In practice, agencies end up with the worst of case-by-case adjudication *and* of rule-making. They try to work without rules in order to live with the loose legislative mandate, and then they try to treat their cases and practices as though they were operating under a rule. For example, most of the applications to the Civil Aeronautics Board have been disposed of without hearings, even where applicants are entitled to them.[7] The so-called flexibility of a case approach is an unconvincing rationalization. Bargaining is involved, but it is reserved for leaders in the field who will not accept mere processing. And those very leaders usually have a stake in keeping the rule implicit or nonexistent.

In contrast, treatment of the same cases by a real administrative rule has most of the advantages claimed for the case-by-case approach, yet possesses few of the disadvantages. A rule can be general and yet can gain clarity and practicality through the specific cases to which it is applied. It was precisely this ability to perceive the public policy implications in complex phenomena that explains our reliance on expert agencies in the first place. The rule in combination with the cases to which it applies can become a known factor in the everyday life of each client. In contrast, although there is an implicit rule

5. Here is one of the few areas where I am not only able to agree with one of the most important authors of interest-group liberal jurisprudence but I am able to draw upon his expertise to sharpen my proposal. See Kenneth Culp Davis, *Administrative Law Treatise* (St. Paul: West Publishing, 1958), especially pp. 9–53 and 144 ff. of the 1965 *Supplement*. See also Henry J. Friendly, *The Federal Administrative Agencies* (Cambridge, Mass.: Harvard University Press, 1962), pp. 141 ff., for similar arguments by a judge and legal scholar who is distinctly not within the interest-group liberal jurisprudence.

6. 60 Stat. 237 (1946), Sec. 2(C) and Sec. 3(A): "Every agency shall separately state and currently publish in the Federal Register . . . (3) substantive rules as authorized by law and statements of general policy. . . . No person shall in any manner be required to resort to organization or procedure not so published."

7. Davis, *Supplement*, p. 151.

in every bargained or adjudicated case, it cannot be known until the outcome of the bargain, and its later applications must be deciphered by lawyers representing potential cases.

Advantages accrue to administrators as well as to clients. First, administrators should want to make rules deliberately focusing broad delegations of power because broad delegations are a menace to formal organization and to the ideal of the neutral civil servant. The pluralistic principle impairs a rational ordering of tasks and the routinization of routines. Broad discretion makes a politician out of a bureaucrat. Many bureaucrats are good politicians, but when political talent becomes the prime criterion of appointment and promotion it tends to contradict the *raison d'être* of administrative independence—neutrality and expertise.

Most important of all—for administrators and for clients and citizens—early rule-making would improve the administrative process by making administrative power more responsible as well as more efficient. Early rule-making forces reflection upon the implications of the original legislation and of the place of the agency in the society. This is juridical in every respect, even though it is not legislative or judicial. This is part of what was referred to in Chapter 5 as "bargaining on the rule" versus "bargaining on the decision." Bargaining on the rule would tend to push the focus of the political process upward toward the highest levels of responsibility rather than downward away from responsibility and away from public scrutiny. In this context, avoidance of rule-making seems to be more of a usurpation than the initiation of rule-making, because clear administrative rules will produce legislative evaluation of whole programs; Congress need not then depend only upon piecemeal committee oversight and narrow appropriations subcommittee scrutiny. Rule-making early in the life of a statute brings on more judicial evaluation before the agency is too much committed to its own existence, and it would almost certainly push at least a few members of Congress to reconsider while there is still time whether the agency is really what was intended.

Finally, early rule-making provides a basis for administrative centralization without the imposition of a heavy Prussian system of hierarchical subordination. When administrative centralization is accomplished around rules, *lesser authority can be subjected to higher authority through criteria relevant to the programs themselves*. An illustration from the judicial process may serve better than an abstract elaboration. Is a leading opinion by the Supreme Court a centralizing or a decentralizing force within the judiciary? Obviously it is both. A strong and clear ruling is an act of centralization toward the Court. Yet at the same time it leads to significant decentralization of case load and a good deal of self-administration by lower courts and by counsel. An area of good leading opinions is thought to be an area of easy law in which few appeals are made; nevertheless the area is centralized in the sense that each decision in each lower judicial unit becomes all the more consistent with other comparable decisions because there is a clear criterion to guide lower-level adjudication or even to head off cases. In contrast, the Supreme Court can inundate itself in areas where it cannot or will not enunciate a leading opinion expressing good governing rules. In such an area there is even greater centralization, but in the worst sense of the word because responsibility can be maintained only through regular, bureaucratic supervision—known in the judiciary as judicial review.

Advantages to formality through early rule-making ought to be obvious to anyone not blinded by an ideology framed for a period when we possibly could not afford legality. But now, when we are not on the edge of economic collapse, and when legality and efficiency tend to go together, it would be foolish not to grasp them.

TOWARD RESTORATION OF CONGRESS:
JURIDICAL DEMOCRACY THROUGH CODIFICATION

The second approach to the problem of Congress's inherent inability to live by the juridical principle, codification, is highly consistent with and complementary to the first. Even if Congress is unable to provide good legislative guidelines at the time of the passage of the original organic act, there is no reason why Congress has to remain permanently incapable. The answer here is codification. Let us consider it in light of the modest proposition that Congress ought to be able to learn from its own experience.

Codification is nothing more than the effort to systematize, digest, and simplify all of the provisions of law relating to a particular subject. The most famous and successful effort at codification was probably that of the French law in 1804 (eventually called Code Napoleon to honor the emperor), which was sought because there were so many sources of law in France: Roman law in the south, customary law in the north, canon law over marriage and family, case law and government edict in an increasing number of areas by the time of the Revolution. Voltaire is said to have observed that travelers in France changed law as often as they changed horses. Demand for codification, beginning well before the Revolution, was a demand for consistency, for accessibility to common people, and for the dominance of the legislature in government. But codification does not require the extensive or rigid approach of the Code Napoleon. This simply defines the mechanism, and it is not a strange and new experience for the United States.

For some years prior to the Legislative Reorganization Act of 1946, Congress had standing committees on revision of laws. These were continued as subcommittees of the Judiciary Committees of the House and Senate after 1946. Some codification had been taking place over the years by the House subcommittee, but it cannot have been very ambitious, inasmuch as a specialized staff of only two persons was assigned to revision of the laws, generally under Subcommittee Number 3 of the House Judiciary Committee after 1946. As of January 1974, twenty of the fifty titles of the United States Code had been revised and enacted into law. However, these actions have two basic shortcomings in terms of the point of concern here. First, apparently in only a few of the twenty instances of title codification were major administrative rulings and court decisions even reviewed, much less incorporated into the Code. In most instances, the relevant administrative actions are simply referred to in the *United States Code Annotated* and have never received any congressional attention at all. Second, and still more to the point, very few of the important titles have been touched, and virtually none in the most important areas of government regulation, including the titles on bankruptcy, banks and banking, commerce and trade, conservation, food and drugs, labor, public contracts, public health, public lands, railroads, shipping, communication, and transportation. In these areas Congress has not yet discovered the need to learn from its own experience. Nevertheless, these efforts of the past thirty years indicate that codification is not foreign to the American experience.

A much richer experience with codification will be found in state law. For example, the state of New York has had an active commission on law revision and codification at least since 1934. Many other states have similar commissions and each of these states seems to have gone much further than Congress in its effort to incorporate administrative and, especially, judicial decisions into later legislative enactments. Perhaps this is why there is more legal integrity in most state laws than in federal laws despite the lower average caliber of state legislators, the smaller professional staffs available to state legislators, and the lower average tenure and specialization of members of state legislatures. American Bar Association Committees have studied this problem as far back as 1914, and recommendations favoring codification of state or federal procedures and substantive clauses will be found in the work of certain legal scholars, most distinguished among them being Ernst Freund.[8] Thus, if we do not engage in codification it is due to the ignorance and incompetence of contemporary legislators and not to anything inherently un-American.

In 1946, a bill was introduced to establish a special office of law-revision counsel in the House. In 1974 a similar proposal was made, was endorsed by the American Bar Association, and was adopted in October of that year. As in the 1946 proposal, the 1974 action (H. Res. 988) provided for

complete compilation, restatement, and review of the general and permanent laws of the United States which conforms to the understood policy, intent, and purpose of the Congress in the original enactments, with such amendments and corrections as will remove ambiguities, contradictions, and other imperfections both of substance and of form, separately stated, with a view to the enactment of each Title as positive law.

8. See, for example, his classic work, *Standards of American Legislation* (Chicago: University of Chicago Press, 1917 and 1965), Chapter VII.

The basis is therefore established, and all that is needed is to push and goad Congress into the implementation of its 1974 decision by establishing a Standing Joint Committee on Revision of Laws that would be given the obligation to incorporate relevant administrative and judicial rulings along with earlier congressional enactments with the goal of proposing to Congress a unified code of positive law in each of the major subject areas of legislation. This committee would have to have a large and professional staff engaged full time in codification and revision of all the titles of the United States Code, especially those that have hitherto not been touched at all. And to repeat, these codifications would go beyond any previous efforts by attempting to sort out, prune, and incorporate administrative and judicial decisions along with past statutory actions.

If Congress got regularly and routinely into the business of serious revision of its laws in light of administrative experience, it would then be perfectly possible for Congress to live according to the juridical principle and yet delegate broad powers to administrators. Everyone would be aware of the fact that the first enactment is only the beginning. Every administrator would be making decisions with an eye toward review for consistency, and every agency would have incentive to influence this process by promulgation of the early rules proposed in the previous section. Every regulated corporation and individual would be pushing the regulatory agency toward general rulings and away from individual decisions because of the knowlege that these are likely to become legislation eventually. Finally, when these rulings are brought back to Congress and put through the regular legislative mill, they will not only be elevated in stature as law but very probably would go through further change and further clarification on their way back to the administrative agency. The regulator would then be participating in the legislative process in a way that is consonant with the Constitution and the juridical principle. This should definitely elevate the status of the regulator and at the same time would be far more honest and open from the standpoint of the regulated corporation and individual.

None of this conflicts in any way with existing congressional procedures. However, a commitment to serious legislative revision which attempted to fuse administrative experience would supplement and could eventually displace much of the futile oversight process. Little in the political science literature is clearer than the analysis of Congress showing the shortcomings of efforts to gain administrative accountability through legislative oversight and through the development of legislative intent. After a brief evaluation of each of these devices, the need for codification ought to appear compelling.

Take legislative intent first, because it involves Congress as an institution, and because it can be dispensed with so quickly. Many responsible members of Congress, many dedicated members of congressional staffs, and many lobbyists pushing for the passage of legislation will rationalize the vagueness of their drafts of bills with the argument that at least the empty statute will get through Congress, and then the administrator can be guided later by the legislative intent that the sponsors can introduce during the debate. The image here is that the administrator, inevitably confused by the emptiness of the statute, will go back and carefully study the *Congressional Record* and be guided by that. But there are two facts about the *Congressional Record*, and it would take a very ignorant and inexperienced administrator not to be aware of them. First, there will be more than one intent expressed in a debate, if there is any debate on the bill. Second, and of far greater importance, most of the *Congressional Record* is phony and therefore is not a good source of intent. Consider the conclusion of the Congressional Commission on Administrative Review following their massive hearings and research in 1976 and 1977:

Under the law, "the *Congressional Record* . . . should be substantially a verbatim report of proceedings" (44 U.S. C. 901). *Currently, approximately 70% of what appears in the* Record *is not actually said on the floor of the House or Senate.* Further, the material is presented in such a way that a reader cannot distinguish what was actually said from what was not. The *Record* not only is a record for the public, but it is also used by agencies as they interpret legislative intent for carrying out the laws. When the *Record* gives an inaccurate reflection of debate, agencies can be misled. [9]

The congressional intent that is brought to bear upon administrators tends to come from individual members of Congress operating as individual lobbyists on their own behalf or on behalf of a particular interest group or constituent. This is not legislative intent at all.

Legislative oversight tends to have two frustrating results. Either it has a marginal influence on substantial problems or a significant influence on marginal problems. It is a myth that programs and administrative agencies are given thorough evaluation at least once a year through normal appropriations processes that extend through the Executive Office of the President to the two Appropriations Committees of Congress and their specialized subcommittees. These yearly evaluations get only at the marginal and incremental aspects of most programs. Substantive questions are most often treated as off limits; while individual members of Congress often ask substantive questions, they are likely to be disregarded or ruled out of order. The very cost-consciousness and care for detail that makes appropriations review functionally rational is also the source of its weakness as a means of achieving any substantive accountability. Review of the basic statute and of the substantive aspects of agency action is well within the authority of the standing committee with jurisdiction over the agency. However, this substantive review is very rare, occurring primarily in those very few instances where the organic statute has

9. *Administrative Reorganization and Legislative Management,* one of the several volumes of Hearings and Meetings before the Commission on Administrative Review, U.S. House of Representatives, 95th Cong., 1st Sess., September 1977, p. 702. Emphasis added.

been brought in for fundamental revision. The pressing need for such a substantive review gives rise to still another reform proposal, which will be taken up in the next section. What is left here is the raw nerve of congressional incapacity to make good law and the need to overcome that incapacity with a desire in the first instance to write better law, and a capacity after the fact to learn from its own experience by regular revision of those original laws in light of administrative experience.

SUNSET LAWS: A TENURE-OF-STATUTES ACT

The juridical principle may be suffering most from the immortality of administrative agencies. Enabling legislation is as indefinite on agency duration as on substantive guidelines. Once an agency is established, its resources favor its own survival, and the longer agencies survive, the more likely they are to continue to survive.[10] The only direct antidote to immortality would appear to be an attack upon the Frankenstein legislation creating each monster, and in that spirit the final reform proposal is for a general statute setting a Jeffersonian limit of from five to ten years on the life of every enabling act.[11] The purpose of this reform is not merely to kill off superfluous and antiquated administrative agencies, desirable though that may be. The purpose is to provide an institutional means for facing up to the basic problem of juridical democracy—the absence of rule of law and the absence of real legislative power to impose it. The guillotine effect of a termination date on an agency enabling act is an opportunity for leverage in favor of imposing the clear rules of law the second time around that were impossible to impose in the original instance. As with codification, we can better live with bad organic laws if we are guaranteed another crack at them.

A termination date should not be considered a death sentence but an op-

10. See especially Herbert Kaufman, *Are Government Organizations Immortal?* (Washington, D.C.: The Brookings Institution, 1976). Though Kaufman tries to keep an open mind on the subject, he tends to agree, on the basis of his extensive research, with the epigramatic statement of Anthony Downs, "The older a bureau is, the less likely it is to die" (quoted by Kaufman in a footnote on p. 69), and with an almost identical generalization by Samuel Huntington drawn from the experience of many other countries (cited on the same page).

11. Since I first proposed such a reform in 1967—and to my knowledge this was the first proposal of this nature anywhere—there have been several serious efforts to implement it. Quite appropriately, its name was changed by Common Cause and others to "Sunset Legislation" and that change of name could very well be the secret of its spread. Several states, including Colorado, Florida, Louisiana, and Alabama, have already adopted sunset laws, and similar legislation is under serious consideration in Illinois, Minnesota, and California. In 1975 an amendment providing for the expiration of the proposed Consumer Protection Agency after seven years, unless specific action to continue it were taken, was attached to the main bill, which was eventually vetoed in its entirety by President Gerald Ford. Later the same year, twenty-five members of the House introduced a bill attaching similar provisions to nine other federal agencies. This kind of reform is now considered such a serious threat that major congressional committees and their fellow travelers in political science and journalism have been moved to denounce explicitly the tenure-of-statute provisions. This may be a solid indication of an idea whose time has come.

portunity to learn from experience. This is why the notion of sunset is appropriate, because it implies a creative time during which the politics of the agency is likely to come unstuck and the opportunity for substantive reconsideration is most propitious. The termination date for the statute and program is, therefore, insufficient in itself and should not be judged alone. Everything depends upon what is made of the opportunity during those months when each agency is approaching its ultimate tenure, when it is likely to be politically most vulnerable. The sunset period is obviously the best period for codification of agency rulings; one could easily imagine a tenure-of-statutes act requiring that the renewal of an agency's enabling act should take the form of a new agency code.

Indeed, most agencies will survive the renewal process, and most will probably be able to avoid any serious alterations in the way they conduct their business. But each agency will be a different one if in the process its true nature has been exposed. My own hypothesis is that few agencies can withstand public scrutiny. And it is not a hypothesis but a certainty that the public will gain immensely from any effort, even when unsuccessful, to codify past rulings and to enact them as a code to guide future conduct—until the next sunset. Those who prefer to be governed by rules rather than authority, must fear the present system, should be opposing almost all existing federal programs, and should be supporting any institution capable of providing rule of law—whether it is the aristocratic Supreme Court through judicial review or technocratic agencies that engage in early rule-making. But those who prefer their rules of law as enacted, at least in part, by elected assemblies should strongly prefer statutory tenure and codification.

The Future as Juridical Democracy

This book began as a general inquiry into the relationship between government, ideology, and public policy in Washington in 1963, scarcely three months before the Kennedy assassination, when confidence in national government and national political institutions was unprecedentedly high. As the first results were being published during the years between 1964 and 1967, confidence remained high but frustration had mounted to such an extent that massive criticisms of national programs and national liberal ideology no longer fell on deaf ears. In 1969 and afterward, there were reasons to be alarmed by the scale of the problem; nevertheless there were grounds for optimism about the prospects for reform. Interest-group liberalism appeared to be undermining itself, and the seeds of self-destruction were still present despite the current triumph of interest-group liberalism in the Second Republic. The likelihood of drastic constitutional change without revolution remains high, because there is at least one practical alternative to interest-group liberalism, juridical democracy, that emerges out of the strongest rather than the weakest traits of the pluralist society and is at the same time more consonant with the strongest constitutional traditions:

1. Interest-group liberalism cannot plan. Juridical democracy can. Laws are plans. Positive law guides; positive law moves in known ways. Yet the juridical principle is not inflexible. Its flexibility comes not from a flabby bargain but from its capacity to be changed in known ways. This capacity to be known and to be changeable in known ways is the basis also of the superior rationality and administrative efficiency of juridical democracy.

2. Interest-group liberalism cannot achieve justice. Juridical democracy can, because its actions derive from known principles and therefore can be judged. Requirement of rule of law leads to a justice-oriented politics just as automatically as the requirement of unguided delegation leads to pluralistic, bargain-oriented politics. The juridical approach to politics produces increments of justice just as surely as the interest-group liberal approach produces increments of equilibrium. And yet, while pluralism eliminates justice from all consideration, the juridical approach does not eliminate pluralist patterns or principles. The juridical approach does not dictate a particular definition of justice, of virtue, or of the good life. Juridical democracy is not popular totalitarianism in disguise. The juridical principle can convert a consumer economy into a just society without altering in any way the virtue of consumption or the freedom to consume. It does not reduce the virtue of political competition but only makes access to some areas of government a bit more difficult to acquire.

3. Interest-group liberalism weakens democratic forms. Juridical democracy strengthens them. Rule of law became unpopular to contemporary liberals because of a widespread belief that it operated as a check against democracy. The truth lies almost altogether the other way round. The decline of Congress, supposedly the popular branch of government, began with Congress's abandonment of rule of law in favor of delegation of power. And Congress usually reasserts itself as a real parliamentary assembly whenever it has a real rule of law to debate. The Civil Rights Act of 1964 still stands as a reminder to anyone who cares to reflect upon it that Congress can, under proper conditions, be the center of government and the source of juridical democracy. Rule of law is no barrier to democracy or democratic forms. The one will not long endure without the other.

4. Interest-group liberalism weakens democratic power. Juridical democracy strengthens it. Here, too, its reputation as a barrier against positive government contributed to the contemporary unpopularity of rule of law and the juridical principle. But again, most of the evidence lies the other way. No government is more powerful than one whose agencies have good laws to implement. Much is spoken and written of the problem of bureaucracy and

how to keep it under presidential control or to insure its effectiveness and its responsibility. But nothing serves better to direct bureaucracy than issuing it clear orders along with powers. One can hardly avoid being impressed with how effective a clear statute or a clear presidential order is upon the behavior of bureaucracies and bureaucrats. It is the broad grant of power without standards that leads to bargaining, to unanticipated commitments, and to the confusions that are the essence of bureaucratic irresponsibility and the illegitimate state. Juridical democracy almost certainly reduces without necessarily eliminating the inconsistency between power and legitimacy.

5. Finally, interst-group liberalism produces an apologetic political science. Juridical democracy produces an independent and critical political science. Interest-group liberalism's focus on realism, equilibrium, and the paraphernalia of political process is at bottom apologetic. Realistic political science is a rationalization of the present. The political scientist is not necessarily a defender of the status quo, but the result is too often the same, because those who are trying to describe reality tend to reaffirm it. Focus on the group, for example, is a commitment to one of the more rigidified aspects of the social process. Stress upon the incremental is apologetic as well. The separation of facts from values is apologetic.

There is no denying that modern pluralistic political science brought science to politics. And that is a good thing. But it did not have to come at the price of making political science an apologetic discipline. But that is exactly what happened. Pluralism required realism and the separation of facts from values because it could not live with the fact that governments make actual moral choices and that for those choices somebody must be held responsible. In embracing facts alone about the process, modern political science embraced the ever-present. In so doing, modern political science took rigor over relevance. Juridical democracy can be scientific even while working toward a fusion of facts and values. In practice this merely amounts to an effort to bring about a fusion of political behavior, public administration, and public law. Rules of law and their consequences—rights, justice, legitimacy—are just as susceptible to scientific generalization as their behavioral equivalents—bargaining, equilibrium, and opinions. Juridical democracy can produce a superior science of politics because it allows rigor but is no enemy of relevance. The juridical approach even permits apology; it simply does not require it. The juridical principle does not even oppose the idea of equilibrium; it simply does not make equilibrium a point of indoctrination. Nor does the juridical principle erect barriers to scientific study of behavior; it only insists that political behavior is only one dimension of the polity. And above all else, the juridical principle would demand constantly that political science look to itself as part of the very political process it presumes to study.

Quite properly, *The End of Liberalism* closes on an academic issue—and it may be the most important issue of all—the influence of theory over practice.

Political science may not produce the theory for the Third Republic, but political scientists can perpetuate the Second Republic by refusing to unmask contemporary theory and its insidious influence upon contemporary government. If the Second Republic should persist, it will be the critics, not the politicians, who are to blame. Meanwhile, the costs of the Second Republic are mounting. The specter of an entrenched Second Republic, while not totalitarianism or turmoil, is nevertheless a profound affront to the American dream: It is a nightmare of administrative boredom.

INDEX